Language Arts and Literacy in the Middle Grades

Planning, Teaching, and Assessing Learning

Second Edition

Margaret J. Finders
University of Wisconsin–La Crosse

Susan Hynds
Syracuse University

Upper Saddle River, New Jersey
Columbus, Ohio

Library of Congress Cataloging-in-Publication Data

Finders, Margaret J.

   Language arts and literacy in the middle grades: planning, teaching, and assessing learning/Margaret J. Finders, Susan Hynds.—2nd ed.

        p. cm.

   Rev. ed. Of: Literacy lessons, c2003.

   ISBN 0-13-175172-7 (alk. paper)

  1. Language arts (Middle school) 2. Middle school teaching. I. Hynds, Susan. II.
Finders, Margaret J. Literacy lessons. III. Title.

LB1631. F56 2007

428.0071'2—dc22

2006023860

Vice President and Executive Publisher: Jeffery W. Johnston
Senior Editor: Linda Ashe Bishop
Senior Production Editor: Mary M. Irvin
Design Coordinator: Diane C. Lorenzo
Senior Editorial Assistant: Laura Weaver
Production Coordination and Text Design: Carlisle Publishing Services
Cover Designer: Kristina Holmes
Cover Image: Corbis
Production Manager: Pamela D. Bennett
Director of Marketing: David Gesell
Marketing Manager: Darey Betts Prybella
Marketing Coordinator: Brian Mounts

This book was set in New Baskerville by Carlisle Publishing Services. It was printed and bound by R. R. Donnelley & Sons Company. The cover was printed by R. R. Donnelley & Sons Company.

Photo credits: All photos by Susan Hynds.

Pearson Prentice Hall™ is a trademark of Pearson Education, Inc.
Pearson® is a registered trademark of Pearson plc
Prentice Hall® is a registered trademark of Pearson Education, Inc.
Merrill® is a registered trademark of Pearson Education, Inc.

Pearson Education Ltd.   Pearson Education Australia PTY, Limited
Pearson Education Singapore, Pte. Ltd.   Pearson Education North Asia Ltd.
Pearson Education Canada, Ltd.   Pearson Educación de Mexico, S.A. de C.V.
Pearson Education—Japan   Pearson Education Malaysia, Pte. Ltd.

10 9 8 7 6 5 4 3 2 1
ISBN: 0-13-175172-7

*To Anna, Sally, and Elizabeth, and to all the
middle school students and their teachers who
have taught us so much*

Preface

Jeez, can I write this over? This is just junk. I thought it was just for you. If we're gonna share it, I want to do it over. I thought this was just for you. This is just junk.

Ryan, 7th grader

Ryan, a seventh-grade student, can teach us much about the significance of the peer dynamic in a middle school literacy classroom. When he thought his writing was just for his teacher, quality was not particularly important, but when his teacher suggested that he share with his peers—well, that was something different.

In this book, you will meet middle school students like Ryan. You'll meet their teachers and their student teachers, and you'll have an opportunity to grapple with the complexities that shape literacy and language arts in the middle grades. Changing school settings, shifting social networks, and fluctuating expectations based on gender roles place middle school students at a pivotal juncture in their lives.

The major difference between being an English *major* and being an English *teacher* is having an intimate knowledge of students and schools. In this text we will focus on that intimate knowledge, specifically for the middle grades. We will examine research and theory as they relate to practice. We will ask you to consider questions such as: What is the teacher's role? What is the student's role? How do current theories translate into practice? What tacit assumptions inform our professional practices? How do we build and implement curriculum? In this text we hope to provide you with the necessary tools to seek answers and grow as professionals.

Our goal in *Language Arts and Literacy in the Middle Grades* is to invite you into the ongoing professional conversations that unite and divide scholars in the field. To do this, we emphasize methods of inquiry rather than mastery of content material. For example, we ask you to look through different lenses to examine what might be lost and gained by a particular teaching approach. Similarly, we ask you to examine a set of national or local standards and consider how these standards might play out differently in diverse classroom settings.

We intend in *Language Arts and Literacy in the Middle Grades* to provide support for you through guided teaching experience, tools for reflection, and an understanding of teaching as a situated process. As you read this book, you'll notice the following features:

- *Guiding Questions.* Each chapter opens with a list of questions that address the focus of the chapter. Here you will be asked to speculate on key issues, examine your own assumptions, connect your experiences to theoretical issues, and articulate your emerging understandings of the chapter content.

- *A Case for Consideration.* Each chapter begins with a short classroom vignette. In these opening cases, we present a range of issues through the words of preservice and inservice teachers reflecting on their classroom experiences. Immediately following each case is a series of prompts for you to address through discussion, writing, or situated role play. We ask you to unpack the embedded issues and speculate on possible teaching strategies to support your students' literacy learning.

- *Standards in Practice.* This feature invites you to consider various aspects of your teaching philosophy and practice in light of such standards as the INTASC English Language Arts Standards, National Board Certification Standards, National Middle School Association recommendations, NCTE/IRA Standards, and your own state standards. You will be asked to consider both the obstacles and opportunities that particular standards pose for you and your middle school students.

- *Fieldwork Journal.* The Fieldwork Journal is designed to support the development of reflective practice by providing tools for inquiry and opportunities for guided reflection. We will ask you to use a variety of informal inquiry techniques to examine the complexities of planning and teaching. You will make observations, conduct interviews, or analyze artifacts as a way of enriching your understanding of teaching and learning in the middle school classroom.

- *Language Lenses.* Chapter 6 introduces the four language lenses: (1) reading and viewing, (2) writing, (3) talking and listening, and (4) language study. In subsequent chapters, you will see how various forms of literacy might look through these lenses. Thus, you are encouraged to think constantly and concretely about how you might integrate the language arts in every aspect of your teaching.

- *Classroom Cases.* Classroom Cases throughout the book showcase teachers working with concrete literacy strategies and teaching techniques such as literature circles, peer response groups, cultural critiques, and grammar mini-lessons. These cases offer multiple models and techniques for approaching literacy teaching and learning. They feature experienced teachers and student teachers who share their successes and struggles in supporting all students. Examining practice through Classroom Cases means taking a critical stance and developing deeper understandings of social, political, and ethical teaching at the middle school level.

- *Resources.* Each chapter concludes with a section of print and electronic resources designed to promote further inquiry and continued professional development.

Still today, texts that address middle school students rarely acknowledge diversity in a richly contextualized manner. In sharing the stories of colleagues who teach in middle schools across the nation and showcasing complex issues at the center of middle school teaching, we hope *Language Arts and Literacy in the Middle Grades* will offer even the most experienced teachers among us the resources to improve our literacy programs. Our aim is to tap your intellectual curiosity and rouse you to continue your professional conversations beyond this text. In the voices of teachers and students that follow, we hope you will recognize your own struggles and successes as teachers and lifetime learners in the middle school classroom.

Acknowledgments

The idea of developing a book for middle school language arts could not have come to fruition without the incredible support and insights of many people. Friends, colleagues, and family members have been supportive, inspiring, and sustaining. We appreciate the conversations and connections with parents, teachers, and students.

In particular, we would like to thank the preservice teachers whose writing appears on these pages. A special note of thanks to Rhiannon Bell, Jason Berrier, Jennifer A. Campbell, Jim DeAngelo, Noah Garfinkel, Connie Gomez, Rebecca Harkavy, Jan Joerling-Leonard, Audra Keiser, Shona Isaacs, Noshin Jihan, Jerry McLaughlin, Tanya M. McRorie, Keith Newvine, Trina Nocerino, Brenna O'Neil, Cari Sue Palma, Ellen Paradise, Jennifer Peters, Cheryl Sawaztke, and James Smith.

We want to acknowledge the generous support of Lawrence L. Cohn. This book is strengthened by the development and implementation of middle school summer programs and teacher education programs designed to prepare teachers to become teacher leaders for urban education, programs funded through The Lawrence L. Cohn Literacy and Learning Laboratory in St. Louis.

We would also like to thank several teachers who have taught us a great deal over the years about working with early adolescents. Some taught across the hall, some opened up their classrooms as research sites, and others shared their stories over cups of coffee. We are particularly grateful to those whose words appear in this book: Ellen Barton, Jonathan Bush, Herm Card, Benjamin Clardy, Amy Craig, Elizabeth Dixon, Debbie Kravitz, Mary McCrone, Sue Peters, Dona Ward, Harry Webb, Joe Wilson, and Gary Zmoleck.

The authors gratefully acknowledge the contributions of reviewers of the second edition: Melissa A. Cain, The University of Findlay; Tracey Meyerhoeffer, College of Southern Idaho; Carol Shepherd, National University; and Charlotte Skinner, Arkansas State University.

Additionally, the first edition of this text benefited from an extensive review by many talented colleagues: Peggy Albers, Georgia State University; Dennise Bartelo, Plymouth State College of the University System of New Hampshire; Marjorie Hancock, Kansas State University; Sandra Hurley, University of Texas at El Paso; Kenneth Kaufman, Loyola University, Chicago; Patricia P. Kelly, Virginia Tech; and Cynthia Leung, North Dakota State University.

Most important, we appreciate the middle school students who have helped us to think deeply about what it means to teach and learn in middle schools. Our special thanks to Jenny Aiken, Cesar Gomez, Casey Grady, Youngin Hahn, Mallory Hohm, Jaclyn Kinney, Jason Mechlin, Shannon Nolan, Stephanie Vaughan, and their classmates across the country.

It is collaboration that has brought this book to life. Our collaboration began with a phone call to a professional colleague and ended in remarkable friendship. We thank each other for the guidance, insights, hard work, and not-so-gentle prodding that we gave to each other. Across the kitchen table and the country, we wrote and talked and wrote together.

Margaret J. Finders
Susan Hynds

Teacher Preparation Classroom

TEACHER PREP

MERRILL
PRENTICE HALL

See a demo at
www.prenhall.com/teacherprep/demo

Your Class. Their Careers. Our Future. Will your students be prepared?

We invite you to explore our new, innovative and engaging website and all that it has to offer you, your course, and tomorrow's educators! Organized around the major courses pre-service teachers take, the Teacher Preparation site provides media, student/teacher artifacts, strategies, research articles, and other resources to equip your students with the quality tools needed to excel in their courses and prepare them for their first classroom.

This ultimate on-line education resource is available at no cost, when packaged with a Merrill text, and will provide you and your students access to:

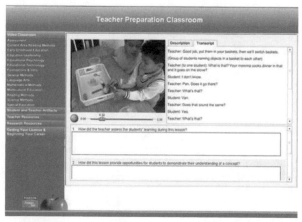

Online Video Library. More than 150 video clips—each tied to a course topic and framed by learning goals and Praxis-type questions—capture real teachers and students working in real classrooms, as well as in-depth interviews with both students and educators.

Student and Teacher Artifacts. More than 200 student and teacher classroom artifacts— each tied to a course topic and framed by learning goals and application questions—provide a wealth of materials and experiences to help make your study to become a professional teacher more concrete and hands-on.

Research Articles. Over 500 articles from ASCD's renowned journal Educational Leadership. The site also includes Research Navigator, a searchable database of additional educational journals.

Teaching Strategies. Over 500 strategies and lesson plans for you to use when you become a practicing professional.

Licensure and Career Tools. Resources devoted to helping you pass your licensure exam; learn standards, law, and public policies; plan a teaching portfolio; and succeed in your first year of teaching.

How to ORDER Teacher Prep for you and your students:
For students to receive a *Teacher Prep* Access Code with this text, instructors must provide a special value pack ISBN number on their textbook order form. To receive this special ISBN, please email **Merrill.marketing@pearsoned.com** and provide the following information:
- Name and Affiliation
- Author/Title/Edition of Merrill text

Upon ordering Teacher Prep for their students, instructors will be given a lifetime Teacher Prep Access Code.

Contents

Chapter

Talking and Listening in the Middle Grades   214

 Chapter

Reading and Viewing in the Middle Grades   254

Part I

Entering the Profession

Entering the Middle School as a Professional

GUIDING QUESTIONS

1. What does it mean to be a middle school teacher?
2. What are the realities of teaching in a middle school?
3. What are the key resources available to you as a middle school teacher of English language arts?

A CASE FOR CONSIDERATION

"So you want to be a middle school teacher. What's wrong with you?"

Connie Garza is a committed preservice middle school teacher. Proudly acknowledging that she has received a large academic scholarship to attend a prestigious university in the Midwest far from home, Connie describes herself as a Latina from south Texas, who "brings a different experience of my own educational background and a passion to help students raised in situations similar to mine see the remarkable world that opens up to them with education." After completing her professional semester in a middle school English language arts classroom, she plans to be a middle school language arts teacher, hopefully back home, for the following fall. Connie was completing her senior year and middle school certification program when she told this story:

> *I went home last summer. It was early May, early enough that schools were in session back home, and so I decided to visit my old middle school. I didn't need to introduce myself to the principal. Mrs. Taylor had been my principal when I went to middle school there. I was excited to tell her that I was going to be a middle school teacher. She met me at the door of the building. When I told her, she didn't say a word. She lifted the back of her hand to my forehead as if she was trying to take my temperature.*

FOR DISCUSSION

After hearing Connie's story in class, Rebecca, another preservice teacher, reported that when she told one of her professors she was going to become a middle school teacher, he said, "Why? You're smart. Why would you want to do that? What's wrong with you?" Some very negative issues appear to be at work here, both obvious and subtle. What are they? What are the assumptions about who would (or should) become a middle school teacher?

PUBLIC PERCEPTIONS AND HARSH REALITIES IN MIDDLE SCHOOL EDUCATION

Middle schools have long been viewed as wastelands. Early adolescence is often characterized as a troubling time. Everywhere in the popular media are stories about adolescents at risk. We are told that adolescents are becoming all the more dangerous to others and to themselves. Amid a growing concern with acts of school violence, rising illegal drug use, and ever-younger teen pregnancies, we invite you to become middle school teachers. In light of the negativity that often surrounds such a choice, why would anyone accept such an invitation?

The narratives that circulate in our culture tell us that middle schools are little more than holding pens whose inhabitants suffer from uncontrollable raging hormones and whose teachers are doomed to controlling rather than teaching their young charges. The counter narratives of engaged learners and dynamic teachers are often reported as surprises and exceptions to these "harsh realities."

As if these exigencies weren't enough, some middle school literacy teachers have little or no preparation in middle schools, little or no preparation with early adolescents, and little or no preparation in English language arts. Clearly, our society has an urgent need to better serve early adolescent learners. Consider the following sobering facts, and ask yourself how you can develop the pedagogical skills and habits of mind to make your classroom a rich and positive environment in which middle school students can thrive:

- The expectation that teachers in today's middle and high schools will teach native speakers and writers of English is outdated (Carroll, Blake, Camalo, & Messer, 1996).
- In her research, Anne Wheelock demonstrates that rising academic requirements and bans on social promotion are pushing kids out of school earlier. Many who might have dropped out in high school are now dropping out in seventh grade. The middle school drop-out rate has jumped 300% in the past 5 years (Ohanian, 2002).
- Approximately 8 million young people between 4th and 12th grade struggle to read at grade level. Some 70% of older readers require some form of remediation.

Very few of these older struggling readers need help to read the words on a page; their most common problem is that they are not able to comprehend what they read (Biancarosa & Snow, 2004).

- For years, ample evidence has shown that U.S. middle schools aren't pulling their weight. Generalizing, one can say that U.S. kids do reasonably well in grades K–4; that their performance falters in grades 5–8; and that (with splendid exceptions) it is dismal in high school. In the middle grades, trouble sets in and disappointment is born (Finn, 2005).

While, indeed, teachers and learners in today's middle schools face many harsh realities, these schools are not, as public perception might suggest, hopeless wastelands or holding pens. Many middle schools are sites of enormous talent and great potential—places where teachers can, indeed, make a remarkable difference in the lives of our future citizens. While it is necessary to face some sobering realities about the needs of early adolescents in contemporary society, it's equally important to question and challenge some of the harmful assumptions and stereotypes that persist about teaching and learning in the middle grades.

Clear and Careful Conceptions

Goodlad (1990) suggests that what is needed is "a clear and careful conception of the educating we expect our schools to do, the conditions most conducive to this educating, as well as the conditions that get in the way" (pp. 3–4). Throughout this book, we will attempt to provide such clear and careful conceptions of teaching and learning with middle school students as well as a host of pedagogical tools to help you examine these challenges and provide for transformative education in the middle grades.

Our goal is not to provide you with a one-size-fits-all set of pedagogical practices, as there exists no such set. We will instead provide an extensive array of pedagogical tools, including knowledge of early adolescents, historical knowledge of middle schools, reading strategies that build from a perspective of strength rather than deficit, research tools to examine practice, and a pedagogical framework to guide your teaching decisions.

We will contrast traditional views of adolescents and assumptions about best practice with views based on current research and theory. Our goal is to help you transform middle schools into learning communities that help students acquire the competencies to participate in and enrich their schools and communities. Although popular media often paint a grave picture, clearly you will find energetic teachers, professional allies, and other professional resources to guide and support your work as a teacher in the middle grades.

Professional Support: Where to Begin?

A professional learning community is vital to ensure your success. So how do you go about locating and joining such a community? There are many resources available locally, nationally, and internationally. The following sections present just a few of these resources.

Professional memberships. Throughout this book, you'll find references to resources available from professional organizations. Many of these organizations offer conferences, books, journals, and other opportunities to help you continue your professional development. Those that might be most beneficial to you as a middle-grades literacy teacher are the International Reading Association, the National Council of Teachers of English, and the National Middle School Association.

The International Reading Association. Information about the International Reading Association can be accessed online at *http://www.ira.org/*. The IRA provides members with access to a broad range of professional meetings, publications, and other resources. Two of its journals may be of particular interest to middle school teachers:

- *The Journal of Adolescent & Adult Literacy* is intended for those involved in the literacy and language arts education of adolescents and older learners. This journal includes practical ways of teaching and studying literacy and also addresses the challenges teachers face in rapidly changing cultural, economic, and social contexts.
- *The Reading Teacher* is intended for those involved with the literacy education of children up to the age of 12. This journal focuses on practices, research, and trends in literacy education and related fields.

The National Council of Teachers of English. The National Council of Teachers of English addresses the teaching and learning of English and the language arts at all levels of education. Information about the NCTE can be accessed online at *http://www.ncte.org/*. The NCTE publishes several professional journals and books. Three of its journals may be of particular interest to those teaching at the middle school level:

- *The English Journal* is intended for middle and secondary English language arts teachers. Issues include articles written by and for teachers on the teaching of writing and reading, literature, and language. Each issue includes reviews of current materials, including books and electronic media.
- *Language Arts* is intended for literacy and language arts teachers of children from pre-kindergarten through the eighth grade. As with other NCTE publications, research-based and practical classroom articles and relevant reviews of professional materials are included.
- *Voices from the Middle* is devoted to literacy and learning at the middle school level. Each issue includes articles written by middle school teachers. Reviews of adolescent literature, a technology column, and professional resources for teachers are also included.

The National Middle School Association. The National Middle School Association offers resources and services for middle school curriculum coordinators, administrators, and teachers in all content areas. Information about the NMSA can be accessed online at *www.nmsa.org*. The NMSA publishes *The Middle School Journal*, a publication focused on all aspects of middle-level education, specifically the educational and developmental needs of young adolescents.

Local, state, and regional affiliates of these organizations or other similar organizations offer professional support in the form of local chapter meetings, conferences, and publications closer to home. You may locate these through the national Web sites or through talking with professional colleagues in your building.

Help down the hall.   In addition to seeking out publications and professional organizations, you should not underestimate the tremendous expertise that is just down the hall from you. Most experienced teachers and other school professionals will view your requests for advice as a compliment and a mark of your professionalism, not a sign of weakness. Here are just a few examples of people who can support you early in your career.

Media specialists.   Get to know the librarian or media specialist in your building as soon as you arrive. Media specialists can provide great resources for you. They know books, Internet resources, available media, and local community resources. They likely know the culture of the school and the official rules for operating there as well.

If you have a project in mind, make sure to go to your media specialists early so that they can help you locate additional resources. Mrs. Peters, a media specialist with more than 20 years of experience, gives the following advice to new teachers: "I can order materials through interlibrary loan. I can purchase materials. I can get audio and videotapes to support most any project that teachers are developing. But I can't do it with a couple of days' notice." She agrees that the media specialist might be a great person to make friends with early in one's career. Here is a list of questions that she offers for beginning teachers to explore during their first weeks at their new school:

1. What is the school's internet use policy?
2. How do I reserve space in the library for my classes?
3. How do I order videos, books, and other materials?
4. How do I sign up for computer use?
5. What are the school policies on censorship?
6. What counts as fair use in terms of copying?
7. What's here in the library?
8. What seems to be popular with my students?

Guidance counselors.   A school guidance counselor's job is configured differently from district to district. You will want to find out how your particular school defines the job of the guidance counselor. In most schools, the counselor works closely with teachers, parents, students, and community support personnel. Counselors may be in charge of programs for students who are facing social, academic, or legal problems. Some schools sponsor peer support activities through the guidance office. In other schools, the guidance office may handle only course and standardized test schedules. Most counselors know a great deal about the local community and can help you to learn what local resource agencies are available to you and your students. Your guidance counselor will likely know a great deal about the standardized tests that are administered in your school. He or she probably works directly with special needs faculty and family support personnel. The counselor can help you get to know your students, their families, and the community.

Social workers.   Some schools have full-time social workers; others do not. If your school has a social worker, you will want to get acquainted and learn what support systems are available to your students and their families. If special support groups are available for middle school students, you will want to know what they are. If you have concerns about a particular student, the social worker or guidance counselor can help you to identify warning signs and locate support or interventions when needed. As a language arts teacher, you may learn, through your students' writing, information that is far beyond your expertise. Don't try to take on the responsibilities of a social worker or guidance counselor. Allow the professional guidance staff to mentor you in knowing when further action may be in the best interest of any particular student. They might suggest referrals, additional testing, or other interventions. The main point to realize is that they are highly trained to help students and to help you.

School nurses.   You will want to know the school policies and practices regarding health and accidents before you *need* to know them in an emergency. Ask your nurse about any concerns you may have regarding the health and well-being of your students. For example, find out the specific ways to handle blood and bodily fluids so you will be prepared in case an accident should occur in your room. You may have students who have special medical needs. Alert the nurse if you have concerns. At this developmental stage, many students are growing and changing quite rapidly. Medications that have been effective in the past may no longer serve early adolescents in the same ways. Girls who begin their menstrual cycles may be unprepared. Work closely and confidentially with your school nurse so that students' medical needs are handled as discreetly and promptly as possible to ensure the well-being of your students and to avoid classroom disruption and student embarrassment.

Special education teachers.   The special education staff can help you design and modify lessons for students with special needs in your classroom. They can help you to determine appropriate levels of support or modification that may be necessary for a student with a disability, and they are good sources of information about adaptations and curricular materials that enable you to support all learners in your classroom. A special education teacher can also offer guidance in working with students and their families. If you are unsure whether a student needs additional help, a special education teacher can help you to request appropriate additional testing and make referrals. If you need advice on how to hold a parent conference, the special education teacher can arrange appropriate meetings, make referrals, or facilitate other supportive interactions among parents, social service providers, and school personnel.

ESL teachers. Your middle school classroom will likely include students whose home language is not English. An English as a second language (ESL) teacher will be a vital resource to help you to design and guide language development for these students. The ESL program may have additional funding for alternative texts and materials for your second-language learners. Even if no additional funding is available, ESL teachers can help you to adapt your instructional materials. They will be able to guide you in understanding some aspects of second language acquisition and help you think about the ways you might support middle school students with a range of language abilities in your classroom.

Mentor teachers and administrators. Seek out a teacher who can help you get acquainted with the school and community. If you do not have a teaching mentor assigned to you, asking your principal to assign one might be a good idea. Experienced teaching colleagues will help you through the hard days and celebrate the small victories with you. They can clarify school routines and help you streamline many of your nonteaching duties such as duplicating class materials, taking attendance, sending sick or disciplined students to the office, collecting tickets at games, distributing books, and creating a record book. Find a colleague who can provide support, even if it's in the form of going out for a cup of coffee after school. This person can, in a very real sense, serve as your advocate and your lifeline.

Parents. Contrary to popular folk wisdom, middle school parents and middle school students are often closely connected, and most like it that way. Although many parents may have jobs that prevent them from participating during regular school hours, most will be happy to assist in any way they can. Some parents may be unfamiliar with how they might contribute to their children's education, and your invitations may not be accepted because of families' diverse home and school obligations. Finders and Lewis (1994) suggest that instead of assuming that absence means not caring, teachers must understand and break through the barriers that hinder some parents from participating in their children's education more fully. They note that parents' own school experiences, diverse economic and time constraints, and varied linguistic and cultural practices at times make parents feel uncomfortable and unwelcome in school settings. You'll want to create opportunities to get to know parents, making them feel confident and comfortable in becoming active participants in your classroom.

In their ground-breaking work in the barrios of Arizona, Luis Moll and his colleagues (1990, 1992) discovered that, particularly with bilingual students of working-class families, teachers need to escape the deficit thinking that relegates such students to meaningless drill-and-practice activities. Instead, Moll urges teachers to investigate the "funds of knowledge" available in students' homes and communities. By engaging students in purposeful activities and relying on the considerable expertise of community and family members, teachers can draw on and develop students' literacy skills in their first and their second languages.

Teachers using a "funds of knowledge" approach regularly invite parents and other knowledgeable adults into the classroom to share their expertise. Such collaborations not only build community relations and student confidence, they also enrich your teaching and build your reputation with parents and caregivers. Though you might be tempted to close your door to parents in your first years of teaching, try inviting selected parents in to share their time and expertise with you and your students. Once you get to know your students' parents and caregivers, you'll be amazed at how much easier talking with them becomes whenever those inevitable problems and conflicts arise with their children. Parents can offer great insight into and assistance for their children. They can be significant collaborators in designing effective literacy lessons and offer a direct link to resources in the local community.

Community organizations. Find out what resources are available in your community for contacting possible guest speakers, enriching your curricular materials, or helping you to design appropriate community projects. Community connections are a hallmark of an effective middle school program; they can make literacy learning real and relevant in your classroom. Each community has rich and unique resources that should be tapped. Begin with your students to find out about such resources. Local libraries, parent advocacy organizations, courts, community centers, technology centers, and health agencies are just a few examples of resources available to you. Through "social action" or "social justice" projects, your students can engage in meaningful and important activities such as volunteering at homeless shelters and facilities for the elderly or working for change in public policies. The process of documenting and publishing such work can provide tremendous real-world opportunities for students to learn valuable literacy skills.

MONITORING YOUR TEACHING: YOUR FIELDWORK JOURNAL

Throughout this book, we ask you to take a critical orientation to teaching in the middle school. Such an orientation "underscores the need to develop the habit of questioning taken-for-granted assumptions about teaching, learning, knowledge, schooling" (Feiman-Nemser, 1990, p. 227). Effective teachers of any age group learn to examine the assumptions that guide their practice, to monitor their own teaching, and to modify instructional approaches to support all learners in their classrooms. Each chapter in this book will include one or more features titled "Fieldwork Journal." The intent of the fieldwork journal is to give you a variety of inquiry methods for the purpose of gathering and examining information about yourself, your students, and your teaching practices.

Your fieldwork journal supports the development of an inquiry-oriented approach to teaching. You'll gain tools to be a teacher researcher, which simply means that you'll learn to make close observations of students and examine your own practice, thinking critically about what you see and do as well as the assumptions that undergird your teaching. The fieldwork journal provides brief, focused writing experiences (short journal entries designed to support reflective thinking) as well as longer classroom inquiry activities (using research strategies such as interviewing, recording observations, and analyzing artifacts). Fieldwork journal 1-1 invites you to think about resources available to you as a middle-grades teacher.

Fieldwork Journal 1-1

A Blanket of Support

Mark Driscoll (1999) uses the term "blanket of support" to characterize the ways in which a district provides professional development support for teachers. We ask you to look at the blanket of support available to serve as your "security blanket" or protection against anxiety, focusing specifically on concrete examples available in your field setting. The term "blanket" encompasses all kinds of assistance from human resources to logistical supports. We suggest that you begin where all good teaching begins—with a real group of students in a real classroom context.

- **Describe the school system:** You might focus on one of the districts in the local area or the one in which you will be doing your student teaching or field placement. Describe this setting in as much detail as possible. If you're having trouble finding information, visit the district Web site or call the district office for information.
- **Identify the community:** Indicate geographic location, size, primary employers, per capita income, average years of education among residents, problems/issues within the community, community support for education, socioeconomic levels, and ethnic diversity.
- **Identify the school:** Include information about the school name, mascot, support for a middle school philosophy, support for community-based education, socioeconomic levels of students' families, and any problems at this middle school such as the presence of gangs or drug and alcohol use. Explore the following questions by contacting the district office or Web site and talking with other teachers in the building:
- What percentage of students are on free or reduced lunch programs?
- What is the racial and ethnic makeup of the school?
- Who decides what and when courses will be taught?
- What formal opportunities are available for parents to be involved in the school?
- Do teachers have common planning time? Do they work in teams for thematic planning?
- Does your school operate on an "inclusive" model in which individuals are placed in the classroom to assist students with special needs, or do students spend some part of their day in a resource room?
- Do any students speak English as a second language? What services, if any, are provided for these students?
- What support services are available for students?
- What support services are available for teachers?

BEGINNING THE JOB SEARCH: IT'S NEVER TOO EARLY

Though it may seem entirely premature, *right now* is the best time to be in the job market, even if you are only beginning to student teach. Remember that your student teaching and field placements will put you in touch with many potential employers and colleagues. In a sense, every time you enter a field site, you are entering a potential place of employment. You never know when you may be "applying" for a job some time in the near future. Even if you don't plan to stay in the geographic area where you currently are, it's amazing how life plans can shift on a moment's notice.

It's a good idea to meet with department chairs and principals during your teaching placements and invite them into your room to observe your teaching. This way, if you do apply for a job, these individuals will have first-hand knowledge of you. It's important to begin seeking out experiences and collecting support materials to enhance your "employment potential" before you actually begin looking for positions in earnest.

If you are just beginning the job search, the news is good: Contrary to popular opinion, teaching positions are available out there, and even more will be available in the coming years. It is estimated that in the next few years, there will be a 50% turnover in current teaching positions. Teaching professionals across the nation are growing older, much of the current teaching force is nearing retirement age, and many teachers are retiring earlier than their predecessors. That means simply that there are, and will continue to be, many job opportunities for you. You may be wondering, however, what is different about working with early adolescents and what specific expectations future employers hold for middle school teachers.

Rising to the Top of the Pile: What Middle School Principals Value

As a way of supporting the preservice teachers in her program, Margaret conducted telephone interviews with 50 middle school principals, asking them, "What in particular makes one candidate's materials rise to the top of the application files?" This section explores the main reasons that principals gave for deciding whom they would interview. The following criteria are rank-ordered by importance to the middle school principals interviewed.

Explicit interest in teaching middle school.   Enthusiasm for this age group was by far the number one consideration that principals expressed in their reasons for inviting a candidate for an interview and for hiring prospective teachers. One principal made the following observation:

> *I want to know that they are looking for a teaching position at the middle school level, not just looking for any teaching position. I read their letters and look for specifics about their interest in middle school students.*

Of course, in some states, certification at the middle level is a requirement. For others, however, middle schools can and do attract applications across certification programs. Scan your cover letter and résumé, making sure you send implicit and explicit messages about your interest in teaching at the middle school level.

Classroom experiences and evidence of success at the middle school level.

According to several principals, letters of reference from middle school teachers and principals who have observed the candidate at this level are important criteria. Principals reported that they scrutinize résumés for evidence of contact time and successful experience with middle school students. "I want to know that they can be successful and happy working in my building," one said.

Some principals mentioned that they were especially interested in finding candidates who had demonstrated leadership with this age group, for example, organizing outings, attending field trips, and overseeing major projects. One noted that, even if the candidate does not have teaching experiences at this level, he looks for individuals who have experiences with young people of middle school age through community clubs, recreational sports organizations, religious groups, and other programs. Well before it's time to think about applying for a teaching position, seek out opportunities to work with early adolescents in school and nonschool settings.

Abilities to work collaboratively.

Quite often teaching is characterized as an individual activity. Some teachers tend to close their doors and work privately. Not so in the middle school. An effective middle school teacher must be a team member. Since middle school teachers often work across disciplinary boundaries, principals want to know how well an individual can work with others. Seek out opportunities to gain experience in working on a team. Then consider ways to demonstrate your emerging competence in this area. An interdisciplinary unit and letters from colleagues in other content areas are two sources of evidence to document your abilities as a team player.

Credentials in more than one content area and/or additional teaching endorsements.

A middle school teacher who has certification in more than one content area is highly desirable. A candidate who can teach math, science, or social studies in addition to language arts will certainly be regarded as more employable than someone with only one teaching credential. Since class sizes may shift from year to year, principals often find they need to cover additional sections of one subject for a short period of time. They may need 1.5 teachers in one subject and .5 in another, for example. Middle school teachers who can teach multiple subjects make it easier for principals to accommodate such needs.

That said, do not add endorsements and certifications just to secure a job. Do so because you have an interest in more than one subject. Although, for a number of reasons, you might not be able to complete a second endorsement at the same time as you complete your literacy certification program, you may find time in your schedule to complete some of the requirements. If so, make it clear to principals and other hiring personnel that you are working toward a second endorsement. You may be hired with the understanding that you can complete the requirements during your first few years of employment.

Abilities to work with students in nonacademic contexts.

Many middle schools offer social and academic programs outside the classroom. In addition to your preparation in English language arts, consider what additional areas of expertise you bring to the middle school. Think about the types of extracurricular outings, explorations, and performances you might be qualified to sponsor. Consider how you might showcase your hobbies, social involvement activities, and expertise in a middle school setting.

Specific course work in middle school. Several principals in the survey asked, "Does this applicant know anything about the middle school philosophy?" Whereas all beginning teachers will need support and guidance, principals hope to hire those who bring a working understanding of middle schools with them. They want to build on that existing knowledge rather than mentor new teachers in every aspect of middle school life. As one administrator put it, "We often have to start from scratch because the new teachers don't know much about middle schools and how they work." In your letter, résumé, and/or portfolio, you will want to make it clear that you understand the central components of effective middle school programs and can put them into practice.

Understanding the needs of students who are deemed "at-risk" and those with special needs. One principal remarked, "I want my teachers to find ways to support all learners. We need to keep them in school. It's in my building where we can lose them for good." As classrooms become more inclusive, middle school teachers work with a wide range of students. We do want all middle school students to complete middle school successfully and go on to high school. We don't want to "lose them for good." Gain as much experience as you can with programs and teachers who are succeeding with students who have not been successful in traditional classroom settings.

As unfair as it may seem, the inexperienced teacher is often the one who is placed with students most in need of extra enrichment and help. Quite frankly, veteran teachers are either exhausted or unwilling to work with such students in many schools. Despite your relative lack of experience, in your first job, you may be expected to "hit the ground running" with strategies and approaches best suited for struggling students. It's important to view this situation as an opportunity and not a burden. Many teachers (your authors included) find these students to be the most refreshing, honest, and often surprisingly capable individuals they encounter in a lifetime of teaching. You can make remarkable gains with students who have "fallen through the cracks" of traditional schooling, students who are most at risk for failure due to poverty or limited English proficiency, and those who enter school with background knowledge and experiences that do not map easily onto school expectations.

In your field placements and other settings, make sure to seek out experiences and document your progress with "struggling" learners. You'll not only be more marketable, but you may be surprised to discover how personally and professionally meaningful such experiences can be.

Ability to integrate technology into classroom instruction. Principals reported that they like to hire individuals who are technologically proficient. Many middle schools do not have a technology teacher, and technological support in a building may be minimal. So middle school teachers must be able to integrate technology into their curriculum. In some states, you may be able to work toward a technology endorsement; but for many principals, demonstrated competence is enough. Successful completion of a single course or workshop can make your application shine. You may want to showcase your technological skills through creating personal teaching Web pages or an electronic portfolio.

Knowledge of local, state, and national standards and standardized tests.
With increasing state and national demands for accountability, principals want to hire teachers with extensive skills in assessment strategies and those who bring a deep understanding of the ways in which state and national standards can be integrated into the local curriculum. You may want to draw from some of the exercises in this book to showcase your understanding of national standards and appropriate assessment strategies. It's also useful to specifically link your goals and objectives in written unit and lesson plans with your state's standards so that administrators and other school personnel can see at a glance how you are meeting mandated standards.

Competence in subject matter.
Clearly, all teachers must have a deep and broad understanding of their subject matter. To design, implement, and adapt teaching strategies, teachers must make appropriate connections between the structure of the discipline and the experiences that students bring to the classroom. In addition to teaching the content effectively, middle school teachers must have a strong content knowledge to be able to work across disciplinary boundaries, specifically to anticipate and make curricular connections through interdisciplinary work.

Knowing about literacy teaching is different from demonstrating your knowledge of theoretical and research perspectives from your discipline. This book contains many references to current research and scholarship. Whenever you have a chance, seek out the articles and books referenced here, and see what you can learn from a closer scrutiny of what they have to say. Consider adding quotations and key ideas to your teaching portfolio, not only to document content knowledge, but to bring coherence and relevance to your planning and teaching.

The foregoing criteria mentioned by principals might serve you in multiple ways. They might guide you early on as you select courses and gain professional experiences in school and community settings. They can also help you later as you prepare for teaching applications and interviews. As the following section reveals, it would be useful to refer back to these criteria often as you create your professional portfolio.

PREPARING A PROFESSIONAL PORTFOLIO FOR TEACHING IN THE MIDDLE GRADES

A professional portfolio is more than a collection of documents that represents your views of teaching and learning. You may want to consider it a process-folio, because it is a way for you to document not only what you and your students do, but also how you think and make decisions as a teacher. The purposes of a professional portfolio are (a) to reflect on your practice and (b) to make visible to colleagues, supervisors, and potential employers what you can do in the classroom and what you know about the subject area, your students, and your teaching. The following questions may serve to facilitate discussions among your teaching colleagues and give some direction for you as you plan for and design your professional portfolio.

In describing what might go into a portfolio for middle school teaching, we might turn to the National Middle School Association's summary of "Seven key developmental needs" of Young Adolescents. The NMSA defines these needs as follows:

> The uniqueness of the phase of early adolescence stems from a variety of developmental needs, variations in the maturation rate, and complexity due to their simultaneous occurrence. Seven key developmental needs (Scales, 1991) characterize early adolescence:
>
> - positive social interaction with adults and peers
> - structure and clear limits
> - physical activity
> - creative expression
> - competence and achievement
> - meaningful participation in families, school and communities
> - opportunities for self-definition
>
> Retrieved January 23, 2006, from The National Middle School Association Website: http://www.nmsa.org/Research/ResearchSummaries/Summary5/tabid/257/Default.aspx

Although the NMSA lists seven developmental needs, we have selected five that seem most relevant to competencies you might document in your teaching portfolio. Figure 1-1 lists a few possibilities for artifacts you might begin collecting as a way of demonstrating your experience and expertise in these five areas.

As digital media become more accessible and pervasive, teacher education programs are moving toward the creation of electronic portfolios. Electronic, as opposed to traditional, print portfolios present many advantages, most obvious is their portability and adaptability for immediate access to print and nonprint artifacts through hyperlinks. While most potential employers or selection committees would be reluctant to sit through a time-consuming presentation of your portfolio, and while you'd be loathe to leave your only copy behind after an interview, many interviewers might appreciate a CD-ROM that they could peruse and pass around in the event that you become a finalist for a teaching position. Better yet, you might place your portfolio on the Web and simply include the Web link on your résumé.

A growing number of software programs is available for anyone wishing to create an electronic portfolio. To attempt a current and inclusive description is beyond the scope of this book. A good beginners' guide for creating a teaching portfolio using "off-the-shelf" software can be accessed at *http://electronicportfolios.org/portfolios/iste2k.html*

If you don't have a software program specifically developed for electronic portfolios, you can use some combination of more generic programs including database software (e.g., FileMaker Pro or Microsoft Access); hypermedia programs (e.g., HyperStudio or HyperCard); multimedia authoring software (e.g., Macromedia Authorware, Microsoft PowerPoint, AppleWorks). You probably can borrow a digital

FIGURE 1-1   Teaching Portfolio

Competencies	Artifacts
Engaging students in positive social interactions with peers and adults	• Photos or videos of students working in collaborative groups, interacting with guest speakers, working in community settings • Copies of discussion guides or other teaching materials created to facilitate small and large group learning • Excerpts of videotaped class discussions and other interactive class sessions • Evidence of your work with students in extracurricular activities
Transforming physical activities into meaningful learning experiences	• Photos or videos of students engaged in dramatic or performative literacy experiences such as skits, plays, or readers' theater productions
Building upon the competence and experiences that students bring to the classroom	• Copies of personal letters and teaching evaluations from students and parents, and documenting your ability to relate to early adolescents • Excerpts from supervisor or host teacher observations, documenting your ability to draw upon student strengths • Reflections from your field work journal, discussing your work with students in and outside the classroom • Photos or diagrams that demonstrate how your classroom is designed to promote collaborative and independent work by early adolescents • Examples of writing and reading response menus that demonstrate your ability to tap into a variety of student learning preferences and needs • Samples of student work before and after a lesson or unit
Promoting meaningful participation with families, school, and the larger world	• Letters regarding their children's progress • Notes, conferences, phone calls, and emails • Photos of caregivers and community members working with students in your classroom • Student writings, photos, and other evidence of class-sponsored involvement in community and/or national concerns
Working collaboratively with other teachers and support personnel to promote the social and academic development of students	• Excerpts of an I.E.P. plan you helped to create as a member of a team (remember to preserve anonymity of all participants) • Notes from or descriptions of your work on interdisciplinary planning teams • Excerpts of case studies or journal entries describing your work with students from diverse backgrounds and a broad spectrum of abilities. • Teaching materials or other artifacts designed for the purpose of adapting lessons for students with special needs • Certificates of attendance or conference programs that demonstrate your continuing commitment to professional development as related to teaching • Excerpts of "adaptations" sections of lesson plans, demonstrating your ability to provide differentiated instruction • Assessment materials designed by you to tap the diverse strengths of learners

camera, video camera, and scanner, as well as video, audio, and photo editing software, from your local library, school system, or college technology center.

There is much to do in the coming weeks and months as you prepare for and seek out a middle school teaching position. But as one of Margaret's student teachers remarked, "Mistakes are the best learning experiences." We can assure you that you'll have an ample supply of both mistakes and learning experiences during your career as a middle school teacher.

CLASSROOM CASES

In the following section, and in each chapter of this book, we will provide you with some "Classroom Cases," which are vignettes involving actual middle school teachers designed to showcase some complexities of teaching, suggest some lessons learned, and help you think about your own current or future teaching. Classroom Case 1-1 introduces you to Joe Jackson and his attempts to support a group of students who call themselves "the techno trio."

Classroom Case 1-1

The Techno Trio: Staying Within the Lines

Roderick, Isaac, and Jimmy, the "techno trio," as they liked to be called, sit in the back of my sixth-grade classroom, most every day huddled together over a notebook, impatiently waiting for their turn at the computer.

"If Samantha knew how to turn the computer on, she might be about done by now," Isaac whispered, loudly enough for me and the girls who were working beside them to hear. Rod chimed in, "Yeah, Sammi and Paris say, 'Let's comb our hair and use the monitor for a mirror. That's what a computer is for, right?' They don't even know how to turn it on! Oh, duh."

The techno trio shared a fascination for monsters and computers and a strong dislike for girls. They avidly devoured comic books and were, in fact, the proud authors of a comic book series, *Monster Mad*. They read, wrote, and drew monsters and super monsters. Notebook after notebook was filled with storyboards for future episodes in the never-ending story of the arch monster rivals, Monster Mad and Dr. Dead.

Although they were avid readers and writers, all three boys were failing my language arts class. They did not participate in literature discussions. They did not write in their learning logs. They did not hand in daily assignments. I didn't think they read anything except comic books, monster web sites, and technology manuals they needed in order to advance the production quality of *Monster Mad*. I struggled with ways to support the techno trio. I struggled with ways to keep them from intimidating less capable computer users. To be honest, I literally struggled to keep them "in line." I hate to admit it but I resorted to placing a masking tape square around their desks with the firm instructions to "keep in your area." The trio knew they couldn't "drive" their desks beyond the taped boundary or they wouldn't be allowed to work together for five days.

One day they were working together, staying within the lines, and trying to finish the next installment of *Monster Mad*. It was difficult, since there was only one computer in my room, and none of the trio was allowed to go to the media center because they had abused that privilege the day before. They hated to wait for their turn at the computer. Smug about their computer skills, which really did far exceed everyone's in the room (even the media specialist often turned to them for help), Roderick, Isaac, and Jimmy often created a disturbance when they were expected to wait for others in their class.

I worked closely with their parents, creating a contract for them to earn and lose privileges at home and at school, but nothing worked. The techno trio simply refused to do anything except create monsters, which sometimes mutilated and murdered other students in the class, especially Samantha and Paris. Although I wanted to give students the chance to express themselves and make personal choices, such choices often resulted in hurtful acts, such as an excerpt from "Monster Mad, Dr. Dead, and the Two-Headed Princess of Darkness" that Isaac shared aloud in class one day. It didn't take Samantha and Paris long to recognize themselves in the thinly veiled caricature called the "two headed princess" in this excerpt of their story:

> It was some horrible thing. Sa-Pa, the two headed princess, was coming right at Dr. Dead. He never had saw anything so hidious. The two-headed creature was talking and talking, "Oh, my hair. Oh, my lip stick," the monster said. She used this to hynotize her victims. She talked ooo so much. She never did shut up. Dr. Dead couldn't stand it. For the first time ever, Dr. Dead agreed with Monster Mad. We must kill this hideous thing, he said. We must cut off their heads. We must, said MM. Let's cut them to pieces. And so we cut off their heads. Blood was everywhere. It was too bloody. Dr. Dead and Monster Mad washed their hands and went out to dinner together. On the way to the restrant, they seen Sa-Pas mom. She cried and cried. So they killed the mom too. They threw her in a paper shredder and it was so bloody.

The Doctor Dead story went unquestioned. I just asked the boys to stop reading and return to their seats. To avoid such potential hurtful acts in the future, I made a band-aid rule about writing. "If it can't be cured by one band-aid, you can't include it in your story." Writers couldn't approach a violence rating over what a band-aid might cover. I'm not really too pleased with myself and this grand solution. Too clever. Too simple, I think, but it's worked so far.

But I really wanted to focus my energies on the need to find productive outlets for these technologically savvy students. Contracts with students and parents have been very effective for many of my students; they weren't working with these three. Punishments and rewards at home and school didn't help me to harness their computer enthusiasm that was so often channeled into hurtful experiences for other students. Finally I hit upon an idea that seemed to work. The boys now serve as specialists in the media center during our activity time. They offer lessons to teachers and other students and are in the process of sharing a regularly scheduled power point slide show entitled "T3-Techno Trio Tips." In the weekly updates, they write about Internet searches, Photoshop, IM, and blogging.

I felt something positive was really happening when I overheard Rod say to Paris, "How about making a web site for your jean zine" the other day. No, they haven't made a complete transformation like some of their monster characters. They are not successfully completing every assignment on time, but together we are finding ways to make literacy learning meaningful to them on their terms.

For Discussion

These sixth-grade boys and girls seem to hold very different computer competencies and literacy interests. How might you support the literacy learning of Jimmy, Isaac, and Roderick? Of Samantha and Paris? What different steps might Mr. Jackson have taken at the time that the Techno Trio was reading "Two-Headed Princess"? What are some assumptions about classroom management in the middle school classroom implicit in Mr. Jackson's case?

CLASSROOM MANAGEMENT AND RULES OF ENGAGEMENT

One of the first things that beginning middle school teachers worry about is classroom management. Classroom management is most often characterized as a set of rules of behavior external to teaching and learning. In Classroom Case 1-1, you may understand the need to "manage the techno trio," but we encourage you to think more deeply and critically about what counts as "good behavior" in your classroom. We find many classroom management plans problematic in two ways.

First, the school's emphasis on the "management" of youth is, according to Luke and Luke (2001), an ideology that normalizes youth as "uncivil, unruly, techno-subjects"(p. 8). Second, traditional models of classroom management that focus on "handling" or "managing" students often deny diversity, ignoring the ways in which we might tap the multiple cultural resources that middle school students bring to the classroom.

Our notions of what is "good" or "correct" behavior are powerfully shaped by our own (typically middle-class) culture. Such notions, though they may soothe our frazzled nerves, are not necessarily held by members of cultures different from our own. "Culturally Responsive Teaching" (Ladson-Billings, 1994) is a pedagogy that recognizes the importance of including students' cultural references in all aspects of learning. It also influences how we define classroom expectations as well as set rules of engagement.

With students from various backgrounds, but particularly with African American students, Ladson-Billings argues for the importance of believing that all students can learn, making strong connections with the community, and inviting students to share aspects of their homes and cultures that might not be understood or appreciated by White, middle-class students. It's not important, Ladson-Billings argues, that teachers attempt to imitate the behaviors and language patterns of their African American students, but that they learn something about all students' culturally shaped verbal and nonverbal behaviors, preferred ways of learning and discussing ideas, religious beliefs, experiences, and attitudes toward schooling. Some students, for example, may be active learners who learn through physical activity and are mistakenly labeled as hyperactive or out of control; others may participate more vocally in class discussions and be labeled loud or impertinent.

There is much to be lost when curricular decisions are made to control middle school students rather than to educate them deeply. Clearly, we are not suggesting an "anything goes" classroom. Rather we suggest that you develop "habits of mind" about diversity and the establishment of explicit rules of engagement for your classroom that lead to an inclusive and participatory middle school classroom that builds on and invites diverse forms of learning.

Classroom management issues can be approached from the same deficit paradigms that attempt to explain the underachievement of students who have historically not been served well by urban schools (Weiner, 2003). Weinstein (2003) discusses culturally responsive classroom management and explains how teachers who create orderly classrooms that are also academically demanding can begin to interrupt the deficit paradigm that is so pervasive in most urban schools.

In Fieldwork Journal 1-2, we'd like you to think about what counts as "good behavior" in your classroom.

Fieldwork Journal 1-2

Exploring Beliefs and Expectations About Classroom Management

As you read the statements in Figure 1-2, rate your opinion in the left-hand column from 1 strongly disagree to 5 strongly agree. In the Thinking Aloud column, note the ease or difficulty you had with the rating and list any questions that you would like to ask of your colleagues.

1. Strongly Disagree
2. Disagree
3. Neutral
4. Agree
5. Strongly Agree

What counts as "good behavior" is most often based on the teacher's own cultural, family, and educational experiences. This is not to suggest that you post no rules, but simply that you keep the focus on learning, not on power, and continue to ask yourself the following two questions as you prepare for entry into your middle school classroom:

1. What behaviors do I deem "non-school-like"? Is there a cultural basis for some of these behaviors?
2. How might I tap students' needs for social and physical activities within the frame of what counts as good behaviors in my classroom?

We all hold a set of beliefs about what is appropriate and inappropriate with regard to classrooms or any other context. Our beliefs are built from our experiences, but

FIGURE 1-2

Rating	Statement	Thinking Aloud
	1. If a student puts her head down, she is being disrespectful to me.	
	2. Students' home life is their private business and shouldn't enter as a factor in the ways in which they behave in school.	
	3. It doesn't bother me if a student goes to get something across the room without asking as long as it doesn't interfere with others.	
	4. If a student turns in a late homework assignment, it is not my problem.	
	5. I don't want to reprimand a student publicly because it might hurt his/her feelings.	
	6. I need to reprimand students publicly to set an example and to show students that I am fair to all with regard to classroom rules.	
	7. By the time students are in middle school, I shouldn't have to explain my rules.	
	8. I will not accept excuses from a student who is tardy.	
	9. I will use rewards such as movies and library time if my students are well behaved.	
	10. I will use punishments such as taking away privileges and small group time if my students misbehave.	
	11. If a student is absent, it is her/his responsibility to make up work, not mine.	
	12. My students understand that they can interrupt my lecture if they have a relevant question.	
	13. If a student requests a hall pass, I never honor the request.	
	14. I want students to face me and have all eyes on me when I am talking.	
	15. Students who call out are rude and disrespectful.	

these experiences seem so readily apparent to us that we come to accept them as true for all. One of the key elements for educating teachers for diversity, according to Zeichner (1993), is equipping preservice teachers to develop a clearer sense of their own ethnic and cultural identities. In Fieldwork Journal 1-3, we ask that you create a vivid snapshot of your culture in an attempt to uncover where your beliefs about appropriate and inappropriate behaviors and practices may have originated.

Fieldwork Journal 1-3

Coming of Age: Home Culture Snapshot

In this exploration, you will consider a family or neighborhood event in terms of how it reveals something about your cultural background and assumptions. The writing you create should help you to think about what was important to you at the time of your own early adolescence.

Like a lens, our culture filters what we know, do, and think. Sometimes, we have to trick ourselves into seeing what our culture defines as "ordinary," "right," or "good." For some time now, researchers in the social sciences and humanities have turned to qualitative research methods, especially ethnography, to understand complex human phenomena. This kind of research does not start with empirical assumptions or hypotheses about the way things are or should be, but with a deep exploration of the question "What's going on here?" Your task is to create a vivid portrait of some recurring event in your family or neighborhood. Try to remove your cultural blinders and write about this event or occasion in a way that attempts to "make the invisible visible." Conclude your snapshot with a discussion of how you have come to hold the particular values and beliefs revealed in your description.

Brenna's Culture Snapshot in the following example may help you to understand how to make visible your own particular cultural assumptions.

Brenna O'Neill

The Scene

My name is Brenna O'Neill. Although I am fourth generation, I identify as Irish American. I was born in California, but my family is originally from and has been living in the mid-west since my great-great grandfather came to this country from Ireland during the potato famine of the mid 1800s. My grandfather's father and his father helped to build the railroads that now connect this country, as many immigrant Irish did. My grandfather however, worked high up in the administration of the Schlitz Brewing Company, one of only a few who did not have a college degree. My grandfather was a talker of the first order and could tell a story like no one I know (except maybe my father), captivating and funny to the point of tears. This I believe to be a main reason as to why my grandfather and father, becoming a college professor, climbed so high up the socioeconomic ladder.

Our extended family is a tightly knit one, spending every holiday or vacation together. This might perhaps be because of the transplant out to California when my father and his siblings were in their early twenties. A central part of these frequent family gatherings were picnics. My family, being new to California, Irish Catholic, and enjoying drink, would generally hold our picnics outside at one vineyard or another, after a morning of tasting in two or more wineries. These picnics took place the day after any major holiday, and consisted of my grandmother's amazing leftovers from the feast the night before. My grandmother was actually German, but her favorite cuisine to cook was Italian, and to this day, never have I tasted better manicotti. The picnics always seemed to me spontaneous, but happened with such regularity, that I now wonder if it wasn't my young age that made it seem that way.

We would manage to squeeze the whole family into three or four cars, and would head south out of Saratoga to the rolling coastal range just beneath San Jose.

These days were almost always sunny, making the dried grass on the hillsides shine a deep gold against the blue sky of autumn. There would be a slight chill in the air that one could combat with a jacket, or simply by standing in the filtered sun of the end of the year. We'd stop at one or two tasting rooms where, while we waited for our parents and grandparents, the cousins would run around outside, or munch on the crackers at the counter used to clean one's palate. After the tasting at the last vineyard, my grandmother would set up the picnic on a table outside, spreading out her reddish tablecloth printed with pink and white flowers, the feast would begin. Soda cans were popped and wine and beer bottles cracked, and then came the whirlwind of talking and laughing. My grandfather did most of the talking—even when others were telling their stories, so that whoever had the loudest voice and the funniest story was the one who was listened to. "I'll never forget the time when dad. . . ." "There was once the hugely fat woman who road a bus across the country. . . ."

Starting at about the age of fourteen, I was able to partake in the wine tasting and more generally, the drink. This heralded the beginning of adulthood. Drink in our family is an important part of any gathering. There was no age until which we had to wait. One was an adult as soon as one thought themselves one, sitting in the room where the adult conversation took place, and similarly one could drink as soon as one took the liberty to fetch a glass and pour themselves a drink. This perspective was either one passed down from our Irish and German ancestors, or due to the fact that my grandfather was the Division Manager for Schlitz Brewing of the states of Ohio, Indiana, and Michigan, always keeping keg of the brew on tap in the house. He knew his way around alcohol.

"By drinking with family, in a safe environment, one is not as likely to view alcohol in a negative way, thus hiding or sneaking it, and creating bad associations and experiences." So said my father to me, and his father to him at the age of sixteen when he sat my father down and had him drink beer until he was drunk enough to have a hangover the next morning, thus taking the mystery and draw out of the drink. Soon enough my cousins and I were no longer running about in the woods outside the winery, but inside learning how to taste a Pinot Noir or a Vigonier. My cousin James is now the youngest side-splitting story teller, and I find that my sister and I often help initiate these spontaneous and habitual picnics, continuing our family tradition of gathering, story telling, day tripping, drinking, and eating outside.

The Analysis

In reading this snapshot objectively, I see a person whose family is very important, where the people are most important in forming her ideas about the self. Indeed, her concept of self starts with her grandparents, and ends with her family. Her family appears to be a jovial and adventurous type, by her descriptions of the outings and what went on there. Humor in story telling and volume in speech are ways this family makes themselves heard within the family context and without. It is also how they identify with the group and communicate, and thus a valuable characteristic to have. The three people she mentions as good storytellers are men: her grandfather, father, and cousin. Her grandmother is mentioned in relation to cuisine, and setting the table. It seems as if traditional gender roles are at work here (even if the women do partake in drink). Men are talking and displaying loud behavior, and the one woman visible in this snapshot is seen preparing food. Similarly, her identification as Irish American is based on her father and grandfather's lineage. Nowhere does she mention her mother or her mother's family.

The destination and activities her family's outings revolved around show that she clearly was raised in a solidly middle class family. . . . As the children grew into adolescence and early adulthood, they too began to learn, and were encouraged not only by the family, but also by the baristas, to develop their palate. And so, the picnic event also illuminates what it means to come of age in this group.

Of course there are a number of ways to realize one's coming of age, but it is evocative that her experience of this transition occurred within the family setting. It was not her peer's opinion that seems to matter as much as it is her family's. She reflects on the object of symbolic meaning in her coming of age: drink. In her family, giving one's confidence to a young person with something potentially hazardous and certainly a type of taboo in American society, encourages the young person and gives them the opportunity to act in the appropriately responsible way.

The Implications

As I begin my teaching career, it is important to keep in mind the situated nature of my values, recognizing that I may, however unconsciously, view my students through a lens that casts them in an unfair light, by no fault of their own. By examining my own values through this snapshot I recognize that I may favor loud boys in the classroom—those who entertain well, and all students that are generally more vocal. . . .

Similarly, I may have a more relaxed or liberal attitude toward the touchy issues in America. What can teachers openly discuss with which students? My snapshot focused on a laissez-faire attitude about alcohol in my family and at the wineries, but this is indicative of the laissez-faire liberal perspective of Californians in general. As a new transplant and new teacher in Missouri, I need to recognize the different local and cultural values while recognizing and putting my own values aside. To understand the students, as well as the school culture, from within their own framework is a goal to continuously work towards. Becoming aware of others different than oneself is the first step.

As we hope you have seen from Brenna's work, our expectations for school will be based on our set of cultural experiences and assumptions. Brenna recognizes that she may hold differing expectations for what counts as "good behavior" for boys and girls, respectively, in her classroom, speculating that she may favor loud boys. Your cultural expectations will influence your rules and expectations for classroom behavior.

After we begin to understand our own cultural assumptions, we can view our beliefs about classroom management in a new light. Based on their cultural assumptions, your students will hold different views about what it means to be a student. For example, though you may want students to look you in the eyes when you are speaking, for some students this is a sign of challenge. Others may not feel comfortable participating actively in classroom discussions because, in their culture, it is considered disrespectful to ask questions of a teacher. What you may regard as plagiarism, some students may view as showing respect to an author.

Brown (2003) argues that all teachers, but particularly those in urban settings, should adopt culturally responsive management styles that balance caring for all students with authority and assertiveness. He also notes the importance of adopting communication patterns that match students' cultural backgrounds. Making your expectations and classrooms' rules explicit is the key to developing competence in literacy and language and life. You should engage your students in conversations about the rules of classroom behavior, letting them know that the rules shift depending on audience and purpose.

For example, you may start a class period by telling students "Today we'll begin with a *write-and-share*. Respond to the prompt on the board for about 10 minutes. Then, when everyone is finished, we'll share what we wrote. Remember to raise your hands and wait until you're called on, speaking one at a time." Later in the period, you might announce, "It's time for a *Jump-in brainstorm* session," reminding students that it's now acceptable to call out answers without raising hands while recorders try to capture all the good ideas on the board. Later you may engage students in a *meeting of the minds*, in which they're expected to get up, talk to their peers, and find someone who agrees with their particular perspective on the issue under discussion. Particularly with young adolescents, it's a good idea to set different rules of engagement, each with its own name (i.e., *write-and-share, jump-in brainstorm, meeting of the minds*). This is not just a silly gimmick. Creating a variety of participant structures and making sure that students know the rules of engagement for each will streamline your lessons, make your expectations clear, and give students the predictability and structure necessary for their engagement in creative and active learning.

Expectations for how students should participate should be clear to all. And clearly there is not one set of rules that will cover all the ways in which your middle school students will engage with learning opportunities in the classroom. As you think about classroom management, remember that you are managing their learning, not simply their behaviors, and that your ultimate goal is encouraging productive participation for all.

TEACHING IN THE MIDDLE: WHY ACCEPT THE INVITATION?

Teaching in the middle school is challenging. Some middle schools seem like holding pens; the middle school drop-out rate continues to rise; and you will surely encounter colleagues with little preparation for teaching in a middle school or in their content area. So why even think about teaching in this setting? Because of the Rodericks and Isaacs and Jimmys, and because of the Samanthas and Parises. Herbert Kohl (1984) describes the difficulties that all teachers face, as well as the reasons for pursuing a teaching career in spite of these difficulties:

> Why teach, then? Are there reasons that override these negatives and can make teaching a wonderful way to spend a life? The answer for some people—and I'm one

of them—is finally yes, because there still are children. The prime reason to teach is wanting to be with young people and help them grow. (p. 162)

Kohl reminds us that the very reasons *not* to teach are, ironically, the very same reasons why we *should* pursue a career in teaching: "because there still are children."

REFERENCES

Biancarosa, G., & Snow, C. E. (2004). *Reading next—A vision for action and research in middle and high school literacy: A report from Carnegie Corporation of New York.* Washington, DC: Alliance for Excellent Education. Retrieved October 20, 2004, from http://www.all$ed.org/publications/ReadingNext/ReadingNext.pdf

Brown, D. (2003). Urban teachers' use of culturally responsive management strategies. *Theory into Practice, 42*(4), 277–282.

Carroll, P. S., Blake, F., Camalo, R. A., & Messer, S. (1996). Why acceptance isn't enough: Helping ESL students become successful writers. *English Journal, 85*, 25–33.

Driscoll, M. (1999). Crafting a sharper lens: Classroom assessment in mathematics. In M. Z. Solomon (Ed.), *The diagnostic teacher: Constructing new approaches to professional development* (pp.78–103). New York: Teachers College Press.

Feiman-Nemser, S. (1990). Teacher preparation: Structural and conceptual alternatives. In W. R. Houston, M. Huberman, & J. Sikula (Eds.), *Handbook of research in teacher education* (pp. 212–233). New York: Macmillan.

Finders, M., & Lewis, C. (1994). Why some parents don't come to school. *Educational Leadership, 51*(9), 50–54.

Finn, C. (2005). Mayhem in the middle. Retrieved December 15, 2005, from http://nationalreview.com/comment/finn200509200817.asp

Goodlad, J.(1990). *Teachers for our nation's schools.* San Francisco: Jossey-Bass Publishers.

Kohl, H. (1984). *Growing minds: On becoming a teacher.* New York: Harper and Row.

Ladson-Billings, G. (1994). *The dreamkeepers: Successful teachers of African American children.* San Francisco: Jossey-Bass Publishers.

Luke, A., & Luke, C. (2001). Adolescence lost/childhood regained: On early intervention and the emergence of the techno-subject. *Journal of Early Childhood Literacy, 1*(2), 91–120.

Moll, L. C., Amanti, C., Neff, D., & González, N. (1992). Funds of knowledge for teaching: Using a qualitative approach to connect homes and classrooms. *Theory into Practice, 31*(2), 132–141.

Moll, L. C., & Greenberg, J. (1990). Creating zones of possibilities: Combining social contexts for instruction. In L. C. Moll (Ed.), *Vygotsky and education* (pp. 319–348). Cambridge: Cambridge University Press.

Ohanian, S. (2002). Interview with Susan Ohanian. Retrieved January 24, 2006, from http://72.14.203.104/search?q=cache:UikEdefO-CQJ:www.jobseducationwis.org/105%2520Interview%2520with%2520Susan%2520Ohanian.doc+Interview+with+Susan+Ohanian++&hl=en&gl=us&ct=clnk&cd=5

Weiner, L. (2003). Why is classroom management so vexing to urban teachers? *Theory into Practice, 42*(4), 334–340.

Weinstein, C. (2003). Culturally responsive classroom management: Awareness into action. *Theory into Practice, 42*(4), 269–276.

Zeichner, K. (1993). *Educating teachers for cultural diversity (NCRTL Special Report).* East Lansing, MI: National Center for Research on Teacher Learning.

RESOURCES

Print

Alvermann, D., Hinchman, K., & Moore, D. (2000). *Reconceptualizing the literacies of adolescents' lives.* Mahwah, NJ: Lawrence Erlbaum.

Burke, J., & Claggett, M. F. (1999). *The English teacher's companion: A complete guide to classroom, curriculum, and the profession.* Montclair, NJ: Boynton/Cook.

Delpit, L. (1995). *Other people's children: Cultural conflict in the classroom.* New York: The New Press.

Howard, G. (1999). *We can't teach what we don't know: White teachers, multiracial schools.* New York: Teachers College Press.

Hubbard, R. S., & Power, B. M. (1993). *The art of classroom inquiry: A handbook for teacher-researchers.* Portsmouth, NH: Heinemann.

Ladson-Billings, G. (2001). *Crossing over to Canaan: The journey of new teachers in diverse classrooms.* San Francisco: Jossey Bass.

Moje, E. B. (2002). *All the stories that we have: Adolescents' insights about literacy and learning in secondary schools.* Newark, DE: International Reading Association.

Moore, D., & Alvermann, D. (2000). *Struggling adolescent readers: A collection of teaching strategies.* Newark, DE: International Reading Association.

Moore, D., Bean, T., Birdyshaw, D., & Rycik, J. (1999). *Adolescent literacy: A position statement for the Commission on Adolescent Literacy of the International Reading Association.* Newark, DE: International Reading Association.

Muth, K. D., & Alvermann, D. (1999). *Teaching and learning in the middle grades.* Needham Heights, MA: Allyn & Bacon.

Phelan, P., Davidson, A. L., & Yu, H. C. (1993). Students' multiple worlds: Navigating the borders of family, peer, and school cultures. In P. Phelan & A. L. Davidson (Eds.), *Renegotiating cultural diversity in American schools* (pp. 52–88). New York: Teachers College Press.

Rubinstein-Avila, E. (2003). Facing reality: English language learners in middle grade classes. *English Education, 35*(2), 122–136.

Tchudi, S., & Tchudi, S. (1999). *The English language arts handbook: Classroom strategies for teachers.* Montclair, NJ: Boynton/Cook.

Vinz, R. (1996). *Composing a teaching life.* Montclair, NJ: Boynton/Cook.

Wilhelm, J. (1996). *Standards in practice, 6–8.* Urbana, IL: National Council of Teachers of English.

Electronic

Assembly on Literature for Adolescents. ALAN is a special-interest group of the NCTE. ALAN's membership includes teachers, authors, librarians, publishers, teacher educators, and others who are particularly interested in the area of young adult literature.

http://www.alan-ya.org/2/

Center for Multilingual Multicultural Research. The CMMR has established an extensive list of resources for beginning teachers.

http://www.usc.edu/dept/education/CMMR/

Center on School, Family and Community Partnerships. The Center supports research and projects aimed at increasing an understanding of practices of partnership that help all children succeed in elementary, middle, and high schools in rural, suburban, and urban areas. The focus is on how members of communities can work together to improve schools, strengthen families, and enhance student learning and development.

http://www.csos.jhu.edu/p2000/center.htm

National Education Association. This organization provides a Parent Involvement Home Page that includes suggestions for how parents can support their children with reading and other content areas. It also lists publications, grant opportunities, and other resources for parents.

http://www.nea.org/parents/

Rethinking Schools. This online publication emphasizes problems and promises facing urban schools, particularly issues of race. It addresses a broad range of educational issues such as vouchers and marketplace-oriented reforms, funding equity, and school-to-work. Articles are written by and for teachers, parents, and students.

http://www.rethinkingschools.org/

The First Days of Middle School. This site is sponsored by Middle Web and offers a rich array of resources for new teachers.

http://www.middleweb.com/1stDResources.html

2

Middle School Students and Middle Schools

GUIDING QUESTIONS

1. How have our views of early adolescents shifted across time?
2. What are the differences between middle school and junior high school?
3. What are the key components of an effective middle school?
4. (How) do those key components influence literacy curricula?

A CASE FOR CONSIDERATION

Teen Mothers in Different Times

A tintype photograph captures a young bride in white eyelet, poised beside her husband, who stands awkwardly in a borrowed suit. Supported by parents, family, and friends, 14-year-old Joy Dunlap married 28-year-old William Walter Meadows. It was considered a beautiful and proper wedding, but Joy's friends whispered that it was "about time" for her to marry. She was, after all, 14, a grown woman still living in her mother's house, still cooking for her father. When Joy was 15, her family celebrated the birth of her son, Walter, who was welcomed into the world by all.

Eighty years later, things are very different for 15-year-old Angel. As a teen mother, Angel describes herself through the eyes of adults in the following manner: "The biggest thing is slut 'cause I had a baby. No teacher called it to my face. But they looked upon me like that. They looked at me like I was nothin' at all 'cause I had a baby when I was 13.'" Angel was expelled from her middle school and ordered by the courts to attend an alternative school because of her frequent truancies and her "early" pregnancy. Angel, pregnant for the second time, explained, "Yeah, they thought, 'You're no good. You'll never amount to anything.' The sheriff, the teachers, and they kept saying it, 'You're no good.' That's what they think, but I take care of myself. I take care of my son. I take care of him when he's sick. I make sure he's got what he needs. I'm a good mom to Tyler."

Although both Joy and Angel had babies as teenagers, teachers and other community members viewed their lives quite differently. In fact, Joy was never considered a "teenager." That word didn't enter our language until about 1938, and Joy turned 14 in 1912. Neither Joy nor Angel completed the eighth grade, but Joy's world was different from Angel's, who turned 14 in 1996. Although Joy Meadows was 15 when she had her first child, she was never considered a "teen mother." She was, in fact, not considered exceptionally young. Angel, on the other hand, was placed in an alternative school for her sexual misconduct, and her middle school teachers worried about her "running around with a man nearly twice her age."

FOR DISCUSSION

Joy wasn't expected to go to school beyond the elementary grades. Angel was court ordered to attend an alternative middle school. What might account for such different perspectives? Assumptions about appropriate schooling for early adolescents have shifted dramatically over the past 100 years. What assumptions do you hold for teaching early adolescents today?

A BUNDLE OF RAGING HORMONES: THE INVENTION OF ADOLESCENCE

Many of us worry that teaching early adolescents will be a negative experience. Some worry that by teaching language arts in a middle school, we will be forced to abandon our subject matter and focus solely on classroom control. As one of our colleagues once remarked, "Most of my students have only heard horror stories about this age group." Another said, "I'd never wanted to teach middle school. They are nothing but a bundle of raging hormones." Even those who express interest in middle school teaching worry. One middle school teacher observes:

I look forward to their enthusiasm. I want to teach middle schoolers because they're still little kids. They still like to have fun with learning. You don't have to worry so much about apathy, but you DO have to worry about classroom control.

It's true that, when thinking about teaching middle school, you may be tempted to focus more on classroom management plans rather than young adult books, integrated curriculum, multiple intelligences, or other important aspects of middle school pedagogy. After working in a middle school with real live middle school students, however, many teachers speak enthusiastically about their amazing students, the ways in which they can think deeply about their work and the world around them. One preservice teacher reported, "You know, I wouldn't want to work anywhere else. Middle school offers the best of both worlds: students young enough to have real fun with learning and old enough to do some real critical thinking."

Another remarked, "I'm embarrassed about how I underestimated my students at first. When we planned our trip to the zoo, my students weren't just little kids going to see some animals. They weren't just getting out of school for the day. They were scientists and authors who got on that bus ready to do some serious study."

Expectations for teaching in a middle school may be based in part on the stories that you have heard or images of early adolescents as presented in the popular media. Stereotypic images of school cafeterias or after-school detention rooms, although often quite humorous on the big screen, may shape how we come to view what it means to be an early adolescent.

Our assumptions about early adolescence will also guide our curricular decisions and shape our daily interactions with students. Classroom Case 2-1 illustrates how assumptions about early adolescence left invisible and unexamined shaped one teacher's interactions with his middle school students. As you read the following vignette, look for Mr. Stone's assumptions about "ordinary" middle school students. What do Mr. Stone's words and actions suggest that we should consider normal at this age? What does he consider inappropriate and out of the ordinary?

Classroom Case 2-1

Mr. Stone Graduates from Elementary School

Mr. Stone was a popular sixth-grade teacher in a self-contained elementary classroom. Students often requested to be in his room. Many said, "He makes learning fun." He did lots of hands-on activities and took great pride in the fact that he knew each of his students well. The students enjoyed the nicknames he gave them, and an overwhelming majority noted that he was their all-time favorite teacher.

After teaching sixth grade for many years, Mr. Stone elected to accept a position as a seventh-grade language arts teacher in a middle school. At the beginning of his first year as a seventh-grade teacher, he worried,

> I won't be able to be so close to them. I won't know them as well. They won't need me in the same way. I won't know their parents or brothers and sisters like I do now. It will definitely be different. I'll just be more distant. That's all there is to it.

Teaching students at the middle school level also had its positive side for Mr. Stone. He looked forward to interacting with students "more academically" as he put it. Still, he had concerns about the move to middle school, remarking, "I like my new students, but it's very, very different. My students are 'hormone hostages,' and Sarah's group serves as the fashion police. Girls tend to run in packs," he laughed. "There's a herd of them coming down the hall now."

Mr. Stone's changes were apparent to his former sixth-grade students. One commented, "He like changed to a totally new person." Another said, "He's meaner." One girl who had been especially fond of Mr. Stone explained, "He acts like he doesn't even know me." Another commented, "He's not as nice as he used to be. He never laughs. He doesn't tell jokes. He doesn't call me Sunny [the nickname he gave her] anymore." Students remarked that Mr. Stone told fewer stories about his family and himself and seemed more distant. "He just sticks to the books now," one student reported.

For a variety of reasons, Mr. Stone dramatically altered his classroom practices to fit into the new environment. Likewise, the head of his English department viewed the role of a middle school teacher as much different from that of an elementary teacher. In a discussion on hiring another new language arts faculty member, she expressed reservations about a candidate who, like Mr. Stone, had been an elementary school teacher:

> *She may not be happy because she'll expect too much contact with the kids. Kids this age don't want teachers to know that much about them. Not even their parents. They want to be on their own. Elementary teachers get too close. She'd better not hug any of them.*

For Discussion

Think about how Mr. Stone's views of early adolescence governed how he treated his students. His students were only about 4 months older than they had been at the end of their sixth-grade year. How did his underlying assumptions about being a middle school teacher and his beliefs about the needs of early adolescents influence his current teaching behaviors?

Like Mr. Stone's, your assumptions about early adolescents will guide your curricular decisions and shape your daily interactions with students. We judge the value and worth of others based on our beliefs about what counts as "normal." Such assumptions have grave consequences for those whose experiences do not match our own. Current public discourse often casts adolescents, in particular, those from urban settings, as problems and promotes policies for controlling them.

Fieldwork Journal 2-1 invites you to examine any expectations or assumptions you may hold about teaching in the middle grades.

Before meeting with this person, create a few open-ended questions, designed to elicit stories about his or her experience as a middle-grades student, and about his or her views of contemporary early adolescents.

In recording what you discovered, use a "double-entry" journal format (see Figure 2-1), carefully noting your informant's recollections in the left-hand column. When you're done, use the right-hand column to reflect on the assumptions that seem to lie beneath the stories or memories you have just recorded.

Now, write a brief reflection about what you learned from this exercise. For example, are there any biological, animal, or other metaphors in your interviewee's descriptions of middle school or early adolescents? What does this person seem to define as "normal," "ordinary," and "unusual" or "surprising" where early adolescents are concerned? Think about the historical period your interviewee described, and consider how his or her middle-grades education compares to or contrasts with more contemporary views, or with your own views as you articulated them in the opening writing task. Do you see evidence of various political or ideological forces that might have shaped your informant's or your own impressions and assumptions?

Fieldwork Journal 2-1

Middle School Experiences: Schooling for Early Adolescents

1. Think back to your experience as a sixth-, seventh-, or eighth-grade student. Describe a scene from your school experience as an early adolescent. Write quickly and try to capture as much detail about your experiences and feelings as you can. Let your pen fly. Try to get lost in the writing.

2. Set up an interview with a friend or relative who is not a middle-level educator. The purpose of your interview is twofold: (a) to document this person's early adolescent schooling experience, and (b) to examine some underlying assumptions about early adolescents and middle-grades education revealed in his or her description.

FIGURE 2-1 Double Entry Journal

Observations	Reflections
Write down what is observed. In making your observations, you may consider the following questions: • What is said? • What is seen (facial expressions, gestures)? • What gets "center stage"?	Jot down inferences about your observations. In making your inferences, you may speculate on some of the following questions: • What is not seen? • What is hidden? • What do these activities suggest that one is supposed to value? • What is considered appropriate/ordinary? • What is taken for granted? • What is considered inappropriate/out of the ordinary?

When you've finished, it would be good to share these experiences with other beginning teachers, attempting to unpack the ways in which your experiences were shaped by the geographic and historic period in which you were raised, as well as your race, class, gender, socioeconomic status, and other factors. Finally, consider how this exercise has challenged, and perhaps changed, your beliefs about what counts as "normal" in early adolescence.

Many of us have humorous, painful, or embarrassing stories to tell about our adolescent experiences. We may remember disagreements with our parents, our naive bravado in entering competitive sports, or our changing bodies that we feared might forsake us in public. Likewise, we receive stories and representations from the larger culture about who early adolescents are or should be. Talk shows fill the airwaves with images of "out-of-control" early adolescents and distraught parents. Popular media images of classrooms often portray the teacher in an even harsher light. Such images tend to pervade our cultural assumptions and shape our views of "normal" adolescent behaviors. It is often difficult to examine our own stories and underlying assumptions because what is considered ordinary is just that—so ordinary as to be invisible. Yet, these invisible assumptions guide what we expect of our students, our colleagues, and ourselves.

At the same time, stereotypes or fears seldom arise from a vacuum. The changes during adolescence are great. Psychological and biological changes during this period are never more rapid. Gender roles become more rigidly enforced. Shifts in social expectations for the early adolescent are equally dramatic. It is no wonder that parents and teachers often voice fear for the impending arrival of adolescence; yet the concept of adolescence did not exist before the last two decades of the 19th century (Klein, 1990). Klein succinctly describes the creation of adolescence based on social and economic factors:

> Basically, industrialization occurring during the later 1800s created the need for a stage of adolescence; the Depression created the legitimized opportunity for adolescence to become differentiated from childhood and adulthood; and the mass media influence/blitz of the 1950s crystallized this stage by giving it a reality all its own. (p. 456)

Adolescence is not a biological truism, but a socially defined life stage that was solidified, due in large part to economic conditions, specifically the Depression. Palladino (1996) explains that up until the 1930s, most people in this age group worked for a living on farms, in factories, and at home. She writes, "They were not considered teenagers yet or even adolescents for that matter" (p. 5). Palladino argues that it was this mass coming together in a school setting that solidified adolescence as a distinct age group. As the next section will reveal, the emergence of "adolescence" as a distinct developmental period had as much to do with economic conditions as it did with "raging hormones," the theory popularized by G. Stanley Hall.

BEYOND BIOLOGY
The Invention of Adolescence

In this country, G. Stanley Hall became known as the father of adolescence with the publication of his 1904 two-volume set *Adolescence*. Hall conceptualized the period of adolescence as biologically determined, with little consideration of social or cultural influences (Santrock, 1993). According to Hall, hormonal factors accounted for the marked fluctuations in adolescent behaviors (Brooks-Gunn & Reiter, 1990). Although we make the case that adolescence as a life stage is based on social and economic conditions, clearly we do not deny the tremendous biological events that occur at this developmental stage. We ask you to consider, however, how those biological changes are perceived and experienced at particular historical moments and how social and cultural conditions dictate what is considered normal. Clearly, you can see how Joy's marriage to a man twice her age in the opening vignette was considered appropriate so she might be better cared for, while Angel's relationship was considered promiscuous. We are not suggesting that one should view either Angel's or Joy's actions as good or bad, right or wrong. Rather we use their stories to demonstrate that coming of age is shaped by the social and historical events of the particular time period in which it occurs. Joy covered her body completely, while Angel's dress revealed her developing body. Even judgment about body shapes and sizes is influenced by historic period. Brumberg (1997), for example, chronicles the historically changing images and expectations of American girls' bodies, noting that attention was, at one time, focused on the size of hands.

Most often, we fail to recognize the historic, economic, social, and cultural complexities that shape the lives of adolescents and promote a singular, biological definition of the "normal" adolescent. Many of us hold stereotypic assumptions such as the following: (a) adolescents sever ties with adults; (b) peer groups become increasingly influential social networks; (c) resistance is a sign of normalcy for the adolescent; and (d) romance and sexual drive govern interests and relations. Yet, this view may be based for the most part on middle-class assumptions (Finders 1997, 1998/99). On the contrary, class, race, gender, and individual life circumstances influence how one comes of age in this country. In cross-cultural anthropological studies, for example, Schlegel and Barry (1991) note that in middle class homes where child labor is not needed, adolescents of both sexes are likely to spend a good deal of time with same-age peers. Girls in working-class homes or in families of Hispanic or of recent Middle Eastern or Asian extraction, on the other hand, may be expected to spend their after-school time at home, while boys in such families may be with peers or at work outside the home.

Lesko (2001) argues that adolescence as a life stage is constructed as a transitional time, trapping those who make up this group in what she refers to as an "expectant time," in which they experience a moratorium on responsibility and power. She writes,

> Static ideas about youth have helped to keep in place a range of assumptions and actions in and out of secondary schools. For example, since adolescents have raging hormones, they cannot be expected to do sustained and critical thinking, reason many educators. Since adolescents are immature, they cannot be given substantive responsibilities in school, at work or at home. (pp. 189–190)

Though early adolescents are individuals with complex histories, the complexities of their lives are sometimes forgotten when we begin to think about the prospect of teaching in the middle school. If we hold narrow, negative views of early adolescents, we can hardly envision an engaging literacy curriculum. "Out of control" as the identifying trait of this life stage serves to solidify adolescence as a period of incompetence. The assumption at the turn of the 20th century was that a holding facility was needed; thus, junior high schools were created. It is no wonder that junior high and middle schools are so often characterized as "wastelands." The following section traces the history of the junior high school and, later, the middle school model in American education.

From "Mini" High School to Middle School

To meet the needs of early adolescents, the first junior high schools appeared in 1909 in Columbus, Ohio, and in Berkeley, California, in 1910 (Everhart, 1983). Everhart describes two factors that occasioned the creation of junior high schools: (a) the perceived need for student retention and (b) the growing recognition of adolescence as a separate stage in the life cycle. Child labor laws and compulsory schooling laws in the early 1900s solidified the demand for a new school structure that could serve the growing population of school-aged children and discourage them from dropping out after the primary grades.

Until the 1960s, schools for early adolescents were constructed as junior or "mini" high schools, with a focus on subject matter knowledge and little consideration for the social, physical, or psychological needs of the early adolescent. Most students left their self-contained elementary classroom and entered a comprehensive junior high school where they met with individual content teachers for discrete blocks of time. Class periods were linked by 3- to 5-minute passing times with little attention to connections across content boundaries or the early adolescent's need for physical activity.

Typically, the structure and schedule of the junior high school—as opposed to the more contemporary concept of "middle school"—divided each day into seven or eight discrete segments in which students received daily instruction in math, science, social studies, and language arts. Often an alternating schedule provided for instruction in music, art, and physical education. Some junior high schools offered an exploratory strand of instruction in such subjects as foreign language, home economics, and industrial arts. Eventually, at the junior high school level, extracurricular activities such as drama, band, orchestra, vocal music, volleyball, tennis, football, basketball, wrestling, and track became available.

Early on, home economics and industrial arts were segregated by gender. Similarly, extracurricular opportunities were segregated and more readily available for boys than for girls. Eventually, the 1972 federal law Title IX prohibited sex discrimination in education and required schools to offer equal opportunity for involvement in athletics and other extracurricular activities to girls and boys alike.

Beginning in the 1960s, the traditional junior high school began to be replaced by the middle school model, which offered a more transitional form of schooling between elementary and high school. While junior high schools were envisioned as preparatory programs for high schools, the middle school model shifted the focus from the subject matter to the early adolescent learner. This change in focus necessitated a change in the grades included in the school. Typically, junior high schools include grades 7–9, while middle schools include grades 6–8 or 5–8 (see Figure 2-2).

Two landmark reports in the 1980s called our attention to the needs of early adolescents in school settings: the Superintendents' Middle Grade Task Force

FIGURE 2-2 School Orientations

Junior High School Orientation	Middle School Orientation
• Focus on subject matter. • Staff schools with teachers who are expert in subject matter. • Establish individual student schedules. • Expect students to take responsibility for their own learning. • Employ a curricular model based on independent subject matter and competition.	• Focus on adolescent learner. • Staff schools with teachers who are expert at teaching early adolescents. • Establish small communities of learners. • Connect learning to local community. • Include families in the education of the early adolescent. • Employ a curricular model based on interdisciplinary teams and collaboration.

Caught in the Middle: Educational Reform for Young Adolescents in California Public Schools (1987) and The Carnegie Council on Adolescent Development's *Turning Points: Preparing Youth for the Twenty-First Century* (1989). The California report represents the work of the Superintendents' Middle Grade Task Force and identifies students in this age group as at risk in the following ways:

- **Intellectually.** Early adolescents face decisions that have the potential to affect major academic values with lifelong consequences.
- **Physically.** At no other point in human development are individuals likely to encounter so much diversity in relation to themselves and others.
- **Socially.** Adult values are largely shaped during adolescence.
- **In the development of moral and ethical choices and behaviors.** Early adolescents want to explore the moral and ethical dimensions of the curriculum, media, and daily interactions they experience in their families and peer groups.

When you consider the tremendous social, intellectual, and physical changes facing early adolescents, you can see that large comprehensive junior high schools were not serving them well.

The Carnegie Council on Adolescent Development, established in 1986, focused the nation's attention on the challenges of the adolescent years. Although published in 1989, the council's recommendations remain consistent with views of effective programs for middle school learners in today's world. The report offers the following recommendations:

1. Create small communities for learning.
2. Teach a core academic program.
3. Ensure success for all students.
4. Empower teachers and administrators to make decisions about the experiences of middle-grade students.
5. Staff schools with teachers who are expert at teaching young adolescents.
6. Improve academic performance by fostering health and fitness.
7. Reengage families in the education of young adolescents.
8. Connect schools with communities.

The National Middle School Association (NMSA, 2002) lists five key components for exemplary middle school programs: interdisciplinary teams, advisory programs, varied instruction, transitional programs, and exploratory programs. As you read through the recommendations for effective middle school education, think back to your own junior high or middle school experience. You may find that regardless of when you went to school and regardless of whether your school was called a middle school or junior high, there are remnants of both orientations in your schooling experience as an early adolescent. Probably no school is purely one or the other. The following sections present some defining characteristics of the middle school model.

Interdisciplinary teams.   In many middle schools, teachers from different disciplines work together as a team, sometimes referred to as a family. Teams of teachers are assigned to the same group of students as a way of creating a small community of learners within a larger school. Teams ranging from two to five members in two, three, or four subject areas provide support for early adolescents by building a greater sense of belonging and continuity across content areas. Usually, the teaching team shares a common planning time, which allows for collaborative teaching across disciplinary boundaries. This structure, with its built-in opportunities for flexible scheduling, allows teachers to collaboratively plan a curriculum that supports both social and academic competencies. Teams may plan field trips or sponsor family activities such as an "Evening with the Stars," a student-organized dinner and star-gazing event. With close contact between teachers and students, teachers are better able to tap students' interests, maintain close connections with parents, and respond to the unique needs of students on their team.

Advisory programs.   Advisory programs foster strong adult-adolescent relationships and a sense of belonging to the school community. A regularly scheduled time is built into the school day for students to meet with their advisor, who may be a teacher, an administrator, or other staff member. To be well known by a significant adult in the school setting enhances an early adolescent's chances for success. Advisory groups are small by design to allow students opportunities to share concerns; explore careers; plan academic programs; discuss local and global issues; or address personal, school, or community issues that may arise. Advisors get to know individual students, their interests, and their families. Advisory time may be used to allow students opportunities to participate in planning school events and even in establishing school policies. In advisory meetings, students gain opportunities to serve as leaders and experts, which builds positive self-esteem and enhances engagement in the learning community.

Varied instruction.   The content of the middle school curriculum starts with students' interests and often emerges from their own real-world questions. "Real" and "relevant" are the keys to success for a middle school curriculum. Opportunities for physical movement and hands-on (maybe even bodies-on) learning are vital in a middle school. The three Cs for learning in a middle school are collaboration, cooperation, and community. Exemplary middle school programs deemphasize competition and support collaboration. Often, classroom learning projects are integrated with community-based activities. Culminating activities are often designed as opportunities for students to both celebrate their learning and contribute to the community. Flexible scheduling may allow for instruction across age groups. Understanding the need for tapping multiple intelligences, middle school teachers try to structure learning opportunities that actively engage students and accommodate individual differences.

Exploratory programs.   In middle schools, early adolescents are often given opportunities to explore a broad range of academic, vocational, and recreational topics. Exploratory strands may be made available for 1-day exploration fairs, 1- or 2-week mini-courses, or full-semester courses. Courses in such areas as career choices, health, foreign languages, or intramural sports give middle school students a chance to explore new challenges beyond the standard school curriculum. Tapping their curiosity may lead to more comprehensive investigations later. For instance, an exploration into student government or local community affairs may pique a student's interest and lead to memberships in school and community organizations. Through exploratory strands, middle school students also get to share their expertise, often serving as teachers or leaders. Exploratory strands allow middle school teachers and students to participate as teachers and learners and to discover that exchanging such roles can be deeply satisfying to all.

Transition programs. To ease the transition into middle school, teachers, counselors, and school administrators often set up opportunities for incoming students to meet them and visit the building before actually making the move to the middle school. Often, a visitation day is set in the spring so incoming students can see the school and meet their new teachers before summer vacation begins. During the first weeks at their new middle school, students often attend orientation sessions that allow for additional opportunities to meet with school personnel, learn about school activities, explore their questions, and calm their fears. Advisory groups can serve an active role in the transition program. Attentiveness to creating a smooth transition can mean the difference between success and failure throughout the middle school years and beyond.

The middle school movement attempted to align the structure and curriculum of the school to better serve early adolescents. Most important were the changing views of what the curriculum should include. The National Middle School Association (NMSA), founded in 1973 to promote effective changes in middle-level education, established a set of guiding principles that have come to define exemplary middle-level education. The responsive middle school, according to the NMSA, is characterized by a shared vision, educators committed to young adolescents, a positive school climate, an adult advocate for every student, family and community partnerships, and high expectations for all.

It should be noted that the concluding report of the Carnegie Task Force on Education for Young Adolescent (1995) suggested that, 10 years after its first report, middle schools were doing much better in the social aspects of schooling for early adolescents, but the recommendation for academic rigor and high expectations for all had been essentially ignored. It's difficult and complex but essential to balance both social and academic competencies in the education of middle school students. The recommendation from *Turning Points 2000* are summarized below:

- Teach a rigorous curriculum, built on academic standards and relevant to the concerns of adolescents.
- Use instructional methods designed to prepare all students to achieve higher standards and become lifelong learners.
- Staff middle-grades schools with teachers who are expert at teaching young adolescents, and engage teachers in ongoing professional development opportunities.
- Create a climate of intellectual development and a caring community of shared educational purpose.
- Govern democratically, through direct or representative participation by the adults who know middle school students best.
- Provide a safe and healthy school environment as part of improving academic performance and developing caring and ethical citizens.
- Involve parents and communities in supporting student learning and healthy development. (Jackson, & Davis, 2000)

Across the nation, one can find safe and healthy middle schools that are showing powerful gains in rigorous academic achievement. One can find effective teachers and enthusiastic learning in middle schools that offer a rich and rigorous curriculum in all core subject areas, with literacy at the center. Such schools run counter to the stereotypic "wastelands" promoted by popular media and folk wisdom.

LITERACY IN THE MIDDLE GRADES

Just as views of what counts as appropriate schooling for early adolescent learners have changed over time, our views of teaching literacy to early adolescents have shifted conceptually as well. Prior to the 1990s, literacy development for adolescents was most often characterized as reading informational texts in content areas. Vacca (1998) writes,

> The term adolescent literacy only recently has entered the lexicon of literary educators and practitioners, having replaced secondary reading as an alternative and more powerful concept to describe literacy learning among young adolescents and teenagers in middle and high school. (p. xv)

The next section briefly describes our changing notions of literacy education in the middle grades, a topic which will be taken up in more depth in chapter 3.

WHAT COUNTS AS ADOLESCENT LITERACY

The shifting definition of the language arts as the isolated activities of reading, writing, talking, and listening to a view of "literacy" that encompasses all forms of language production and use grew out of several developments within the last century. In the fall of 1992, the United States Department of Education awarded a grant to educators at the Center for the Study of Reading at the University of Illinois, in collaboration with the International Reading Association and National Council of Teachers of English, for the purpose of developing a set of standards for the English language arts. The NCTE/IRA standards present a vision of "literacy" education that includes the use of print, oral, and visual language, and addresses six *interrelated* English language arts: reading, writing, speaking, listening, viewing, and visually representing. In 1996 the NCTE/IRA published *Standards in Practice, 6–8* (Wilhelm, 1996), which presents adolescent literacy practices as situated within unique social and cultural contexts.

The term "literacy" has also been adopted by several professional organizations and journals. For example, in 1995 the *Journal of Reading* was changed to the *Journal of Adolescent and Adult Literacy*. The International Reading Association created the "Commission on Adolescent Literacy" in 1997. These and other changes made visible an expanded definition of what counts as literacy for adolescents. The tenets of adolescent literacy as characterized in *Reconceptualizing the Literacies in Adolescents' Lives* (Alvermann, Hinchman, Moore, Phelps, & Waff, 1998) include the following: (a) adolescent literacy as more complex and sophisticated than what is traditionally considered in school; (b) adolescents as engaging in multiple literacies with a variety of print and nonprint texts, including films, CD-ROMs, the

Internet, popular music, television, magazines, and newspapers; (c) literacy as essential to the development of adolescents' individual and social identities; and (d) adolescents' need for opportunities to explore and experiment with multiple literacies and receive feedback from peers and adults (Moje, Young, Readence, & Moore, 2000, p. 402).

The 1999 position statement by the International Reading Association called for renewed attention to the literacy of adolescents as follows:

> Adolescents entering the adult world in the 21st century will read and write more than at any other time in human history. They will need advanced levels of literacy to perform their jobs, run their households, act as citizens, and conduct their personal lives. They will need literacy to cope with the flood of information they will find everywhere they turn. They will need literacy to feed their imaginations so they can create the world of the future. In a complex and sometimes even dangerous world, their ability to read will be crucial. Continual instruction beyond the early grades is needed (Moore, Bean, Birdyshaw, & Rycik, 1999, p. 99).

HOW WE THINK ABOUT LITERACY LEARNING IN THE MIDDLE SCHOOL

Throughout the pages of this book, we will ask you to consider the incredible complexity of what it means to be and become literate as an early adolescent in today's society. Beyond the ability to create and understand the printed word, literacy in this larger sense involves using language to learn, influence, and ultimately, transform our personal and social worlds. As you think about this broad definition of literacy, or what has been called "multiple literacies," ask yourself: How many different ways do middle school students produce and consume language within and outside school? What are the difficulties my students might face with any particular materials they may encounter? How can I provide support? What are the multiple contexts in which my students live and work? What literacies are important in each? How can I address their real-world literacy needs in my middle school classroom?

In the next chapter, we will present a more thorough description of historical shifts in the field of adolescent literacy. For now, let's begin to see how the issues posed in this chapter might play out in your curriculum planning according to the tenets of effective middle school programs. To help you start thinking from the perspective of a middle school teacher, Classroom Case 2-2 opens with the project overview and rationale for an integrated language arts/science unit written by a teaching team. Jennifer and Noah, two language arts student teachers worked with Robert and Rachel, two science student teachers. The unit is their first attempt at designing plans for middle school learners. You may want to revisit this plan and your responses to it after you complete chapters 3 and 4 to monitor your own emerging competencies as a middle school teacher. As you read about their planning, look for specific places where they infused components of effective middle school practices and places where their planning might have been strengthened. The plan is written in the student teachers' own words.

Classroom Case 2-2

A Smashing Unit Plan

This is a unit plan to die for! Incorporating topics that students have learned in their science and English classes, eighth graders will work together to construct an "educational" haunted trail. The trail will consist of traditional elements of haunted house types of displays, but it will include a number of stations that will, in their own eerie way, demonstrate and celebrate learning in science and language arts.

The trail will be made up of a number of different stations that students will work together to conceive and build. They will be asked to create items that integrate the things that they have been studying in class. For example, students will read original and found poems and stories. Also, students will be introduced to the art of oral history, and they may share stories that they have written or collected from the community. A guest speaker will introduce students to Dia de los Muertos (Day of the Dead), so students may share the memorials to their friends and loved ones that they have written and read. Students will make observations of the cemetery ecosystem. They will identify different flora and fauna. Students may share their contour maps and research projects on life in the cemeteries. They may decide to set up a rock sample station and ask guests to identify rocks and minerals.

The haunted trail is designed as an opportunity for our students to "show off" what they have been learning. They will invite parents and friends to adventure on this trail of "horrors," allowing students to share and enjoy the conclusion to the unit that we call "The Graveyard Smash."

A Graveyard Smash Rationale

By now, upon mentioning to others that our integrated studies unit topic is cemeteries, we have become accustomed to the double takes and raised eyebrows. Typical remarks include, "What'ya goin to teach the kids to do, dig their own graves?" Well, er, no. Snide comments aside, cemeteries constitute one of those rare topics that easily bridge the sciences and the humanities. More important, we are convinced that students will be engaged. How can we be so sure? As a subject, cemeteries are not typically addressed in the classroom; confronted with this novel area of study, students will not feel as though they are revisiting materials that they have previously encountered year in and year out. Equally important, cemeteries are a vital aspect of most any community. Also, as students progress through adolescence, they become increasingly curious about issues pertaining to death and mortality. The relevance and potential for engagement, we believe, will encourage students to exhibit a positive attitude toward learning. Inasmuch as we believe in our topic's worthiness, excitement has characterized the planning stages of our unit design, consequently we have generated an abundance of ideas. Incidentally, we are consciously providing more activities than we would need for 10 days. (Fifteen days, in all likelihood, would be more ideal.) At any rate, the choice of cemeteries has proven to be a fertile topic, and we imagine it would be an enlightening experience for students and teachers alike.

In our efforts to make this unit design as educational and stimulating as possible, we plan for the eighth-grade class to take a field trip to one of the large public cemeteries in the local community. As safety is a strong consideration here, teachers and parents will act as chaperones for this half-day outing. We expect either a community historian or groundskeeper will be present to give an introduction to some aspects of the graveyard we intend to visit. Language arts and science teachers will have visited the graveyard beforehand and be ready to explore topics of interest. (We have in mind, for example, finding and recording particularly compelling or witty epitaphs and finding and recording aspects of the graveyard's faunae and florae.)

We are confident that our integrated unit design incorporates many Indiana English/Language Arts Proficiencies and Essential Skills. Some of our curricular goals include, but are not limited to, the following: Students will view themselves as readers, using school and public libraries/media centers to collect stories, reading a variety of materials (including the Internet), constructing meaning through collaboration with others, and critically examining what they read. As far as writing is concerned, students will view themselves as writers. They will generate ideas for writing from research and from collaboration with others and use process strategies to create and revise their writing. Particularly with our inclusion of guest speakers from the community, students will become more proficient listeners in a pleasant environment of learning. Students will also be expected to examine critically what they hear and not just become passive participants during these presentations. Proficiencies specific to the culminating activity include the following: selecting reading materials and sharing what they read, speaking to learn, collaborating with other speakers, and adapting their speech to different audiences.

The science curriculum for this unit plan incorporates a wide variety of the Indiana Proficiencies. Lesson topics involving the life sciences include ecosystems of the cemetery, human life expectancies, and even animals (blood-sucking animals). These lessons would integrate proficiencies that address interdependence of life, human identity, and physical health. Other integrated science studies would include lessons of the undetectable motions of the ground called creep, mineral and rock identification of tombstones, and the creation of a scale map of the cemetery with age contour lines. This project helps kids learn about research methods as well as the direct study of contour and scale. The cemetery has proved to be a wonderful way to integrate the various aspects of science while at the same time involving the community.

For Discussion

As you think back through the hallmarks of the exemplary middle school, consider how the graveyard project infused components of effective middle school practices. In what ways might the literacy component be strengthened? Do you see any possibilities to strengthen the connections between students' home experiences and the goals of this unit? In what ways might the connections between science and literacy be strengthened?

EFFECTIVE MIDDLE SCHOOL PRACTICES: OPPORTUNITIES AND OBSTACLES

Because of ongoing scheduling conflicts within their teams, Jennifer and Noah were never able to implement their unit. In working on the "Graveyard Smash" project, these student teachers faced great challenges in working across the disciplines.

One reflected, "Working together has definitely NOT been easy. Time to plan is doubled." Another observed, "Those science teachers, ugh, they don't think like we do." Science student teachers voiced similar concerns about "those English teachers." In reflecting about her interdisciplinary team, another student teacher remarked, "I hate group projects. You never have time to do them well." She concluded her reflection on a brighter note, however:

> *In working through this project, I really learned how teachers with diverse specialties can enhance overall learning. Because of her biology background, Stephanie was able to introduce aspects of frontier life that I would never have considered, like land and climate issues. Because of her English background, Shonda was able to develop the ideas of genre and bring in literature of the period and writing to have real-life implications for students.*

For Jennifer, Noah, and others, the opportunities were greater than the obstacles in interdisciplinary planning. Although interdisciplinary teams are considered to be a vital element of the exemplary middle school, many factors are at work to make middle schools unable to enact this recommended practice. Financial constraints, for example, may make scheduling classes difficult for interdisciplinary groups. Likewise, team planning time is often dropped. Shifting orientations can be challenging at the teaching level as well. Often, teachers have had little or no experience in working across disciplines.

In addition to the many economic and structural reasons middle schools have failed to create exemplary programs such as those described early by the NMSA, perhaps one of the key reasons is the lack of trained professionals to teach early adolescents. For more than 60 years, the professional literature has been calling for teacher preparation programs specifically geared to middle school; yet the majority of middle school teachers have no such specialized preparation (McEwin, Dickinson, Erb, & Scales, 1995, p. 3). Many schools have not been philosophically or financially able to undertake such dramatic changes from the junior high school to the middle school model. Some schools have changed in name only; others have changed building configurations, housing children from grades 6–8 as opposed to grades 7–9, for example. Such superficial changes do not encompass the shift in philosophy or practice necessary for the move from junior high school to middle school. Even today, many middle schools remain "mini" high schools.

What does all of this mean for you as an English language arts teacher of young adolescents? What are the specialized knowledge, skills, and dispositions needed to be a highly successful English language arts teacher? Unfortunately, we can't give you a single list. We don't believe there is a singular, tried-and-true view of effective literacy instruction for middle school teaching. We believe that instruction must be contextualized. Certainly, we believe that specific practices lend themselves to effective literacy teaching and learning in the middle grades; otherwise we wouldn't be writing this book.

In the next chapter, you'll see how views of English language arts, like views of early adolescence, are situated historically. We invite you to consider how English language arts teaching and learning has shifted across time.

Throughout the remainder of this book, we will ask you to look at sets of standards and recommendations, examining how these standards might play out differently in diverse classroom settings. In the following Standards in Practice section, we ask you to examine two sets of recommendations related to middle school teaching. We do not ask you to embrace them uncritically; rather, we want you to become critically aware of them, to examine them to understand the ways in which your classroom might be supported or constrained by external agencies.

Standards in Practice

Go back and skim some of the major ideas of this chapter. Based on your review, make a list of what you consider to be the five most important things a middle school language arts teacher should do, think, and/or be? (Keep each item concise.)

Top Five List of "Shoulds" for Middle School Teachers

1. A middle school language arts teacher should . . .
2. A middle school language arts teacher should . . .
3. A middle school language arts teacher should . . .
4. A middle school language arts teacher should . . .
5. A middle school language arts teacher should . . .

Now, compare your "top five" list with the standards for English language arts teachers of early adolescents suggested by the National Board for Professional Teaching Standards. The NBPTS offers advanced voluntary certification for experienced, highly competent teachers. You can download its standards for board certification in Early Adolescence/English Language Arts (EA/ELA) from the following address: *http://www.nbpts.org/candidates/guide/whichcert/07EarlyAdolEnglish2004.html*

As you look over the board's 16 standards, can you identify any additions or changes you'd like to make to your "top five" list? Do you have items on your list that the NBPTS didn't mention? What seem to be the assumptions about early adolescents that underlie the items on the NBPTS list, and how do these assumptions compare to yours?

You might want to keep the list of portfolio requirements from the NBPTS handy as you prepare your teaching portfolio and in the event that you decide to apply for National Board Certification some day. The NBPTS requires you to document your ability to meet the following objectives in the required portfolio:

- demonstrate that your teaching practice meets the Early Adolescence/English Language Arts Standards
- have access to a class of at least 6 students, in which 51% of the students are ages 11 through 15 during the 12 months prior to the submission of your portfolio entries
- submit student work samples and videotapes in English showing your interactions with your students
- demonstrate how you help students grow as readers and writers
- show the teaching strategies you use for whole-class discussion
- show the teaching strategies you use for small group instruction
- present evidence of how you impact student learning through your work with students' families and community and through your development as a learner and as a leader/collaborator

(Retrieved February 8, 2006, from The National Board for Professional Teaching Standards Web site: *http://www.nbpts.org/candidates/guide/whichcert/07EarlyAdolEnglish 2004.html*)

REFERENCES

Alvermann, D. E., Hinchman, K. A., Moore, D. W., Phelps, S. F., & Waff, D. R., (Eds.). (1998). *Reconceptualizing the literacies in adolescents' lives.* Mahwah, NJ: Lawrence Erlbaum Associates.

Brooks-Gunn, J., & Reiter, E. O. (1990). *At the threshold: The developing adolescent.* Cambridge, MA: Harvard University Press.

Brumberg, J. J. (1997). *The body project: An intimate history of American girls.* New York: Random House.

Carnegie Task Force on Education for Young Adolescents. (1989). *Turning points: Preparing youth for the twenty-first century.* Washington, DC: Carnegie Council on Adolescent Development.

Carnegie Task Force on Education for Young Adolescents. (1995). *Great transitions: Preparing adolescents for a new century.* Washington, DC: Carnegie Council on Adolescent Development.

Everhart, R. (1983). *Reading, writing and resistance: Adolescence and labor in a junior high school.* Boston: Routledge & Kegan Paul.

Finders, M. (1997). *Just girls: Hidden literacies and life in junior high.* New York: Teachers College Press.

Finders, M. (1998/99). Raging hormones: Stories of adolescence and implications for teacher education. *Journal of Adolescent and Adult Literacy, 42,* 252–263.

Jackson, A. W., & Davis G. A. (2000). *Turning points 2000: Educating adolescents in the 21st century.* New York: Teachers College Press.

Klein, H. (1990). Adolescence, youth and young adulthood: Rethinking current conceptualizations of life stage. *Youth and Society, 21,* 446–471.

Lesko, N. (2001). *Act your age! A cultural construction of adolescence.* New York: Routledge.

McEwin, C., Dickinson, T., Erb, T., & Scales, P. (1995). *A vision of excellence: Organizing principles for middle grade teacher preparation.* Westerville, OH: Center for Early Adolescence and National Middle School Association.

Moje, E. B., Young, J., Readence, J. E., & Moore, D. W. (2000). Reinventing adolescent literacy for new times: A commentary on perennial and millennial issues in adolescent literacy. *Journal of Adolescent and Adult Literacy, 43,* 400–411.

Moore, D. W., Bean, T. W., Birdyshaw, D., & Rycik, J. A. (1999). Adolescent literacy: A position statement. *Journal of Adolescent and Adult Literacy, 43,* 97–112.

National Middle School Association. (1995). *This we believe: Developmentally responsive middle level schools.* Columbus, OH: Author.

National Middle School Association. (2002). Research Summary #5 "Young adolescents' developmental needs." Retrieved January 17, 2006 from http://www.nmsa.org/research/ressum5.htm

Palladino, G. (1996). *Teenagers: An American history.* New York: Basic Books.

Santrock, J. W. (1993). *Adolescence.* Dubuque, IA: Wm. C. Brown.

Schlegel, A., & Barry, H., III. (1991). *Adolescence: An anthropological inquiry.* New York: Free Press.

Superintendents' Middle Grade Task Force. (1987). *Caught in the middle: Educational reform for young adolescents in California Public Schools.* Sacramento: California State Department of Education.

Vacca, R. T. (1998). Foreword. In D. E. Alvermann, K. A. Hinchman, D. W. Moore, S. F. Phelps, & D. R. Waff, (Eds.) *Reconceptualizing the literacies in adolescents' lives* (pp. xv–xvi). Mahwah, NJ: Lawrence Erlbaum Associates.

Wilhelm, J. (1996). *Standards in practice, 6–8.* Urbana, IL: National Council of Teachers of English Press.

RESOURCES

Print

Allen, H. A., Splittgerber, F., & Manning, M. L. (1993). *Teaching and learning in the middle level school.* Upper Saddle River, NJ: Merrill/Prentice Hall.

Beane, J. A. (1993). *A middle school curriculum: From rhetoric to reality.* Columbus, OH: National Middle School Association (NMSA).

Coleman, J. S. (1961). *The adolescent society.* New York: Free Press.

Dickinson, T. (1993). *Readings in middle school curriculum: A continuing conversation.* Columbus, OH: NMSA.

Eccles, J., Lord, S., & Midgley, C. (1991). What are we doing to early adolescents? The impact of educational contexts on early adolescents. *American Journal of Education, 99,* 521–542.

Eccles, J., Wigfield, A., Midgley, C., Reuman, D., Iver, D. M., & Feldlaufer, H. (1993). Negative effects of traditional middle schools on student's motivations. *The Elementary School Journal, 93,* 553–574.

Feldman, S., & Elliott, G. (1990). *At the threshold: The developing adolescent.* Cambridge, MA: Harvard University Press.

Hynds, S. (1997). *On the brink: Negotiating literature and life with adolescents.* New York: Teachers College Press.

Kellough, R. D., & Kellough, N. G. (1999). *Middle school teaching: A guide to methods and resources.* Upper Saddle River, NJ: Merrill/Prentice Hall.

Mahiri, J. (2004). *What they don't learn in school: Literacy in the lives of urban youth.* New York: Peter Lang.

Manning, M. L., & Bucher, K. T. (2001). *Teaching in the middle school.* Upper Saddle River, NJ: Merrill/Prentice Hall.

McEwin, C., Dickinson, T., Erb, T., & Scales, P. (1995). *A vision of excellence: Organizing principles for middle grade teacher preparation.* Westerville, OH: Center for Early Adolescence and National Middle School Association.

Moore, D., Bean, T., Birdyshaw, D., & Rycik, J. (1999). *Adolescent literacy: A position statement for the Commission on Adolescent Literacy of the International Reading Association.* Newark, DE: The International Reading Association.

Muth, K. D., & Alvermann, D. (1999). *Teaching and learning in the middle grades.* Needham Heights, MA: Allyn and Bacon.

Takanishi, R. (1993). Changing views of adolescence in contemporary society. In R. Takanishi (Ed.), *Adolescence in the 1990s* (pp. 1–7). New York: Teachers College Press.

Walley, C. W., & Gerrick, W. G. (1999). *Affirming middle grades education.* Needham Heights, MA: Allyn and Bacon.

Watson, C. R. (1997). *Middle school case studies: Challenges, perceptions, and practices.* Upper Saddle River, NJ: Merrill/Prentice Hall.

Wiles, J., & Bondi, J. (1993). *The essential middle school.* Upper Saddle River, NJ: Merrill/Prentice Hall.

Electronic

Adolescence Directory On Line. ADOL is a directory of Web documents that focus on the social, emotional, and developmental needs of adolescents. ADOL exists as a way to help educators, parents, health practitioners, researchers, and adolescents access Web resources.

http://education.indiana.edu/cas/adol/welcome.html

Center for Adolescent and Family Studies. The Center states that its mission is to advance the understanding of the psychological, biological, and social features of adolescence. It serves as a resource of research on transition into adolescence.

http://www.indiana.edu/~cafs/

Middle Web Resources. This Web site explores the challenges of middle school reform and provides resources for educators and parents.

http://middleweb.com/index1.html

National Board for Professional Teaching Standards. The NBPTS is an independent organization governed by a 63-member board of directors. Its mission is to establish high and rigorous standards for what accomplished teachers should know and be able to do to develop and operate a national, voluntary system to assess and certify teachers who meet these high standards.

http://www.nbpts.org/

National Council of Teachers of English. The NCTE middle-level strand offers research and resources for middle-level English language arts teachers.

http://www.ncte.org/middle/

National Middle School Association. The NMSA is an organization of professionals, parents, and others interested in the educational and developmental needs of young adolescents. The NMSA is the only national educational association exclusively devoted to improving the educational experiences of young adolescents. Its website includes publications for purchase and exclusive Web-based materials to support teachers in the middle grades.

http://www.nmsa.org/

3

English Language Arts from Mid-Century to the Millennium

GUIDING QUESTIONS

1. How have our assumptions about literacy teaching in the middle grades changed over the past 50 years?
2. How have these changing assumptions influenced the teaching materials and techniques of junior high and middle school teachers?
3. How have your experiences as a student influenced your current assumptions about literacy and its teaching?

A CASE FOR CONSIDERATION

The World Across the Hall

In Mr. Owens's seventh-grade English classroom, students sit in rows of desks waiting for the class period to begin. Some are chatting with neighbors and friends; others are tearing paper out of notebooks or stuffing personal items temporarily inside their wooden desks. Steam escapes from a row of radiators beneath the large classroom windows. On a table along the back wall is a yellow cardboard box, with colored dividers, that seems to hold teaching materials of some kind. A stack of worn grammar books sits in the corner, flanked by a filmstrip projector and a pile of dittoed multiple-choice quizzes. An American flag and the teacher's heavy wooden desk dominate the front of the room. Some due dates and a few spelling words are written on the dusty blackboard.

After a few moments, Mr. Owens steps to the front of the room and tells students to take out their grammar books. Students each turn to different pages in large workbooks with slick green covers. They are supposed to work at their own pace, completing as many pages in one class period as they can. Some of them start right away, while others shuffle to the back of the room to sharpen pencils or dig in purses and pants pockets for pens. Suddenly, the activity stops as the principal, Mr. Jones, enters the doorway. There are some nervous looks as Mr. Jones begins:

> Good afternoon, students. I have an announcement to make. As you know, last week was the end of the first marking period. Some of you worked very hard this term, and we're very proud of you. You did much better than your classmates, and your efforts have paid off. Will the following people please gather up your things and move to the "A" classroom across the hall?

As Mr. Jones calls out the names, the mix of apprehension and relief in the room is almost palpable. Some students shift uneasily in their desks; others gather their books and belongings for the move across the hall. As soon as the three students leave the room, Mr. Jones's face turns somber.

> Now, just as there are those who worked up to their full potential, there are others who, unfortunately, failed to live up to our expectations. Will the following people please take your belongings and move to the "C" classroom next door?

The students watch in stunned silence as their classmates file out the door.

FOR DISCUSSION

You probably suspected that this story didn't happen in a modern-day classroom. In what historical period do you think this incident took place? As you read this story, in what ways does this picture compare or contrast with the memories of your own middle or junior high school? How do you think students would respond to a scenario like this today?

Scenes like this one happened routinely in the junior high school Susan Hynds attended from 1959 to 1961. Though his name has been changed, "Mr. Jones" was Susan's principal. Every marking period, without fail, Mr. Jones marched into her classroom with THE LIST, as Susan and her classmates waited in nervous anticipation. Compare Susan's account with that of someone who attended an urban middle school from 1988 to 1990. Noshin is a doctoral student in literacy education whose middle school experience in language arts provides a stunning contrast to Susan's description in the opening scenario.

> In seventh grade we read A Day No Pigs Would Die. I will never forget that book. I remember feeling disgust (like I really wanted to throw up). The author must have used vivid language for me to remember and feel so much. I don't remember so much about my teacher teaching, except that she asked a lot of questions and we had to take a test on it. But I do remember that she seemed to enjoy the story, too.

I remember other things, too. That I had to do a paper. I wrote about the homeless, and that was really my first research paper. That I studied so much about Shakers that I never wanted to know another thing about them, though I was fascinated at the time. That my friend Holly did a research paper on building plans for a local mall that was so thorough that all seventh graders were made to listen to her presentation (it was interesting). That we had to read a story written by a local author about an overweight girl who develops better eating habits and slowly gains self-awareness and self-esteem, and the author came to our class and visited and talked with us. I felt I could relate to that book, I think because I was overly anxious and self-critical during that time. It helped me to see that things can get better and you can do something about your own life.

What I remember about eighth-grade English, more than anything, is the ambience. I couldn't tell you what we wrote or did, but I do remember that most of the time it was a nice change from most other rooms. We had a stage in our room and lots of books and different areas in which we could do things. It's funny, but I don't have any recollection of the teacher talking or doing things; I can kind of picture her in the background somewhere. I do remember having discussions with other students and also that I used to hang out in different parts of the room. I also have a vague memory of being in a certain part of the room that was very colorful. I also remember there was an area with stuff to read, and there was a Redbook *magazine that I used to enjoy reading. I would sometimes read* Redbook *after that time in my life. I think we also had computers in the room, but I don't remember using them.*

At this point, you are probably marveling at what a difference a decade—or, more accurately, three decades—can make in the life of a middle school student. The "ambience" that Noshin talks about, the room with its stage platform and comfortable reading spaces, the fact that she could read *Redbook* magazine during English class, the opportunities for social interaction and for researching current topics like homelessness—all these factors stand in striking contrast to Susan's memories of multiple-choice quizzes, spelling lists, and fierce academic competition.

There's an adage that we never remember what our teachers taught us; we remember only how they treated us. If you think back to your own memories as an early adolescent, chances are, you'll remember bits and pieces of things that distressed or impressed you about English class. Like Noshin, you may not remember exactly what your teachers said or did, but you will surely remember how you felt. If you trace these feelings back far enough, you may make some important discoveries about the assumptions from which your teachers might have been operating in each historical period. The purpose of this chapter is to help you understand the social and historical roots of some of these assumptions.

EXPLORING YOUR TEACHING HISTORY

We begin this chapter from the premise that those who don't know their history as teachers and learners are condemned to repeat it. Often it's hard to put a finger on exactly why we resonate or clash with others about teaching, but when those "others" have power over our lives, these disagreements can be devastating. Although there are surely many uncaring or ill-prepared teachers in the world, sometimes it's all too easy to pronounce someone else's teaching as mindless or cruel. Often, teachers eye each other with suspicion because they don't understand the historical origins or recognize the good intentions behind each other's teaching practices. It's also easy for any teacher—especially in an age in which teaching materials and assessment techniques are a big-business enterprise—to combine various teaching approaches in a kind of mindless eclecticism, failing to understand the historical and possibly contradictory assumptions behind those approaches.

In Fieldwork Journal 3-1, we invite you to think back to your own days as an early adolescent. What materials and other artifacts dotted the landscape of your teachers' classrooms? As you engage in this imaginative excavation, consider the assumptions and, perhaps most important, the good intentions that may have been behind your teachers' practices.

Fieldwork Journal 3-1

Artifact Analysis: Revisiting Your Teachers and Textbooks

If you are lucky enough to have lived in the same place for most of your life, or if your family has saved some of your old schoolwork, you might want to do a little archeological excavation. Go up to your attic or storeroom and dig out any of the writings that you produced for your English teachers in middle or junior high school, as well as any textbooks or other materials you may have saved. Perhaps you used workbooks or worksheets. You may have an old literature anthology, grammar workbook, or writing textbook from this time in your life. If you're like most of us, and you've long ago lost track of such artifacts from your past life as a middle or junior high school student, jot down what you can remember about the classroom structures, assignments, textbooks, and other materials your teachers used, just as Noshin did in the previous example.

Now, do a mini-study of these artifacts. Consider what assumptions may have been behind your teachers' practices and teaching materials. Analyze any textbooks or materials you gathered or remembered. What seem to be the assumptions behind these published or teacher-created materials? You might want to create a double-entry journal like the example in Figure 3-1. In the left-hand column, jot down a description of the textbook, assignment, or other artifact from your days as a young adolescent. In the right-hand column next to each description, make a list of your teachers' "Assumptions About Literacy Learning." That is, what beliefs about reading, writing, oral language, and/or listening seem to underlie their choices of materials or teaching strategies (see Figure 3-1)?

When you are finished, think about the similarities or differences between your current beliefs about the teaching of literacy and your former teachers' beliefs. What examples can you find in your personal experiences, classroom discussions, or conversations with teachers of the current tensions in literacy teaching?

For example, can you see evidence of a "building blocks" approach to language study in your personal experience and classroom materials? How does this approach

FIGURE 3-1

Textbook, Teaching Material, Assignment	Assumptions About Literacy Learning
Grammar Workbook Page: "Parts of Speech." This is set up as a matching exercise where the names of the parts of speech are at the top and a list of definitions are below. Students are supposed to write the letter of the correct part of speech next to the matching definition below.	• Knowing the names of the parts of speech will make a person a better writer. • Memorizing definitions is important to the development of writing abilities. • Writing is an orderly process that begins with a knowledge of words, then sentences, paragraphs, and finally, longer pieces.

resonate or contrast with your own beliefs about literacy teaching? Do you see evidence of "reading-as-decoding" or "New Critical" approaches in your own experiences as a student or as a teacher? What "intelligences" do your middle school students seem to draw upon? Do their school experiences seem to support the development of these intelligences? What challenges do you face as classrooms become more diverse? Are all teaching decisions inherently political?

FROM TEXTS TO POLITICAL CONTEXTS: LITERACY LEARNING THEN AND NOW

As a way of comparing approaches and artifacts from several historical periods, Susan often asks her preservice teachers (who range in age from their 20s to their mid-50s) to make a list of the various approaches and materials they can remember from their own experiences as students in English language arts classes. As they share their memories of school, she makes a list similar to the one in Figure 3-2.

Looking closely at this chart, you can see a kind of shift in the assumptions about literacy and its teaching over the years. In the first half of the 20th century, teachers seemed preoccupied with the products of student learning. Gradually, this preoccupation turned to a more learner-centered focus on the social, emotional, and intellectual development of individual students. Eventually, teachers' concerns expanded to include the social (and sometimes political) contexts that influenced this development. Although approaches like spelling bees and sentence diagramming may have lingered from one decade to the next, we gradually began to see teaching approaches like journals, writing groups, independent reading programs, and inquiry projects in the English language arts classroom. The appearance of these approaches signaled some basic shifts in our assumptions about teaching, learning, and literacy.

You'll notice that the sheer number of approaches and materials seems to grow with each decade. Indeed, teaching materials, high-stakes assessment programs, and

FIGURE 3-2   Teaching Artifacts and Approaches

1950s	1960s	1970s	1980s
• sentence diagramming • parts of speech • quizzes, essay & multiple-choice tests on literature • spelling bees • "college-bound" literature lists • research papers (on teacher-selected topics)	• sentence diagramming • parts of speech • quizzes, essay & multiple-choice tests on literature • vocabulary cards • language workbooks • "college-bound" literature lists • research papers (on teacher-selected topics) • grammar worksheets • "SRA" kits	• sentence diagramming • parts of speech • quizzes, essay & multiple-choice tests on literature • research papers (on teacher-selected topics) • grammar worksheets • "SRA" kits • sentence combining • "framed" paragraphs • "The Writing Process" • prewriting and prereading activities • peer writing groups • collaborative inquiries • free-choice independent reading of "young adult" paperbacks • literature and reading circles • "I-Search" projects • collaborative learning activities	• sentence diagramming • parts of speech • quizzes, essay & multiple-choice tests on literature • grammar worksheets • sentence combining exercises • grammar mini-lessons • collaborative inquiries • service learning projects • "The Writing Process" • prewriting and prereading activities • peer writing groups • negotiated grading in assessment conferences • free-choice independent reading of "young adult" paperbacks • "I-Search" projects • literature and reading circles • word processors used in writing activities • grammar & spell checkers • computer-assisted writing programs

a burgeoning educational consulting market have proliferated over the past 50 years. This commercialization of the educational enterprise makes it all the more imperative for us to become critical consumers of the many teaching materials and approaches available to us today. As a way of developing a more critical stance, this chapter will examine some of the classroom approaches and artifacts over the past half century, attempting to put our own beliefs about literacy teaching in the middle grades into historical perspective.

OUR SHIFTING VIEWS OF LITERACY AND ITS TEACHING

As we explore the major changes in our thinking about literacy teaching from roughly the middle of the 20th century to the beginning of the 21st, it's important to remember that these shifts are not neat, tidy, nor clearly bounded by historical periods. That is, what we might call the text- or product-centered approaches such as sentence diagramming and memorization of grammar rules are still alive and well in some classrooms today.

Historically, a constant tension has existed between a preoccupation with standardized testing and teacher accountability on the one hand, and a concern for students' personal growth and development on the other. As a result, even today, high-stakes testing, state standards, and teacher accountability, with their heavy attention to the products of learning, often coexist in a sort of schizophrenic relationship with more process-centered, social, or sociopolitical approaches, which situate student learning and achievement within the context of complex social and political forces. Perhaps it's helpful to think about English language arts teaching over the past half century in terms of five major shifts: (a) literacy as text, (b) literacy as cognitive process, (c) literacy as personal growth, (d) literacy as sociocultural process, and (e) literacy as sociopolitical practice (see Figure 3-3).

The categories in Figure 3-3 give us a language for examining our own views and understanding the assumptions behind the materials and methods in most classrooms. They should not, however, be used to stereotype individual teachers. Instead, we hope that they will serve as a frame for examining the often rough and uneven

FIGURE 3-3   Approaches to Literacy Teaching

	Product-Centered	Process-Centered		Social/Contextual	
Aspects of the Learning Climate		**Cognitive/ Developmental**	**Personal/ Expressive**	**Sociocultural**	**Sociopolitical**
Focus of Curriculum	**Literacy as Text** • Part-to-whole approach to reading, writing, and grammar • Stress on correctness in grammar, spelling, and handwriting • Reading as decoding • Oral language as memorizing or answering teacher questions • Assessment through tests, quizzes, workbooks, formal writing	**Literacy as Cognitive Process** • Cognitive stages of literacy development • Writing and reading as thinking processes • Language as a way of learning across the curriculum • Assessment of processes as well as products • Prereading and prewriting strategies • Emphasis on revision • Portfolios for error analysis and assessment	**Literacy as Personal Growth** • Stress on self-expression and discovery • Student choice in topics and reading materials • Learning to write by writing • Wide variety of "young adult" literature • Oral language as a way of learning and sharing • Individualized, qualitative assessment through portfolios	**Literacy as Sociocultural Process** • Community-building • Collaborative learning activities • Peer and teacher-pupil conferencing • Stress on "authentic" audiences for student writing and talk • Curriculum and assessment negotiated between students and teachers • Literacy as cultural understanding and tolerance	**Literacy as Sociopolitical Practice** • Classroom as democracy • Emphasis on social justice and/or community action • Critical analysis of published texts and popular culture • Assessment and grading negotiated with students

	Product-Centered	Process-Centered		Social/Contextual	
Aspects of the Learning Climate		**Cognitive/ Developmental**	**Personal/ Expressive**	**Sociocultural**	**Sociopolitical**
Responsibilities of Teacher	• Dispense knowledge • Correct student errors • Keep records • Produce good citizens • Develop cultural literacy • Administer tests and quizzes • Monitor student progress on independent learning activities	• Develop "higher order" thinking skills • Develop strategies for reading, writing, and speaking in a variety of contexts • Make learning strategies explicit • Develop metacognitive awareness • Give substantive feedback to students • Teach stages of and strategies for reading and writing processes • Recognize developmental patterns in student ability and error	• Create safe classrooms • Celebrate personal expression and growth • Promote personally relevant independent language activities • Legitimize student texts • Expand the canon and curriculum to include a variety of cultural and social perspectives • Promote student choice • Read and write along with students	• Create classroom community • Foster student collaboration • Expand contexts for students' reading, talking, and writing • Promote cultural tolerance through literacy • Expand the canon and curriculum to include a variety of cultural and social perspectives • Set goals collaboratively • Teach grammar and usage "in context"	• Create a democratic classroom where all voices can be heard • Recognize influence of race, class, gender and other sociopolitical aspects of learning • Teach critical and political skills • Empower students as members of a democracy • Create opportunities for students to use literacy as a form of social action
Teaching Approaches and Materials	• Lecture • Whole class discussion • Programmed instruction • Formal speaking, reading, writing, and research activities • Workbooks • Book reports • Vocabulary cards • Spelling bees • Grammar handbooks • Reading machines • Programmed learning kits • Research papers	• Cross-curricular projects • Learning logs • "Think alouds" • Guided reading and writing activities • Sentence combining • Framed paragraphs • Slotted sentences • Portfolios for analyzing drafts, revision processes, and patterns of error in writing	• Reading and writing workshops or learning centers • Informal language experiences • Sharing circles • Student-authored publications • Informal research (or "I-Search") • Response journals • Writer's notebooks • Personal folders • Classroom libraries of young adult paperbacks • Portfolios for qualitative analysis of student learning	• Authentic audiences and purposes beyond the classroom • Project learning • Use of Internet, electronic mail, and other communication technologies • Peer response groups • Collaborative inquiry • Multiculturalism • Young adult books • Dialogue journals • Reading/writing circles • Portfolios for student-teacher conferencing • "Development" and "Showcase" portfolios for demonstrating growth to others	• "Social action," "service teaming," or "community action" projects • Reading, writing, and talking about politically relevant topics • "Antibias" or "antiracist" curricula • Multiculturalism as cultural critique • Exploration and critique of popular culture • Use and critique of Internet, electronic mail, and other communication technologies • Portfolios as opportunities for demonstrating growth and negotiating grades

ways in which English language arts teaching has evolved through the latter half of the 20th century. Most of us probably incorporate aspects of all five perspectives to one degree or another in our teaching. The point is not to see any one perspective as necessarily better or worse than the others, but to understand our ideas about literacy and its teaching as they developed over the past half century.

Literacy as Text: Product-Centered Approaches

Around the mid- to late 1960s, texts—their production and comprehension—were the centerpiece of the English language arts classroom. For Susan, the text that set the course of her entire junior high school experience was the standardized test. Given at the end of the sixth grade, this was the benchmark by which students would be sorted into the A, B, and C classes in the school's first experiment with "homogeneous grouping." Because this was Susan's first brush with standardized tests, she got stuck on the first few items, never finishing the examination. As a result she entered the B class for the first year of junior high school.

For a different set of reasons, Margaret was also placed in the B class. She had gone to a tiny rural elementary school, which had not given the standardized tests upon which students could be tracked. In addition, her administrators assumed that since she had gone to a rural school, she wouldn't be prepared to compete with children from the city.

The '50s and early '60s were highly competitive times, when classroom practices like spelling bees and the public sharing of everything from class rank to individual grades were commonplace. This focus on competition wasn't all bad; for academically successful students, a certain degree of competition actually enhanced learning. For kids like Susan and Margaret who were placed in the B track, however, their resistance to this competition often surfaced in antisocial and disruptive ways. Susan quickly mastered the art of becoming the class clown. At first, her homeroom teacher gave her "write-offs" and then eventually moved her desk into the cloakroom as a way of controlling her distracting attempts to amuse her classmates. Junior high school students in the '50s and '60s sat in rows, often working silently on independent activities. Sentence diagramming and workbooks were commonplace. Writing, if it was taught at all, typically focused on product-centered goals such as developing good handwriting and correct grammar, usage, or spelling. No research had yet been done on the thinking processes in which real writers engage, so writing instruction was dominated by a classical "building blocks" assumption that students should first learn words (vocabulary) before developing the ability to produce phrases, sentences, paragraphs, and finally, longer pieces of writing. If you happen to have a workbook or grammar handbook from the '50s or '60s, or even a more contemporary version, you'll probably see evidence of this building-block approach, in which punctuation and grammar at the sentence level are treated in the early chapters and rules for paragraphing and organizational structures for longer pieces of writing come later.

Similarly, reading instruction was dominated by what might be called a "decoding" perspective, in which teachers often presented students with short bits of texts in workbooks or readers and tested their comprehension at the word, sentence, or paragraph level. Unless teachers read aloud to students from stories or novels, or unless a school was fortunate to have class sets of literature anthologies, reading usually focused more on the study of these short contrived texts than it did on longer pieces of literature.

Often, if literature was taught at all, teachers, in the tradition of "New Criticism" (Brooks, 1947; Ransom, 1979), conducted discussions and gave tests and quizzes on the "correct" understanding of whatever the class was reading. Textbooks usually included a series of questions after each selection for teachers to use in assessing whether students understood what they read or, more likely, whether they read at all. Book reports were also common. Oral language opportunities consisted of oral book reports, large group discussions, an occasional assignment to memorize and present a short piece of literature, or a chance to compete in a spelling bee. Occasionally, students would stay after school to practice for skits or assemblies. Talk was usually reserved for demonstrating rather than creating knowledge.

Lest we paint an entirely dismal and oppressive picture of the junior high school English classroom at mid-century, we need to point out that, in many ways, we both flourished in this atmosphere. Margaret was good at answering questions about her reading and managed to use the same book report on *Across Five Aprils* (Hunt, 1964) three times from the sixth to the eighth grade. Always an extrovert, Susan loved to perform the poems she memorized and compete in spelling bees. Both of us were adept at diagramming sentences and enjoyed being tested on our reading. After all, we both became English teachers, so our own teachers must have done something right. Now that we've become teacher educators, however, we are struck by how many horror stories we hear from teachers in our workshops and classes about feeling "stupid" in class discussions and receiving papers that were viciously "red-penned" by grammar-obsessed teachers.

This product-centered view of literacy came out of the behaviorist notion that the mind is a "black box," inaccessible by any means (Skinner, 1976). Because strict behaviorists believe that only behaviors can be empirically measured, most teachers were pushed to produce "behavioral objectives" in which their goals for students had to be phrased in terms of easily measurable outcomes.

In addition, beginning with the launch of Sputnik by the Soviets in 1957, Americans were consumed by what became known as the "space race," and students were under tremendous pressure to excel in science and mathematics. It's not surprising that in an era of fierce national competition, standardized testing grew so powerful. Tests provided a set of neatly hierarchical and objective scores on which students could be judged against one another and placed in tracks according to "ability."

Although this text-centered view may seem altogether superficial and rigid, we should not dismiss its importance entirely. As teachers, we all bear the responsibility of teaching students how to craft and polish their writing, understand literary devices, learn appropriate grammar and usage conventions, master the arts of performing and publishing, and pass the standardized examinations they will surely face. If we fail to prepare them for these tasks, we have ignored one of our primary responsibilities as teachers.

When we focus too heavily on texts, however, we can easily lose sight of individual differences among students and the way social issues such as race, class, and gender complicate their literacy practices. It wasn't until the early 1970s that educators began to question the individualistic, competitive view of literacy education, opening up the mind's "black box" and daring to speculate on the unique and varied thinking processes that lie beneath the surface.

Process-Centered Approaches

In the early '70s, classrooms were slowly beginning to change in appearance and structure. Within what has been called the process movement were two major views of literacy: literacy as a cognitive process and literacy as personal growth.

Literacy as a cognitive process. In the early '70s, teacher-centered arrangements like desks in rows began to be replaced with circles of desks or small tables to accommodate collaborative learning projects. Occasionally, students were invited to depart from the standard canon of literature and choose from an array of what came to be called young adult novels or "YA" books.

During the famous Dartmouth Conference in 1966, an internationally renowned group of literacy scholars and researchers assembled for the purpose of reflecting on the past and future of English teaching. The early work of the conference participants had already begun to filter into professional conversations about teaching (Dixon, 1967). The early '70s heralded what promised to be an exciting new era in the teaching of English, in which a text-centered view, dominated by New Criticism, prescriptive grammars, and classical approaches to writing, was challenged by a student-centered approach that focused on the unique abilities and needs of individual learners.

Books like *Teaching as a Subversive Activity* (Postman & Weingartner, 1969), *Uptaught* (Macrorie, 1970), and *Hooked on Books* (Fader, 1966) became the new staples of college methods courses in the '70s. Writers like Postman and Weingartner, Macrorie, and Fader argued passionately for the need to depart from traditional focus on correctness and conformity—to let students read freely from books written especially for them, choose their own topics in writing, and have a say in direction and content of their own learning. Despite the urgings of a few revolutionaries, though, the innovations of the '70s were slow to filter down into real classrooms. In most English classrooms, sentence diagramming, workbooks, and desks in rows were still pretty much the order of the day.

Harris (1991) has written about this stark contrast between the "progressivist" rhetoric of the early '70s and the daily realities of most schools. He argues that this "heroic view" (p. 631) of Dartmouth as the catalyst for progressive education in America was inaccurate. In fact, there was a noticeable difference between the basic philosophies of the American and British participants at the conference—a difference that persists in the profession today. Harris argues that the British educators at Dartmouth largely supported a "growth model," informed by developmentalists such as Piaget (1950; Piaget & Inhelder, 1969), Vygotsky (1962), and Bruner (1960). This view celebrated the personal experiences of students and the expressive nature of language. In their zeal to beat the Russians in the space race, the Americans, on the other hand, were struggling to define English as an academic discipline. Inspired by the work of linguists such as Chomsky (1957) and literary critics such as Frye (1957), they were attempting to establish the legitimacy of English as a formal subject of study with distinct bodies of knowledge and subsets of skills to be mastered. This tension between knowledge and skills on one hand and personal growth on the other remains with us today.

By the early '70s, a group of writing researchers, inspired by the work of scholars such as Piaget (1950; Piaget & Inhelder, 1969), Vygotsky (1962), and Bruner (1960), began to peer inside the "black box" of literacy to explore how real readers, writers, and speakers created and comprehended language.

The earliest studies of writing were based on analyses of texts. Braddock (1975) discovered that, contrary to popular wisdom, published writers did not always have what English teachers called "topic sentences" in their paragraphs. Hunt (1970) discovered that students' sentences grew larger and more complex as they grew older. As a result, approaches like sentence combining slowly began to replace sentence diagramming, as teachers tried to give students practical ways to build the complexity and length of their sentences by creating and combining what they called "kernel sentences" in different patterns.

A group of early writing researchers (Emig, 1971; Flower & Hayes, 1977, 1981; Perl, 1979) argued that, contrary to the classical building-block assumptions, writing is a messy, often recursive process that proceeds in different ways for different writers. More experienced writers, for example, tend to make larger, more global revisions, in contrast to novice writers who typically revise at a surface level, rarely moving beyond cosmetic changes of words or phrases (Flower, 1979; Sommers, 1980). As this research gained a foothold in American education, we began to hear now-familiar phrases like "teach process, not product." Although grammar handbooks still lined the shelves and windowsills of most middle and junior high school classrooms, posters of the stages of the composing process—from prewriting to revising—gradually began to appear.

In some classrooms, early adolescents would pull up chairs in pairs or small groups to give each other feedback on texts in process, and it became fashionable to turn in a series of "messy" drafts before final products were completed. What came to be called the Writing Across the Curriculum (WAC) movement grew out of the idea that writing could be used not just as a way of demonstrating knowledge but also as a way of learning in all subject areas. Eventually, teachers beyond the English classroom were urged to use writing as a regular way of encouraging more active learning of their course content.

Inspired by Louise Rosenblatt's landmark work, *Literature as Exploration* (1995, originally published in 1938), researchers from a "reader response" perspective (Beach, 1974; Holland, 1973; Purves & Ripperre, 1972) discovered—again, no surprise to many teachers—that each student had a unique and individual response to literature. Teachers began to understand that literary reading (as opposed to informational reading) offered what Langer (1995) would later call a "horizon of interpretive possibilities" in contrast to a "steady reference point" of correct interpretation. Tests and quizzes on literature were sometimes replaced or supplemented by "guided response" activities in which students were led through a series of strategies designed to capture their unfolding responses as they read. The traditional questions-at-the-back-of-the-book started to reflect a developmental orientation, beginning with literal questions about literature and moving toward more interpretive levels.

At the same time, definitions of literacy were being expanded beyond the traditional triad of reading, writing, and language study. Barnes (1975) from the United

Kingdom showed how oral language, like writing, could be a way of learning and not just a way of demonstrating knowledge. As a result, the traditional research paper sometimes gave way to informal collaborative inquiry through which students explored a topic of interest with a group of their peers. Heathcote (1970) and Moffett and Wagner (Moffett, 1968; Moffett & Wagner, 1992) introduced the importance of drama in the English classroom. Oral language activities ranging from panel discussions, public speeches, and debates to creative dramatics, oral interpretation, and readers' theater entered the literacy classroom. This approach was especially exciting and engaging for middle school students, whose keen sense of adventure and need for social interaction and physical activity were not yet dampened by the increasing peer pressure of high school.

Despite a flourishing body of research and the work of innovative teachers, however, large-scale studies of how literacy was actually taught in the '70s and '80s revealed a rather bleak picture. Britton and his colleagues (1975) from the United Kingdom reported that adolescents had few opportunities to engage in what he called "expressive" or "poetic" writing; instead, most students wrote for a narrow audience of teachers/examiners. Similarly, Applebee (1981), in his large-scale survey of students and teachers in the United States, concluded that English teachers assigned few writing projects longer than a paragraph. Other content-area teachers in his study relied almost solely on multiple-choice and fill-in-the-blank tests.

Later, in his study of American literature classrooms, Applebee (1993) discovered that, despite growing interest in expanding the canon of literature available to secondary students, teachers still clung to the traditional Eurocentric canon and held to the principles of New Criticism in their teaching. Although such studies were crucial to our understanding of the teaching practices of the times, it's interesting that those including the middle grades tended to lump early and older adolescents together in their discussion, reflecting little or no recognition of the unique needs and abilities of early adolescents.

Nevertheless, during the '70s and early '80s, many teachers gradually moved from a focus on products to a focus on the processes behind them. In some classrooms, student-centered learning logs and journals replaced workbooks and worksheets as teachers recognized the value of informal, exploratory writing and self-selected reading. Teachers sought to find authentic audiences for student writing beyond themselves and engaged students in brainstorming, drafting, and revising as well as regular goal-setting and evaluation conferences throughout the various stages of the composing process. Standardized tests were still present in many states and, largely as a result of the cognitive process movement, state and local curricula were often based on hierarchies or taxonomies of skills that were expected to develop as students moved through the grade levels.

Eventually, we began to realize that the strong focus on skills and knowledge, made even more pressing by the push to become an intellectually superior nation, had blinded us to important affective and personal aspects of literacy teaching.

Literacy as personal growth.   Largely inspired by the early work of cognitive psychologists, advocates of a student-centered curriculum argued passionately for the benefits of student choice and "authentic" literacy practices. One approach promised teachers a way to provide students with choice and personally meaningful literacy experiences while still maintaining a comfortable structure and routine. This approach became known as "workshop teaching."

Nancie Atwell's landmark work, *In the Middle* (1987), provided middle school teachers with concrete examples of early adolescents exercising choice in reading, writing, and oral language within a flexible setting. In a workshop arrangement, students often worked individually or in small groups, and teachers acted more as guides or facilitators rather than the sole arbiters of students' learning. Teachers learned to move among groups of students, conferring with individuals or giving suggestions to groups as they worked on a variety of projects. Perhaps because of their need for constant movement, change, and choice, early adolescents seemed uniquely suited for workshop models of literacy learning. Even today, it is more common to see workshop teaching in a middle than a high school classroom.

With the aim of developing students personally and intellectually, teachers and researchers began to focus on the affective and aesthetic as well as cognitive dimensions of language learning. In the late '70s, Rosenblatt wrote *The Reader, The Text, The Poem* (1994, originally published in 1978), noting the differences between "aesthetic" and "efferent" reading. Literature, she argued, should be read aesthetically (with a near-total absorption in the reading process); yet, in classrooms, students often read literature efferently (from the Latin *effere*, "to carry away") for the purpose of remembering bits of trivia for a test or quiz. Based largely on the work of humanistic psychologists such as Rogers (1969) and the work on aesthetic reading by Rosenblatt (1994, 1995), teachers acknowledged the complex interplay of personal response, motivation, and authenticity in literacy learning. Atwell (1987), Graves (1983), Calkins (1986), and Murray (1985), among others, urged teachers to give students choices in their reading and writing activities and to encourage the development of "authentic voice" in writing and personal response in reading.

In some classrooms, as a result of the reader-response movement, reading workbooks were replaced by more personal "response journals," and the competitive forum of the large-group discussion gave way to more informal approaches, in which small circles of students might discuss paperback young adult novels with their peers. Teachers began to install book racks or set aside areas for classroom libraries of these paperbacks for students' independent reading.

With the publication of Hinton's *The Outsiders* in 1967, a healthy market emerged for books written especially for teenage readers. Today, although YA novels are supposed to be for both middle-grades and high school students, they are typically viewed as more appropriate for early adolescents. Perhaps because they face less pressure for college preparation, middle school teachers are more likely than high school teachers to embrace adolescent literature and independent reading programs.

In the early '70s, the Assembly on Literature for Adolescents (ALAN) was created within the National Council of Teachers of English to help teachers discover and evaluate the burgeoning supply of literature for young adults. *The ALAN Review*, Carlsen's *Books and the Teenage Reader* (1980), Fader's *Hooked on Books* (1966), and *Your Reading* (an annotated bibliography of young adult books published and updated regularly by the National Council of Teachers of English) helped teachers to expand the canon of literature available to students beyond the traditional. At the same time, the Bay Area Writing Project and its offshoot, the National Writing Project, offered hands-on staff development and a support network for teachers interested in implementing a process-centered approach to writing in schools across the nation.

In the early '90s, student-centered approaches to literacy were enriched by the work of Howard Gardner (1993) and his theory of multiple intelligences. Anyone who has taught in the middle grades can attest to the tremendous range of preferences and abilities among early adolescents. Perhaps no other period of development captures students at so many different points on the intellectual and social spectrum. It is no wonder that Gardner's work was so relevant to teachers in the middle grades, inspiring them to look beyond the logical and linguistic (the intelligences most valued in schools) and discover the vast wealth of other capacities in young learners.

Especially during this personal growth movement, artistic, spatial, kinesthetic, and other "alternative" intelligences were recognized and valued in the middle school English language arts classroom. It was not uncommon for students to include drawing or other artistic representations in portfolios and journals as teachers discovered the value of assessing students on their abilities beyond the logical and linguistic.

Beginning in the '80s, rigid developmental sequences and hierarchies of skills were challenged by the work of Ken and Yetta Goodman and the "whole language" movement. This movement started in the elementary grades and gradually worked its way into middle and (occasionally) high school classrooms (Goodman, 1986; Goodman, Goodman, & Hood, 1989). Although the movement is far more complicated than we can describe here, it is founded on the notion that literacy skills are best developed as learners encounter whole texts rather than the "manufactured" atomistic stuff of the workbooks, quizzes, and basal readers of the '60s. Rather than relying on standardized tests and quizzes or rigid taxonomies of skills that students are supposed to master at certain age levels, the whole language movement encouraged teachers to become "kid watchers" and researchers in their own classrooms, developing curricula and evaluation materials sensitive to the unique groups of students they served.

Perhaps because some middle school teachers have an elementary education background or because the middle school is not as rigidly segmented by subject matter areas as high school, it seems that middle school teachers have been more accepting of whole language than secondary teachers, though not perhaps quite as accepting as their colleagues in elementary settings.

Considering the rather rigid and simplistic text-based views of literacy teaching being advocated by politicians and test makers today, this learner-centered perspective seems too good to be true, as, in a sense, it still is. Gradually, some limitations of this personal growth approach became apparent. First, although teachers experienced the satisfaction of offering students choices and inviting their unique personal perspectives into the literacy classroom, it became difficult to assign grades or to assess student progress without appearing to squelch their creativity and enthusiasm. Second, even though techniques like personal sharing and collaborative learning worked well in relatively homogeneous classrooms, the increasing cultural diversity of our schools made such approaches complicated for children of different cultures, especially those who spoke English as a second language. Finally, we began to realize that, considering the incredibly social nature of language, there was really no such thing as the "individual" response to literature or even what came to be called "personal" writing. Language learning occurred not in a vacuum, but in a complicated web of social relationships. As the next section will discuss, we are both created by and the creators of our language acts.

Social/Contextual Approaches to Literacy Teaching

Literacy as a sociocultural process. Eventually, as approaches like workshop teaching began to bring students and teachers into closer collaboration, it became apparent that literacy was not simply an isolated activity in which students' reading, writing, and oral language processes operated independently of the social contexts surrounding them. Although the goal of most English language arts teaching still focused heavily on the development of individual language skills, we began to recognize that social, cultural, academic, and other experiences all influenced the development of those skills.

Through the work of Vygotsky (1962), we began to realize that what students could do on their own was only a small part of what they could do with the help of peers, teachers, and other adults. Vygotsky's "zone of proximal development" referred to the spectrum of language activities that individuals could accomplish with the assistance of more able individuals in their social realm.

A movement known as "constructivism" promoted the idea that students should be viewed not as passive learners, but as active in constructing their own knowledge, often in social interaction with teachers and more able peers (see Hiebert, 1991).

In contrast to more private, individualistic approaches to literacy learning, students in constructivist classrooms discovered the power of engaging in such collaborative activities as writing conferences, peer response groups, literature circles, and collaborative inquiry. This social view of language stood in stark contrast to the assumptions of the '50s and '60s that students should be taught and tested independently, without outside help. Fifty years ago, collaborating with others on tests and papers was considered cheating. By the mid- to late 1970s, collaboration on everything from writing to research projects became the order of the day. Such collaborative approaches became even more popular in the middle grades where early adolescents' need for social interaction is paramount.

At the same time, as more and more children of diverse cultures and languages began to enter the public schools, it became vividly apparent that the experiences of young women and children of color were not represented in textbooks, classroom libraries, or even standardized tests. The term "multiculturalism" entered our vocabularies as we strove to make our students more tolerant of difference through their reading, writing, listening, and talking. In its early days, multiculturalism became associated with building cultural tolerance. Teachers and students began reading and writing about the holidays and traditions of particular cultural groups. For example, literature by African American, Latino/Latina, and Asian writers, among other racial and ethnic groups, began to make its way into some classrooms.

In the '70s and early '80s, however, literature by women and writers of color was still hard to come by, and most teachers continued to teach from a primarily White European canon. Our views of the "individual" language learner were challenged by anthropologists and psycholinguists (Heath, 1983), who argued that race, culture, and class profoundly influenced the ways in which students used language and, consequently, the impressions their teachers developed about them.

Scholars such as Smitherman (1986) and Labov (1972) popularized the notion that the language of some African American children, in contrast to popular stereotypes, is rich with nuance and complexity and not, as many teachers suspected, a sign of laziness or sloppiness. As a result of such work, teachers began to question the legitimacy of Eurocentric approaches to grammar and language study that had long been the mainstay of American public education. "Correctness" began to be viewed within the context of the varied cultural and social expectations that students encountered in their daily lives.

A view of literacy as a sociocultural process went a long way in promoting the value of collaboration in the English language arts classroom and encouraged an understanding and tolerance of diversity. In the latter part of the 20th century, however, we were confronted by difference and diversity in ways we had never imagined. Understanding the vital role of literacy in a democratic society, we began to believe that students could use literacy, not only to understand, but also to transform the world around them.

Literacy as sociopolitical practice. As scholars such as Luke (1988), Edelsky (1994), and Willinsky (1990) began to make their mark upon the field of literacy education, teachers were urged to move beyond the goal of developing individual students' cognitive and social skills toward a greater awareness of the role of literacy in a democracy. For the past several decades, whether represented by the individualized learning approaches of the '50s and '60s or learner-centered approaches such as reader response to literature and the process approach to writing, English language arts teaching had been largely focused toward developing the skills and capacities of individual learners. This highly individualized view of literacy has recently been criticized on many fronts.

In a more politically situated approach, students are challenged to use their literacy as a way of promoting social change. On one end of this spectrum, English language arts teachers might engage students in a service-learning curriculum, creating projects aimed at helping others or improving community life. On the other end of the continuum, teachers might create an antibias, antiracist, or social-justice curriculum, in which students work collaboratively on social and political issues such as the environment, crime, and political reform. When literacy is viewed as a sociopolitical practice, it is not enough to simply include multicultural literature or promote tolerance of others in the classroom. We are challenged today as never before to make issues of race, class, gender, and injustice explicit aspects of our literacy teaching.

Through the influence of movements such as postmodernism, feminism, and cultural studies, we are also urged to become more sensitive to the ways in which issues like race, class, gender, and other sociopolitical factors influence the literacy practices of students. As Edelsky (1992) has argued, every curricular choice, from textbook selection to assessment practices, has political implications:

> Many people, especially in the United States, think of politics only as dirty and "backroom stuff." As a result, we regard it as not polite to engage in controversial arguments or politics; we don't want to politicize. . . . The schools, because they are public schools, supposedly do not advocate any particular position. But we ignore

the fact that embedded in every textbook, every basal reader, and every classroom discussion is a political perspective. (p. 325)

In a similar vein, work on gender in the literacy classroom (Barbieri, 1995; Finders, 1997; Smith & Wilhelm, 2002) has made teachers more sensitive to the fact that young girls are often socialized toward silence. Young men, on the other hand, are steeped in a tradition of competition and aggressiveness; they often demand more "air time" in class discussions, are reluctant for male peers to see them reading books or writing poetry, and place more value on "real-world" than classroom reading.

In her study of early adolescent girls in two middle school groups (the "social queens" and the "tough cookies"), Margaret Finders (1997) contrasted the "sanctioned literacy practices" of school with the practices constituting their "literate underlife." Outside school, girls in both groups engaged in a variety of literacy activities such as creating bathroom graffiti, passing notes, reading teen 'zines, and signing yearbooks. Arguing the importance of this "literate underlife" in the identity formation of early adolescent girls, Finders concluded the following:

> Rhetoric about becoming an adolescent revolves around issues of freedom, independence, and responsibility; yet, for the queens and the cookies, these expectations did not hold true. In junior high, the girls' actual experiences in the school context were constricted time, movement, and talk. Only through literate underlife were these girls provided any opportunity for more freedom, independence or responsibility. (p. 129)

The recent decline in academic performance and test scores among males has focused much attention on boys and their experience in schooling. Smith and Wilhelm (2002), in their study of adolescent males, found that, contrary to popular belief, many young men have a rich relationship with reading and literacy in their daily lives, but their preferences and practices aren't often sanctioned in school. The typical English curriculum, focused largely on literary texts, often fails to capture the attention of many boys, who favor more "real-world" texts such as those found in popular newspapers and magazines, electronic peer networks, the Internet, and informational television shows. Smith and Wilhelm's suggestions seem beneficial for boys and girls alike: Give ample opportunities for students to choose their own reading materials in an inquiry-oriented curriculum that fosters active learning and promotes strong social relationships.

In a sociopolitical approach to literacy, teachers have an increasingly difficult role to play. In contrast to their role in the teacher-centered classrooms of the '70s and '80s, they are urged to create classroom democracies in which all voices can be heard and no students are silenced because of race, class, gender, or privilege. This is no easy task, since engaging middle school students in grappling with issues they might not have sought out on their own requires a new kind of "teacher-centeredness." In contrast to their experiences as student-centered teachers in the '70s and '80s, today's English language arts teachers cannot afford to simply step out of the way and allow students total choice in the topics and products of their learning. Sometimes, students and teachers alike must step into uncomfortable positions as the literacy classroom becomes a crucible for the divisiveness and discomfort that often accompany social awareness and change.

In addition to adopting new roles in their literacy classrooms, teachers are also challenged to compete with the ever-expanding array of reading, writing, talking, and interactive literacies available to their middle school students through technological advances such as the Internet. More important, they must teach their students to become more critical of the barrage of popular culture in their daily lives. This is no easy task for early adolescents, who often define themselves and others by choices in everything from fashions to music groups to popular magazines.

It's important to reiterate that the move from product to process to social and political contexts over the past 50 years is neither neat nor clearly represented by historical epochs. Although different ideas about the nature of literacy learning have been more popular at certain historical points than others, the relationship between theory and practice has never been tidy. Often, historical shifts in practice have come more from classroom constraints than published journal articles. Text- or teacher-centered approaches have appeared and disappeared in different guises throughout the latter half of the century, just as some approaches have dropped out altogether. Our aim in this chapter has been to give you a lens for viewing what you see in classrooms—your own and those of other teachers—from a social and historical perspective.

In brief, studies of adolescent literacies now address the ways in which gender shapes literacy experiences (Chandler-Olcott & Mahar, 2003; Finders, 2005; Gilbert, 1997), how technological tools mediate writing (Beach & Bruce, 2002; Luke, 2002), how race and ethnicity shape school experiences (Fecho, 1998; Mahiri, 2004; Willis, 1995), and how class influences how one experiences school (Gee & Crawford, 1998). Equally important, in recent years, more attention has been given to the dichotomous nature of in-school and out-of-school literacies for adolescents (Alvermann, Hinchman, Moore, Phelps, & Waff, 1998; Finders, 1997; Hull & Schultz, 2002; Rymes, 2001; Smith & Wilhelm, 2002). Alvermann et al. (1998) posed the question,

> How is it that schooled literacy makes the other literacies in adolescents' lives less valuable or less commendable—especially given that it is the nonacademic literacies that are most likely to sustain students' interests in further schooling?... School literacy is assumed to be more desirable than nonacademic literacies, at least by educators' standards and perhaps by some adolescents as well. (pp. 355–356)

In short, the field of adolescent literacy has expanded to include deeper and broader definitions of literacies as well as deeper and more complex understandings of the lives of early adolescents. As Martha Ivery's experience in Classroom Case 3-1 demonstrates, however, this is often easier said than done.

POLITICAL REALITIES AND PENDULUM SWINGS: CHALLENGES FOR MIDDLE SCHOOL TEACHERS AT THE MILLENNIUM

While current definitions of literacy are being expanded to include the reading, writing, and viewing of print and nonprint texts in multiple contexts, current political and popular rhetoric seems to call for a narrowing of the field and a return to a definition of literacy as reading, and even more narrowly, to reading in school.

Classroom Case 3-1

Pets and Projects: Processes and Products

Martha Ivery is a sixth-grade teacher in a rural middle school. During the first few weeks of class, she decided to try a community-building activity that she hoped would develop her students' skills as researchers and language users. Her goals were to build community within the classroom as well as to help her students see themselves as important members of the larger community. Since many of her students rode the bus and thus did not have opportunities to participate in her classroom community beyond the school day, she divided them into groups, carefully considering the ways in which each student might become a valued member of that group. For instance, since she knew Velma had had many experiences with animals but was not presently a fluent writer in English, she placed Velma within a group that had fluent Spanish-speaking students as well as English language users who did not bring experiences with animals.

After dividing her class into small groups, Martha asked them to research the necessary supplies and expenses of owning particular classroom pets. Some students immediately went to the Internet to research exotic pets and their habitats. Some students interviewed pet owners and pet store employees. She invited Velma's older brothers to class to talk about caring for animals.

Martha's students were enthused and articulate during their class presentations in which they shared their research. After a week of researching and a day of sharing their discoveries, students then turned in their letters to the administration, asking for permission to purchase a pet of their choosing for their classroom and requesting money for the project. They were excited to hear what the principal would decide.

Martha was terribly disappointed when students handed in their letters. While students' levels of interest, collaboration, research practices, even the real-life desire to acquire a pet for the classroom were high, the letters were short, messy, and rife with grammatical errors. She would be too embarrassed to hand these over to Mrs. Wilton, the middle school principal. Martha took the stack of letters home, struggling with how to respond tactfully and honestly to her students without squelching their enthusiasm or demeaning their hard work and accomplishment.

For Discussion

Many middle school students, for any number of reasons, make tremendous leaps in learning but do not complete an acceptable final product. In Martha's case, the vast array of knowledge and skills the students required to complete their project was not visible in their letters to the principal. Think for a moment of all the skills Martha's students drew upon during the course of this project: social skills, research skills, mathematical and problem-solving skills, oral language and listening skills, writing and language skills. In the end, their final grade would hinge upon one small aspect of those skills: their ability to edit and proofread for standard spelling and usage. Think about the five major perspectives on literacy presented earlier in Figure 3-3: (a) literacy as text, (b) literacy as cognitive process, (c) literacy as personal growth, (d) literacy as sociocultural process, and (e) literacy as sociopolitical practice. If you had to put Martha's teaching goals and assessment practices into one of these categories, where would you place them? How might Martha have designed a set of assessments to document the range of competencies that students needed to complete this project?

Despite all the effort that students put into a project, eventually they will be judged on the quality and correctness of the final product. Even when students' enthusiasm and inspiration are high, you still have to grapple with how to teach them the fundamentals of edited American English. And the pressures to value this part of the language arts curriculum over all others will be strong.

In a report commissioned by the National Reading Conference, Alvermann (2001) writes,

> More often than not in the United States, newspaper headlines and feature stories on national television networks focus on early literacy instruction and the so-called reading wars between advocates of direct skills instruction and those who favor more holistic approaches to teaching young children to read print text. (p. 3)

Similarly, a report by the American Association of Colleges for Teacher Education (2002) expresses concern that the *No Child Left Behind* legislation will force states to adopt a "one-size-fits-all approach . . . [to the] . . . unnecessary exclusion of other sound approaches that can build strong literacy skills with the diverse groups of students represented in our classroom today"(p. 3). The AACTE further argues that this legislation "excludes or undermines writing as part of literacy" (2002, p. 3).

What does this mean for middle school literacy teachers? As Lonsdale and Mc-Curry (2004) argue, the definition of literacy used by policy makers and public officials

> has implications for governments, workplaces and institutions, for which aspects of literacy are favoured and supported, which research is funded, how literacy is measured and valued and the teaching and learning approaches adopted. How we define literacy can lead to different conclusions about the extent of illiteracy. (p. 13)

Such a return toward more narrow definitions of adolescent literacy holds grave implications for our future work and for the adolescents we teach.

It might be valuable at this juncture to place some of what you've just learned into the context of your own beliefs about teaching literacy in the middle grades. Fieldwork Journal 3-2 should help you to consider some of the major ideas in this chapter in a more concrete and personal way.

Fieldwork Journal 3-2

Cutting the Pie: Your Approach to Literacy Teaching

Now that you've read about the five approaches to literacy teaching in the past 50 years, we'd like you to try your hand at mapping out your own assumptions about literacy at this point in your career. Think about what aspects and approaches to literacy teaching you value most and least. Then sketch out a pie chart like the one in Figure 3-4, allotting the space that you think each approach deserves in your philosophy of teaching.

FIGURE 3-4 My Approach to Literacy Teaching

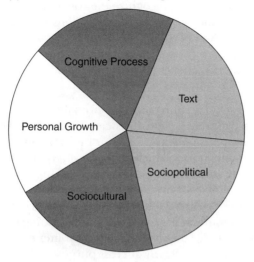

To jump-start your thinking, consider the degree to which the following are important in your middle school classroom:

- **Literacy as Text:** To what extent do you think it's important for middle school students to craft and perfect their writing? To read and comprehend complex texts that they might not seek out on their own? To recognize and use literary techniques in their reading and writing? To learn about principles of correct grammar and usage? To present or perform in front of a large group? To participate in a whole class discussion? To succeed in standardized examinations?
- **Literacy as Cognitive Process:** To what extent do you think it's important for middle school students to develop metacognitive and higher order thinking skills? To draw upon a variety of strategies for composing and revising texts? To develop a repertoire of strategies for understanding and analyzing literature and nonfiction? To use both exploratory and more formal language as a way of learning?
- **Literacy as Personal Growth:** To what extent do you think it's important for middle school students to use literacy for self-expression and personal growth? To make their own choices about reading, writing, talking, and listening? To share reading and writing with others? To feel safe and respect others in the classroom community? To see themselves as competent readers, writers, and language users?
- **Literacy as Sociocultural Practice:** To what extent do you think it's important for middle school students to understand how social and cultural contexts shape language? To engage in collaborative projects? To reach out to others in the larger world through their literacy practices? To appreciate culturally and socially diverse perspectives? To read from an array of multicultural literature and nonfiction? To respond to each other's writing critically and sensitively? To use language in a variety of social and cultural contexts?

- **Literacy as Sociopolitical Process:** To what extent do you think it's important for middle school students to recognize the role of literacy in a democracy? To understand and critique the political motivations of texts from print to electronic to multimedia and beyond? To use literacy as a tool for social action and change? To become critical consumers and producers of popular culture? To recognize the influence of race, class, gender, and other sociopolitical aspects of literacy?

If you're like most teachers, your pie chart probably contains aspects of all five approaches to literacy teaching. Few of us can afford the luxury (or the narrow-mindedness) of philosophical purity where our beliefs about teaching and learning are concerned. A certain amount of eclecticism is not only healthy but necessary in the midst of real-world concerns like high-stakes testing and increasingly diverse classrooms.

The point here is not to aim for a mindless consistency, but to consider where some of our assumptions about literacy may be undercutting others. For example, if we believe in nurturing an aesthetic appreciation of literature, yet base our grades on short-answer quizzes, we are clearly at cross purposes with our own goals. As you read through the other chapters of this book, keep this chart handy. You may find yourself questioning your original choices or wondering about how they play out in the real world of the middle school English language arts classroom. Perhaps by the end of the book, you'll revisit and rework your original chart, based on the insights and ideas you encounter along the way.

In the next chapter, we invite you to step more firmly into your role as teacher as you consider the process of planning instruction for your middle school students.

Standards in Practice

Charting the Assumptions of Your State Standards

For this exploration, we'd like you to consider the assumptions behind your statewide English language arts standards. First, find a copy of your state standards. Try finding them on the *Developing Educational Standards* Web site (*http://edstandards.org/Standards. html*) or locate a printed copy. Find the section on the middle grades, and read closely the parts that address what early adolescents should know and do. Your task is to unpack the assumptions on which the standards are based according to the five historical perspectives on literacy presented earlier in this chapter: literacy as text, literacy as cognitive process, literacy as personal growth, literacy as sociocultural process, and literacy as sociopolitical practice.

We realize that this is a difficult task with which teachers, teacher educators, and legislators continue to struggle. But try to tease out the ways in which a particular standard (or standards) is built from a set of assumptions about literacy and its teaching. For example, if one of your state standards specifies that all students should be able to "use language for literary response and understanding," what perspective (or perspectives) about literacy is represented? How might the assumptions be different if the standard were worded "reading comprehension and analysis" or "cultural and political critique" instead of "literary response and understanding"?

Don't Stop with the General Standards Statements

Look for places where your state might specify certain tasks that students should be able to perform at different grade levels. For instance, if the standard says "literary response and understanding," but the examples of what students should be able to do focus mostly on knowledge of literary historical periods, recognition of genre features, and the ability to arrive at a "correct" interpretation of a literary text, then you can be pretty sure that the state is working from a text-centered rather than a personal response perspective about the reading of literature.

After you've completed this informal analysis, go back to the pie chart you just created and sketch out another chart, this time mapping out what seem to be the guiding assumptions of your state standards. How do your beliefs match what your state says you and your students should be doing? Consider where you are likely to have problems "teaching to the standards" or preparing your middle school students for the standardized tests based upon them. Then consider which standards embody perspectives on literacy teaching that you can support in your classroom.

As you plan your future lessons, it's a good idea to return constantly to your state standards, asking yourself which aspects of the standards are represented in your overall goals and your daily teaching. This kind of cross checking and informal documenting can be invaluable in conversations with supervisors, administrators, and parents. It can also help you to prepare your middle school students for the standardized tests in a way that won't diminish your overall goals for their literacy learning.

REFERENCES

Alvermann, D. E. (2001). Effective literacy instruction for adolescents. Executive Summary and Paper Commissioned by the National Reading Conference. Chicago, IL: National Reading Conference. Retrieved September 19, 2004, from http://www.coe.uga.edu/reading/faculty/alvermann/effective.pdf

Alvermann, K., Hinchman, K., Moore, S., & Phelps, D. (1998). *Reconceptualizing the literacies in adolescents' lives.* Mahwah, NJ: Lawrence Erlbaum Associates.

American Association of Colleges for Teacher Education (2002). Research-based literacy instruction: Implications for teacher education. A White Paper of the American Association of Colleges for Teacher Education. Focus Council on Literacy. Retrieved September 19, 2004, from http://www.aacte.org/Membership_Governance_literacy.pdf

Applebee, A. N. (1981). *Writing in the secondary school: English and the content areas.* Urbana, IL: National Council of Teachers of English.

Applebee, A. N. (1993). *Literature in the secondary school: Studies of curriculum and instruction in the United States.* Urbana, IL: National Council of Teachers of English.

Atwell, N. (1987). *In the middle: Writing, reading, and learning with adolescents.* Montclair, NJ: Boynton/Cook.

Barbieri, M. (1995). *Sounds from the heart: Learning to listen to girls.* Portsmouth, NH: Heinemann.

Barnes, D. (1975). *From communication to curriculum.* Harmondsworth, UK: Penguin.

Beach, R. (1974). Conceiving of characters. *Journal of Reading, 17*(7), 546–551.

Beach, R., & Bruce, B. (2002). Using digital tools to foster critical inquiry. In D. Alvermann (Ed.), *Adolescents and literacies in a digital world* (pp. 147–163). New York: Peter Lang.

Braddock, R. (1975). The frequency and placement of topic sentences in expository prose. *Research in the Teaching of English, 8*(3), 287–302.

Britton, J., Burgess, T., Martin, N., McLeod, A., & Rosen, H. (1975). *The development of writing abilities.* London: Macmillan.

Brooks, C. (1947). *The well wrought urn: Studies in the structure of poetry.* New York: Harcourt, Brace & World.

Bruner, J. (1960). *The process of education.* New York: Vintage.

Calkins, L. M. (1986). *The art of teaching writing.* Portsmouth, NH: Heinemann.

Carlsen, G. R. (1980). *Books and the teenage reader: A guide for teachers, librarians, and parents* (2nd ed.). New York: Harper & Row.

Chandler-Olcott, K., & Mahar, D. (2003). "Tech-savviness" meets multiliteracies: Exploring adolescent girls' technology-mediated literacy practices. *Reading Research Quarterly, 38,* 356–385.

Chomsky, N. (1957). *Syntactic structures.* The Hague: Morton.

Dixon, J. (1967). *Growth through English.* Urbana, IL: National Council of Teachers of English.

Edelsky, C. (1992). A talk with Carole Edelsky about politics and literacy. *Language Arts, 69*(5), 324–329.

Edelsky, C. (1994). Education for democracy. *Language Arts, 71*(4), 252–257.

Emig, J. (1971). *The composing processes of twelfth graders.* Champaign, IL: National Council of Teachers of English.

Fader, D. (1966). *Hooked on books.* New York: Berkeley Medallion.

Fecho, B. (1998). Crossing boundaries of race in a critical literacy classroom. In D. Alvermann, K. Hinchman, D. Moore, S. Phelps, & D. Waff (Eds.), *Reconceptualizing the literacies in adolescents' lives* (pp. 75–102). Mahwah, NJ: Lawrence Erlbaum Associates.

Finders, M. (1997). *Just girls: Hidden literacies and life in junior high.* New York: Teachers College Press.

Finders, M. J. (2005). Gotta be worse: Literacy, schooling and adolescent youth offenders. In. J. Vadeboncoeur & L. P. Stevens (Eds.), *Re/constructing the adolescent: Sign, symbol and body* (pp. 97–122). New York: Peter Lang.

Flower, L. (1979). Writer-based prose: A cognitive basis for problems in writing. *College English, 41,* 19–37.

Flower, L., & Hayes, J. R. (1977). Problem solving strategies and the writing process. *College English, 39*(4), 449–461.

Flower, L., & Hayes, J. R. (1981). The pregnant pause: An inquiry into the nature of planning. *Research in the Teaching of English, 15*(3), 229–243.

Frye, N. (1957). *Anatomy of criticism, four essays.* Princeton, NJ: Princeton University Press.

Gardner, H. (1993). *Multiple intelligences.* New York: Basic Books.

Gee, J. P., & Crawford, V. M. (1998). Two kinds of teenagers: Language, identity and social class. In D. Alvermann, K. Hinchman, D. Moore, S. Phelps, & D. Waff (Eds.), *Reconceptualizing the literacies in adolescents' lives* (pp. 225–246). Mahwah, NJ: Lawrence Erlbaum Associates.

Gilbert, P. (1997). Discoursed on gender and literacy. In S. Muspratt, A. Luke, & P. Freebody (Eds.), *Constructing critical literacies* (pp. 69–75). Cresskill, NJ: Hampton Press.

Goodman, K. (1986). *What's whole in whole language?* Portsmouth, NH: Heinemann.

Goodman, K., Goodman, Y., & Hood, W. (1989). *The whole language evaluation book.* Portsmouth, NH: Heinemann.

Graves, D. H. (1983). *Writing: Teachers and children at work.* Exeter, NH: Heinemann.

Harris, J. (1991). After Dartmouth: Growth and conflict in English. *College English, 53*(6), 631–646.

Heath, S. B. (1983). *Ways with words: Language, life, and work in communities and classrooms.* New York: Cambridge University Press.

Heathcote, D. (1970). How does drama serve thinking, talking, and writing? *Elementary English, 47*(8), 1077–1081.

Hiebert, E. H. (1991). Literacy for a diverse society: Perspectives, practices, and policies. New York: Teachers College Press.

Hinton, S. E. (1967). *The outsiders.* New York: Viking.

Holland, N. N. (1973). *Five readers reading.* New Haven, CT: Yale University Press.

Hull, G., & Schultz, K. (2002). *School's out: Bridging out-of-school literacies with classroom practice.* New York: Teachers College Press.

Hunt, I. (1964). *Across five Aprils.* New York: Follett.

Hunt, K. W. (1970). Syntactic maturity in school children and adults. *Monographs of the Society of Research in Child Development, 35*(1), 1–67.

Labov, W. (1972). *Language in the inner city: Studies in the black English vernacular.* Philadelphia: University of Pennsylvania Press.

Langer, J. (1995). *Envisioning literature: Literary understanding and literature instruction.* New York: Teachers College Press.

Lonsdale, M., & McCurry, D. (2004) *Literacy in the new millennium.* Adelaide, SA, Australia: NCVER. Retrieved November 19, 2004, from http://www.ncver.edu.au/research/proj/nr2L22/Longsdale&McCurry.pdf

Luke, A. (1988). *Literacy, textbooks and ideology: Postwar literacy instruction and the mythology of Dick and Jane.* Bristol, PA: Taylor & Francis.

Luke, A. (2002). What happens to literacies old and new when they're turned into policy. In D. Alvermann (Ed.), *Adolescents and literacies in a digital world* (pp. 186–203). New York: Peter Lang.

Macrorie, K. (1970). *Uptaught.* New York: Hayden.

Mahiri, J. (2004). *What they don't learn in school: Literacy in the lives of urban youth.* New York: Peter Lang.

Moffett, J. (1968). *Teaching the universe of discourse.* Boston: Houghton Mifflin.

Moffett, J., & Wagner, B. J. (1992). *Student-centered language arts, K–12* (4th ed.). Portsmouth, NH: Boynton/Cook.

Murray, D. M. (1985). *A writer teaches writing.* Boston: Houghton Mifflin.

Perl, S. (1979). The composing processes of unskilled college writers. *Research in the Teaching of English, 13*(4), 317–336.

Piaget, J. (1950). *The psychology of intelligence.* London: Routledge & Kegan Paul.

Piaget, J., & Inhelder, B. (1969). *The psychology of the child.* New York: Basic Books.

Postman, N., & Weingartner, C. (1969). *Teaching as a subversive activity.* New York: Delacorte Press.

Purves, A., & Ripperre, V. (1972). *Elements of writing about a literary work: A study of response to literature.* Urbana, IL: National Council of Teachers of English.

Ransom, J. C. (1979). *The New Criticism.* Westport, CT: Greenwood Press.

Rogers, C. R. (1969). *Freedom to learn: A view of what education may become.* Upper Saddle River, NJ: Merrill/Prentice Hall.

Rosenblatt, L. M. (1994). *The reader, the text, the poem: The transactional theory of the literary work* (with a new preface and epilogue). Carbondale, IL: Southern Illinois University Press.

Rosenblatt, L. M. (1995). *Literature as exploration* (5th ed.). New York: Modern Language Association.

Rymes, B. (2001). *Conversational borderlands: Language and identity in an alternative urban high school.* New York: Teachers College Press.

Skinner, B. F. (1976). *About behaviorism.* New York: Vintage Books.

Smith, M. W., & Wilhelm, J. D. (2002). *Reading don't fix no Chevys: Literacy in the lives of young men.* Portsmouth, NH: Heinemann.

Smitherman, G. (1986). *Talkin and testifyin: The language of black America.* Detroit, MI: Wayne State University Press.

Sommers, N. (1980). Revision strategies of student writers and experienced adult writers. *College Composition and Communication, 31*(4), 378–388.

Vygotsky, L. (1962). *Thought and language.* Cambridge, MA: Harvard University Press.

Willinsky, J. (1990). *The new literacy: Redefining reading and writing in the schools.* New York: Routledge.

Willis, A. I. (1995). Reading the world of school literacy: Contextualizing the experience of a young African American male. *Harvard Educational Review, 65,* 30–49.

RESOURCES

Print

Historical and Critical Accounts of English Teaching Theory and Practice

Applebee, A. N. (1974). *Tradition and reform in the teaching of English.* Urbana, IL: National Council of Teachers of English.

Applebee, A. N. (1996). *Curriculum as conversation: Transforming traditions of teaching and learning.* Urbana, IL: National Council of Teachers of English.

Beach, R. (1993). *A teacher's introduction to reader response theories.* Urbana, IL: National Council of Teachers of English.

Eagleton, T. (1983). *Literary theory: An introduction.* Minneapolis: University of Minnesota.

Elbow, P. (1990). *What is English?* New York: Modern Language Association.

Farrell, E. J., & Squire, J. (1990). *Transactions with literature: A fifty-year perspective.* Urbana, IL: National Council of Teachers of English.

Hook, J. N. (1980). *A long way together.* Urbana, IL: National Council of Teachers of English.

North, S. M. (1987). *The making of knowledge in composition: Portrait of an emerging field.* Upper Montclair, NJ: Boynton/Cook.

Purves, A. (1973). *Literature education in ten countries: An empirical study.* Urbana, IL: National Council of Teachers of English.

Purves, A. (1981). *Reading and literature: American achievement in international perspective.* Urbana, IL: National Council of Teachers of English.

Tobin, L., & Newkirk, T. (1994). *Taking stock: The writing process movement in the '90s.* Portsmouth, NH: Boynton/Cook.

Willinsky, J. (1991). *The triumph of literature/the fate of literacy: English in the secondary curriculum.* New York: Teachers College Press.

Annotated Bibliographies

Beach, R., & Hynds, S. (1991). Research on response to literature. In R. Barr, M. L. Kamil, P. Mosenthal, & P. D. Pearson (Eds.), *Handbook of reading research* (Vol. II, pp. 453–489). White Plains, NY: Longmans.

Purves, A., & Beach, R. (1972). *Literature and the reader: Research on response to literature, reading interests, and teaching of literature.* Urbana, IL: National Council of Teachers of English.

Handbooks and Encyclopedias

Cushman, E., Kintgen, E. R., Kroll, B. M., & Rose, M. (2001). *Literacy: A critical sourcebook.* Boston, MA: Bedford/St. Martin's.

Flood, J., Jensen, J. M., Lapp, D., &. Squire, J. R. (Eds.). (1991). *Handbook of research on teaching the English language arts.* New York: Macmillan.

Purves, A. (1994). *Encyclopedia of English studies and language arts: A project of the National Council of Teachers of English.* Jefferson City, MO: Scholastic.

Electronic

Developing Educational Standards. This is a comprehensive annotated list of Internet sites for K–12 educational standards, curricula, frameworks, and documents listed by state. The site provides a great resource for looking up your own state standards and related Web sites by state.

http://edstandards.org/Standards.html

The Educator's Reference Desk. This site encompasses material from the ERIC database. It contains, among other things, one of the most useful bibliographies for educators available. The online catalog includes an index of journal articles (CIJE) and ERIC publications (RIE) as well as book-length publications and reports from 1966 to the present. Extended bibliographies and access to Web sites are available by subject area.

http://www.eduref.org/

International Reading Association. An organization with more than 90,000 members, the IRA sponsors a host of national and regional conferences and has an extensive publications department. The site includes a number of helpful literacy links, notices of upcoming events, and access to current research, and innovative practices in the teaching of reading and literacy.

http://www.reading.org/

National Center for the Study of Writing and Literacy. Sponsored by the U.S. Department of Education, this center is a cooperative venture between the University of California at Berkeley and Carnegie Mellon University. The site provides access to publications and resources, information about current research projects, and information about interactive workshops available through the center for classroom teachers.

http://www-gse.berkeley.edu/research/NCSWL

National Research Center on English Learning and Achievement. CELA is a nationally funded center for study of the learning and teaching of literature. The site includes links to more than 600 research reports from other OERI (Office of Educational Research and Improvement) centers nationwide. The site includes a discussion board, newsletter, highlights of current research in literature, and notices of upcoming presentations.

http://cela.albany.edu

National Writing Project. The NWP started in the 1970s for the purpose of helping classroom teachers learn how to teach the composing process to their students. Based on a grassroots model of teacher change, the organization has been holding institutes and workshops for teachers across the country for the past 30 years. The site includes access to NWP publications, presentations, workshops, institutes, and support networks.

http://writingproject.org/

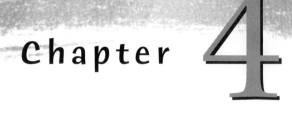
Designing for Excellence and Equity with Middle School Students

GUIDING QUESTIONS

1. How do you design instruction to support each of the learners in your classroom?
2. How might you tap your students' social, physical, cultural, and academic competencies to support their peers?
3. How do you balance middle school students' need for social support and your academic goals?

A CASE FOR CONSIDERATION

Mr. Carlisle's First Days

Steve Carlisle is a new eighth-grade language arts teacher at Adams Middle School. He completed a successful student teaching semester with ninth-grade students and feels well prepared for teaching middle school language arts. During the orientation week, he is given his class roster and, for the first time, reviews the names of the 125 students he will teach each day. His room is ready. He has set up the desks in working groups of six. He has created a conference area in one corner and a cozy author's circle in the other. He bought an attractive tray to place on the shelf by the door where students will place their written masterpieces. As his first day of teaching approaches, he feels ready and excited.

Following his first day of school, Mr. Carlisle discovers his classes are not what he had envisioned. Almost immediately he realizes that his groupings of desks, although pedagogically sound, make his room wheelchair inaccessible. He notes that two of his students seem inappropriately active. He suspects that one is not able to read. He has received a note from Ms. Gomez, the ESL teacher, that one student is proficient in a language other than English. He feels overwhelmed and unprepared.

Steve doesn't want to appear incompetent on his first day, and besides, as a newcomer to the community and school, he has no idea where to turn for help. He leaves school that day less excited for the second day to begin and completely unsure of his ability to teach all the learners in his classroom.

The next morning Ms. Perkins, the special education teacher, approaches Steve in the teacher's lounge. She asks him about his first day and mentions that she will stop by after school to give him copies of the instructional objectives for the students with disabilities who are in his classes and to answer any questions he might have about particular students. Mr. Carlisle realizes he doesn't even know what questions to ask. He doesn't want to appear incompetent to Ms. Perkins, Ms. Gomez, or the other teachers, but he has no idea of how to support these students or how to teach them language arts.

FOR DISCUSSION

Mr. Carlisle is not unusual, and neither is his teaching situation. Teachers are expected to reach a variety of students with various learning needs and from various backgrounds. This includes students with disabilities and students who come to the classroom proficient in languages other than English. What are the main issues that Mr. Carlisle will need to address? What role should Mr. Carlisle take in this situation? How might he tap the "blanket of support" that appears to be readily available to him?

Teachers entering the classroom for the first time often do so with a naive idea of the students they will teach, the layout of their room, and the specific methods they will use to teach their students. As noted in chapter 2, we all need to think deeply about adolescents and to understand their lives and literacy experiences in more complex ways. In this chapter, we ask you to examine and reexamine the rigid boundaries that may prevent schools and other social institutions from providing the kinds of rich and diverse classroom experiences in which adolescents thrive. Let's begin by considering a phrase that seems all too pervasive in contemporary society: The Mainstream.

"MAINSTREAM" METAPHORS

main·stream. (mān´strēm´)
The prevailing current of thought, influence, or activity *adj.* Representing the prevalent attitudes, values, and practices of a society or group

tr.v. **main·streamed, main·stream·ing, main·streams**
1. To integrate (a student with special needs) into regular school classes.
2. To incorporate into a prevailing group.*

As the foregoing definitions reveal, the term "mainstream classroom" builds from an assumption that anyone not in the mainstream is somehow deficient or devalued. This model situates teachers and learners in imbalanced and unequal relationships. In the "mainstream classroom," there are students who fall within the mainstream—the "prevailing current of thought, influence, or activity"—and those who do not. As you might imagine, labeling students in this way can be severely disabling. As Lewis and Finders (2002) argue, "The ways that teachers envision their adolescent learners have everything to do with how they will teach these learners" (p. 102). Equally important, the ways that teachers envision their adolescent learners have everything to do with how these learners will learn in their classrooms. Similarly, Moore and Hinchman (2002) write,

> Personal identities and resulting actions frequently are shaped by outside influences. For instance, individuals view themselves according to their gender, family income, ethnicity, home language, immigrant status, test proficiency and career aspirations. Such markers are powerful: they position students to think of themselves and act in certain ways. (p. 17)

In the face of such positioning, students can experience a loss of power in the classroom, as their labels typically describe how they do not fit into the mainstream.

For example, the label "Limited English Proficient" (LEP) highlights students' lack of proficiency in English rather than more positive attributes such as being bilingual or multilingual. When faced with the disabling power of labeling, students may lose confidence in their cultural and linguistic identity as well as in their ability to learn and their confidence in school. Evelyn Reid (1995; personal communication, February 7, 2006), a leading scholar on multicultural education, notes that often biracial children who have satisfying relationships in elementary school may become marginalized upon entering middle school. In middle school, Reid argues, biracial students often receive negative and conflicting messages about who they are.

As Cohen and Steele (2002) note, "Being a member of a socially devalued group can cause a student to question whether teachers, schools or societal institutions more generally will provide reliable fair and kind treatment" (p. 304). Similarly, Theresa Perry (2005) explains the dilemmas of academic achievement for African American students in the following way: How can they commit themselves to achieve, to work hard over time in school, if they cannot predict (in school or out of school) when or under what circumstance this hard work will be acknowledged and recognized?

Students in your "mainstream" classroom who repeatedly hear the overt or unspoken message "you can't learn" must either accept the message or mistrust the messengers. Both choices have devastating implications for their academic futures. Implications for teachers are equally negative. King and O'Brien (2002) point out that "The very terms 'educationally handicapped,' 'educationally disadvantaged,'

---

*Retrieved on January 24, 2006, from The Free Dictionary Web site: *http://www.thefreedictionary. com/mainstream* 'at-risk,' 'struggling' subtly but effectively grant immunity to school with regard to blame for their students' failures" (p. 45).

While the metaphor of the "mainstream classroom" persists at every grade level, we feel it is particularly damaging at the middle school level. There are a number of reasons for this conclusion. First, middle school students may have moved from small elementary classrooms where they were well known by significant adults. In middle school, teachers and support persons do not know them well as individuals, and the labels can serve to further distance them from teachers and peers. Second, middle school students are keenly aware of the labels that schools attach to them. Equally damaging to the learning community is the implicit assumption that some students are, in fact, "mainstream," and that early adolescents are a homogeneous group who want and need the same things. Finally, by the time students reach the middle grades, the stakes for learning become much higher, with serious consequences for students' academic futures. As one middle school principal noted, "Everyone enters middle school, but not everyone leaves. This is where we lose them."

As you read through Classroom Case 4-1, notice the importance of looking beyond assumptions about who students *are* and focusing on who they *can be*. Consider the following description of the suburban middle school where Evan, a preservice teacher, will do his student teaching. Notice how Evan has forced himself to look beyond the obvious in describing what at first glance may appear to be a "homogeneous," White, upper-middle-class setting.

Classroom Case 4-1

Looking Beyond the "Obvious"

Evan describes his student teaching placement as follows:

> *Eastvale Middle School is located in a newly renovated, very modern building. The building was refurbished last year, as teachers and students (seventh and eighth graders) were temporarily housed in a nearby elementary school. The hallways are bright and cheery, matching the personalities of the teachers I have met thus far. The spacious library has plenty of room for students to spread out and several computers for their use. There is also soothing, quiet music from a "light hits" radio station continually being played through the hallways. The bell system is actually not a bell at all, but three soft tones that signal the end of each 40-minute period. The principal says that the tones are so students don't view the end of a period as a harsh, abrupt stop to one subject and the beginning of another.*
>
> *Team teaching is the norm at EMS. One team consists of the English, math, science, and social studies teachers. Collaboration with the art teacher is also common. The resource teacher is in constant contact with the content teachers, giving them feedback not only about students' work but also about what is happening in their often incomprehensible day-to-day lives. The members of my team meet informally every day and formally when needed. Judging from their rooms, my*

teammates are firm believers in displaying student work. Projects most recently completed occupy every spare inch of wall space.

My host teacher's room is situated as such. Jackie designs units so that there will be some sort of artifacts to hang on the back wall when they are finished. The room itself is a little small for how many seventh graders she has, but with desks in traditional rows, the students don't feel cramped. Huge windows and billowing plants give the room a more spacious feel. Jackie's loud, cheerful voice keeps most students highly engaged. She also gives students a lot of freedom. She allows students to come in during her lunch period to work or talk. She has them make out their own passes when leaving the room. She treats students with a great deal of respect, and they reciprocate that, feeling perfectly comfortable to come up and talk to her in a friendly way.

At a glance, the students at EMS are racially homogeneous, with white students making up the majority. That, however, is basically the only way in which my students are homogeneous. The range of socioeconomic status in the Eastvale school district stretches from wealthy to near poverty, with each and all between represented in Jackie's classes. Many students who are financially disadvantaged come from homes where at least one parent is alcoholic, siblings are dropouts or have run away, or parents simply don't have the time between jobs to spend going over schoolwork.

The students represent a vast array of ability levels as well. Eastvale's commitment to inclusion is evident in Jackie's classes. There are four students with IEPs. Each IEP is necessary because of severe reading and writing deficiencies. Other students possibly should be considered for an IEP. Several students have poor reading and/or writing skills. One boy's reading level, according to Jackie, is not higher than third grade.

One boy recently transferred from another school, where he was the head of his class. Since coming to Eastvale, he has done absolutely no work. . . . Another boy needs constant reminders to keep him from sleeping through every class. He appears completely uninspired by whatever the class is engaged in, but is seldom openly disruptive. Yet another boy has recently come off of a two-week suspension for possession of drugs. . . . Divorce, abuse, and alcoholism are common themes among the struggling students in Jackie's class.

Six students in my classes have been labeled as "gifted." Unlike my own middle school experience, the gifted students are not put on a pedestal in Jackie's classes. Each student is treated with the same respect in the classroom.

As I think about it, the girls in the classes do not stand out as gifted, nerdy, disciplinary problems, etc. There are some girls who are very bright and there is one with an IEP. Discipline has not been an issue with them thus far in my experience. They seem to try hard and work well together, often acting as leaders when put in groups that include both sexes. I think this is a perfect example of the beginning of the physiological changes in boys and girls. Girls generally mature faster and earlier than boys do. The differences will be much more evident in a couple of years when they are in ninth grade.

Nearly all of the students were extremely eager to talk to me and "check me out." They seemed enthusiastic about having me in their classes. In my few initial visits, I feel that I have definitely been accepted into their world.

For Discussion

This case illuminates a few of the complexities surrounding diversity. While Evan is beginning to disrupt assumptions about this "homogeneous group," like all new teachers, he still holds some assumptions that may prevent him from addressing the varied needs of all learners in his classroom. Try to tease out some of the assumptions that Evan holds regarding, for example, the connection between abuse, alcoholism, and "financial disadvantage." How does Evan appear to define the term "problem students"? Now think about your own classroom or field setting. What assumptions do you hold about students on the basis of their race, socioeconomic status, gender, and other characteristics? Consider what assumptions and cultural expectations you may need to get past to build from a perspective of ability rather than disability.

THE MIDDLE SCHOOL CLASSROOM: FROM MAINSTREAM TO ECOSYSTEM

The metaphor of a "mainstream" classroom is just that, a metaphor. It presumes that students are carried along by a rapidly moving stream of normalcy and that those who are not swept into the mainstream quite literally "miss the boat."

Kenneth Burke (1990) explains how language works like different colored photographic lenses to filter attention toward or away from particular versions of reality. Lenses may be tinted or may have surfaces that seem to transform what the viewer sees. The "mainstream" metaphor filters teachers' decisions every day. It colors the way they assess the classroom context, reflect on their practices, and design programs and learning opportunities in response to student needs. Consider what happens if we shift metaphors from "mainstream" to "ecosystem." In an ecosystem, if one organism is removed, the entire system is threatened. Ecological balance has been defined by various online dictionaries as "a system formed by the interaction of a community of organisms with their physical environment" and "an ecological community together with its environment, functioning as a unit." (Accessed on January 26, 2006, from Answers.com Web site: *http://www.answers.com/topic/ecosystem*). The idea of an intricate balance among all members of a community or classroom should be at the heart of middle school teaching. The representation of adolescents by teachers and other adults is the topic of Fieldwork Journal 4-1.

Fieldwork Journal 4-1

Adolescents in Action

This fieldwork journal experience serves several purposes: to bring into focus the ways in which adults construct adolescents and their lives; to explore the implications for schools created by these representations of adolescents; and to develop critical awareness about the role of education for early adolescent learners. You have two options for this exploration:

Option One: Ethnographic Interview.   Select two middle school students from your field site to interview. The first should be someone whom you would guess, from outward appearances, is most like you in terms of race, class, gender, and so on. Select a second student whom you would guess is unlike you in terms of these same markers. Spend a few minutes talking with each student and taking notes.

After you've finished, create a richly textured portrait of each adolescent, his or her interests, beliefs, and activities. Remember that you are basically answering the question "What is going on here?" from the perspective of the adolescent. Next, write about what surprised or puzzled you. In what ways were your assumptions reinforced, confirmed, or disrupted? What do your interviews tell you about your perspectives on who your students are or should be? Remember to change the names of your informants to protect their privacy.

Option Two: Troubled Teens: Popular Representations of Adolescents.   Explore what messages adolescents receive from the larger culture about who they are and should be. What assumptions do adults and policy makers seem to operate within as they talk about how schools and other social institutions should be structured? Seek out images of adolescents and their school experiences portrayed in advertisements, sitcoms, news, movies, newspapers, and other media.

When you've finished, write about whether you think these representations are culturally and historically bound. Did the images you examined seem to challenge or reinforce what you think are current social constructions of adolescence as a life stage? Now think about middle schooling. In what specific ways do you think school policy and practice promote these constructions? Finally, write about any ways in which you feel adolescents or adults acting on their behalf can challenge these ideas and expectations.

Jan Joerling-Leonard, a student in Margaret's class on middle school education conducted an ethnographic case study of a 12-year-old student in a suburban middle school. In Classroom Case 4-2 notice how Jan's own memories of middle school contrast with the contemporary setting in which she suddenly finds herself. As you read through her portrait of Chris, her middle school informant, notice how many of her assumptions about adolescence are challenged and how many of your own rise to the surface.

Classroom Case 4-2

A Dose of "Adolescent Reality"

Jan begins by describing the school:

Passing through the doors of a quiet Midwestern suburban middle school as a college student feels a little like stepping back in time. Familiar hand-made posters sag dog-eared from the cement walls, while announcements still crackle unintelligibly as always over the address system. Although it is yet morning, the unforgettable smell of fish and French fries nevertheless permeates the air, enveloping my senses and evoking "painful" memories of days gone by when my own adolescent mindset could justify a Hostess fruit pie and a chocolate shake into a meal containing nearly three of the four food groups! My wistful reverie is jolted for a moment by the sight of a local squad car and a courteous nod from the police officer manning the entry to the school, but the warm smile and friendly greeting of the office receptionist soon have me feeling reassured once again that, after all, kids are kids, and surely not much has changed since my own middle school days.

Emerging into the quiet hallway, I glance at the clock just in time to hear the first period bell. Suddenly, and somewhat incongruent to the Rockwellian scenes I've been enjoying, a giant wave of laughing, talking, stumbling, and at times, playfully 'shoving' adolescents swells up the stairway from within the depths of this austere and cavernous building in a sweeping expanse of color, movement and, most of all, sound. Slender arms of chatting girls gesture dramatically to emphasize their conversation, while the laces on the boys' untied shoes flap wildly about as if to mimic the girls' activity. Books and papers collapse loudly to the floor as students descend on their lockers and voices and laughter ranging all depths and pitches continues to overlap in the commotion. Gauging the momentum and speed of the crowd, I realize I had better move quickly or be engulfed, as it soon becomes obvious these adolescents are nearly oblivious to anything other than their all-important focus for the moment: navigating the social scene before they have to get to class.

To my surprise, as easy as it had seemed for me to conjure my own public middle school experiences just moments before that first period bell, the sight of the tiny skirts, designer shirts and "baggy" jeans soon reminded me that, sentimental memories aside, it was not just the police officer at the door that has changed since middle school in the 1970s. As a pre-service middle school teacher interested in understanding the adolescent perspective, therefore, I soon realized that if I intended to teach to what is relevant to students today, that relevance could only be found within the voices of these students, not fond memories of the past. . . .

My initial enthusiasm at the prospect of this venture soon met with its first dose of "adolescent reality," when my first two candidates for interview politely turned me down! It was then that I remembered lesson number one: how dearly adolescents value their privacy at this age. Fortunately, a favorite student of mine, Chris (all names in this study have been changed to respect confidentiality) agreed to participate in an interview during his lunch break. Chris is a slender, 12-year-old African American seventh grader with luminous eyes and a winning smile that complement his quick wit and insightful remarks. Every day I have seen him, he appears sharply dressed in clean blue jeans and tennis shoes, wearing a pressed, button-down shirt with the tails out, which serves to emphasize his already lanky profile. A keen observer, Chris has already become adept at navigating through the hallway chaos, gliding down the hallways alongside the walls, wisely keeping his thin frame away from the main "fray" of adolescent traffic as he flashes a smile to his teachers and students he knows. In class, one can again see him studying the dynamics and interactions of his environment, engaging in whole class discussions enthusiastically, yet only after his watchful eyes and thoughtful expressions indicate that he has carefully weighed the contributions of his peers before venturing his opinion on a topic.

Surprisingly, this observation stands in sharp contrast to his comments during our interview about how his friends have come to identify him within his peer culture at school. When asked whether he was aware of any social "cliques" or nicknames for groups of students in his middle school class, he quickly volunteered his knowledge of this social phenomenon, remarking, "Oh yeah. There's the 'Dexters'(slang term adopted from "Dexter's Laboratory," a cartoon depicting an exaggerated "boy-genius"). They're the 'smart' kids. An' there's the 'Goths,' who dress up in black and stuff." When asked whether he, too, was a member of a 'group,' with a name, he sat up straight in his chair and beamed proudly, "Yeah. The 'Clowns'!" We laughed about this, but, wanting to be sure I understood the social connotations this label implied, I pressed the question further, asking, "So, is being in 'The Clowns' a 'good' thing? What does it mean to be in 'The Clowns'?" Between huge bites of pizza, Chris seemed happy to explain, "You see, 'The Clowns' means you're funny. You're the class clown." It was obvious not only from his expression, but the pride with which he spoke, that he not only accepts, but relishes this identity, as it clearly carries a significant amount of social capital within his adolescent peer culture. Although there is a potential for trouble his identification with this label could have for placing him at odds with the behavior demanded and valued by his academic culture, Chris demonstrates that, as a maturing adolescent, he recognizes a distinction between what is appropriate for "free-time," and what is appropriate in class. As such, it has not been my observation that he is overtly disruptive in the classroom. It is actually quite the reverse, as it is the skillful way in which he quietly assesses the classroom environment that usually results in his contributing his well-timed, if sometimes wry, observations. . . .

As the time for our interview was about to end, I thought I would round out my perspective on his day by inquiring about his favorite activities outside of school. His response, "To rest," caused me to circle his answer in the margin of my notes in curiosity. Not certain what to make of this, I dismissed it for the time being, asking instead whether there were any other activities he liked to do. Chris cheerfully responded he likes to "play football and race car video games on [his] PlayStation," noting with no small amount of pride that he plays "defensive tackle" on an outside-school football team. It was not surprising to me that he would seek out an off-campus sports activity, as he noted with some disappointment that his middle school does not participate in organized team sports outside of Physical Education class. I wondered privately what impact maintaining a football game and practice schedule had on his studies, as he had previously made the observation that, contrary to sixth grade, he found his seventh grade teachers "really strict about having homework in on time," and "really strict about being on time for class." When I shared my concerns with him about balancing homework, school, free-time, and football, however, he shrugged it all off, adding he did not think football interfered with his studies, "that much."

Just as we were preparing to part, I found I could not help but feel that, despite his lack of concern about balancing his time, I remained nevertheless puzzled over his response about wanting "to rest" as his favorite activity. Unable to solve the mystery on my own, I asked him plainly why he thought that was his favorite activity. "Cuz I'm tired!" came the predictable response with a curious but respectful look that seemed to say, "What else?" It was here the interview took a dramatic turn. Realizing the rhetorical nature of my question, I asked Chris what time he wakes up for school. "I dunno . . .," he mused, "six . . . six-thirty or something . . . I have to catch the bus at two minutes after seven." It was then I understood that Chris's experience as a middle school student was anything but typical. As one of a handful of students who participate in a voluntary bussing program at this school, bringing students from what is typically a distant and underserved urban community, I realized that, to Chris, this experience was indeed so culturally "normal" to him, he did not even think to volunteer the information! As for me, I was ashamed to admit that, though I strive to consider myself a culturally sensitive educator, I had nevertheless come very close to ignoring the clues Chris was providing that truly served to unlock the depth and richness of his cultural and adolescent perspective on his school experience.

Suddenly, my image of Chris as just an ordinary adolescent was transformed into a young man who was nothing short of heroic for the efforts he must undergo to obtain an education. I realized with no small amount of awe that not only does his middle school experience challenge him on a cognitive, physical, and psychological level, like his peers; but further, his commitment to his education requires that he and his family must coordinate a great deal of effort attending to the added pressure for time, energy, and socialization opportunities that are inherent to being a student who is, in essence, displaced from his own familiar community and expected to thrive. Hence we hear the true precision to which Chris must attend to scheduling his time as we hear him note he must catch the bus at "two minutes after seven."

Needless to say, the implications of my experience with Chris made an enormous impact on me as a pre-service teacher, as I reflected on just how critical it can be for an educator to pay attention to even the slightest subtleties of a student's responses. Without this attention to detail, I discovered first-hand how easily an educator can slip into the habit of making generalized assumptions about the adolescent experience—a practice that could very well have a significant, and likely negative, effect on the learning experiences of a child. . . . As I began this research, I thought I could define the "typical teen"; however, I see now that there is very little about the adolescent experience that can be defined as "typical" at all. Like seeds in a "cognitive garden" called "middle school," they are destined to develop physically, morally and intellectually at all different rates and with various social and emotional results. Thus I have learned that there are indeed many things that have changed since I was a middle school student, and yet, many things will perhaps never change. As I prepare now to enter the teaching profession, I nevertheless look forward to the challenges these experiences hold for me, and to the possibility that I can be an educator of the kind who truly makes a difference in these young students' lives.

For Discussion

As you read over Jan's description, think about moments when you were surprised or brought up short by her unfolding discoveries about Chris. Did you make any immediate assumptions about Chris based on his race, physical stature, interest in sports, or identity as a class clown that were later challenged by any new information in Jan's ethnographic case? Can you think of students in your own experience who defy the quick assumptions that you or other teachers might make about them?

A QUESTION OF BALANCE: NAVIGATING THE MIDDLE SCHOOL ECOSYSTEM

Considering the diversity of interests, abilities, and experiences that students bring to the classroom, we ask you to see all teaching as a set of balances or tensions. Issues of class, race, and gender complicate issues of effective instruction. As teachers, we have many demands placed on our time and energy, balancing our students' needs with our curricular demands, balancing our attentions to both social and academic competencies. In the following pages, we discuss a few such balancing acts that middle school teachers must perform on a daily basis.

Comfort and Challenge

Creating a comfortable classroom with students at the center is not as easy as it may seem. Comfort is a cultural construct. What may appear comfortable to some may create great discomfort for others. The familiar routines that students bring to your classroom may not match your expectations, and they may not match those of their peers.

As students continue to grow past early adolescence, they will work with people less like themselves. They may have just moved from a small rural elementary school, or they may have been bussed from one part of the city to a less-familiar area. To support early adolescents, especially those who are new to middle school or who have other circumstances that make school difficult for them, you need to establish and make explicit a set of predictable routines for your classroom. By creating these comfortable routines, you will allow students to concentrate on the content of your teaching rather than on guessing at what might happen next.

When you begin with a set of comfortable and familiar expectations, you privilege all students, not just those who come to your classroom already understanding the social and academic dynamics of the school setting. When students know, for instance, that they must sit down and write the day's agenda in their notebooks or devote a few minutes to journal writing before going to literature circles, they develop a sense of comfort and safety that, paradoxically, allow them to be creative and take intellectual risks.

Comfort does not mean reducing the academic rigor of the curriculum. Middle schools have come under attack from critics who feel that middle schools focus too much on social development at the expense of challenging academics. This criticism is especially relevant in a climate of high-stakes testing and accountability. At the middle school level, a focus on social support and academic rigor should not be viewed as an either/or proposition.

FIGURE 4-1 Model of Academic Language Development

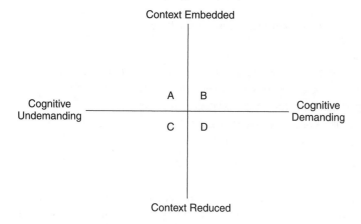

James Cummins's (1981) Model for Academic Language Development may serve as a heuristic for designing a rigorous and supportive curriculum (see Figure 4-1). While his model was designed to support second language learners, we feel it may prove useful for all middle school teachers. In this model, tasks range in difficulty along one continuum from cognitively undemanding to cognitively demanding, and along another continuum from context reduced to context embedded. Context reduced tasks include listening to a lecture, reading a textbook, or working on isolated grammar skills. Any task in which there are no other sources of help other than the language itself is context reduced. A context embedded task is one in which the student has access to a range of additional visual and oral cues.

Referring to Figure 4-1, a task that is both cognitively demanding and context reduced is likely to be the most difficult for your middle school students, particularly for second language learners or those with language disabilities. Yet, it's vital that all middle school students develop competencies with such tasks.

Too often, we assume that middle school students are not yet ready for cognitively demanding activities. As noted in chapter 2, the Carnegie Task Force on Education for Young Adolescents (1995) reported that many middle schools are unable to balance academic rigor and high expectations for all. Middle school teachers should focus their teaching on tasks that are both cognitively demanding and context enriched (quadrant B). But often many of the materials used in the language arts classroom are cognitively demanding and context reduced (quadrant D). One's instructional design should include moving materials from context reduced (quadrant D) to context embedded (quadrant B) by enriching the context with a number of strategies. This can be done in a number of ways, as shown in Figure 4-2.

Extending Cummins's model to include the social and cultural dimensions of learning, we might draw upon work by Gloria Ladson-Billings (1994) and Luis Moll and his colleagues (1990, 1992). An important way to enrich the context of literacy tasks is to connect the tasks to the rich cultural resources that students bring to school. Such context enrichment might come from tapping what Luis Moll calls

FIGURE 4-2   Enriching the Context of Language Activities

Enriching the Context of Language Activities
• Bring in real objects. • Include photographs, maps, illustrations, and other relevant visual materials. • Include manipulatives, props, and graphic/cognitive organizers. • Facilitate rich, oral language activities with peers. • Make explicit connections to home, families, and communities. • Invite middle school students to share their stories.

"Funds of Knowledge." Linguistically and culturally diverse students emerge from households rich in social and intellectual resources. For example, imagine that you are a member of a multidisciplinary team of teachers who have chosen the theme of "Our Amazing Planet" as a way of providing continuity across the content areas. Some of your language minority students may come from households with expertise in farming, pesticide-free gardening, or folk medicines, which they or their parents can share with the class.

When you can tap the strategic knowledge, skills, and practices that students bring to your classroom, you provide an enabling and enriching context for learning cognitively challenging tasks. If students are allowed to choose topics that fall close to areas of expertise already available in their homes and communities, you allow them to engage in challenging tasks at the same time as they are developing skills in English. The cognitive demands of academic tasks are influenced by the cultural and social capital that students bring to the classroom. Thus, employing Culturally Relevant Pedagogy moves tasks from context reduced to context embedded.

Culturally Responsive Teaching recognizes the importance of including students' cultural references in all aspects of learning (Ladson-Billings, 1994). You will have the greatest success with all students if you seek to understand and become culturally sensitive to the cultures represented in your classroom. By providing culturally mediated instruction and culturally valued knowledge in curriculum content, you can turn context-reduced tasks into context-enriched tasks, thus facilitating learning for all.

You might be wondering what culturally mediated instruction and culturally responsive teaching might look like. There is a terrific explanation of these models, replete with classroom examples on the Web site "Teaching Diverse Learners," sponsored by the Education Alliance at Brown University. A link to "The Knowledge Loom" on this Web site provides classroom stories as well as links to research and resources (see *http://knowledgeloom.org/practices3.jsp?t= 1&bpid= 1125&storyid= 1197&aspect= 2&location= 1&parentid= 1110&bpinterid= 1110&spotlightid= 1110&t estflag= yes*).

We will briefly discuss some basics of culturally relevant teaching in the following section.

PRINCIPLES AND PRACTICES OF CULTURALLY RELEVANT TEACHING

To begin, culturally responsive teachers have high expectations for all students. Most middle school students respect teachers who set high expectations and believe that success is possible. Communicate to your students that you believe they can succeed, and create structures so they can. You can accomplish this by making a few small changes in your teaching. Make sure to call on all students some of the time, rather than privileging the most verbal or academically successful. Talk informally with students in free moments about their families and neighborhoods. Discover their areas of expertise, and encourage them to share their knowledge with others. You'd be surprised at how much they know beyond traditional academic learning. Invite parents and caregivers into the classroom to share expertise or just to lend a helping hand when students are doing projects that require adult guidance.

Developing cultural sensitivity means going beyond the simplistic notions of "celebrating diversity" and avoiding the urge to classify racial and cultural groups on the basis of stereotypes about food, clothing, speech, and mannerisms perpetuated by popular media. Some teachers misjudge a student as lazy or as lacking academic abilities if the student speaks a variant of what has come to be called "standard" English. You can allow students to use home languages in informal tasks such as journals or informal notes, but teach them to use what you might call "edited English" in their more formal written work. If you have bilingual students in your room, find texts written in students' home languages that correspond with texts you're currently teaching. Ask them to read aloud in the original language as class members listen to the ways in which the nuances of phrasing and pronunciation change from one language to another. Ask your bilingual students to explain any words or phrases that have no exact translations in English, and see how the meanings of texts are shaped by the language in which they are written.

Students who talk while you are talking or who get up and move around the room may seem disruptive or disobedient, but may actually come from cultures or families that value physical activity and a more open participatory conversational style. Make sure to provide lots of opportunities for students to get out of their seats, especially if you have 80-minute class periods. All students will benefit, as early adolescents are bursting with energy most of the time. Get students involved in collaborative inquiry projects, and capitalize on the strengths of more verbal students by sponsoring activities such as creative dramatics, readers' theater, panel discussions, and debates.

When approaching cognitively challenging tasks, then, you can create context enrichment by providing visual and oral cues, tapping the funds of knowledge that students bring to the classroom, and being sensitive to diverse cultural backgrounds. Balancing the cognitive demands of learning tasks means creating a place of comfort and safety within which you can nudge students into those sometimes uncomfortable spaces where learning occurs. You must help them to reach the intellectual places that they cannot yet reach independently—what Vygotsky (1978) has called the Zone of Proximal Development (ZPD), or the place that learners can traverse only with the help of an adult or a more knowledgeable peer.

Richard Lloyd-Jones, a rhetorician and leading scholar of writing instruction, provides a useful metaphor to help us think about how to balance comfort and challenge in the classroom. He says, "It's the sand in the oyster. You don't want to have so much sand that you kill the oyster, but you want enough to have a pearl every now and then" (quoted in Finders, 1992, p. 507). Your instruction should be based on rigorous but reachable goals for all of your middle school students.

Collaboration and Independence

You should have plenty of opportunities for both independent and group work in your classroom, as students usually have a preference for one or the other, and most can benefit from a balance of the two.

Peer group interactions and collaborative learning are centrally important in the middle grades; yet, they demand much guidance and structuring on your part. For any number of reasons, students may be uncomfortable sharing with peers. Simply assigning students into groups does not ensure positive social interaction. Tim Lensmire (1994), for example, discusses the social tensions that surround groups in a writing workshop. Making sure that students see valid purposes for the collaborative effort is a necessary first step. But most important, you must make sure that you "do no harm" by placing students from divergent backgrounds in the same group and expecting them to work out the social complexities on their own.

Attending explicitly to the purposes for tasks and designing instruction to support positive interactions are vital. Students need to know up front what procedures will be followed by each member and what the outcomes will be. You need to be clear about whether students will be producing a collaborative product (in task groups), discussing an issue and reporting back to the whole class (in study groups), responding to writing in progress (in peer response groups), or sharing their ideas about literature (in book clubs or literature circles). Will individual roles be assigned or open ended? How will groups be evaluated? Will you walk around the room, informally gauging whether groups are on task, or will you ask students to write brief "progress reports" at the end of each group session?

Most often, group activities fail when students see little purpose for collaboration beyond filling out worksheets or killing time. Opportunities that extend beyond the classroom walls to students' homes and neighborhoods can make collaborative groups more meaningful and social interaction more productive. Groups that are committed to a task and can see the tangible results of their work in the world beyond the classroom are less likely to drift off task or succumb to boredom.

Just as it's important to provide meaningful opportunities for group interaction, it's equally important for students to have time for working independently. Providing a regular time and space for independent reading or private writing lets students know that not all work needs to be shared or formally evaluated. This is especially important for some early adolescents who are uncomfortable in groups or who simply learn and work better alone.

The trick is in allowing students independence to complete tasks, while still monitoring the degree to which they might need extra help or the gentle nudge of your praise or evaluation to keep them engaged. Because all students have different needs where social and independent learning are concerned, it's often helpful to set up at least some days during the week or the school year when students have the choice of working collaboratively or independently. A workshop model can allow some students to read or write quietly while others are working in small task groups. Remember also that just as some students abhor working in groups, others prefer the social interaction of collaborative work. Varying your approaches and expectations and balancing collaboration and independence can go a long way in providing an atmosphere in which all middle school learners can prosper.

CHOICE AND CONTROL

You need to consider the obstacles and opportunities your classroom structures might create for particular students. Think carefully about how and when students should be given choices, not only about what to read, write, view, and talk about, but about the social structures of the classroom as well. Clearly, no one structure is best for all students under all circumstances. You must often negotiate a fine balancing act between careful planning of activities and a willingness to adjust the moment-to-moment orchestration of your lessons when the social dynamics shift.

Many teachers would say that student choice is clearly a hallmark of any successful literacy program. On the surface, we agree heartily with this idea. Many students relish the idea of exploring topics of their own choosing through language. Although many students flourish in an atmosphere of free choice, you must remember that choice is never really free from the tangle of the peer dynamic, and the stakes of marking oneself as an "insider" or "outsider" can be quite high. For example, Darius, a seventh-grade boy in one of Margaret's research projects, reported privately that he loved fairy tales. He liked to read and write them and had been doing so for a couple of years until he entered junior high school. "It's like not okay to write fairy tales anymore," he explained. Boys like Darius are beginning to encounter more rigid gender roles that come with what may seem like strict unwritten rules in middle school classrooms. Perhaps Darius was saying that in seventh grade, "real men don't write about childish things." Early adolescents are often extremely vigilant not to mark themselves as childish. Andrea is a case in point.

In Andrea's sixth-grade classroom, Mr. Adams set up workshop time every Tuesday and Thursday for students to write about self-selected topics. He did not give prompts or require certain genres. Students kept their notebooks up-to-date with daily entries that included what they wrote, how much they had written, and a list of particular skills they were working on. Almost all students wrote fiction. The boys, for the most part, wrote stories about sports and fast-action adventure stories that often included killing and other violent acts. The girls often wrote about friendships and romance.

Andrea found such writing silly. She viewed herself as a writer and dreamed of becoming published. As an avid reader of nonfiction and the newspaper, Andrea liked essays addressing the inequalities that she observed in the world. To support her arguments, Andrea turned to autobiography and historical documents. She became fascinated with the Women's Liberation Movement of the 1960s, reading about Betty Friedan and Gloria Steinem. After she stumbled onto the *Roe v. Wade* court case on the Internet, Andrea became determined to write an editorial for *The*

Nugget, the middle school newsletter that went out to all fifth-, sixth-, and seventh-grade students in her school. Her essay, titled "The Women's Movement," focused on the history of the Women's Movement and expressed her views on how women's rights were declining. Her essay stood in sharp contrast to the fiction written by all of the other students. Boys began derisively calling her "the feminist." Whispers about Andrea's sexual orientation began to circulate. Needless to say, Andrea didn't submit another piece for publication.

We're sure you wonder what to do about the Andreas in your own classrooms, especially when these students are often forced into the background and rarely share such embarrassing information with their teachers. As you know, free choice is clearly not "free" in the social world of school where words and actions may mark students as immature, or worse yet for early adolescents, make their sexual orientation suspect.

Choice in the curriculum is never as simple as telling students to "write or read whatever you like." A curriculum built entirely around students' "free choices" will make some students like Darius and Andrea very uncomfortable in accepting such invitations. Choices about topic selection, genre, and publication are witnessed by peers, who may assign meanings that mark a student as an outsider in the group. As a result, young men like Darius must keep their interest in fairy tales secret for fear of abandoning their fragile sense of masculinity, and young women like Andrea may feel silenced for a lifetime.

It's important to understand that we are not advocating placing rigid limits on students' choices, but simply asserting the need to recognize the possible consequences of our well-intentioned instructional choices. Often these consequences are beyond our conscious attention or control. You'll need to create a classroom that openly challenges the notion that real men don't have feelings or that real women can't be strong or assertive. An "antiracist" (Hall, 1981; Ng, Staton, & Scane, 1995) or "antibias" curriculum in which issues like gender, race, culture, and sexual orientation are a conscious part of students' reading, writing, and talk can go a long way in opening up choices for students like Darius and Andrea.

Beyond this responsibility, however, teachers need to help all students to understand the consequences of "going public" in unfamiliar and potentially hostile environments. It may be a positive, affirming experience for a gay student to "come out" in the comfortable environment of the language arts classroom, but teacher cannot guarantee that student safe passage in the often cruel social networks that adolescents build in the hallways, playing fields, or cafeteria.

By the same token, however, a curriculum built on free choice may make some students far too comfortable. Students offered a steady diet of choice may not stretch intellectually. They may continue doing what they are comfortable doing and not venture beyond those comfort zones.

Correctness and Creativity

Teachers must also walk a shaky tightrope between correctness and creativity in the literacy classroom. Students may be so concerned with issues of correctness that they doubt their ability to speak or write at all. Standardized testing and state-mandated curricula loom large. Issues of correctness may become more compelling as students prepare for high school placement exams and standardized tests. At every level, students will need to employ conventions of edited English to have their voices heard beyond the classroom. Lisa Delpit (1996, 2002), among others, advocates for explicit instruction so children who are not born into the dominant dialect may gain access to further opportunities that are often denied them due to linguistic stereotyping and prejudice. In the face of this pressing need for access to what has been called "the language of power," students need to explore their own interests, and a strong focus on correction may constrain and stifle that exploration.

Issues of edited English such as grammar, punctuation, and spelling are best taught in the context of students' own language activities. Concentrating on patterns of error rather than editing every error; helping students to keep personal skills inventories of spelling, punctuation, and usage errors; and making "progress, not perfection" your ultimate goal will go a long way in developing your students' knowledge of language conventions without stifling their enthusiasm and creativity.

Private and Public Learning

Just as there is a need to create opportunities for social interactions, there is a vital need to respect the privacy of our students. Students need to explore their views without fearing the judgments of their peers or the evaluation of their teachers. Many of our students thrive on the personal understanding gained through private writing in journals or diaries. Just as we may have kept personal journals over the years, our students often bring notebooks or diaries to school in backpacks or keep them hidden in a special place at home. These personal writings serve as a repository of feelings and insights; at the same time, they mark moments in students' lives and document their personal histories. Other students would rather die than keep journals, viewing them as mindless busywork or "girl stuff."

It's also important to remember that assumptions about privacy have social and cultural origins. Some students are taught to keep their home business at home; others come from families in which private matters are discussed freely over dinner. Schools are incredibly public places. Sponsoring private literacies as one part of our curriculum means providing ways for students to fold and staple personal entries in journals or to simply spend some quiet time with work that is not seen by anyone else.

At the same time, we must make it perfectly clear that we are not therapists or guidance counselors. As students enter adolescence, a whole host of personal issues may emerge on the pages of journals: thoughts of suicide, parental abuse, sexual experiences, and other delicate issues with which we, as literacy teachers, are not prepared to deal. Before assigning journals or logs, we must tell students up front (and with occasional reminders) that if, as a result of reading their journals, we suspect that they may be in danger or may hurt themselves, it is our duty to inform others who can help them. Often, conscious or not, our students' private writings may be a call for help, and students will eventually welcome our interventions. But we and they must understand that we are in no position to prevent suicide or mediate child abuse without the help of competent professionals.

Just as privacy is important to students, as their world expands, they will seek out opportunities to gain meaningful relationships beyond their neighborhoods. This is often a time when students see the school's curriculum as less meaningful to their lives. Our job as teachers includes making meaningful connections between the school's curriculum and the students' lived experiences. Public venues are a means by which the language arts curriculum can become real and relevant, especially if students are given opportunities to make contributions to their local community and beyond. Sometimes this will demand rigid adherence to particular conventions of edited American English that will allow them to have an impact on others. At other times, rigid adherence to one set of conventions that do not carry currency in a particular context will prevent their voices from being heard. It is the ability to move among multiple discourse communities and make appropriate choices for particular contexts that will allow students to write and speak their ways into the larger world.

MULTIPLE ENTRY POINTS AND ESCAPE ROUTES

All of this balancing may seem a daunting juggling act for the middle school teacher. Clearly, there is a lot to think about in designing learning experiences that support all students. While it may appear almost overwhelming, we need to re-member that our middle school students are likely to meet tasks with eagerness, especially if we approach these learning opportunities with enthusiasm, a confidence that all students have something important to say, and a belief that all students can learn.

One way of negotiating these balancing acts and involving all students can be better understood through a children's story. In Randall Jarrell's *The Bat Poet* (1964), a bat writes a poem about an owl. After the chipmunk hears the bat's poem, he worries that he doesn't have enough holes dug to be protected from something as terrible as the owl. The bat confirms, "If it weren't for that hole in the oak he'd have got me" (p. 17). The chipmunk agrees to have the bat write a poem about him and asks the bat to put lots of nuts and seeds and especially lots of holes in it so the owl or other predators won't eat him.

As middle school teachers, we should provide not only nuts and seeds to nur-ture our young students, but plenty of holes in the oak tree for them to feel safe. Pro-viding multiple entry points and escape routes for classroom activities can give all students the chance to succeed and free them from worries about the censure of their peers. Never underestimate the power of the peer dynamic. If you have ever spent time in a middle school classroom, you have witnessed incredible cruelty and astonishing compassion. Some of these events are a result of your planning, but of-ten they seem to spring from nowhere. Suddenly, before your eyes, someone is cry-ing and you have no idea why.

Because classrooms are such public places, you'll need to attend to the many ways that student participation can occur and be evaluated. As a new teacher, you may wonder why students don't volunteer to answer questions in class discussion. You might begin by looking closely at patterns of classroom talk.

Most classroom discussion follows an IRE, three-part sequence, in which the teacher initiates (I), a student responds (R), and the teacher evaluates (E) the student's response. Evaluation is essential to the initiation-reply-evaluation (IRE) pattern (Cazden, 1988; Mehan, 1979). Large-group discussions are often constrained within this typical turn-taking pattern. Fearing the public evaluation, some middle school students will simply opt out of the discussion. You can consciously disrupt this pattern in a variety of ways. For example, you might try replacing the IRE pattern with the IAR pattern. The IAR pattern begins with the teacher's taking two simultaneous turns. The teacher initiates (I), and then before any student responds, the teacher acknowledges (A) the student's contribution, and finally a student responds (R). The IAR might look something like this.

(I) Teacher: We've been working on community invitations.

(A) Teacher: Kenisha, when you were working in your small group, you were commenting about ways you might interview the principal. You had some great insights into some of the problems that might come up. Would you share with us?

While clearly there is a flavor of evaluation in her comments, the teacher has provided the student with assurance that her contribution would be of value to her classmates. The teacher may set up this kind of participation opportunity by talking to a student very briefly in the hallway or listening in during small groups. Here's another example.

Teacher **(privately to student in small group):** Corrier, I wonder if I could call on you when we come back together as a large group because you understand how to use key words in the search engine very effectively. You're fast at finding relevant materials on the Internet, and you know how to examine the site to see if it's likely to be reliable. Would you be willing to tell the class about how you are researching your bikes?

To make students comfortable talking with their peers, the teacher may alert the students before class to give time for rehearsal, reducing some of the affective dimensions of public talk. This is especially true for those students who are proficient in languages other than English. Notice, for example, how his teacher invites Tommie into the discussion of *Esperanza Rising* by Pam Munoz Ryan (2000).

Teacher: Tommie, during read aloud today, I'm going to give a book talk on the novel *Esperanza Rising.* Since you know Spanish, do you want to tell the students what the word *Esperanza* means in English? I know you've lived in California, so do you think you could talk about some of the fruits and vegetables that grow there that kids in our class might not know about?

In this example, Tommie's teacher privately scaffolds some things he might say in the upcoming discussion of the book, giving him language for ideas he might not have been ready to articulate on his own.

"Revoicing" (O'Connor & Michaels, 1993) is another strategy for promoting powerful class participation. The teacher "revoices" what the student has said by responding with a summarizing statement, something like, "So what you are saying is that. . . ." This allows the teacher to extend students' language beyond what they might say on their own. Students can then agree or disagree with the teacher's phrasing and be encouraged to say more. This sequence is subtly but powerfully different from the IRE pattern in that it moves the teacher out of the evaluative role and positions the teacher more as a collaborator in the conversation. When students are not quite able to articulate their views, this type of support may serve as a scaffold for more formal academic language.

Students who are proficient in languages other than English may be asked to be involved in activities that do not require language production such as observing, pointing, collecting, or constructing, for example. Allow students to practice academic language with peers in small groups and then report to the whole class about what they discovered. Assigning individual roles based on students' current level of language development allows for multiple entry points and avoids setting up students who are learning English to fail in front of peers.

Another way to create multiple entry points and escape routes is to frame your questions with linguistic hedges to allow students opportunities to participate without fear of exposing themselves. Ask, for example, "What might someone say about . . .?" or "What have you heard about . . .?" as opposed to "What do you know about . . .?" Most teachers are familiar with the KWL chart, in which students list what they already know (K) about a topic in the first column, list what they want (W) to learn in the second column, then, after a lesson or a task, list what they have learned (L) in the third column.

The KWL strategy assumes that students have accurate knowledge of some event prior to the task and that they do, in fact, want to learn something about it. As most middle school teachers know, some students will resist presenting themselves as active, engaged learners to their peers. The KWL strategy also requires that students commit to a list of facts that may include some inaccurate information to paper; as a result, some students may be embarrassed, while others may hold on to prior misunderstandings.

By contrast, a strategy that Margaret calls "HRQ" asks students to share what they have heard (H) about a topic before engaging in the learning task. Because what they have heard may or may not be true, students can save face before, during, and after the activity. This approach also allows any misconceptions to be placed on the table so they can be addressed prior to a learning activity. In filling out the "H" column, encourage students to list things they've read, heard, or seen in public media, even if they suspect that some information may be wrong.

In the next phase, students engage in a bit of reading or informal research. Ask them to fill in the second (R) column with anything that confirms or refutes what they wrote in the first column. In the final (Q) column, ask students to list lingering or new questions that have emerged as a result of their inquiry. In this way, they see learning as ongoing and learn to view their reading as biased, partial, and capable of interpretation from multiple perspectives. Questions generated from this process may be followed up as a whole class, individually, or simply allowed to linger unanswered for a time.

Designing for multiple entry points allows all students to be active and valued members of your middle school classroom. As you strive to lessen the affective dimensions of students' being wrong in front of peers, consider the multiple ways that students of varying abilities can positively engage with their peers.

PERFORMANCE ASSESSMENT OF AUTHENTIC LEARNING TASKS

Provide multiple pathways for your students to demonstrate emerging competencies. Critiques of traditional assessment methods and strategies are now commonplace. Educational reformers call for the replacement of multiple-choice and fill-in-the-blank tests with more authentic performances, as opposed to atomized tasks (Herman, Aschbacher, & Winters, 1992; Kirst, 1991; O'Neil, 1992). Performance assessments and portfolio assessments can be designed to support all students' language development. This is vitally important for students who are proficient in languages other than English (Moya & O'Malley, 1994; Pierce & O'Malley, 1992).

Wiggins (1989) and many others have argued that we should test competencies and habits essential to real-world work and that we need to test them in authentic contexts. Performance assessments may include recitals, debates, plays, radio broadcasts, or games (and the criteria by which they are judged). If you want to tap the competencies of all students, however, it's important to define "performance" in rather broad strokes. Some of your middle school students might, for example, design and build an animal habitat for an elementary classroom. Others might identify community resources on a topic and make a handbook for parents.

Rather than test isolated skills, aim to place your assessments in real-life contexts whenever possible. We will discuss the integration of assessments throughout the remaining chapters. See the Resources section at the end of this chapter for more valuable information on portfolios and performance assessments.

Middle school presents a precarious juncture in students' school experience. Here, we can tap their interests, engage them in authentic and demanding tasks, or lose them for good. In a sense, we are always at risk of failing our middle school students. While we have addressed the complexities of teaching effectively for all, we conclude with a list of guidelines to help you monitor the ways in which you are planning for excellence as well as equity:

- Abandon all hope for a one-size-fits-all curriculum.
- Recognize that middle school students may experience schooling in varied ways.
- Don't reduce students' complex lives to mere labels.
- Group heterogeneously for specific instructional purposes.
- Draw upon specialists, such as ESL teachers, as part of interdisciplinary teams.
- Plan for both achievement and belonging for all learners.
- Provide for multiple entry points and escape routes to reduce affective pressure and cognitive demands.
- Work to contextualize cognitively demanding activities and assessments.

In this chapter we have focused on teaching all students, holding high expectations, and designing a rich and rigorous curriculum. In the next chapter we will address a population of students who face great barriers to school success: those who have documented physical, medical, and/or psychological conditions and need individualized services.

Standards in Practice

CREDE is a federally funded research and development program focused on improving the education of students whose ability to reach their potential is challenged by language or cultural barriers, race, geographic location, or poverty. From 1996 to 2001, CREDE funded 31 research projects around the country. Researchers in these projects gathered data and tested curriculum models in wide-ranging settings and with diverse student populations—from classrooms with predominantly Zuni-speaking students in New Mexico to inner city schools in Florida to California elementary schools with large populations of native Spanish-speaking students. CREDE's philosophy can be summarized in the following statements:

- All children can learn. Children learn best when challenged by high standards.
- English proficiency is an attainable goal for all students.
- Bilingual proficiency is desirable for all students.
- Language and cultural diversity can be assets for teaching and learning.
- Teaching and learning must accommodate individuals.
- Schools can mitigate risk factors by teaching social and learning skills.
- Solutions to risk factors must be grounded in a valid general theory of developmental, teaching, and schooling processes.

(Accessed on January 26, 2006, from the Center for Research on Education, Diversity & Excellence (CREDE) Web site: *http://www.crede.org/standards/standards.html*)

For this Standards in Practice activity, visit the CREDE Web site:

- A Rubric for Observing Classroom Enactments of CREDE's Standards for Effective Pedagogy: *http://www.crede.org/standards/spac.shtml*

After carefully examining the Rubric, focus your attention on Strand III Contextualization, "Making Meaning: Connecting School to Students' Lives." Make a chart like the one in Figure 4-3 and add in some specific details for an English language arts curriculum.

In other words, what would you expect to see and hear in a middle school classroom if the language arts teacher was attending to the need to contextualize learning?

FIGURE 4-3 Connecting the English Language Arts Curriculum to Students' Lives

	Emerging	Developing	Enacting	Integrating
Contextualization: Making Meaning: Connecting the Middle School to Student' Lives Through the Language Arts				

REFERENCES

Burke, K. (1990). Language and symbolic action. In P. Bizzell & B. Herzberg (Eds.), *The rhetorical tradition: Readings from classical times to the present* (pp. 1034–1041). Boston: Bedford Books of St. Martins's Press.

Carnegie Task Force on Education for Young Adolescents. (1995). *Great transitions: Preparing adolescents for a new century.* Washington, DC: Carnegie Task Force on Adolescent Development.

Cazden, C. (1988). *Classroom discourse: The language of teaching and learning.* Portsmouth, NH: Heinemann.

Cohen, G. L., & Steele, C. M. (2002). A barrier of mistrust: How negative stereotypes affect cross-race mentoring. In J. Aronson (Ed.), *Improving academic achievement: Impact of psychological factors on education* (pp. 303–337). San Diego, CA: Academic Press.

Cummins, J. (1981). The role of primary language development in promoting educational success for language-minority students. In *Schooling and minority students: A theoretical framework* (pp. 3–49). Los Angeles: Evaluation, Assessment, and Dissemination Center, California State Department of Education.

Delpit, L. (1996). *Other people's children: Cultural conflict in the classroom.* New York: New Press.

Delpit, L. (2002). What should teachers do? Ebonics and culturally responsive instruction. In B. Power & R. Hubbard (Eds.), *Language development: A reader for teachers* (2nd ed., pp. 124–128). Upper Saddle River, NJ: Merrill/Prentice Hall.

Finders, M. (1992). With Jix. *College Composition and Communication, 43,* 497–507.

Hall, S. (1981). Teaching about race. In A. James & R. Jeffcoate (Eds.), *The school in the multicultural society* (pp. 58–69). London: Harper.

Herman, J. L., Aschbacher, P. R. & Winters L. (1992). *A practical guide to alternative assessment.* Alexandria, VA: Association for Supervision and Curriculum Development.

Jarrell, R. (1964). *The Bat Poet.* New York: Macmillan.

King, J. R., & O'Brien, D. G. (2002). Adolescents' multiliteracies and their teachers' needs to know: Toward a digital détente. In D. E. Alvermann (Ed.), *Adolescents and literacies in a digital world* (pp. 40–50). New York: Peter Lang.

Kirst, M.W. (1991). Interview on assessment issues with Lorrie Shepard. *Educational Researcher, 20*(2), 21–23.

Ladson-Billings, G. (1994). *The dreamkeepers: Successful teachers of African American children.* San Francisco: Jossey-Bass Publishers.

Lensmire, T. (1994). *When children write: Critical re-visions of the writing workshop.* New York: Teachers College Press.

Lewis, C., & Finders, M. (2002). Implied adolescents and implied teachers: A generation gap for new times. In D. E. Alvermann (Ed.), *New literacies and digital technologies: A focus on adolescent learners in new times* (pp. 101–113). New York: Peter Lang Publisher.

Mehan, H. (1979). *Learning lessons.* Cambridge, MA: Harvard University Press.

Moll, L. C., Amanti, C., Neff, D., & González, N. (1992). Funds of knowledge for teaching: Using a qualitative approach to connect homes and classrooms. *Theory into Practice, 31*(2), 132–141.

Moll, L. C., & Greenberg, J. (1990). Creating zones of possibilities: Combining social contexts for instruction. In L. C. Moll (Ed.), *Vygotsky and education* (pp. 319–348). Cambridge: Cambridge University Press.

Moore, D., & Hinchman, K. (2002). *Starting out: A guide to teaching adolescents who struggle with reading.* Boston, MA: Allyn & Bacon.

Moya, S. S., & O'Malley, J. M. (1994). A portfolio assessment model for ESL. *The Journal of Educational Issues of Language Minority Students, 13*, 13–36.

Ng, R., Staton, P., & Scane, J. (1995). *Anti-racism, feminism, and critical approaches to education.* Westport, CT: Bergin and Garvey.

O'Connor, M. C., & Michaels, S. (1993). Aligning academic task and participation status through revoicing: Analysis of a classroom discourse strategy. *Anthropology and Education Quarterly, 24*(4), 318–335.

O'Neil, J. 1992. Putting performance assessment to the test. *Educational Leadership, 49*(8), 14–19.

Perry, T. (2005, March 1–2). A workshop with Theresa Perry. Sponsored by the St. Louis Racism and Achievement Partnership and Educational Equity Consultants, LLC. St. Louis, MO.

Pierce, L. V., & O'Malley, J. M. (1992). *Performance and portfolio assessment for language minority students.* Washington, DC: National Clearinghouse for Bilingual Education.

Reid, E. (1995). Waiting to excel: Biracial students in American classrooms. In C. Grant (Ed.), *Educating for diversity: An anthology of multicultural voices.* Boston, MA: Allyn and Bacon.

Ryan, P. M. (2000). *Esperanza Rising.* New York: Scholastic Press.

Vygotsky, L. S. (1978). *Mind and society: The development of higher mental processes.* Cambridge, MA: Harvard University Press.

Wiggins, G. (1989). Teaching to the (authentic) test. *Educational Leadership, 46*(7), 41–47.

RESOURCES

Print

Applebee, A. (1994). English language arts assessment: Lessons from the past. *English Journal, 83*, 40–46.

Banks, J. A. (1993). Multicultural education for young children: Racial and ethnic attitudes and their modification. In D. Spodek (Ed.), *Handbook of research on the education of young children* (pp. 236–250). New York: Macmillan.

Banks, J. A., & Banks, C. A. M. (1993). *Multicultural education: Issues and perspectives* (2nd ed.). Boston: Allyn and Bacon.

Beach, R., & Myers, J. (2001). *Inquiry-based English instruction: Engaging students in life and literature.* New York: Teachers College Press.

Brown, R. (1989, April). Testing and thoughtfulness. *Educational Leadership, 46*, 31–33.

Capper, J. (1996). *Testing to learn—learning to test.* Newark, DE: International Reading Association.

Dana, T., & Tippins, D. (1993). Considering alternative assessments for middle level learners. *Middle School Journal, 25*, 3–5.

Edelsky, C. (1991). *With literacy and justice for all: Rethinking the social in language and education.* New York: Falmer Press.

Gay, G. (2000). *Culturally responsive teaching: Theory, research, and practice.* New York: Teachers College Press.

Gill, K. (1993). *Process and portfolios in writing instruction.* Urbana, IL: NCTE Press.

Grant, C., & Sleeter, C. (1989). *Turning on learning: Five approaches for multicultural teaching plans for race, class, gender, and disability.* Columbus, OH: Merrill.

Graves, D., & Sunstein, B. (1992). *Portfolio portraits.* Portsmouth, NH: Heinemann.

International Reading Association. (1999). *High-stakes assessments in reading: A position statement of the International Reading Association.* Newark, DE: International Reading Association.

International Reading Association and National Council of Teachers of English Joint Task Force on Assessment. (1994). *Standards for the assessment of reading and writing.* Newark, DE: International Reading Association.

Lewin, L., & Shoemaker, B. J. (1998). *Great performances creating classroom-based assessment tasks.* Alexandria, VA: The Association for Supervision and Curriculum Development.

Lustig, K. (1996). *Portfolio assessment: A handbook for middle level teachers.* Westerville, OH: National Middle School Association.

Nieto, S. (1996). *Affirming diversity: The sociopolitical context of multicultural education* (2nd ed.). White Plains, NY: Longman.

Perrone, V. (Ed.). (1991). *Expanding student assessment.* Alexandria, VA: Association for Supervision and Curriculum Development.

Perry, T., Steele, C., & Hilliard, III, A. (2003). *Young, gifted and black: Promoting high achievement among African-American students.* New York: Beacon Press.

Reif, L. (1990). Finding the value in evaluation: Self-assessment in a middle school classroom. *Educational Leadership, 47*(6), 24–29.

Schurr, S. (1999). *Authentic assessment using product, performance, and portfolio measures from A to Z.* Westerville, OH: National Middle School Association.

Sleeter, C. E., & Grant, C. A. (1988). *Making choices for multicultural education: Five approaches to race, class, and gender.* Upper Saddle River, NJ: Merrill/Prentice Hall.

Stiggins, R. J. (2001). *Student-involved classroom assessment* (3rd ed.). Upper Saddle River, NJ: Merrill/Prentice Hall.

Sunstein, B., & Cheville, J. (1995). *Assessing portfolios: A portfolio.* Iowa English Bulletin. Urbana, IL: NCTE Press.

Tchudi, S. (1997). *Alternatives to grading student writing.* Urbana, IL: NCTE Press.

Wiener, R., & Cohen, J. (1997). *Literacy portfolios: Using assessment to guide instruction.* Upper Saddle River, NJ: Merrill/Prentice Hall.

Wiggins, G. (1994). Toward better report cards. *Educational Leadership, 52*(2), 28–37.

Winograd, G. (1994). Developing alternative assessments: Six problems worth solving. *The Reading Teacher, 47,* 420–423.

Yancie, K. (1992). *Portfolios in the writing classroom: An introduction.* Urbana, IL: NCTE Press.

Yancie, K. B., & Weiser, I. (1997). *Situating portfolios: Four perspectives.* Logan: Utah State University Press.

Zeichner, K. M. (1995). Educating teachers to close the achievement gap: Issues of pedagogy, knowledge, and teacher preparation. In B. Williams (Ed.), *Closing the achievement gap: A vision to guide change in beliefs and practice* (pp. 39–52). Washington, DC: U.S. Department of Education, Office of Educational Research and Improvement.

Electronic

Equity and Culturally Relevant Resources

Américas Book Award for Children's and Young Adult Literature. The Américas Award is given in recognition of U.S. works of fiction, poetry, folklore, or selected nonfiction (from picture books to works for young adults) published in the previous year in English or Spanish that authentically and engagingly portray Latin America, the Caribbean, or Latinos in the United States.

http://www.uwm.edu/Dept/CLACS/outreach/americas.html

The Center for Research on Education, Diversity & Excellence. CREDE is a federally funded research and development program focused on improving the education of students whose ability to reach their potential is challenged by language or cultural barriers, race, geographic location, or poverty.

http://www.crede.org/

The Coretta Scott King Award. The American Library Association presents the Coretta Scott King Award annually to authors and illustrators of African descent whose distinguished books promote an understanding and appreciation of the "American Dream."

http://www.ala.org/ala/emiert/corettascottkingbookawards/abouttheawarda/cskabout.htm

Empowering Multicultural Initiatives. This initiative specializes in antiracist education. This Web site offers teacher resources and lesson plans.

http://www.edcollab.org/EMI/EmpoweringMulticultural.html

The National Association for Multicultural Education. NAME's membership encompasses the spectrum of professional educators and specialists, including early childhood, classroom, and higher education faculty; administrators; psychologists; social workers; counselors; curriculum specialists; librarians; scholars; and researchers. This Web site includes diversity/inclusive teaching tips, lesson plans with a multicultural focus, and a wealth of resources and links to other Web sites.

http://www.nameorg.org/resources/defining_multicultural_education.htm

Oyate. This organization works to see that Native Americans' lives and histories are portrayed authentically in texts. This site includes evaluation of texts, resource materials, and fiction by and about native peoples and includes a "books to avoid" list.

http://www.oyate.org/aboutus.html

Parents for Public Schools. This national organization of grassroots chapters is dedicated to involving parents in more meaningful roles as decision makers in their children's education.

http://www.parents4publicschools.com

Teaching Tolerance. Founded in 1991 by the Southern Poverty Law Center, Teaching Tolerance provides educators with free educational materials that promote respect for differences and appreciation of diversity in the classroom and beyond.

http://www.tolerance.org/teach/

Tomas Rivera Mexican American Children's Book Award. The award was established in 1995 by the College of Education at Texas State University–San Marcos to encourage authors, illustrators, and publishers of books that authentically reflect the lives of Mexican American children and young adults in the United States.

http://www.education.txstate.edu/subpages/tomasrivera/

Assessments and Excellence

Practical Assessment, Research and Evaluation. PARE is an online journal that provides access to refereed articles relevant to researchers and teachers with an interest in assessment and evaluation.

http://pareonline.net/Home.htm

National Center for Fair & Open Testing (FairTest). This advocacy organization works to end the abuses, misuses, and flaws of standardized testing and ensure that evaluation of students and workers is fair, open, and educationally sound.

http://www.fairtest.org

North Central Regional Educational Laboratory's "Alternative Assessment" Page. NCREL is one of 10 not-for-profit Regional Educational Laboratories. The organization is dedicated to helping schools and students reach their full potential. The "alternative assessment" page provides links to useful resources.

http://www.ncrel.org/sdrs/areas/issues/methods/assment/as8lk30.htm

Chapter 5

Supporting Middle School Learners with Disabilities

Written with Teresa Taber, *Purdue University*

GUIDING QUESTIONS

1. Who are the support personnel in the middle school to assist you and your students?
2. How do you adapt instruction to support each of the learners in your classroom?
3. How might you tap your students' social, physical, and academic abilities to support their peers?

A CASE FOR CONSIDERATION

Emily's Plan

At F. E. Gates Middle School, as Emily's Individual Education Program (IEP) meeting begins, Ms. Collier introduces each member. In addition to Ms. Collier, the special education teacher, those in attendance include Mr. Hill (Emily's teacher, a first year sixth- and seventh-grade language arts teacher), Mr. and Mrs. Grabosky (Emily's parents), Emily, the physical therapist, the speech and language pathologist, and the school counselor. Following introductions, Ms. Collier reviews Emily's current level of functioning, which includes her strengths and weaknesses in the areas of academic, social, motor, and communication skills.

During the review of Emily's current level of functioning, Mr. Hill learns that Emily is a 13-year-old student with cerebral palsy who uses a wheelchair. According to her test scores, previous educational progress, and teacher and parent observations, Emily has numerous academic and social strengths. She has participated in a grade-level curriculum for her entire school career and plans to attend college one day. Her areas of weakness are her motor and communication skills. To provide maximum opportunities for Emily to be educated alongside her peers, modifications have been provided to accommodate her motor and communication needs in previous years.

As Emily's IEP meeting progresses, Ms. Collier leads the team through the decision-making process for determining Emily's instructional goals and objectives, needed modifications and supports, educational placements in the Least Restrictive Environment (LRE), additional settings or activities that would provide Emily with opportunities for interaction with peers, and ways to evaluate her performance on IEP objectives.

The IEP committee identifies six objectives. In addition to continuing her education in regular academic subject areas over the next school year, Emily's teachers will work with her on (a) improving oral communication skills, (b) enhancing written expression skills (which includes addressing her need for improvement in fine motor coordination), (c) decreasing the time it takes for her to transition between classes, (d) improving her dressing skills, (e) using public forms of transportation, and (f) increasing her skills in using a motorized wheelchair.

FOR DISCUSSION

As you can see, both Emily and Mr. Hill have a blanket of support already in place at Gates Middle School. The transition from elementary to middle school will pose new problems for Emily, however. For example, the committee needs to address the question of how to facilitate Emily's involvement in after-school clubs and activities. In addition, because each student has a locker, and because there are more changes of classes than there were in elementary school, transition times between class periods will be a more complicated issue for Emily. The middle school cafeteria is much larger than the one in Emily's elementary school, and her wheelchair will barely fit through the narrow lunch line, so she will need some assistance in ordering and paying for her lunch. Because Emily has difficulty speaking and uses a special augmentative communication device, her classmates in the past have shown some impatience when she contributes to class discussion or attempts to communicate informally with them. Because social relationships in middle school are often more complicated and intense than they were in elementary school, Emily may need help in making the social as well as the academic transition to middle school.

As the meeting proceeds, Douglas Hill begins thinking about the types of modifications that might support Emily in his English class for each of the objectives identified by the committee. As you look at each of the six objectives, think about what types of concrete support Doug might provide for Emily in his language arts class. If you're feeling unsure of where to begin, you have a lot in common with Doug. The purpose of this chapter is to get you started in thinking about some tangible ways you might support students like Emily in your own middle school classroom.

Because of their disabilities, students in your classroom may learn or behave in ways that may be significantly different from the majority of their peers. These students may experience learning disabilities, behavior disorders, physical or sensory disabilities, autism, and/or mental retardation. Although these students typically require some level of support or modification to be able to learn, they can all be productive and valuable members of your classroom. This chapter focuses on an extended Classroom Case featuring Doug Hill, Emily, and several of Doug's other students. Through Doug's experiences, you'll learn where to find support and how to adapt instruction for your own students with disabilities.

Teaching students with disabilities in regular education classrooms is becoming more common across the country as school administrators and teachers begin implementing components of the law that governs the education of students with disabilities. This law, known as the Individuals with Disabilities Education Act (IDEA), mandates that students with disabilities be taught in the Least Restrictive Environment (LRE) with maximum opportunities to be educated alongside their peers (IDEA, 1997).

Specifically, the IDEA (see *http://www.nichcy.org*) describes the LRE as based on the presumption that children with disabilities are most appropriately educated with their peers, and that special classes, separate schooling, or other removal of children with disabilities from the regular educational environment occurs only when the nature or severity of the disability is such that education in regular classes with the use of supplementary aids and services cannot be achieved satisfactorily.

In other words, the law begins with the assumption that all students with disabilities should be members of regular education classes for at least some part of their school day. Students with disabilities may be removed from the regular education classroom and taught in other school or community settings only when an Individual Education Program committee (of which regular education teachers are members) documents and determines that a student's educational goals and objectives cannot be achieved satisfactorily, even with the use of modifications.

THE INDIVIDUAL EDUCATIONAL PROGRAM

All students with a disability who receive special education services must have an Individual Education Program (IEP). This legal document and the information it contains serve as the framework for the provision of instruction to a student with a disability. The IEP contains the following information:

- a student's academic, social, behavioral, and communication strengths and weaknesses
- long-term annual goals
- measurable, short-term instructional objectives
- the provision of related services such as speech therapy or occupational therapy
- the frequency of these services
- a program of study and transition plan if the student is aged 14 or older
- the settings in which the student will receive instruction in the LRE
- a description of the modifications needed and considered

An IEP is written on an annual basis and includes input from an IEP committee. Members of the IEP committee include the following: the parents of the child with a disability, at least one regular education teacher, at least one special education teacher, a representative of the local education agency, and, whenever appropriate, the child with a disability. What does all of this mean to the middle school language arts teacher? Classroom Case 5-1 focus on this question.

Classroom Case 5-1

Defining the Least Restrictive Environment

Complete inclusion in the regular education classroom does not always constitute the Least Restrictive Environment for all students. Some students have disabilities that require a mix of "pull out" (instruction in a self-contained setting) and "push in" (special educators or aides co-teaching with regular educators) instruction. Consider the case of Jason, a student with a reading comprehension learning disability, and Beth, a student with severe mental retardation and physical disabilities. In separate IEP meetings at Gates Middle School in the spring, the committee considered LRE placement options for these two students.

Jason. Members of his IEP committee noted that Jason had been following the regular education program for sixth-grade students with modifications made to accommodate his specific learning needs. Ms. Kaplan, his sixth-grade English language arts teacher, began the IEP meeting by stating that Jason had been successful in her class. She explained the modifications that worked well for Jason previously. Specifically, she recommended that next year's English teacher adapt written assignments specifically regarding length requirements and adapt assessments for Jason's cognitive abilities. In addition, she noted that his seventh-grade teacher would need to evaluate all textual materials to determine difficulty level and make alternative selections when necessary. In addition, Jason would require additional time for reading assignments. As a result of these suggestions, members of the IEP committee confirmed that the LRE for Jason to learn English language arts would be Mr. Hill's seventh-grade English class during the next school year. Jason's parents and other members of the committee agreed that pulling him out of the classroom for special services, even for short periods, would result in his missing valuable classroom activities and would compromise his overall educational experience. As a result, he will receive the agreed-upon modifications within the context of the regular school day.

Beth. In a separate IEP meeting, the committee considered educational options for Beth. Because Beth would be in the seventh grade next year, the IEP committee considered whether a placement in Mr. Hill's English class would best address her specific IEP objectives. These objectives included learning to read color words and numbers to 20, learning to write these same words, and learning to compose sentences with at least 4 words. After reviewing each of her IEP objectives and considering a variety of modifications, the IEP committee determined that, in light of Beth's particular educational needs and academic goals, a seventh-grade English class would be a more restrictive placement for Beth. Instead, instruction in a mix of special and regular education classes was identified as the LRE that would provide maximum opportunities for her to be educated alongside her peers. Beth will not be in Mr. Hill's English class. Instead, she will spend approximately 60% of her school day in a self-contained classroom where she will receive direct instruction appropriate for her cognitive level in mathematics, English, science, and social studies. The remaining 40% of her school day will be spent with her peers in physical education, health and safety, art, and music classes. She will also go to the cafeteria with her same-age peers. Because she has physical disabilities and would have difficulty locating her classrooms, she will have an aide escorting her to various locations during the day.

For Discussion

As Mr. Hill attempted to implement inclusive practices, he knew he would need support. He understood that he needed help from other professionals in the school, but he didn't know exactly where to begin. Where might Doug turn to provide a positive learning climate for Jason? How might he learn about specific adaptations for Jason in the English language arts?

Whereas instruction in the LRE is legally mandated, the philosophy of inclusion is not. However, we believe that components of the inclusion ideal should be incorporated to the greatest extent possible into the provision of instruction to students with disabilities. Implementing inclusive practices involves ensuring whenever possible that students with disabilities (a) are members of chronologically age-appropriate grades and classes, (b) attend the same schools as their siblings and the other children in their neighborhood, (c) receive support as needed across school and community settings, and (d) are actively engaged in learning within the context of classroom activities.

Teaching all middle school students is the responsibility of all teachers in a building. Yet, you may feel a little like Doug Hill and not know how to get started or who is in your building to support you and your students. In Fieldwork Journal 5-1, you will explore the blanket of support available in your school setting.

Fieldwork Journal 5-1

Learning From Support Personnel

Select a teacher, administrator, or support service provider who works with students with disabilities in your school or field placement, and arrange an interview with that person. Find out how he or she works with other individuals to provide for the needs of all students in the school. Here is a list of questions to begin your interview:

1. Do all students with disabilities participate in inclusive settings in this school?
2. How does the school administration work with teachers to ensure an appropriate number of students with disabilities for each teacher? In this school, who determines when the number of students with disabilities is in "natural proportion" to those without disabilities?

3. What are some tips you would give to new teachers about the most effective and appropriate approach for serving students who experience various disabilities?
4. Who provides guidance to regular education teachers in the areas of data collection, behavior management, instructional strategies, and social skills development?

You may want to add questions of your own, depending on whether the person you interview is an administrator, special education teacher, related service provider, or regular education teacher. After you have completed your interview, it may be valuable to share what you have learned with your teaching colleagues.

Once you know who your support personnel are and which of your students have IEPs, you will be ready to begin the process of actively engaging the student with disabilities in literacy learning. In Classroom Case 5-2, Mr. Hill seeks the advice of special education teacher Naomi Collier and begins the process of envisioning a more inclusive pedagogy for all of his students.

Classroom Case 5-2

A Conversation With the Special Education Teacher

Doug Hill approached his meeting with Naomi Collier armed with a host of questions about his students with disabilities and how best to teach them. Their conversation begins.

Doug: Hi, Naomi. Thanks for getting together with me. I'm really wondering how I can help the students with disabilities in my classes, but I feel clueless right now. I guess the first thing I need to know is who are the students with disabilities, and what kinds of modifications do they need?

Naomi: Well, at the moment you have five students with disabilities taking seventh-grade English.

Doug: At the moment?

Naomi: Yes. There's a possibility one more student with a disability will be assigned to your class after her IEP meeting next week.

Doug: Oh, that's right. Lannie. I heard about her IEP meeting the other day. I'll find out more about her in the meeting, I guess. But for now, what can you tell me about the kids with disabilities who are in my class already?

Naomi: Well, it looks like you have Jason, Todd, and Maria. Even though they're each labeled with a learning disability, as you can imagine, the disability is different for each one. Jason has significant problems with reading comprehension. Todd's is primarily in math, and he has some difficulties in organizational skills. Maria has problems with organizational skills too, but she also has difficulty with note taking. Then you have Larry. He has mental retardation and will be working on his IEP goals within your seventh-grade English curriculum. Right now, he's learning to read functional reading materials like grocery labels and street maps that will lead to independent living, so it would be good to incorporate tasks like these into your assignments for him. Your fifth student is Emily, and since you attended her IEP meeting, you know where she is right now.

Doug: Wow, I don't know how I'm going to do this. I have to tell you I feel overwhelmed. I have no idea what to do. I've had some courses in my teacher ed. program, but right now I feel like I've forgotten everything I learned!

Naomi: Not to worry. That's why I'm here. As the special education teacher, I go wherever my students are being served. In this case, I'll be meeting regularly with you to develop modifications for each of these students.

Doug: Will you also be helping me teach each day?

Naomi: At the moment, no. The IEP committee decided that none of these students requires daily direct one-on-one support from a second adult while they're in your class. But I'll try to visit your class as much as possible to get you started teaching, and I promise that I'll provide support to you and the students throughout the year. Sometimes we'll meet outside class, and sometimes I'll come into your class to work with individual students. I'll help you select appropriate materials and adapt instruction to support these students, so it would help me to know if you're planning to teach something that might pose a problem for any of these kids.

Doug: That's a relief—kind of. But, I still don't know where to start.

Naomi: Let's take a look at the specific modifications identified by the IEP committees last spring for each of these students, and we can talk about how they'll translate to what you're planning for your English class this year. When we get together next week for Lannie's IEP meeting, you'll see more about how placements and modifications are decided. In the meantime, I have a list of modifications that have been used in the past with students who have different disabilities. I'll put it in your box, so you can read it over before Lannie's meeting.

For Discussion

Like Doug, you may be eager to learn more about the disabilities your students have and feel desperate to learn about modifications you can make to ensure their success. While these issues are crucially important, you might have noticed that there was little or no discussion in that first meeting between Doug and Naomi of students' strengths, interests, or areas of expertise. If Doug is designing for learning from a strength perspective, he will need to know more about who these students are as active, complicated middle school learners. Thinking back to the CREDE Standards for Effective Pedagogy in chapter 4, consider what questions Doug might ask at Lannie's IEP meeting.

Making Modifications

The type of modification developed for a student depends on the goal of instruction. Modifications considered for students should be age appropriate and allow for increasing numbers of independent interactions with peers. For example, in fifth grade, Emily, a 13-year-old student with poor fine motor coordination, used a large grip or Velcro strap to hold a pencil instead of being required to use the large pencils and crayons typically used by elementary-age children when writing. The ability to write independently now that she's in middle school would allow Emily to work on writing projects with her peers without having to rely on an adult or peer to write for her. The use of a laptop computer might also help her to take notes and complete assignments with greater ease.

As you will see in the following sections, modifications generally fall into four categories: activity, instructional, material, and environmental. Modifications may be made to accommodate learning, cognitive, behavioral, physical, and/or sensory issues.

Activity modifications.   These changes are made to an activity to allow for active student participation. Activity modifications may include allowing a student who is nonverbal to respond by using a switch to activate a computer or an augmentative communication device. Partial participation (allowing students to participate in an activity to their maximum level, as opposed to denying access to the activity because the student could not complete the task) would also be considered an appropriate activity modification.

Instructional modifications.   These modifications require a change in the delivery of instruction. A teacher may modify instruction by using large and small group as well as peer-mediated and individualized instruction. The delivery of instruction may also be modified by shortening the length of a lesson and/or decreasing the rate at which instruction is delivered. A teacher may also use a simpler vocabulary, use visuals, and provide a student with additional opportunities to practice learned skills within and across lessons. To assist with note taking, the teacher may provide copies of any overheads and class notes or record class discussions for later playback.

Material modifications.   Materials may be modified in several ways to allow student learning and participation to occur. Modifying the format of materials such as using real objects and/or manipulatives instead of words or pictures can reduce the cognitive demand and make the materials more functional and concrete for the students. Teachers may also alter the motor or sensory requirements of materials by changing their size, highlighting specific parts, and using a computer or other assistive technology to help students access materials. If a student is unable to use textual materials through traditional means, worksheets, handouts, and tests may be adapted to include more spacing, fewer items, and bold or highlighted directions and key concepts.

Environmental modifications. These modifications may be made to accommodate student behaviors and physical or sensory needs. Teachers may use visual daily schedules for a student who is working on self-management skills, proximity seating for a student who uses a wheelchair to be able to sit with his or her peers, or lamps instead of overhead lighting to reduce the glare for a student with a visual impairment. An FM system can be provided by the school for students with hearing difficulties.

In Emily's case, Mr. Hill can make several modifications to support her IEP objectives. Since Emily's oral and written competencies are most relevant to his English class, he needs to focus on the following objectives most closely:

> *Objective 1:* When presented with an opportunity to engage in conversation during lunch and in classes, Emily will ask a question to engage a listener in a conversation during 75% of opportunities for 3 consecutive weeks.
>
> *Modification:* Emily will learn to use an electronic augmentative communication device that is preprogrammed with age-appropriate vocabulary enabling her to ask desired questions to others and engage in conversations.
>
> *Objective 2:* During writing exercises, Emily will write sentences and paragraphs following an outline, writing at least three sentences per day for 6 consecutive weeks.
>
> *Modification(s):* Emily will use a laptop computer with a modified keyboard and switch to engage in writing activities in her classes.

During their meeting, the IEP committee identified a few additional modifications that would enable Emily to become a more active participant in her classes. These modifications included having a table instead of a desk in each of her classrooms to accommodate her wheelchair and use of a laptop, widening the aisles between desks in classes, providing a copy of the lecture notes or allowing tape recording of lectures, and allowing Emily to take tests either with her communication device or on the computer.

Since Mr. Hill's class is divided into general daily activities, corresponding modifications for each activity are indicated per IEP objective and her general class participation needs. According to a schedule analysis, to accommodate her writing IEP objective, Emily will require a material (M) modification during all activities in which writing is required. In Emily's case, use of a laptop computer for writing and either lecture note copies or a tape recording of lectures would be the modifications implemented. To address her IEP objective of engaging in conversations, the modifications would include a material (M) modification (an augmentative communication device), an environmental (E) modification (widening the aisles to navigate her wheelchair closer to her peers or teacher), and possibly an instructional (I) modification in which students would break into small groups for discussion.

Once Emily's IEP team identifies the modifications she will require to participate actively in her classes, members then address the issue of supports. In other words, will Emily require a second adult to assist her in her classes? Do the academic and special education teachers need to consult regularly to develop modifications? If so, how often? Will peers be used to support Emily in her classes?

Supports

To ensure the effectiveness of instruction in the LRE, various levels of support may be implemented. A student may require different types of support for different IEP objectives and different settings. Even within a single setting, the type of support may change over time or incorporate various types of assistance. Supports available to a student include consultative support, collaborative teaching, individual support, and peer support.

Consultative support. This kind of support involves the special education teacher jointly planning with the regular education teacher in determining modifications for a student. Planning time may be regularly scheduled, or teachers may meet more informally during lunch or on an as-needed basis. With this level of support, the special education teacher is not present in the classroom on a daily basis; however, he or she maintains regular contact with students as specified by the IEP. For example, Mr. Hill and Ms. Collier will meet every Tuesday morning during their second period planning time to review the next week's lessons, identify the IEP objectives that will be addressed for the students who are served in the regular education class, and discuss needed modifications for each student.

Collaborative teaching. This is also known as co-teaching or "push-in" support and involves settings in which the regular and special education teacher share the responsibility for providing instruction to all students during a lesson segment. Formal planning occurs regularly throughout the school year. This planning includes jointly developing lesson plans and modifications for all students in the class. Schools frequently provide this type of support by reassigning a teacher from an existing special education class to rotate between regular education classes throughout the day. For example, Ms. Fenske, another special education teacher, collaboratively teaches with Mr. Wilson during the first 2 hours of each day in their math and language arts classes. During the 4th and 5th hours, Ms. Fenske collaboratively teaches with Ms. Johnson during language arts and social studies.

Individual support. This kind of support involves providing one-on-one support to a particular student so he or she can participate in a specific setting. Support may be required for academic, behavioral, and/or physical reasons. Although the primary responsibility is to work individually with the student with a disability, the support person should do this within the context of small group activities with nondisabled students to prevent isolation from the rest of the class. For example, Mr. Hill will provide individual support for Jason during individualized reading time. Since Jason has difficulty with reading, Ms. Collier will assist him as he learns to participate in group reading activities with his classmates. In addition, Mr. Hill will work with Jason's classmates in making them aware of how they can best support Jason.

Occasionally, while Jason is being supported by his peers or independently participating, Ms. Collier will assist other students or Mr. Hill. Related service professionals (e.g., the speech and language pathologist, occupational therapist, physical therapist) will also be part of Mr. Hill's class, providing services to particular students while participating in more general educational activities as well. While providing support to the classroom teacher, related service providers are often able to serve several students on their caseload simultaneously within the regular education classroom.

Peer support. This kind of support is vitally important and requires delicate handling by significant adults if it is to succeed. Peer support is often used in conjunction with other models of support. Although never a substitute for the teacher, peers assist the student with a disability in a variety of ways. In academic settings, peers guide and encourage involvement in various components of lessons and materials. For example, they can help students with disabilities to practice particular skills. Peers can also encourage students in the use of their augmentative communication systems and assist in transitions from one school setting to another.

In order for the student with a disability to engage in a structured manner with classmates, and for the nondisabled students to share the responsibility of providing support, peer responsibilities should be rotated on a regular basis. Teachers may also facilitate peer relationships by reformatting the manner in which information is presented in their classes. Use of hands-on, experiential learning and heterogeneous small groups tends to foster peer collaboration and the development of peer relationships. The student with a disability is provided with the same materials as other students in a class (e.g., workbooks, handouts, notebooks, supplies) and is expected to participate actively in class activities. Peers can support students not only in classroom settings but also in the school cafeteria, on field trips, and during after-school activities.

Supports are often modified over time to lead students toward independence. For example, Emily's IEP team concluded that peer support should be used during all of her classes as well as during some of the transitions between classes. Because Emily demonstrates significant motor and communication challenges, the team decided that for the first 3 weeks, individual supports would be provided in each of her classes. After the first 3 weeks, support would then be shifted to consultative. In her social studies class, a co-teaching (collaborative) model would be used.

Because the time it takes Emily to transition between classes was a concern, team members wanted to ensure that Emily's classes were located in proximity to her previous classes. Thus, the time it will take for her to move between classes should be decreased. Because at least two teachers in each academic area teach seventh grade, the team chose classes according to their proximity to Emily's previous classes and provided her with a schedule that accommodated her mobility needs.

When a student's IEP indicates that he or she needs to learn skills that cannot be taught in a regular education class, even with the use of modifications and supports, the committee must consider another step in the LRE decision-making process. In which special education or community settings will IEP objectives be taught?

Interaction with peers. When students receive instruction in settings other than the regular education classroom, the IEP committee must consider another question, "What additional settings or activities will provide opportunities for interaction with peers?" Opportunities for interaction may occur during lunch, recess/break, assemblies, dances, field trips, plays, school programs, sporting events, clubs, extracurricular activities, homeroom, hallways, walking together to classes, and transportation to and from school.

In Emily's case, the IEP committee identified transportation to and from school as an additional opportunity for her to interact with her peers. Because Emily uses a wheelchair, a school bus equipped with a lift was required. Although the only buses with lifts were mini buses, the school system agreed to use one of these buses to transport Emily and several of her neighborhood peers to and from school and other activities. Emily's committee decided that she should participate in community-based instruction during the assemblies/clubs/computer period two times per week to address the objectives on the use of public transportation and navigating her wheelchair in a variety of settings. On the three days she remains in the school building, she would meet with the drama club on club day and receive instruction in computer class.

As a means of encouraging peer interactions, some schools implement a peer support system in which students without disabilities are paired with students with disabilities for extracurricular and integrated activities throughout the school (e.g., clubs, breaks, homeroom, lunch, athletic practice, band). Typically, students with disabilities would then be included in the same classes that their peer support partners attend. In this way, students with disabilities have access to an immediate support network for social interactions and academic assistance.

BALANCING THE SOCIAL AND THE ACADEMIC

Teachers all too often focus on the class as a whole and gloss over the needs of individuals. When teachers think about individuals with disabilities, they may focus on the individual, but the focus is mainly on just that, the disabilities, whether they are social or cognitive. An effective middle school teacher attempts to recognize and tap the social and academic competencies of each student. But how do you accomplish this? Fieldwork Journal 5-2 offers some practice in thinking about supporting the social and academic competencies of your students.

Fieldwork Journal 5-2

Adapting Instruction to Support All Learners

We'd like you to think about planning one lesson in terms of some students you have met in this chapter. You already know a lot about Emily's disabilities but little about her interests. That is perhaps too often the case for students who are "labeled." If students are known only by their labels and their disabilities, you cannot possibly design learning activites in which you tap their interests or expertise. You need to know your middle school students well beyond any academic or behavioral labels they may carry with them.

As the school year progresses, Mr. Hill gets to know many things about Emily, Larry, and Maria. As you read the descriptions of each student, think about how much more multidimensional each student seems, compared with the impressions you may have formed from Naomi Collier's brief description of them in her first meeting with Doug Hill.

Emily

Emily is White and lives in the suburbs. She loves music. Although she does not sing, she has an extensive CD and video collection of music, including pop, classical, country, and Latin. Emily is a serious student who plans to attend college to prepare for a career in music history. Because of her inattentiveness to dress and her difficulty with oral expression, Emily has a difficult time making friends. She is consciously aware of this need and has been making tremendous progress with the help of her parents and teachers. She works closely with a seventh-grade peer named Ronda who has helped her to integrate into lunch hour social activities. Ronda has also signed them both up for Mr. Hill's drama club to serve on the props and make-up crew.

Larry

Larry is a 13-year-old White male who loves to be the center of attention. He has a pleasing personality, and his teachers and peers enjoy being around him. However, at times, Larry doesn't know when to stop seeking attention. He is occasionally reinforced when others laugh at what he says, so he frequently makes comments or repeats jokes when they are no longer funny. In addition, he often interrupts conversations between others to gain attention. Larry loves country and western music and often brings in a CD for Mr. Hill. He also loves cartoons and likes to draw pictures of his favorite super heroes from movies and television. He says he wants to be a cowboy singer when he grows up or draw pictures for *TV Guide.*

Academically, Larry is working on a variety of skills. Because Larry experiences a moderate level of mental retardation, his academic objectives are focused on learning and maintaining functional skills that will increase his independence as he gets older. Presently, he can recognize and read approximately 120 functional sight words and is now beginning to focus on reading those words in context, such as reading the movie section of a newspaper, the washing instructions on the labels of garments, the TV program guide, and basic instructions for completing vocational tasks. Some of his other learning objectives include identifying various types of jobs in the community, using a calculator to determine the costs of various items purchased at a store, appropriately engaging in conversations with peers and teachers (refraining from interrupting), and working cooperatively in a group with peers.

Maria

Maria is a tall, White, 13-year-old who has numerous friends in school and her neighborhood. She likes to go to the mall with her girlfriends, and she has started to make an online zine that tells about hair styles and accessories. She thinks she will be a fashion designer when she is older and is proud of her dog, which she has entered in competitive local dog shows.

Maria is easily distracted by others during lunch and physical education, in group tasks, and between classes. She is especially distracted by boys, who often tease her and call her a "bubble-headed girl." In addition to being distracted, Maria is extremely disorganized and has difficulty with note taking. Both of these characteristics are a result of her learning disability and directly affect her ability to understand and retain information. Prior to being officially identified as having a learning disability, Maria had low self-esteem because she thought she was "dumb." She struggled daily to keep up with assignments and frequently received low grades. When Maria was tested, results confirmed the presence of a learning disability but also indicated that she had an above average level of intelligence. Encouraged by these results, Maria began working with a special education teacher to learn strategies that would assist her in learning. Now, as long as she receives a few modifications and reminders for note taking, she does extremely well academically.

As noted previously, the classroom context is a dynamic ecosystem, and you can't ever design foolproof plans. You can, however, anticipate how a literacy lesson might unfold, as well as the needs and possible obstacles that some of your students will encounter. Effective teachers consider the strengths and weaknesses of their students and plan modifications and additional supports for specific difficulties that students are likely to experience.

Think about some lessons you have planned or are in the process of planning. If possible, locate a lesson plan that you've already used or one you are planning to use. Reconsider how you might modify this plan to address the unique needs and strengths of Larry, Maria, and Emily. Write notes in the margin about how particular aspects of the plan might be modified to support all students in your classroom.

PROMOTING AND DOCUMENTING STUDENT PROGRESS IN ENGLISH LANGUAGE ARTS

At this point, you may be wondering how all of this information about students with disabilities specifically relates to adapting instruction in the English language arts classroom. In Classroom Case 5-3, you see this process in action as Doug Hill designs a collaborative project for a literature unit.

Classroom Case 5-3

Providing Assistance and Tapping Expertise

Doug Hill learns early in the year that many of his students do not seem connected to literature in ways he would like. In fact, many enter the room saying, "I hate reading." He wants to create a learning opportunity that engages all of his students in reading. He also wants his students to work together, especially early in the year, so they learn to depend on each other for social and academic support. Since all teachers have been asked to organize some sort of showcase for the upcoming Parents' Night, Doug decides to organize and videotape students' reading of literature in a sort of "Beatnik Café" format. He knows from team meetings that his students are studying the 1950s in an exploration strand for another class. Dramatic readings with accompanying music might be just the thing to engage students, and they can work collaboratively to create the stage, organize the music, and set the whole thing in motion. His seventh-grade students will have a real audience of parents and siblings for their performances.

"Will any students have difficulty in selecting and presenting poetry and short stories?" Doug Hill asks himself. Clearly, yes. But this activity accommodates the vast range of interests and abilities in each of his classes. He decides to make available a range of difficult and more accessible reading materials. Length of reading materials will be equally varied.

He builds in peer support for Emily by inviting students to read with partners and small groups. Because Brad, one of Emily's classmates, has learned to program and operate her communication device, he can help Emily to share her piece without adult assistance on the night of the performance. Mr. Hill plans to build in support for Jason by inviting him to serve as video technician. Although he would be challenged by oral reading, Jason can lend expertise in videotaping.

Doug realizes that he needs to build in modifications for Todd and Maria, who demonstrate difficulties in organizational skills. He designs a step-by-step guide to help them select materials, rehearse in the company of their peers, and be ready to perform for the video camera. Actually, he knows that this early in the year, all students will benefit from such support structures. For Larry, who has mild mental retardation and is working on his IEP objectives within the context of his seventh-grade English curriculum, Mr. Hill will need to order special textual materials from interlibrary loan.

Doug thinks about the ways in which this Beatnik Café can tap students' interest and expertise. He knows he can count on Larry to run the lights. Emily, who loves to tell him about her CD collection, can be part of the group that organizes the music. Several students will surely sign up to bring in dark glasses, props, and any other costumes or visual materials, he thinks.

For Discussion

You can see how Doug is attempting to position each student in a positive participatory role for the event. Can you think of ways that Doug might solicit his students' help and counsel in designing this dramatic event? Are there some specific ways in which he might draw from the larger community?

GETTING TO KNOW ALL STUDENTS: MOVING BEYOND THE IEP

Just as Doug has done with his Beatnik Café project, you'll want to think about the ways that you can provide support for your students with disabilities; however, focusing solely on the issue of "support" can lead to the assumption that such students have little or nothing in common with their same-age peers. It's important to remember that Emily, Jason, and Larry are, despite some limitations, still early adolescents with many of the same developmental needs as their peers. Remember that an IEP is only one small part of the equation in which providing quality instruction for all students is concerned. As a classroom teacher, you will come to know things about your students that even their parents and support personnel may not know. From what you know about Emily, consider how you might provide support "beyond the IEP" for her in terms of four "key developmental needs" of early adolescents outlined by the NMSA as presented in chapter 1.

- Middle school students need positive social interactions with peers and adults.
  - Although Emily does need physical assistance for certain activities, how can she rely less on her adult aide and more on her peers for such assistance?
  - How can her peers be encouraged to become familiar and comfortable with Emily's use of her communication device in informal conversations?
  - How might the classroom be arranged so that Emily can be in close physical proximity to her peers during informal work times?
- Middle school students need physical activities to develop and showcase their competencies.
  - What classroom tasks might Emily be responsible for each day (e.g., taking roll, choosing music for independent reading and journal writing time)?
  - What nonlinguistic activities might Emily engage in to support her learning? Are there technologies to assist her in these alternative forms of learning?
  - What alternatives to paper-and-pencil or word-processed examinations are there for evaluating Emily's work?
- Middle school students need opportunities for self-definition, creative expression, and a sense of competence and achievement in their learning experiences.
  - What special interests or talents could Emily share with the class? For example, since she is interested in music and has a CD burner at home, could she create a CD of early rock n' roll music for Doug's Beatnik Café project?
  - How might Emily work on projects and other performances in collaborative teams that allow her to showcase her abilities with little or no adult intervention?
  - Are all of Emily's instructional modifications age-appropriate? Do support personnel sometimes act as intermediaries when her peers try to communicate with her or ask her questions, for example?
- Middle school students need opportunities that promote meaningful participation in families, school, and the larger world.
  - Would Emily be comfortable with a family member coming in to explain to the class about her communication device and what some of her other adaptive needs might be?
  - How might Emily be encouraged to become involved in social or political action projects ranging from her neighborhood to the larger world? What technologies might assist her in doing so?

EVALUATION OF STUDENT PERFORMANCE

An IEP committee must consider how student performance on IEP objectives will be evaluated. For students with disabilities, regular education teachers will need to collect data to determine if a placement is appropriate and student learning is occurring. For example, one of Emily's IEP objectives is that she ask questions and engage in conversations. Data might be collected on the number of questions Emily asks during a class period, the length of her conversations, and the number of times she initiates interactions with her peers.

The individual responsible for data collection is generally based on the type of support provided to a student. For example, in classes in which co-teaching exists,

FIGURE 5-1   Lesson Plan and Data Collection Format

Lesson Plan for 7th Grade English	
Student: Emily Grabosky	Special Education Teacher: Ms. Collier
Weeks of: September 4–25	Regular Education Teacher: Mr. Hill

Objectives	Dates
Wheelchair navigation	
	P
	P
	P
Engage in conversation	
	V
	V
	I
	I
Transition between classes	
	V
	V
	V
	V
Writing	
	V
	V
	M
	M

Key:	I	Independent			
	V	Verbal Prompt		√	Correct
	M	Model	OR	X	Incorrect
	P	Physical Guidance		O	No Response
	NR	No Response			

Adapted from *A Guide to the Instruction of Students with Disabilities in the Least Restrictive Environment,* by S. A. Brozovic, T. A. Taber, P. A. Alberto, & M. A. Hughes, 1999, unpublished manuscript, Atlanta: Georgia State University. Used with permission.

general and special education teachers are responsible for gathering the data, depending on who is working with the student at any given time. If a paraprofessional is present, he or she may collect data. In addition, the teacher may train peers to collect data on each other's learning, making sure that all students are involved and the student with disabilities is not singled out. However, in classes in which only one adult is present, that adult is typically responsible for collecting data on student learning.

When discussion turns to data collection, you probably have many questions and concerns. First, you may be unfamiliar with how to collect data on IEP objectives. Second, you may fear that you will not have time to collect data in the midst of a busy school day. Most often, however, you will not be the sole person responsible for data collection. You will work closely with the special education teacher and other teachers on the IEP team. Ms. Collier, for example, worked with Mr. Hill to review the data collection form with him and demonstrated during class how to record progress on Emily's, Jason's, and other students' IEP objectives.

A sample lesson plan in Mr. Hill's class and the data collected on four of Emily's IEP objectives are presented in Figure 5-1.

This combination lesson plan and data form provides teachers with a quick glance at what instruction will take place for the whole class, and it highlights a student's specific IEP objectives. It could be used during collaborative planning meetings between teachers to identify lessons and modifications or individually for general planning.

BUILDING FROM STRENGTH: REMEDIATING DEFICIT THINKING

At the end of the school year, Doug Hill was pleasantly surprised to discover some remarkable things about his students with disabilities. For example, despite her learning disability, Maria brought tremendous social skills to the classroom, making sure that Emily's backpack and other belongings were put away before she went to lunch each day, and often acting as a mediator when other students got into arguments. Despite his sometimes annoying attention-seeking behaviors, Jason worked successfully with a group of boys on a final writing project, providing several illustrations for a graphic novel based on the Marvel comics X-men series. Emily learned to use a portable word processor for in-class work and, with the help of Ms. Collier, created a set of templates for recurring class assignments which streamline repetitive tasks like typing her name and the date on homework pages. She has begun participating in an Internet email exchange for teenagers with cerebral palsy and has made several online friends this way. Emily's collaborative group produced a stunning project on paper recycling for the school's science fair. She is now reconsidering her original goal of being a music historian and is thinking about a career in environmental biology.

The Standards in Practice activity in the following section is based on material from the Council for Exceptional Children. The Council for Exceptional Children (CEC) is the largest international professional organization dedicated to improving educational outcomes for individuals with exceptionalities. The CEC advocates for appropriate governmental policies, sets professional standards, provides continual professional development, advocates for newly and historically underserved individuals with exceptionalities, and helps professionals obtain conditions and resources necessary for effective professional practice.

Standards in Practice

The CEC has created a set of standards for beginning teachers. Although these standards apply to special educators, you may find these guidelines useful in understanding how special educators can support you and how you can increase your disability-specific knowledge and skill base. The CEC home page can be found at *http://www.cec.sped.org/index.html*. The Standards of Practice for beginning teachers are located at the following Web address: *http://www.cec.sped.org/ps/perf_based_stds/common_core_4-21-01.html*

Select one activity below and prepare to share what you learned with your classmates:

1. What does this set of standards implicitly advocate for all teachers? Looking at the 10 standards, how might you characterize the role of the English language arts teacher? Write a paragraph or two about the ways in which this list could serve as a set of standards for all classroom teachers.
2. Use the Council for Exceptional Children Web site as a starting point and search for additional Web sites or other resources for teaching literacy to individuals with disabilities. Make an annotated list of these resources to share with your colleagues.

REFERENCES

Brozovic, S. A., Taber, T. A., Alberto, P. A., & Hughes, M. A. (1999). *A guide to the instruction of students with disabilities in the least restrictive environment.* Unpublished manuscript, Georgia State University, Atlanta.

Individuals with Disabilities Education Act Amendments of 1997, Public Law 105-17, 105th Congress, 1st session.

Morrocco, C. C., & Solomon, M. Z. (1999). Revitalizing professional development. In M. Solomon (Ed.), *The diagnostic teacher: Constructing new approaches to professional development* (pp. 247–267). New York: Teachers College Press.

RESOURCES

Print

Bender, W. (1997). *Understanding ADHD: A practical guide for teachers and parents.* Upper Saddle River, NJ: Merrill/Prentice Hall.

Carger, C. L. (1996). *Of borders and dreams: A Mexican American experience of urban education.* New York: Teachers College Press.

Dunn, P. (1995). *Learning re-abled: The learning disability controversy and composition studies.* Portsmouth, NH: Boynton/Cook.

Falvey, M. A., Grenot-Scheyer, M., Coots, J. J., & Bishop, K. D. (1995). Services for students with disabilities: Past and present. In M. A. Falvey (Ed.), *Inclusive and heterogeneous schooling: Assessment, curriculum, and instruction* (pp. 23–39). Baltimore, MD: Paul H. Brookes.

Friend, M. (2002). *Including students with special needs: A practical guide for classroom teachers.* Needham Heights, MA: Allyn & Bacon.

Lang, G., & Berberich, C. (1995). *All children are special: Creating an inclusive classroom.* Portland, ME: Stenhouse.

Lee, C., & Jackson, R. (1992). *Faking it: A look into the mind of a creative learner.* Portsmouth, NH: Boynton/Cook.

Murphy, S. (1992). *On being L.D.: Perspectives and strategies of young adults.* New York: Teachers College Press.

Pierangelo, R., & Crane, R. (2000). *The special education yellow pages.* Upper Saddle River, NJ: Merrill/Prentice Hall.

Sailor, W. (2002). *Whole-school success and inclusive education: Building partnerships for learning, achievement, and accountability.* New York: Teachers College Press.

Smith, T., Polloway, R., Patton, J., & Dowdy, C. (2001). *Teaching students with special needs in inclusive settings* (3rd ed.). Needham Heights, MA: Allyn & Bacon.

Uphan, D., & Trumbull, V. (1997). *Making the grade: Reflections on being learning disabled.* Portsmouth, NH: Heinemann.

Electronic

Council for Exceptional Children. The CEC is the largest international professional organization dedicated to improving educational outcomes for individuals with exceptionalities, students with disabilities, and/or the gifted. This Web site includes policies, practices, and standards regarding exceptionalities.

http://www.cec.sped.org/index.html

The National Center for Learning Disabilities. The NCLD works to ensure that the nation's 15 million children, adolescents, and adults with learning disabilities have every opportunity to succeed in school, work, and life. This site includes practical suggestions for parents and teachers and promotes research and advocacy to strengthen educational rights and opportunities.

http://www.ncld.org/index.php?option=content&task=view&id=523

National Information Center for Handicapped Children and Youth. The NICHCY is the national information and referral center that provides information on disabilities and disability-related issues for families, educators, and other professionals. The special focus is children and youth (birth to age 22). The Web site includes publications, personal responses to specific questions, and links to other Web sites.

http://www.nichcy.org

Recordings for the Blind and Dyslexic. The RFB&D is an invaluable educational resource for those with print disabilities. Established in 1948, this service provides recorded textbooks and other textual materials to those who cannot effectively read standard print because of a visual, perceptual, or other physical disability.

http://www.rfbd.org

Special Education Resources on the Internet. SERI provides links to Web sites related to special education. Teachers can locate resources, teaching ideas, chat groups, and a host of helpful information about various disabilities.

http://www.seriweb.com/

Part II

Planning the Language Arts Curriculum

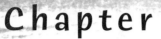

Chapter 6

Language Lenses: Integrating the Language Arts

GUIDING QUESTIONS

1. What does the phrase "integrated language arts" mean to you?
2. How are reading, writing, talking, and listening alike, yet different?
3. How can you create experiences with language that help all students to succeed?

A CASE FOR CONSIDERATION

A Constant Voyeur

Mary McCrone is a seventh- and eighth-grade teacher at Roberts school, a K–8 building in the city school system of Syracuse, New York. Although her building includes children from the primary grades, there are approximately 170 seventh and eighth graders who, along with their middle school teachers, occupy the entire top floor of the building. This "school-within-a-school" has adopted many aspects of the middle school model such as team advisement, 80-minute block scheduling, cross-curricular planning, and team teaching.

Students stay with the same English teacher for the entire 2 years of middle school, so Mary will have her seventh-grade students again next year. In fact, she teaches all 170 middle school students in the school on a 6-day schedule. On days 1, 3, and 5, she teaches the seventh-grade students, while on days 2, 4, and 6, she teaches eighth-grade students. This arrangement is possible because her students have math and science every day but take English and social studies on a rotating basis. On days when a group isn't with Mary, that group is with the social studies teacher. The following story is from Mary's seventh-grade classroom. She tells it in her own words.

At eight o'clock in the morning the school is buzzing with a familiar mixture of sounds. I hear voices in the hall, collectively. The agitated hum of adolescence. Busses pull away. The crossing guard yells to a motorist. A bell rings. Announcements begin. My eighth-grade homeroom has gone to its first period, and I await my first seventh-grade class of the day. For now, all noise stops at my door. Room 303 is silent, except for my soft classical music that floats from the corner. That music will strive all day to help me maintain an atmosphere of peace. Now it is my companion as I quickly rummage through my desk for my attendance cards. Another bell rings and students begin to prance, saunter, leap, stroll, and drag into my classroom. "Good morning," I say, momentarily looking up from an overstuffed desk drawer. They kind of ignore me, which is okay for now, because I am rabid to find these stupid attendance records. By the time I am victorious, students are seated at their tables. Some have started to copy what's on the overhead screen. Some are chatting and some are staring into space, waiting for my invitation to begin. One boy has his nose in a book, one girl is frantically finishing a note, and one girl has already fallen asleep. I scan the room. They are all so different, yet even before I look up to greet them, I know which class they are. The sound of them. Their patterns of movement. They have group characteristics as well as individual ones. I walk from behind my desk and slip through the maze of tables, couches, chairs, plants, bookshelves, lamps, and computers to the destination of my wind chimes. I run my fingers across them and, magically, all becomes quiet. (Surprise!) I welcome them again and begin to review what is on the screen (see Figure 6-1). The opening task gets their attention. Some "oooh" and "ahh." Some hide in their notebooks.

FIGURE 6-1 Opening Task

OPENING TASK

KEY POINT: One purpose for real-life writing is to record memories.

AGENDA: March 30–Day 3

1. opening procedures: task and silent reading
2. choice: Literature Circle—the poem "Oranges" (Gary Soto)

    OR Reading/Writing Workshop

3. closure: class meeting; follow-up choices

OPENING TASK: Write about a time when you had a crush on someone, or write about a character in a movie you have watched or a book you have read who has experienced a crush.

Some roll their eyes. "Mrs. McCrone, you need to stay 'out of the business'!" I assure them that I don't want to be "IN the business," that they can keep this writing private if they like. Heads bow in unison.

The music plays. I find my writer's notebook, have a seat on couch, put my feet up on the coffee table, and begin writing. Even though there are 25 kids in the room, I momentarily get lost in the memory of my first crush. We write separately, yet the sound of our sliding pens and pencils makes us one. After about 10 minutes, some kids are bursting to share, while others would die first. As I finish my writing, I scan them. I feel a sudden pang for those students who have never been "crushed out" on anyone or, worse yet, have never had anyone be infatuated with them. I realize that this topic will evoke very different memories, thoughts, and self-perceptions.

My eyes skip from face to face as we read the poem. I am a constant voyeur with my students, watching them from the back of my head or out of the corner of my eye to see their unrehearsed reactions. Today we are reading the poem, "Oranges," by Gary Soto (2000). It's about a young man on his first date with a girl. He walks to her house with a nickel and two oranges in his pocket. Together, they walk through city streets on a winter day until they come upon a drugstore. Soon, they are standing before the candy counter, and he tells her to pick out something. When she chooses a candy that costs a dime, he doesn't say a word. Instead, he places his only nickel and an orange on the counter. There is a moment of suspense as he waits to see if the shopkeeper will trade these for the dime candy the girl has chosen. The poem ends on a happy note as the girl unwraps the candy, he peels the orange he has left, and they continue on their first walk together.

We are halfway through, and I can almost see the individual "movies of the mind" that they are creating as they read. The films dance in front of them and over their heads. Some visions hold them close, like a first hug, as it dawns on them that this is exactly what this poem is about—first love. As I continue my peeking, I am jerked to a halt by one student who is (of course) not paying the slightest bit of attention. "He hasn't loved a girl yet," I think. "There is no movie for him." Another student seems almost to be crying. "OK, whom does she have a crush on now?" I take a deep breath as I realize that it's now up to me to think of a way to get all these different students to respond to this poem.

When we prepare to teach anything, we have so many decisions to make. Is this primarily a literature lesson? Do I want to focus on reading skills or appreciation? What about writing? Is the lesson going to inspire a creative piece because we are going to reach down into their gut and pull it out? Or, do we need to focus on organization, grammar, spelling, punctuation, sentence structure? OR should the previous OR be an AND? What about style, organization, and audience? Maybe we'll concentrate on their speaking skills—let's see, formal or informal? With audiovisuals or not? Probably we have to bring in Howard Gardner's eight intelligences and let them act, draw, build, blah, blah, blah. . . . Maybe we should let them use this as a journal piece? Or, do we get this to publication in their folders? Should they work in groups or alone? Should they make the choice, or should I?

One of the hardest decisions has to do with the language experiences I offer. Some of my kids are born readers, preferring to bury themselves in a good book;

others would rather die than be caught reading. Some love to write in journals or diaries, while others find them too "touchy-feely." Some of my students are natural performers and sharers. Put them in a group and they're in heaven. Others sit shyly on the sidelines, preferring to write or read silently in the privacy of their own thoughts. And, let's face it, nobody likes to study grammar. As a language arts teacher, I know you can't please all students all of the time. But how can you at least create enough variety so that all students have an equal chance to succeed?

FOR DISCUSSION

What are your own strengths and preferences where different language arts are concerned? As an early adolescent, how would you have preferred to respond to a poem about first love? If you were teaching this poem to this particular group of middle school students, what kinds of language activities might you design to allow all students a chance to succeed? What can you tell about the ways in which Mary sets her class up to allow for her students' diversity?

INTEGRATING THE LANGUAGE ARTS: TEACHING FOR DIVERSITY

For roughly a year, Mary and Susan have been working on a collaborative teaching and research project with Mary's seventh-grade students. Although they have taught seventh grade as a team for most of the past semester, Mary taught the lesson described here during a week when Susan was not there. What Mary had planned to be a one-day experience ended up taking on a life of its own and stretched out over several days.

We're sure you'll agree that Mary's class load of 170 middle school students is daunting enough, but the diversity of these students makes her life as an English teacher even more complicated. For the rest of this chapter, we will do something a little unusual. Instead of profiling the experiences of different teachers in our classroom cases, we will present an extended lesson that Mary taught over the course of several days.

In this chapter, we ask you to consider the different ways that language can be put to use in classrooms like Mary's and to accept the premise that, regardless of how similar the students in any classroom may appear on the surface—particularly at the middle school level—there is no such thing as a homogeneous classroom. Not only does each student come from a slightly different racial, cultural, and family background, each has also developed particular preferences and predispositions toward different language acts, from reading and viewing to writing, talking, listening, and language study. Your constant challenge as a middle school teacher is to provide ways for reluctant readers, writers, and language users to succeed alongside those who seem to be more eager and flexible.

We'd like to begin by introducing you to the concept of language lenses that forms the organizing framework for the following chapters in this book. After this introduction, we'll bring you back into Mary's classroom for a look at how students themselves can learn to view their literate acts through these lenses. We hope that this chapter will provide you with a set of tools to assist you in helping students like Mary's in your current and future classrooms. Let's begin, though, with some common misconceptions that seem, at least on the surface, to work against the idea of integrating the language arts.

CHALLENGING SOME MYTHS ABOUT LANGUAGE

Somewhere in your teacher education program or on the pages of professional journals you've probably encountered the phrase "integrated language arts." Although we believe this is an excellent idea (we wouldn't be writing this chapter if we didn't), we need to point out that integrating doesn't mean throwing reading and viewing, writing, talking, and listening activities together haphazardly or assuming that one language form is the same as all the others. Creating an integrated curriculum must be done mindfully, just as you would sequence a good lesson or unit plan. Although your particular students and circumstances will dictate many of your decisions, you bear the ultimate responsibility for deciding exactly how and in what form different language acts will support and enrich each other. This is a difficult process, especially when your administrators, colleagues, or former teachers may have been operating on some myths about language that seem to argue against an integrated approach to English language arts teaching. Let's consider three of the most common.

Myth: Speech Is an Inferior Form of Language

James Britton explains that talk is the sea upon which all else floats (1970). This is true in two senses. First, talk is our first language. From the moment of birth, we are immersed in talk. Our fledgling attempts at communication are in the form of sounds, which later become words and eventually the longer utterances we call oral language. We have been talking longer than we've been writing or reading, and much of our thinking, conscious or otherwise, is accomplished through talk.

Second, just as fish are the least likely creatures to be aware of water, young people in schools are not often taught how to make oral language work for them in their learning processes (see Hynds & Rubin, 1990). In addition, English language arts teachers, most of whom are not trained as speech or drama teachers, are sometimes reluctant to bring oral language into their classrooms. Even if teachers are comfortable with oral activities, there is often a misconception that writing is more formal and therefore more appropriate for the English classroom than talk.

Oral language includes pauses, repetition, slang, and other evidence of informality. It "leans upon" context in a way that writing does not. That is, you might say to a friend, "Get that!" as you gesture toward something that is blowing away. Your nonverbal behaviors assist your talk. Sometimes they're quite literally worth a thousand words, or at least a few. If you were writing about the same incident, you might say, "Get that napkin! It's blowing away!" Notice how much more formal and explicit the written sentence is. Because of the formality of most writing done in schools, the mistaken belief is that students who "write as they talk" fail to write in cogent, coherent ways. This simply isn't true. As Elbow (1985) points out, talk not only helps the development of writing skills, it's essential to that development. And talk, like writing, can be permanent (try to take back something you said when you thought no one was listening) or what Elbow calls evanescent and inconsequential, like singing in the shower or "practicing" a conversation in a private moment.

As you help your students to become writers, you need to engage them in this kind of informal "talking to learn." Brainstorming informally with teachers and peers in pairs or groups helps students to develop and create ideas for writing. Later in the process, peer- and teacher-student conferencing can help them to craft and polish their writing. Finally, reading their writing aloud to others not only builds confidence, but also lets them "hear" their words as others may perceive them. Thus, contrary to our former beliefs, oral language is not an inferior form of language, but an integral aspect of literacy learning.

Myth: Learning to Read Must Precede Learning to Write

For years, it was assumed that elementary school children had to learn to read before they could be taught to write. As a result, many children prior to the 1970s were denied the opportunity to play with written language through what's known today as "invented spelling." As we explained earlier in this book, both of our elementary school teachers focused on reading, with perhaps a little attention to writing in the form of copying words from lists or printing the alphabet. Today, however, young children in many elementary classrooms are encouraged to interweave drawing and "invented spelling" (their fledgling attempts at sounding out and spelling words) as part of their early writing processes.

Today, reading/viewing and writing are often taught in tandem, not in some kind of arbitrary sequence. This same principle holds true for middle school students. Some still need to draw before (or during) writing; others become writers before they discover the power and pleasure of reading and viewing. Although the processes are different, reading/viewing, writing, talking, and listening can enrich and enhance each other. It's your job to find a way to make all of these language activities work together.

Let's say you have an avid writer who hates to read. Encouraging that student to "read like a writer" (Smith, 1984), with an eye to a published author's techniques, may allow you to turn an enthusiasm for writing into a love of reading. Another student may shy away from reading or writing but produce elaborate drawings or cartoons. This student's attraction to drawing may be a key to thinking skills just waiting to be tapped and transformed into literate behaviors. Through talking about their art or illustrating their own writing, students may develop other literacies. In an integrated approach to English language arts, students should always be shuttling from among a variety of language experiences that support and enrich each other.

Myth: Fluency in One Language Interferes With Fluency in Another

In fact, one supports the other. Perhaps you have students in your classroom whose family members speak Spanish or Hmong or a dialect of Chinese. For years, America was seen as a "melting pot" in which teachers were supposed to turn students quickly and permanently away from their home language to help them to master English. If you have ESL learners in your classroom, it is not your responsibility to eradicate their first language, often called "L1" by linguists. In fact, research consistently bears out the fact that children who are supported in two or more languages can actually develop superior language competency to that of monolingual students. Occasionally providing reading materials in a student's home language or allowing the use of L1 in the context of informal logs or journals gives students whose first language is not English the opportunity to read and write with fluency without always having to "translate" ideas from or into an unfamiliar language. This isn't to say that ESL learners should never have to speak, write, or read in formal English. A good literacy program supports the development of both languages, fostering a kind of back-and-forth process, in which one language "teaches" the learner about the other.

We need to point out that by asking you to integrate the language arts, we are not assuming that all language processes are the same. In fact, different thinking and linguistic processes underlie each language act. Reading is not writing, is not talking, is not listening. More important, students view these processes very differently. Some love to write and share in large groups; others, like some of Mary's students, "would rather die first." Some will write, but only in the privacy of journals or notes to trusted friends. Others won't write at all, preferring to lose themselves in a good book or chat with classmates. Some students are natural performers; others shrink from group discussions or oral performance.

All of these students will be sitting side by side in your classroom. What's a middle school teacher to do? The trick is learning to create lessons with enough diversity of language choices that students of all stripes can succeed and prosper. This means helping them to view their learning through what we call "language lenses."

LANGUAGE LENSES

Perhaps a metaphor will help you to envision the integration of language arts in a more concrete way. First, consider these four aspects of English language arts teaching: (a) reading and viewing, (b) writing, (c) talking and listening, and (d) language study. Think of each aspect of language learning as a lens through which you might view all of the other possibilities available to create a lesson, a unit, or an entire curriculum. Lenses may be tinted particular colors or may have surfaces that seem to transform what the viewer sees. Think, for example, how the color and thickness of an eyeglass changes your view, or how objects look when seen through a multifaceted lens. Each language lens changes the appearance and array of the other language options in some way. The possibilities for supportive language activities change when viewed through different language lenses.

Before explaining this concept in more depth, we'd like to define a few key terms. According to the *NCTE/IRA Standards for the English Language Arts* (1996),

> we use the term text broadly to refer not only to printed texts, but also to spoken language, graphics, and technological communication. Language . . . encompasses visual communication in addition to spoken and written forms of expression. And reading refers to listening and viewing in addition to print-oriented reading. (p. 2)

By this definition, reading can encompass all manner of "texts" from printed materials to film and other media, including visual art, television, and different forms of electronic communication. Similarly, "writing" can include drawing, photographing, and producing computer graphics, among other forms of nonprint representations.

To further clarify our notion of language lenses, we'll begin with an example. Suppose you want to focus your students' attention on reading and viewing. Maybe they seem to be struggling readers, or you have been spending a lot of time on other types of language activities in the past several weeks and want to focus more particularly on reading and viewing. When seen through the lens of reading and viewing, the other language arts available to you take on new dimensions and possibilities.

Just as a lens may highlight certain aspects of an object over others or even change the shape and array of a set of objects, the lens through which we view different aspects of language learning renders new possibilities for how we use them. Notice in Figure 6-2,

FIGURE 6-2 The Lens of Reading and Viewing

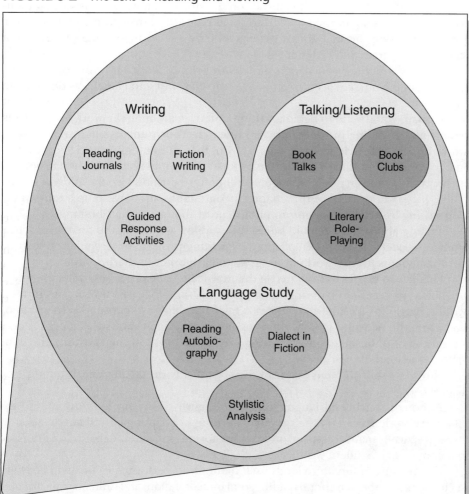

for example, the ways in which the possibilities for talking/listening, writing, and language study take shape when seen through the lens of reading and viewing.

You might bring the other three aspects of language learning into your reading and viewing instruction in several ways. If, for example, your students are reading literature, you can engage them in a variety of oral language experiences such as book clubs in which five or six students meet regularly to talk about a group-selected novel. At various points in their reading, you might ask different students to role-play events or scenes alluded to but not directly presented by an author. Or, you could invite a librarian in to model the art of book talks, in which readers create lively, dramatic renditions of favorite books, designed to entice their classmates into reading the same book.

Your students might begin writing their own fictional pieces, writing informally about their reading and viewing in logs or journals, or following guided response opportunities.

You might want to focus specifically on the study of language by asking students to write memoirs about their own histories as readers, studying the use of dialect in published fiction, or analyzing a writer's style by comparing several pieces by the same author across different genres.

Now try switching your language lens to writing. Notice how the options and possibilities for other aspects of language learning shift and change, as depicted in Figure 6-3.

Perhaps you decide to begin a writing unit by examining the work of published writers and engaging in some informal research. Your students might read several works by a favorite writer, read a biography of that author, or engage in some informal research about him or her. In the process, they could read published reviews by literary critics or even other teenagers on literature listservs (see the address for the NCTE listserv at the end of this chapter). You might want to wrap up a unit on fiction writing by helping students to publish an anthology of their best pieces.

Talking and listening could be used to support writing in the form of teacher-student or peer conferences, collaborative writing projects, and regular opportunities for students to read works-in-progress to each other in sharing circles.

Finally, you can focus students on their own language processes by helping them to analyze patterns of error and keep personal "skills-to-learn" inventories in their writing portfolios. Periodically, students might exchange papers and respond to or edit each others' work. Finally, they might compare their own stylistic preferences with those of published authors through regular analysis of their writing with your help or the help of their peers.

Now let's shift the lens again to focus explicitly on talking and listening (see Figure 6-4).

Although much oral language in the English classroom is informal and exploratory, students can try their hands at writing or scripting of oral language activities, preparing manuscripts or outlines for formal speeches, debates, or dramatic performances of student writing.

The reading of literature lends itself naturally to performance through activities such as readers' theater, choral reading, oral interpretation, and dramatic enactments. More informally, students can talk about their reading and viewing in pair-shares,

FIGURE 6-3 The Lens of Writing

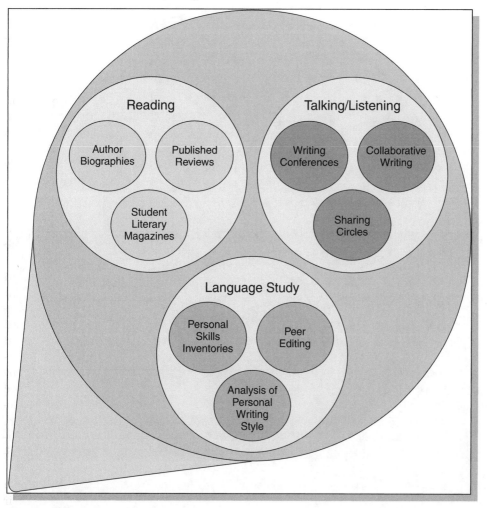

small groups, or larger forums such as literature circles, in which volunteers meet in a comfortable place to read and talk about a piece of literature while other class members are working on independent projects.

Language study takes on a new richness as students explore different facets of oral language. Perhaps they might want to conduct a bit of informal research by taping and analyzing the conversational patterns in a social gathering or a workplace setting. The study of slang and regional usage patterns helps students to understand that language is constantly changing and often bonds people together on the basis of neighborhood, family, or age group. Students might also be urged to study the dynamics of group discussion by sitting in a circle and watching a small group as they note "helpful" and "unhelpful" discussion patterns in a "fishbowl" arrangement.

FIGURE 6-4 The Lens of Talking and Listening

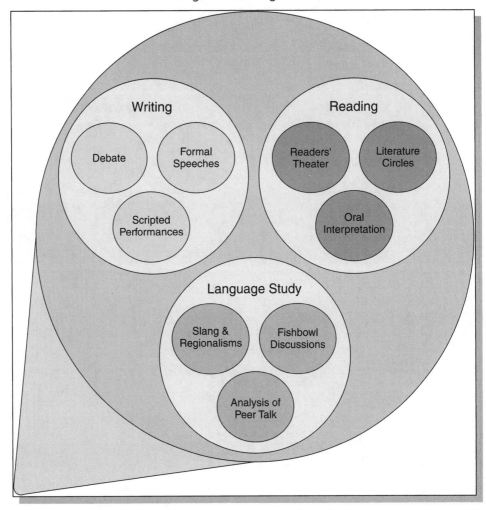

Finally, let's say that you want to focus explicitly on the study of language (see Figure 6-5). Students might begin their study of language by researching and writing about the origins of words or the history of family names.

If they have been studying different aspects of an author's style or have been reading literary or film criticism, they might be encouraged to write critical reviews of their own, paying particular attention to the language of writers or the visual "language" of film makers.

Each day might start off with a bit of oral language as students present mini-lessons in groups or individually on various aspects of style, grammar, and usage. As a regular part of writing instruction, students could work in collaborative teams of "editorial experts," in which each team is responsible for a particular skill, such as subject-verb agreement, and all drafts must be analyzed by different "expert groups"

FIGURE 6-5 The Lens of Language Study

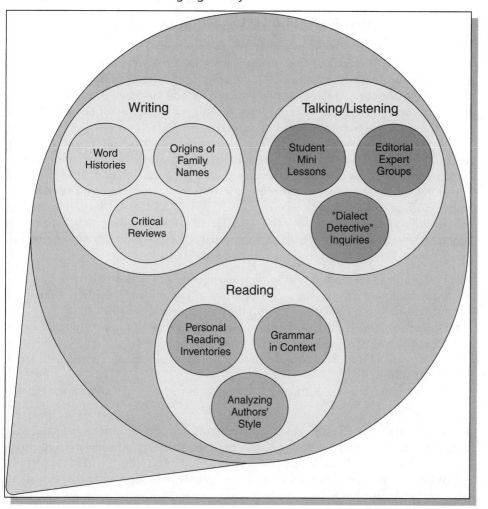

before being handed in. Small groups of students could become "dialect detectives," taping and/or studying the language of people in different occupations such as restaurant workers, computer programmers, or mechanics.

Reading and viewing can be enlivened by asking students to examine how published authors use language or by studying their own reading preferences and keeping regular personal reading inventories. Finally, principles of grammar, vocabulary, and usage can be taught by asking students to focus explicitly on structures peculiar to certain authors whose work they have been reading.

To more fully understand the concept of language lenses, try the brief classroom inquiry project in Fieldwork Journal 6-1.

At this point, the concept of language lenses may still be a bit fuzzy to you. After all, this whole business of integrating the language arts sounds good, but as you have

Fieldwork Journal 6-1

Classroom Inquiry: Viewing a Lesson Through Language Lenses

Now that you've learned a bit about language lenses, find a lesson plan that you have created or one on which you are currently working. First, decide if your overriding goal can be captured in one or more of the language lenses presented earlier in this chapter. Maybe your main goal involves reading or oral language. Don't worry if you can't narrow everything down to one lens. Teaching is messy and not easily captured in simple diagrams like those you've just seen.

Begin with the lens that seems most salient in this particular lesson; then, examine the language activities you have created. If your goal is reading and viewing, look for any examples of writing, listening, talking, or language study that you could use in the service of your goals for reading and viewing. Underline and label any instances such as these with abbreviations ("W," "T&L," "LS"). Don't forget, by the way, that different language acts can take on different guises. Drawing or artistic representation, for example, can be an important part of the writing or reading process. When you're done, ask yourself the following questions:

- Does my lesson focus too heavily on one language lens to the exclusion of others?
- Can struggling readers be given options to use informal writing, talking, or other forms of language to develop their reading and viewing skills?
- Do the writing experiences I provide include a range of opportunities from informal to more formal?
- Have I missed important opportunities for talking, listening, or language study in this lesson?
- Can students' reading and viewing experiences include their own choices as well as mine?

Remember that every lesson does not have to incorporate options from all four lenses. At the same time, identify places where you can expand your offerings to include options that help all language learners to succeed.

When you've finished with this informal analysis, write a paragraph or two about what you've learned. Or perhaps better yet, revise this lesson with an eye to expanding the language possibilities available to your students.

---

probably guessed, it can get pretty dicey in real classrooms with real students. Sometimes, though, our students can help us with this process if we share our goals and allow them to shape their own learning experiences.

In Classroom Case 6-1, Mary McCrone does just that. As the lesson begins, her students have just finished writing about their first crush and are now getting ready to choose whether they want to gather together for "literature circle," to explore Soto's poem in more depth, or to participate in what Mary calls "reading/writing workshop." Those who choose reading/writing workshop work quietly outside the circle individually, in pairs, or small groups on independent reading, writing, or inquiry projects.

Classroom Case 6-1

Decisions, Decisions

One of the hardest things about teaching, for me at least, is striking the balance between letting the students construct their own learning and knowing when to step in with my expertise and facilitate. Because this poem is about a pretty personal topic, I'm glad I am presenting it in a voluntary literature circle. Some kids might need to opt out.

I stand, walk, ring the chimes again, and without a word, open my record book. "When I call your name, please tell me if you are doing reading/writing workshop or joining us in literature circle for the poem, 'Oranges.'" I give them a trailer for the poem and promise that if they want to share what they've written, they can do so in literature circle. I start reading names. There is a bustle of movement. "Can I go to the library today to finish my research?" "Can I get online?" "How long is the poem?" "Where are you going to sit, Mrs. McCrone?" "Can I go to the bathroom?" Finally we are settled. I have 15 students lounged around me in the couch area, 9 students sprinkled around the room reading silently, working on writing pieces (oops, that one child is asleep again), and 3 students in the library. There are 60 minutes of class left. We begin.

We get to the last line of the poem—the one that talks about the young man's orange, "so bright against the grey of December that someone might have thought I was making a fire in my hands" (Soto, 2000, p. 339). There is a pause, then Danielle says, "That reminds me of my parents. I bet they fell in love like that." Tim says, "Yeah, nobody had any money in the days—not like now." Then Bruce yells from somewhere on the floor of literature circle, "I think they were black; what he did was so 'ghetto.'"

Some kids talk about a time when they liked someone. We tease each other about who is going out with whom. I relate stories of my first love (which, of course, really put them in a tizzy). We dissect why the boy told the girl to buy anything when he knew he didn't have much money. We put all the metaphors of the weather and time of day under a microscope. We create the voice of the girl, remarking how silent she is in the poem. What was she thinking and feeling anyway, and just how do we know? We take turns pretending to be the saleslady, acting out the look on her face when she saw the orange and the nickel on the counter. Then we write:

Jomell: I think the boy really liked the girl because of the way he went to her house in the winter, but then it didn't seem like winter.

Katy: I liked how the girl put makeup on to see him. She must think he was going to ask her out.

Alicia: The poem made me sad. I used to like somebody, but now he goes with someone else.

Shaliah: When people are young, love is so sweet. But I don't think it's that way when they get older. People just fight.

Brooke: I would like to be that girl, and have a boy do that for me. Now, boys don't buy you anything. Not even when you go to the movies.

Tim: That's how my mom and dad must have met, or something like that. Sometimes we drive by a little store on a corner where they used to live.

Some students draw pictures of porches with one light brilliantly on, of girls with too much rouge, of two oranges on a counter, of candy on a shelf, of a cold day, lit by a small fire. Because I am blessed with block scheduling, they are all still sitting in front of me. Waiting. Looking. OK, I guess it is my turn. So I say, "Now it's time to go deeper. Now it's time to learn more about communication and how we can connect this piece of writing with our lives."

They still sit there, rather empty. They have just written, discussed, created art, and I am asking for more. But, they are used to this from me. So one boy yells out, "Class meeting." My students know that whenever they want choices in what they do, they can call for a class meeting and I will try to negotiate their choices with them. Ben's announcement breaks the quiet moment, and we all laugh a little. So I say, "The class meeting concerning where we go next with the poem 'Oranges' is now in session." Corny, I know, but it works.

I have to think fast. I reach back into my (not so distant) memory and remember that Susan had asked me to write something she calls a "Case for Consideration" for the book she has been writing. In typical style, I haven't done it yet, though we've both been thinking about the concept of "language lenses" for some time now. I pull out the diagram she gave me a few weeks ago, and before I know it, I'm standing in front of the overhead projector.

"I'm going to let you create the possibilities for what you want to do next with the poem we just read." I decide for the moment not to get into explaining what a "language lens" is, since I'm not even sure I know what it is myself yet. Instead, I draw four circles on the transparency: "reading," "talking and listening," "writing," and "language study." I have to explain what language study is for a few minutes. Even though I teach grammar and usage some of the time and even though I try to teach kids how to be aware of the ways in which language works, I usually do it in ways that don't overwhelm them—in the context of informal conferences or mini-lessons.

After a brief explanation that language study can include everything from examining a published writer's technique to improving their own grammar and writing style, I say, "All right now, let's fill up each of these circles with things we might do in response to 'Oranges.' Anybody have any ideas?" The silence almost kills me, as usual. But suddenly Tara steps up to the plate. She crawls over several people and stands by the projector next to me. I am impressed that this 4-foot-tall blond is so gutsy all the time. "What about reading choices?" she asks. Silence. I tap my overhead marker against the side of the machine. "I want to read more poems like this. Can we find poems about falling in love or liking people?" She grabs the marker from my hand (they do that sometimes) and writes "find poems" in the reading circle. A couple other girls grab the marker and scrawl "write our own poems" in the circle I have labeled "writing."

The boys sit on the sidelines, waiting for the next choice. Interesting, as this poem is written from the male perspective. Another hand. Pat: "How about if we read other stuff and compare it to characters in movies? People are always falling in love in movies." Sounds good, I say, and I grab the marker from Theresa, writing "compare characters" in the "reading" circle, though I realize this could be a writing choice as well. Another student asks if we can figure out how the author wrote the poem and then try to write like the author. Inside I'm thinking, "Wow, someone really wants to do that? Cool!" This is the only entry so far in the "language study" circle.

"Time to move on," I say. Tara moves us to the writing circle. "What if we pretend we were these two kids and wrote letters to each other after the date?" Her best friend Maggie says, "Yeah, then we could do a reading of the letters and act it out." Selwyn looks like he is ready to say something, but he would never volunteer, so I say, "Selwyn, what's on your mind?" He smiles shyly and says, "I want to write about why people fall in love, about love in general." Everyone laughs. Selwyn is always our class philosopher. In large groups, he masquerades as a nonwriter and a reluctant reader, yet he just finished reading *Care of the Soul* (Moore, 1994) for independent reading and is working his way through *Tuesdays with Morrie* (Albom, 1997).

"That sounds good, Selwyn. Why don't you see what you can find?" I say. Tara moves on, "What about talking and listening?" Time is ticking away. Brittney, our resident actress, pipes up: "Listening sometimes happens without words. Maybe we could do a play without words about this poem. Act out all the looks and stuff. Remember the last readers' theater we did? We could put all this stuff together, all our writing, and do one of those again." Brittney is satisfied with this category, and so am I.

We go on for a bit, adding options to the different circles. Then Tara says, "Language study looks pretty empty." Some kids chuckle uneasily; then there is nothing. Silence. Heads down. So I say, "What if you picked another poem like this one and taught it to us as a language study option?" I don't think they care at this point, but heads nod. Jessica asks, "Can we use the board and overhead?" "Yes," I say. That creates interest. Kids will do almost anything if you let them use chalk or transparencies. Then I say, "How about if I work up a mini-lesson on the writing techniques that I know are used in this poem." They groan, but agree, because they know I'll do it anyway. "Are we done?" I ask, feeling guilty because I know I am rushing them.

They take my question as a cue to be dismissed. I run for my chimes. I won't see them for 2 days and I am suddenly frustrated. "Think about these choices, make up new ones if you like, and come to class on Wednesday ready to tell us what you are doing." I'm struggling to be heard over the sounds of backpack zippers and chairs and rising conversations. "I wish I was better at this closure stuff," I moan to myself. "Goodbye. Have a good lunch." Then they are gone. I am invisible to the stragglers, and I wonder what this poem will do to their hearts, souls, and minds while they are away from me. I guess a little incubation time never hurts.

It's Wednesday. I am ready for them. I have set up a table strewn with markers, newspapers, magazines, poetry books, construction paper, drawing pencils, and so on. It is the last period, unfortunately. We rotate our schedule, so now I get them after lunch and after what we call "study and support" time. The last time we met was the beginning of the school day when they were still waking up. This isn't the best time, but we'll roll with it. They enter in a fury of conversation, arguments, a little slapping, and exhaustion.

I sigh to myself but smile and greet them. It takes a little bit more to settle them down. They can't hear the music or the chimes. "Just keep smiling," I say to myself.

They eventually calm down and begin to write down the agenda (Figure 6-6). A moment of suspense for me. I know some are walking in with more than I sent them away with last time, some come with less, some with nothing. Today's agenda looks like this:

FIGURE 6-6 Agenda

> ## Agenda
>
> **KEY POINT:** All of our communication skills overlap. We are never using just one.
>
> **AGENDA:** April 1–Day 5
>
> 1. opening procedures
> 2. lens activity time
>
>   OR reading/writing workshop
>
> 3. performance plans
>
> **OPENING TASK:** Write down your choice of activity in response to "Oranges," or write about what you accomplished during reading/writing workshop last class.

I begin by explaining that each of the circles we drew last time represents what we'll call a "language lens." I am grateful for the 2 days of thinking that led me to the explanation I'm about to give. It's funny how teaching something forces you to learn it yourself. I tell them that although we began by reading the poem "Oranges," there are many other kinds of language activities we can create whenever we "put on our reading and viewing lenses." Reading and viewing can lead to everything from written responses to oral performances to studying a published author's style. I explain that just as a pair of sunglasses seems to change the color of a landscape or a kaleidoscope seems to create a new "picture" every time we move it, our reading and viewing lens brings into focus a variety of options for other language activities.

"Today," I explain, "we're going to look at the reading of 'Oranges' through all four language lenses. As you think about what you'd like to do next with the poem, think about each of the lenses. Try on different language lenses and see which seem to suit you best. Are you more of a writer than a reader or vice versa? Do you like to talk and perform? Look through your favorite lens and create an option for yourself. Or better yet, try a lens you don't usually use. Take risks. Try something different for a change. You can work with a partner or a group if you'd like."

After a few minutes of settling in, they write. I hop from student to student and put in my two cents about their choice. I coax students without a choice. I listen to why students who were not technically part of the last literature circle want to join us in the activities. This all takes about 20 minutes. We are ready to begin. Now, you have to have some tolerance for chaos, noise, and constant movement to proceed. It is the end of the day after all, and I am questioning my own tolerance levels. I am kind of wishing that

I was just passing out dittos. A period-long, silent test would be nice, I think. But, I shake off those fantasies and begin to arrange the kids.

We do what I call a "four corners." I put up signs around the room: Reading and viewing lens, Writing lens, Talking/listening lens, and Language study lens. (I'm so clever!) I ask them to move to the category of the project they chose. All but three students get up and move. The three left behind are opting out for other work, and I ask them to find a space. Then I survey the results. They're always interesting. Let's see, we have eight in the reading and viewing, four in the writing, six in talking/listening, and zero in the language study corners. Guess I'm the only one for that category.

I give them time to discuss their ideas and ask them to find a space in the room where they can work together. Some will choose to do the activity with a classmate or two; some will work alone. Ten minutes later, we are settled. I announce that they have the rest of the period to work. One group asks to work in the library so that they can do a literature search. One group wants to use the Internet. Their quest has taken them to searching song lyrics to compare to the poem. One student has crawled under my classroom stage with a piece of drawing paper and a flashlight. Forget the classical music. A student puts a tape of "15A" in the boom box and we let each song fuel our work. When the period is over, the room is a mess, I am exhausted, and they are cranky. Some are done, and others will continue for homework. "Presentations on Friday!" I announce.

Two days later, I simply write PRESENTATION DAY on the overhead. They come in, laden with props. Some have sob stories about why they didn't finish. I give them 10 minutes to rehearse, get their materials together, and generally get organized. Then I call them, table by table, to the couch area. Some sit on the soft furniture, some pull up chairs, some sit on the floor. I ask who wants to go first. Many hands are raised. Good sign. I sit back and enjoy the show which includes:

- A collage of pictures of couples of all ages, with a poem about love through the years.
- Two letters written by the characters in the poem.
- Clips from three movies about young love, with commentary on how the emotions were like the ones in the poem.
- A humorous poem about how embarrassing it can be to like someone.
- A copy of a love letter that was written by a student's parents, all written in song titles from the '60s. Pat talks about how his parents fell in love.
- A readers' theater of Jessica and Alicia's love poems, mixed with other poems they have found.
- A poster about safe sex (don't ask).
- An essay called When Love Dies, in which a student writes about his parents' divorce.
- One group, not ready, saved for next time.

Because time is running out, I agree to do my mini-lesson next time. By the end of class, I am amazed at the dimensions of this one work of literature. I am amazed at how much these young people understand about the intricacies of love, and I am shocked that they, for the most part, worked so hard and learned so much.

As you can see by Mary's story, nothing ever works seamlessly, especially when you have to make so many spur-of-the-moment decisions. Since she barely understood the concept of "language lenses" herself, she didn't even try to teach it to her students. Her instinct told her that this abstract concept was something she and her students could do without for the moment.

By drawing circles on a transparency and asking students to think about the different language possibilities available to them, she was making them conscious of their options for integrating reading, writing, talking, listening, and language study in a concrete and nonthreatening way. After some time to think, she introduced the idea of language lenses and helped her students to look through those lenses in creating their own language activities. The next phase happened 2 days later.

We want to stress the fact that Mary is a veteran teacher with many years of trial-and-error under her belt. These lessons may seem to have been planned on the spot, but they aren't quite that spontaneous. Mary has honed her instincts about what works with her students and has carefully paved the way for such "teachable moments" to unfold. Choice—or rather negotiating options—is a regular part of her curriculum. Most of her lessons "integrate" the language arts, so her students are already comfortable with the idea that writing can spring from reading and viewing or that oral performance can be a regular part of language study.

You may decide that a concept as complicated as language lenses can be a part of your teacher toolkit, but that right now, it's too difficult for your students to grasp. That's fine. You know your own comfort zone. If the "lenses" concept works for your students, as it did for Mary's, that's great. If it doesn't, put it in the back of your mind and be willing to pull it out later when you've strengthened your confidence and sharpened your teaching practices. As you read the remaining chapters of this book, we'll return often to the concept of language lenses, so you'll become better acquainted with the idea as time goes by.

MAKING A FIRE IN OUR HANDS: ONE FINAL THOUGHT

After reflecting for some time on the myriad ways her students combine reading and viewing, writing, talking, listening, and language study, Mary was still left with a nagging feeling that teaching English language arts involves far more than just language. Her reflections are important for all of us to ponder. Again, we present Mary's own words:

> *Obviously, I found the concept of lenses to be a great help. Although we were focusing on reading at first, we quickly ran the gamut of other possibilities from writing to talk and listening, extended reading, and even (with a little help from me) language study. The idea of language lenses helps me to put my choices for language learning in focus and helps to ensure that I am teaching evenly, giving equal air time to all facets of what I teach.*
>
> *But I think something less tangible lurks beneath the language activities in my classroom; just like a lens, that "something" colors everything students do. I think that Bruce and Danielle and Tim and Phillip bring it with them to class every day. It has to do with their own experiences, past and present, their personality and their family*

life, their neighborhoods and their friendships. It has to do with what they did or didn't have for breakfast that morning, who hugged or didn't hug them as they walked out the door. It's small enough to fit in a pocket or a pencil case next to the white-out.

However, some kids wear it on their sleeve. At the end of the year, as I leave the building, final exams bursting from my book bag, I stop, lean against the fence, and watch the girls' softball game. "Hi, Mrs. McCrone," Danielle yells to me as she waits to bat. I watch them. I think of that certain "something" that lies beneath all of the language activities I provide. The something that students bring with them every day. And I continue my walk home. I realize as I do so that every day we teach, it is a combination of their needs and our choices. If we work together, some days we'll get it right. And, just like the boy and girl in the poem, we can make "fire in our hands."

Standards in Practice

NCTE/IRA Standards

Locate a copy of the *NCTE/IRA Standards for the English Language Arts* (1996). For an explanation of the standards, as well as a table of contents for the volume, an annotated listing of each standard, and chapter excerpts, consult the NCTE Web site at this address: *http://www.ncte.org/standards.*

To begin, look over the list on page 3 of the *Standards for the English Language Arts.* At first glance, what do the NCTE and IRA seem to believe about integrating the language arts? What evidence do you find that the standards support (or fail to support) an integrated approach?

Next, we'd like you to practice looking at the standards through the four language lenses presented in this chapter. For this particular exercise, focus only on the first standard, but it would be useful to think about all 12 standards in this way.

> **Standard One states**: Students read a wide range of print and non-print texts to build an understanding of texts, of themselves, and of the cultures of the United States and the world; to acquire new information; to respond to the needs and demands of society and the workplace; and for personal fulfillment. Among these texts are fiction and nonfiction, classic and contemporary works.

Obviously this standard asks teachers to look at instruction through the lens of reading and viewing. Its intent appears focused on providing a variety of reading and viewing genres, as well as spanning a broad spectrum of historical and cultural perspectives.

- Begin by reading the "Standards in Detail" section on pages 27–46.
- Next, brainstorm a list of different kinds of reading materials and activities suggested by this first standard. For example, the section titled "Standards in Detail" suggests reading Katherine Patterson's *Lyddie,* a story about textile workers in 19th-century New England.
- Finally, refer back to Figure 6-2 ("The Lens of Reading and Viewing"). Draw a similar diagram and fill in each of the smaller circles with possibilities for integrating writing, talking/listening, and language study with the kinds of reading experiences

suggested by this standard. For example, in reading Patterson's novel, students might create a 19th-century newspaper (for the "writing" lens), perform a readers' theater of women's letters from the period (for the "talking/listening" lens), and so on. If possible, share your diagram with others when you're done. If you're working with a larger group, you might want to divide up all 12 standards among your group members and follow a similar process with each one.

REFERENCES

Albom, M. (1997). *Tuesdays with Morrie: An old man, a young man and life's greatest lesson.* New York: Doubleday.

Britton, J. (1970). *Language and learning.* Harmondsworth, England: Pelican Books.

Elbow, P. (1985). The shifting relationships between speech and writing. *College Composition and Communication, 36*(3), 283–303.

Hynds, S., & Rubin, D. L. (1990). *Perspectives on talk and learning.* Urbana, IL: NCTE.

Moore, T. (1994). *Care of the soul: A guide for cultivating depth and sacredness in everyday life.* New York: Harper Perennial.

Smith, F. (1984). Reading like a writer. In J. Jensen (Ed.), *Composing and comprehending* (pp. 47–56). Urbana, IL: NCTE.

Soto, G. (2000). Oranges. In *The language of literature, grade nine* (p. 339). Evanston, IL: McDougal, Littell.

Standards for the English language arts. (1996). Urbana, IL: National Council of Teachers of English/International Reading Association.

RESOURCES

Print

Resources Relevant to the NCTE/IRA Standards

The standards themselves are detailed in the publication *Standards for the English Language Arts.* (1996). Urbana, IL: National Council of Teachers of English/International Reading Association. Vignettes describing how the standards play themselves out in a variety of middle school settings are available from the Standards in Practice series of NCTE and IRA: Wilhelm, J. (1996). *Standards in Practice 6–8.* Urbana, IL: NCTE.

Two publications of interest to middle school teachers from the NCTE/IRA Standards Consensus Series are *Motivating Writing in Middle School* (NCTE, 1996) and *Teaching Literature in Middle School: Fiction* (NCTE, 1996).

Assessment issues related to the NCTE/IRA standards are presented in International Reading Association and National Council of Teachers of English Joint Task Force on Assessment. (1994). *Standards for the Assessment of Reading and Writing.* Newark, DE: International Reading Association.

Resources on Integrated Language Arts Relevant to Middle School Teachers

Anders, P. L., & Pritchard, T. G. (1993). Integrated language curriculum and instruction for the middle grades. *Elementary School Journal, 93*(5), 611–624.

Beane, J. A. (1993). Problems and possibilities for an integrative curriculum. *Middle School Journal, 25*(1), 18–23.

Beane, J. A. (1997). *Curriculum integration: Designing the core of democratic education.* New York: Teachers College Press.

Flurkey, A. D., & Meyer, R. J. (Eds.). (1994). *Under the whole language umbrella: Many cultures, many voices.* Urbana, IL: NCTE and Whole Language Umbrella.

Gaveleck, J. R., Raphael, T. E., Biondo, S. M., & Wang, D. (2000). Integrated literacy instruction. In M. L. Kamil, P. B. Mosenthal, P. D. Pearson, & R. Barr (Eds.), *Handbook of reading research: Volume III* (pp. 587–607). Mahwah, NJ: Lawrence Erlbaum Associates.

Pearson, P. D. (1994). Integrated language arts: Sources of controversy and seeds of consensus. In L. M. Morrow, J. K. Smith, & L. C. Wilkinson (Eds.), *Integrated language arts: Controversy to consensus* (pp. 11–31). Needham Heights, MA: Allyn & Bacon.

Powell, R., & Skoog, G. (1995). Students' perspectives on integrative curricula: The case of Brown Barge Middle School. *Research in Middle Level Education Quarterly, 19*(1), 85–115.

Smagorinsky, P. (1991). *Multiple intelligences in the English class.* Urbana, IL: NCTE.

Tchudi, S. (Ed.). (1993). *The astonishing curriculum: Integrating science and humanities through language.* Urbana, IL: NCTE.

Wilhelm, J. (1996). *You gotta be the book.* New York: Teachers College Press.

Wixson, K., Peters, C. W., & Potter, S. A. (1996). The case for integrated standards in English language arts. *Language Arts, 73*(1), 20–29.

Electronic

NCTE/IRA standards.

The standards can be accessed at the following Web site:

http://www.ncte.org/standards

7

Language Study in the Middle Grades

GUIDING QUESTIONS

1. What does language study include?
2. How can you help students understand how language varies and changes in different regions, across different cultural groups, and across time periods?
3. How does a middle school teacher foster and monitor language development?

A CASE FOR CONSIDERATION

"I Never Thought About Words Before"

Mr. Williams had his back turned to the empty class as he quickly attempted to erase from the blackboard all traces of the words that his third-period class had been discussing. Suddenly, Anna came tumbling into his seventh-grade classroom with her best friend Sarah. She could barely contain her enthusiasm or the scraps of paper that seemed to be exploding out of her writer's notebook.

"Mr. W., you won't believe what I found! You won't believe it! Did you know that there are really word detectives? Did you know that there are people who go around listening? That's their job. I'm not kidding. Someone has the job to go out and just listen. And did you know," she interrupted herself in her excitement, "you won't believe what Aunt Mary said about dictionaries. She knows, and she heard on the radio, that a dictionary has a life span. And if it is too old it is dead, because the words may be too old."

Mr. Williams tried to quiet her. "Anna, can you wait until the bell rings? I'd like you to tell everybody what you found in your detective work." Like Anna, Mr. Williams could barely contain his pleasure in learning that a student was really excited about language. In his 10 years of teaching seventh-grade language arts, he had struggled to find ways to make language study not only fun but, more important, to make it meaningful for his students. This project seemed to interest at least one student. He hoped there would be more in the days to come.

A week before, he had filled the room with old books of Victorian and Elizabethan poetry, 19th-century novels, even a few textbooks that were written around the turn of the century. Some he had gotten from the school librarian who brought them to his room on a cart, and some he had been collecting over the years from thrift shops, used bookstores, and garage sales. He told his students up front that some of the words in these books would seem foreign to them. They might have dropped out of current usage altogether. Others might have changed meaning since they were used in an earlier time period—words like "gay" or "radical" or "awesome."

His students discussed current slang terms that probably had different meanings in earlier times. For example, Morgan suggested that the word "ridiculous" (pronounced REEEEdiculous) could be used to describe something that a person really loved or really hated. Rolf explained, "If my dad asked me how I liked a concert, I'd say, 'REEEEdiculous!' If it was good or bad depended on how I said the word."

After a bit of fun discussing popular slang terms, Mr. Williams asked his students to read as many pieces as they could and keep a word notebook, listing all of the words or phrases they found interesting or those that had changed meaning since the time they were written. "For the next few weeks, you're going to become 'word detectives,'" Mr. Williams challenged.

After creating their word lists, he explained, students would choose three words and do some detective work, finding out not only the multiple meanings of the words, but the way they have changed over time. As a start, they could use one of the dictionaries on his bookshelves, but they should try to move beyond these sources, eventually searching Web sites or even going to the public library to consult the *Oxford English Dictionary*. As a culminating activity, students would create visuals displaying their three words, their current definitions, and a brief explanation of their different meanings over time. On a selected day, Mr. Williams planned to have a poster session in which students could walk around the room, visiting each other's word detective displays.

Anna's class had been working on the project for the past 5 days. As other students began filing into their seats, there was the usual commotion as they dropped their notebooks and backpacks on the tables and began to settle in. The room was still abuzz, but Anna's voice could be heard above the others as she began opening her notebook, "You know, I never thought about words before!"

FOR DISCUSSION

What might you assume about Mr. Williams's goals for the word detective's notebook? What might Mr. Williams have students do next with their detective work? What are some other means by which a middle school teacher might help students to "think about words"?

WHAT COUNTS AS LANGUAGE STUDY

In thinking about middle school teaching, preservice teachers often have a long list of questions and concerns about language study:

- "I don't know all of the rules. I don't remember what an adverbial clause is. How can I ever teach grammar?"
- "Is there a handbook I can buy?"
- "Don't middle school students hate language arts because of all of the grammar stuff?"

Many of us had (and still have) similar worries about language study. We tend to equate this term with grammar and feel ill prepared to teach the tiny particulars about parts of speech and punctuation that we once knew but have long since forgotten. Worrisome questions flood our minds: What's a dangling participle, a gerund, a predicate nominative? What's the difference between a predicate and a verb? These questions plague us every time we consider teaching about language. We probably learned to read, write, and speak with some semblance of grace, or we wouldn't be teaching English language arts.

But is that enough? Do we need to know all the parts of speech to be able to write? What technical terms do we need to teach our students so they'll become competent writers, readers, and language users? Do you need to know all the parts of a sewing machine to make a dress? Of course not! But still, those worries nag us. We're afraid we'll be at a party with a bunch of English teachers and won't know the difference between a dangling modifier and a dangling participle.

Let's begin by recognizing that the study of formal language and grammar is only one small (however important) part of the study of language. What "counts" as language study, you might ask? The answer to that question is "many things." First, it's an understanding of the social and political aspects of language use—the multiple language communities within which we and our students live, the rules of communicative competence within those different communities, and the political implications of being a language "outsider." Next, it involves the history of language.

Much as Mr. Williams' students were discovering in the opening Case for Consideration, our students should see language as fluid, flexible, and changing. Language study also includes discovering how words function across the curriculum—discovering how scientists, mathematicians, and historians write and speak. We need to help our students as they write reports for earth science or unpack the language of story problems in mathematics.

Your classroom should be a place where students openly discuss issues of language diversity, including the study of dialect issues and what counts as "correctness" in different social contexts. They need to value the language of home and neighborhood at the same time as they master the conventions needed to succeed in a wider sphere. Of course, the study of grammar and usage should be integrated into every aspect of your English language arts curriculum, from reading and viewing to writing, oral language, and listening.

We know from research and from our own common sense as teachers that teaching isolated rules from grammar textbooks or making copious editorial marks on student papers rarely results in better or more "correct" language. Issues of grammar and usage should emerge naturally at the point of use, when students are most ready to learn about them and incorporate them into their daily language activities. Finally, and most important, your middle school students will embrace language study most willingly if you set aside some time in your teaching for language play. Language games and activities go a long way in teaching students how to exploit the fun as well as the power of language in their daily lives.

Language study is much more than imparting rules of correctness. English is a living language. Words change. Rules change. Yes, language study is the study of correctness, but it is the study of correctness in context. You might say it is the study of appropriateness. It's also the study of language play. It is the study of the history of language and the study of language in use. It encompasses the critical study of the language of power and the social and political consequences of language use. In other words, language study is the study of words and how they circulate, live, change, and die. In this chapter we want to shift the lens of language study from the texts (whether they be oral or written) to learners and contexts.

Throughout this chapter, think about the lens of reading and viewing, the lens of writing, and the lens of oral language. Consider how language study can be contextualized and integrated into meaningful literacy lessons. We begin by reflecting on what is unique about approaching the study of language with early adolescents, based on some of the NMSA key developmental needs of young adolescents presented in earlier chapters. Think about these questions as you consider how you might incorporate language study into your own classroom.

DISCOURSE COMMUNITIES AND COMMUNICATIVE COMPETENCE

Sociolinguist James Paul Gee (1990) argues that to appreciate language in its social context, we need to focus not on language but rather on what he calls "Discourses." He writes, "A Discourse is a sort of 'identity kit,' which comes complete with the appropriate costume, and instructions of how to act, talk, and often write, so as to take on a particular social role that others will recognize" (p. 142). He notes that another way to think about discourses is to approach them as "clubs with (tacit) rules about who is a member and who is not and (tacit) rules about how members ought to behave (if they want to continue being accepted as members)" (p. 143).

> An integrated approach to language study focuses on the contexts and communicative competence demanded by them. The goal of language study is to help students move adeptly among multiple communities of readers, writers, speakers, viewers, and listeners.

Students learn how to interact in multiple discourse communities. Different groups have different ways of talking, thinking, acting, and even dressing. A child who grows up in a "soccer family," for example, learns the rules of the game in terms far beyond the playing field. She learns how to talk, think, act, and dress "soccer," and she learns what linguists call "code switching" when she prepares for other memberships. She knows how to talk, think, act, and dress "soccer" and can easily shift to talk, think, act, and dress "church choir." Because social practices valued in one discourse community may not be valued in another, students learn to switch codes across different contexts. A student who is a member of advanced choir is expected to dress, talk, and even walk across the stage in a particular manner. That same student may need to change "costumes" and "scripts" when she or he prepares for a poetry slam or performs in a basement band.

Most middle school students know how to talk, think, act, and dress "school"— or at least their version of school. It is easy to identify those students who, for any number of reasons, do not. Our job as literacy teachers is to help students move effectively into different contexts. In much the same way, students in different disciplines need to learn the rules of multiple communities, discovering how scientists talk about experiments or how artists critique a painting, for instance. Learning to participate in each of these communities requires that students learn certain social practices valued in these different communities. In looking through the lens of language study, you might ask yourself, "What are the multiple contexts or 'discourse communities' in which members of my middle school classroom and their families live and work?"

> In looking through the lens of language study your might ask. "What do students need to do and know to participate fully in a particular context?"

Anthropologist Dell Hymes (1972) defines communicative competence as "what it is a member of society knows in knowing how to participate" (p. 66). Hymes (1996) notes that the term "competence" "should not be a synonym for ideal grammatical knowledge" (p. 58) but should be understood in terms of actual communities and the consequences for persons in that community. Our judgments of middle school students' competence with language in use must be expanded beyond issues of grammar.

Fieldwork Journal 7-1

Discourse Detectives

For this activity, explore a couple of your own Discourse communities. First, select two settings: (1) an informal setting where you are with a group of close friends or family, and (2) one in which you are in a formal learning setting such as a university classroom or a professional organization. If possible, bring in a tape recorder and tape the talk in each setting. If not, make some quick notes about the language you used in each setting. Try to capture both verbal and nonverbal practices in which each community engages. Now for the detective work: What must a member of this group know to be able to participate?

If you were able to tape record the talk, listen to the first tape and try to make explicit at least three "rules" that someone must follow to indicate that he or she is a fully functioning member of this community. Your rules can include verbal and nonverbal actions. For example, you might list such things as

- "Address members by humorous nicknames."
- "Raise your hand and wait to be called on before speaking."
- "End your conversational turn taking by calling on the next speaker by name."

Now do the same thing with the second tape. When you're finished, try to create at least three language rules that are exactly the same for both contexts. Record these rules in a Venn diagram like the one in Figure 7-1.

Now listen to the tape or consult your notes again and think about any language infractions that mark someone as an outsider to this discourse community. What

FIGURE 7-1 Language Rules in Context

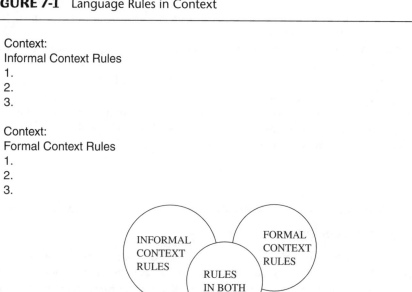

Context:
Informal Context Rules
1.
2.
3.

Context:
Formal Context Rules
1.
2.
3.

behaviors might mark someone as less than a fully functioning member of this group? If someone were to break the rules, what might the members do to "school" this individual in more appropriate ways with words? Write these infractions in the area surrounding each side of the Venn diagram.

Keep in mind what you learned from this exercise as you think through the ways in which you can create a language-rich classroom for your students. Ask yourself, "What are the multiple contexts or discourse communities in which members of my middle school classroom and their families live and work? What do students need to do/know to be able to participate in a particular context, and how can I help them in my classroom to do this?"

Both oral and written communicative competence should include attention to intentions and expectations within a context. Begin by examining your own discourse communities in Fieldwork Journal 7-1.

HELPING STUDENTS TO UNDERSTAND THEIR DISCOURSE COMMUNITIES

Heath (1983) notes that children learn language through the process of socialization in their neighborhoods, communities, and schools. The idea that there is one "correct" English denies our own practices as we talk on the telephone to our best friends, our professors, our families, or our doctors. In both fostering and monitoring language study in your middle school classroom, you might begin by asking your students to help you to examine the demands and expectations of particular contexts in which they live, learn, and play.

A simple way to help students to understand the role of language as a social practice is to ask them to list the different language groups to which they belong. This is also a good way to get to know your students. In Classroom Case 7-1, Ms. Harmatuk asks her students to explore their multiple discourse communities. When Ms. Harmatuk asked her students to do this at the beginning of their sixth-grade year, she wasn't surprised to find that many of her students were fluent speakers of many languages. She explains her teaching approach in her own words.

Classroom Case 7-1

"I Speak French Cooking."

I begin with an official language; that's easy. And they are usually amazed at the many languages spoken by their peers. And then I want to lead them to a more complex understanding of the ways we talk. I start with myself. I brainstorm with them to deepen their understanding of language in use. I tease them with the ways in which I can talk like an English teacher, but that is not the only way I know how to talk. I talk differently to my family and friends, to telemarketers, and to Dr. Gonzalez, the principal.

I like to bring in a phone and talk into it and ask students to tell me whom they think I am talking to and what evidence they have to support their views. They can quickly see that it is word choice, body language (even over the phone), tone, and inflections that give clues as to whom I am talking to and what my relationship is with that person. For example, I pretend to talk to my grandbaby. Then we talk about the "rules" for motherese. Students will often ask to try out a particular way of talking to challenge their classmates. They are actually quite savvy and quite aware of particular sets of language rules.

Next, on the blackboard, I begin with my own personal list of memberships in language groups. I write something like: school English, Spanish, French cooking, the language of bridge playing. When I wrote "French cooking," one of my students interrupted, "Ms. Harmatuk, I didn't know you spoke French."

"Well, I don't speak French," I replied, "I speak French cooking. I understand and use the language of French cookbooks." I then gave her some examples: "Chiffonnade means vegetables cut into ribbons or shreds, aromates means herbs and spices, and à la Broche means to cook on a skewer over a flame. I need to know how to use these words so I can cook and follow recipes." I told her that she probably spoke a little French cooking too. I asked, "Do you know what à la mode means?"

She said, "Yeah, it means you want ice cream on top."

"See, you do speak French cooking."

This is how I start the class thinking about the different rules we use when we talk or write. I begin where they are experts. I ask them to list their memberships and list three words they must know to be a member. Because I start by talking about my grandbaby and my hobbies, I think they can see and hear that it isn't only official clubs that influence the ways people talk. This too eases any sense that I think talking like an English teacher is the only right way to talk.

For Discussion

Language study in the middle school classroom should consist of fostering students' understanding of language purposefully, critically, and creatively. If Ms. Harmatuk's teaching goals include (1) engaging students in meaningful experiences that extend their abilities to use language both creatively and as shaped by accepted conventions, and (2) creating opportunities for students to analyze and create messages shaped by social, cultural, intellectual, and political contexts, how might she extend this lesson further? Consider the next steps that you might take to move students further into understanding how membership in groups and contexts influence language rules and conventions.

Many middle school teachers underestimate their students' abilities to interpret and analyze the social and political consequences of language use. Some teachers fear that a focus on more political aspects of language use will embarrass or offend students, so they focus on things like French cooking. That is not to say that Ms. Harmatuk didn't create and orchestrate a powerful learning opportunity. It is simply to suggest that many teachers, fearful of offending, don't go quite far enough.

In Classroom Case 7-2, Vickie, a 23-year-old White student teacher, struggles with teaching about racist language in a school that is 91% African American.

Classroom Case 7-2

The "N" Word: Silence Isn't the Answer

During her student teaching semester, Vickie prepared to teach the novel *Words by Heart* by Ouida Sebestyen (1997) to her seventh-grade students. While her host teacher suggested that Vickie should skip over the "N" word, Vickie felt addressing the issue was important. She wanted to sponsor a serious discussion, even though her students might prefer not to talk about it. Vickie recalled,

> *As I was preparing to create a lesson on Ch. 7, I noticed right away that the n-word was used on the first page of the chapter. Instead of ignoring or just telling the students that we weren't going to use it, I felt that it was important to address it in some way. This is also due to the fact that the students use the word frequently in everyday conversation. I felt that it was important for them to know the background and historical meaning of the word and to be more thoughtful in the words they choose to speak.*
>
> *So, I started to look online to see if I could find an article that would work well for engaging in this type of discussion. I showed the article and presented this idea to my host teacher, Ms. Randolf. She said that in the past, she had not spent much time on the word. From what I understand, she mostly told them that they would not be using the word in the class when they came across it in the novel or at any other time.*

Though she was reluctant to disregard her host teacher's advice, and although she too was afraid of possible repercussions, Vickie felt uncomfortable skirting the obvious racial implications of this word. She reasoned,

> *You don't want your students to feel left out or singled out. Yes it's risky but if you start out so concerned that you are going to offend somebody then you won't do critical literacy at all. You don't want to always stay at the safe side. At the same time, I wanted to be very careful that they didn't see me as a white woman telling them they can't say the N word.*

After seeking the advice of her university supervisor, Vickie went to the Social Justice Cadre (a group of teachers within her school) for advice. She asked whether an African American teacher might participate in the discussion to represent multiple perspectives. This was a first step, but it wasn't always possible, and didn't completely solve her dilemma of being a White teacher sponsoring a discussion about the touchy subject of race in a primarily African American classroom. Vickie remarked,

> *Twice, an African-American member of the Social Justice Cadre came in, but the problem was that they didn't have free periods when I taught. But I was able to draw on what some of the African-American teachers had said. That helped me too.*
>
> *Some of the students brought up the fact that their families use the word, their mothers have called them that word, and that it is in their vocabularies. I worried about telling them that what their mothers tell them is not right. So how much of it is my place? Should I be doing this?*

For Discussion

Examine the questions that Vickie poses for herself: "So how much of it is my place? Should I be doing this?" Look back through this brief case and think about what you would do in Vickie's situation. What are the risks of sponsoring overt discussions of racism and racist language when you are a White teacher in a primarily African American setting? Teachers like Vickie cannot leave their White privilege at the door in such situations. As she wonders, how do you confront issues of racist language without appearing to tell students that "what their mothers tell them is not right"?

We believe that, no matter what your race or ethnic background, there is a great deal of value in exploring and confronting uncomfortable issues such as racist language in your classroom. You don't have to disparage someone's family in discussing why, for instance, members of a group may use racial or other epithets as a satiric way of building group solidarity or critiquing the social order. The difference is one of power: When people in power use language to attack those with less power, it becomes hate speech. When the "N" word is used in literature or other writings for the purpose of exposing and critiquing racism, as opposed to damaging or defaming African American people, it is not necessarily "racist language." At the same time, many may still be offended by such language, no matter who says it, why, or in what context.

As teachers, we need to lay some ground rules about racist, sexist, homophobic, or other kinds of potentially offensive language. You can tell your students that because such language has been used in damaging and hurtful ways, you will not tolerate name calling or other hate speech in your classroom. You may also, as Vickie's teacher did, decide to skip over words in a literature text or sponsor another book that does not contain such words, for fear that your middle school students may be too young to distance themselves from the hurt and anger such words evoke, regardless of an author's intentions. Consider two important points as you make your decisions about what you will address and what you will "skip over." First, teachers often underestimate middle school students' abilities to examine and critique language. Second, silence sends powerful messages too.

Most important, the power of words to hurt and exclude cannot be underestimated, even when the author's intentions seem noble. As you can see, there is no "right answer" to Vickie's dilemma. There are also no racial or ethnic boundaries to hate speech. As a Jewish woman, Vickie might have talked about moments in her own life when words had the power to wound and exclude. Her students could have talked about name calling and other forms of hate speech in their neighborhoods, the shopping mall, or the school cafeteria. Middle school students such as Vickie's might do a bit of informal research, not only about racist language, but about hate in all of its varieties, exploring the use of stereotyping and hate speech from the time of Nazi Germany to more recent examples from Christian Identity Groups, members of the Aryan Nation, and gangsta rappers, to name a few.

Such an exploration is not easy, but if we don't begin to address such topics with our students, who will? As a start, you might want to look at a report and curriculum guide, sponsored by the The New Jersey Commission on Holocaust Education, titled "The Hitler Legacy: A Dilemma of Hate Speech and Hate Crime in a Post-Holocaust World" (accessed on February 6, 2006, from *http://www.state.nj.us/njded/holocaust/ downloads/curriculum/hate_doc_complete.pdf*). Many of the texts and other materials suggested in this curriculum guide would be too sensitive for young adolescents, so you should exercise careful judgment and discuss your ideas with colleagues and mentors in your planning process. But remember that the peaceable classroom is not always the "safe" classroom. Sometimes we must sponsor uncomfortable discussions about hateful and destructive uses of language so that our students of color or members of other subordinated groups do not have to.

Just as Anna exclaimed in the opening case—"I never thought about words before!",—middle school students need opportunities to think about words and structures of the language they use in written and oral texts. They need to make intentional decisions and employ strategies to engage, persuade, and interact with others. They also need chances to critically examine texts and the social contexts in which they were produced. Equally important, they need to understand the social nature of texts, examining the rules in terms of who uses them and for what purposes. At the same time, middle school students need opportunities to play with language, to engage creatively with the rhythms, repetitions, cadences, humor, and beauty in language.

One question you may want to revisit as you progress through this chapter is "How does language study support reading, viewing, oral language, and writing?" By itself, language study can be interesting, motivating, and engaging. Most students will probably enjoy researching how and for what purposes words come into being. For example, they might study the arrival of the computer and how it transformed our language—that is, how "computerese" has slipped into our everyday language. Similarly, dialect journals, designed to capture language in use in multiple contexts, may be a fun way for middle school students to keep track of how context shapes meaning.

Middle school teachers can help students understand the differences demanded in formal and informal contexts by asking them to create dramatic scripts or role plays in which they act out how their language changes in different settings or with different people. For example, one teacher asked her fifth-grade students to work in groups and create a short skit in which they were to explain something to three different individuals. She gave them several open-ended prompts from which to choose such as, "You borrowed your sibling's jacket without permission and tore it while performing a spectacular acrobatic feat on your bike. Now, confess this to your sibling, your best friend, and your parent." When designing oral language activities, give students a free rein to take the lead in creating situations that best match their experiences and needs.

Note the ways in which the study of language can integrate the multiple language arts. Here, we see how looking through the lens of language study can expand students understanding of oral and written texts.

It's also important to share with students the ways in which oral and written texts shape meanings differently. They might, for example, compare the language of essays with those of extemporaneous and formal public speeches on the same or similar topics. Or, closer to home, they might compare how they talk to a friend, email that same friend, and write a schoolwide invitation that all students and parents will receive.

STANDARDIZATION AND "POWERFUL" LANGUAGE

Just as we can explore the social dimensions of language with students, we should also look at its political dimensions. Such a study may seem pretty risky at first glance. After all, we're English language arts teachers, not politicians. Clearly, though, a study of language *is* a study of politics, and it's important not to deny it. As Edelsky (1992) so eloquently argues,

> Many people, especially in the United States, think of politics only as dirty and "backroom stuff." As a result, we regard it as not polite to engage in controversial arguments or politics; we don't want to politicize. . . . The schools, because they are public schools, supposedly do not advocate any particular position. But we ignore the fact that embedded in every textbook, every basal reader, and every classroom discussion is a political perspective. (p. 325)

Christensen (2002) says,

> Asking my students to memorize the rules without asking who makes the rules, who enforces the rules, who benefits from the rules, who loses from the rules, who uses the rules to keep some in and others out, legitimates a social system that devalues my students' knowledge and language. (p. 176)

A wide variety of activities can help middle school students learn about how language varies and changes in different regions, across different cultural groups, and across different time periods. Equally important, students can teach you and their peers about the multiple ways they adapt their language for work and play. This is also a great opportunity to include family and community members in your language study.

Middle school teachers may find themselves torn between honoring the language of the home and helping students to acquire "standard" English or what we call "edited English" in this book. Delpit (2002), a leading scholar on teaching and learning language in settings of cultural diversity, addresses this dilemma and notes that teachers must understand that language

> . . . is intimately connected with loved ones, community and personal identity. To suggest that this form is "wrong" or, even worse, ignorant is to suggest that something is wrong with the student and his or her family. To denigrate your language is, then, in African-American terms, to "talk about your mama." Anyone who knows anything about African-American culture knows the consequences of that speech act! (p. 125)

On the other hand, Delpit goes on to say that to deny students access to a politically powerful dialect denies these students access to succeed economically. So the answer to a middle school teacher's question about which approach to take with language is quite simple: Do both. But how?

Before we go further, we need to address briefly what "standard" we are talking about. The very label standard indicates that some students in our classrooms are below standard. Those students who do not come with the social and cultural background that gives them access to what has been called the "language of power" or the "language of wider communication" are often viewed as deficient in classrooms. For that reason, many scholars refuse to call one particular code "standard." Instead, they choose terms like "edited American English," "cash code," or "power code." Beyond our own classrooms, we know our students will be judged according to some version of "standard" language use, and our language study can address the politics of such definitions.

To understand how social context affects language, middle school students can monitor their own language use. Explicit attention to language variations of all kinds can help them learn to make appropriate language choices for a wide array of settings such as home, school, and workplaces. Middle school students are not too young to understand the politics of language choices. In fact, they are keenly aware of the power of language to mark them as insiders or outsiders, of who controls and enforces the rules, and who benefits from them.

Gee's (1990) notion of discourse communities is not beyond the understanding of middle school students. During middle school, friendship networks often flourish around literacy activities that come with a need to create new language variations. For example, when Margaret was visiting a middle school, one group of sixth-grade boys spent their leisure-time activities creating monster magazines and using electronic publishing on the Web to showcase their new creations. For whatever reasons, new vocabulary sprang up around these activities. A "Mo-Mo," for instance, was someone within the group who had created his own monster. And a "Mo-Te" was a writer who used other writers' monsters in his writing. Likewise, many students in this middle school classroom began to create words around their interests— music, fashion, and technology—to name a few.

When adults or other outsiders attempt to co-opt their language, early adolescents usually poke fun at these feeble attempts to enter their discourse community. The reason is that, in the life of the average middle school student, there are many "languages of power." It's useful for us to keep our perspective as we teach about "standard language." Remember that talking like an English teacher would make many of our students seem "deficient" in their elaborate social networks of peers.

Remember also that you can have a great deal of fun asking your students to teach you the language of their peer groups. They, and you, will get a kick out of your bumbling attempts to be "cool." Your students might also enjoy a visit to the "Urban Dictionary," where they can find 64 definitions for the word "cool" (*http://www.urbandictionary.com/define.php?term5cool*).

Guiding Practice With Varieties of English

Middle school students can learn the rules of standard English when they understand the multiple rule systems in operation. But what exactly might this look like?

Rhonda Ricketts, a seventh-grade teacher, asked her students to examine the ways in which adolescent boys and girls were characterized in popular teen magazines. She brought in copies of popular magazines targeted for boys (*Sports Illustrated*) and girls (*Seventeen*). They examined the cover art, tables of contents, advertisements, and articles. Students began collecting snippets of language that seemed to characterize the ways in which the magazine publishers constructed what it meant to be a boy or a girl through their language use.

Rhonda's seventh-grade students came up with all sorts of questions: Why weren't girls encouraged to be strong and powerful? Why were there so many boys in the girls' magazines but not any girls in the boys' magazines? Why did the boys' magazines use technical language about playing a game, but girls' magazines focused mainly on romance and beauty? What would happen if magazines didn't follow these gender-bound rules?

Rhonda's students enjoyed making magazine pages for boys and girls that seemed to "break the rules." This activity made students more keenly aware of how language rule systems work and how such unwritten rules constrain the ways we think and act.

Similarly, Mr. Williams, the teacher in the opening case study, wanted his students to investigate language use, not just in texts, but in their own lived worlds. He discovered that his students were often quite savvy about the ways in which they needed to move among multiple discourse communities, but he also found that they did so without explicit critical attention to these moves. He often found them ridiculing a friend for what they perceived to be acting, talking, or dressing in inappropriate ways. Sometimes he'd overhear his students making fun of the way someone talked, and was disappointed to hear the word "poser" used among friends to describe peers who appeared to sell themselves out and make moves that were not "true" to their character.

To disrupt the notion that there is only one "correct" or "true" way to talk and be in the world, Mr. Williams asked his students to select an individual from the sporting or entertainment world and to examine the ways that this person talked and acted in different settings. As an example, he brought in video clips of one of his favorite singers performing on *Sesame Street*, on *Saturday Night Live*, and at a concert. He also brought video clips of a professional football player talking about winning a big game, and then on a public service announcement asking parents to read with their children.

He directed students in a whole-class inquiry project in which they compared the news as it was broadcast on different stations. Together they teased out the rules for appropriate words, actions, and dress in different situations. He also asked students to articulate the ways in which teenagers typically talk among their friends and then to design skits for "alien adolescents," teaching them how to "get it right" in different settings such as the classroom, the cafeteria, the playing field, and even with probation officers or in the courtroom.

In an attempt to help students understand the necessary shifts that all effective language users make and the politics of their language choices, Mr. Williams designed many language study activities, including the "word detectives" exercise described in the opening case study.

Following are some additional suggestions for activities and projects to help students to (a) understand how and why the English language varies and changes, (b) learn English appropriate for many settings, and (c) analyze how social context affects language use.

Language histories.   In addition to studying language in textual and real worlds, middle school students can investigate the ways in which language changes over time. This can be done in a variety of ways. Ms. Evans, for example, asked her sixth-grade students to interview family members who were at least 20 years older than they. Their task was to investigate the ways in which "teenage talk" has shifted over time. Students interviewed grandparents, aunts, uncles, and parents about their ways of talking about friends, about music, about parents in their teenage years.

The students then prepared oral presentations of what they discovered. Some dressed in their parents' clothes, some played music, and all were amused with the silly ways their "elders" spoke. As a reflection on the experience, Ms. Evans asked them to collaborate on creating a time capsule of contemporary teen language and to predict what might amuse their grandchildren.

Word detective inquiry projects.   Word detective inquiries can be drawn from old television programs or books. Students can look for the ways that words, phrases, and even sentence patterns shift over time, geographic region, or cultural groups. Students can create and mail out surveys to investigate the study of language in use across regions. Middle school students might create translation dictionaries based on technical language, generational language, or peer group language. These dictionaries can be created individually or in small groups. They can be the result of interviews, Internet searches, or text-based research.

Language locks.   Language codes work like locks to keep some people out. Students can create codebooks to record secret friendship codes. They can select a hobby or profession and look at highly specialized language that is accessible only to those few who have the technical expertise, social competence, and/or language "keys" to unlock the codes. The Internet is a helpful source for students to use in investigating such codes, as are instant messaging, emails, and their own understandings of how language is used to "lock" someone out of a club or peer group.

Language bias. Even at the middle school level, students can look for bias in language. A comfortable place to begin is with the way sports reporters describe men and women, respectively. Students can look at newspapers or listen to television news and record the ways in which some teams are given priority treatment over others. A bit closer to home, they can examine how their neighborhoods or schools are characterized in the media or the ways in which teenagers are portrayed in the local newspaper.

For example, in one middle school classroom, 15-year-old Angel noted that students from her urban school were portrayed differently than students from suburban schools in the local paper. "They make it look like we are all in trouble or on welfare or something like that. They try to make it look like we are all wards of the court. That's BS." Angel set out to right the characterizations of students in her school, writing and submitting an editorial to the newspaper that began, "We the students of TLC would like to speak out on our own behalf and rights. We are not all troubled kids or wards of the welfare system."

PLAYING WITH LANGUAGE

Be sure to make space for language play in your classroom. Poetry, word games, rhymes, puns, and riddles can make language visible to students in creative and fun ways. Such activities work like finger exercises on a piano, helping students to gain control over their language. Working with homonyms, for example, students can play with understandings and twist meanings for the pleasure of their peers.

Ms. Vingant's fifth-grade students each selected a set of homonyms and created very short "poems" such as "I'll visit you on the Isle of Capri if you walk down the aisle with me." They also began to understand how poetry could work on multiple levels by looking for and then creating "hidden meanings" in poems. One girl came up to Ms. Vingant excited with this secret message in the poem she had just composed:

> Craig is some boy
> He stole her heart
> And then your hand
> Kept in golden pens

She asked, "Do you get it? Can you see my secret meaning?" Ms. V. studied the poem and asked, "Is it that golden means more than just the color?"

"No. No. Read it across."

After a few attempts, Ms. V. read diagonally, beginning with "Craig," and the secret revealed itself: "Craig stole your pens." She then asked Craig to return the missing pen set.

Getting the Knack (1992), by Stafford and Dunning, has many accessible poetry exercises that allow students to play with language. Another rich source is *The Weighty Word Book* (Levitt, Guralnick, & Stevens, 1999), which offers one-page stories that playfully illustrate difficult vocabulary words. One, for example, illustrates the word "bifurcate" in a story of two sisters who always go everywhere together until one of the sisters, Kate, decides she will take a trip without her sister, so friends will have to say a separate "bye for Kate." Students may groan when you read one of these stories aloud, but you can use them to create a bit of language play. Ask students to turn the stories into short scripts for performance, or to create their own "weighty word" stories, illustrating the meaning of a challenging word through drawing and writing.

Middle school students may connect with language through visual, dramatic, or kinesthetic activities. For example, they might illustrate adjectives through art, pantomime, or performance, making them look, feel, or even smell like what they are. They might create short skits to illustrate the literal meanings of euphemisms or colloquialisms. Bring in large cookies and ask students to write on them with frosting tubes so they can "eat their words." The Internet offers great sources for playing with words. Students can examine and/or create Web sites in which playful language is employed for multiple uses: to amuse and entertain, to include and exclude, or to attend to particular groups, for example.

LANGUAGE STUDY ACROSS THE CURRICULUM

History, mathematics, and science each have a language. The specialized languages of subject matter and professions are a rich source for inquiry. Especially as they move into the upper grades, middle school students need explicit attention to content-specific languages. Specialized vocabularies and language uses can be taught across disciplinary boundaries with the other middle school teachers on the team. It might be a rich opportunity for the guidance counselor, parents, and community members to share their specialized language competencies. Students may interview or invite guest speakers from professions that they are considering for their future. Such activities can be informal and ongoing or can culminate in activities like career fairs.

In Ms. Robinson's sixth-grade class, for example, students created storyboards and career dictionaries about their chosen professions. They each wrote a short script and enlisted one or two classmates to help them demonstrate the ways in which dentists, mathematicians, electricians, and other professionals might talk. Following is a snippet of Sally's script. Can you guess her chosen profession?

Sally: The galleys are late.

C'Koh: Well, have you seen the copy?

Sally: I have to have them proofed within 48 hours. We need the galley proofs right away.

Language Diversity and Grammar Instruction

Teaching grammar should still be a central part of any literacy program. But as we have said throughout this chapter, grammar should not be reduced to isolated drills. You've probably heard the phrase "teach grammar in context," but you might be wondering how this works out in practice. Clearly, standard written English is not identical to standard oral English. Opportunities for grammar instruction may arise within writing, reading, or oral language activities. Likewise, rather than rigidly adhere to traditional drills, teachers can design mini-lessons according to the needs of the students they are teaching. As a way of taking the sting out of correcting students' work, mini-lessons might focus on a published story in which students look at the ways the author selected language to situate a story in a particular region or period of history. They might study an author's use of dialect and practice, transforming it into Edited American English.

The study of language through literature or film can expose students to language in use in a particular context, helping them to acquire words, phrases, and language structures. Delpit (2002) suggests that role play and drama to practice standard English are viable alternatives because they remove the threat and embarrassment of correction. Videotaped or audiotaped conversations allow students the opportunities to listen to language in use. This is a useful means to help students learn to monitor their own language use. Read-alouds by the teacher are another viable means to support language learning. Reading to your middle school students is especially beneficial to second language learners who may benefit from hearing language in use.

Teaching Grammar and Usage to Early Adolescents

Much of a middle school language arts curriculum may be devoted to the teaching of grammar. As noted previously, a focus on grammar is not a focus on a singular rule system, but clearly, you will need to attend the rules of Edited American English as a central part of your language study. Weaver (1996) documents an overwhelming body of research demonstrating that the teaching of grammar in isolation does little to improve reading, writing, or even standardized test scores. In *Teaching Grammar in Context* (1996), Weaver provides a wealth of resources, examples, and strategies for teachers to use in teaching grammar and usage within the context of students' own language. Weaver recommends that, in teaching grammar, teachers shift the focus of their instruction from labeling mistakes to making students aware of the various functions of language. Figure 7-2 may be useful as you think about designing language study for your middle school students.

FIGURE 7-2   Teaching Grammar in Context

Less Attention	More Attention
• The use of terminology • Memorization of definitions • Analysis of sentences • Usage exercises	• Inquiry • Effective grammatical structures in reading • Production of effective sentences • Discussion and investigation of questions of usage • Exploration of the power of dialects through literature and film • Consideration of different effects that differing dialects have in different circumstances.

Source: Adapted from *Teaching Grammar in Context* by C. Weaver, 1996, New Jersey: Boyton/Cook.

Understanding Second Language Acquisition

It's likely that your middle school classroom will include a diverse student population. There will be students whose home language is not English. Unfortunately, many middle schools do not have an ESL teacher to help you design ways of helping these students to develop competence in English. It's important to understand theory and research in second language acquisition so you don't base your program on common myths about second language learners. Likewise, it's important to understand that learning standard English varies from individual learner to individual learner within and across cultural groups. Samway and McKeon (2002) list some features of second language acquisition, which might help you think about the ways you can support your middle school students:

- Language learning involves hypothesis testing. Errors are integral to language learning.
- Understanding language usually precedes language production. A "silent period" is normal.
- Mastering academic language may take second language learners up to 7 years.
- Second language acquisition and academic success are influenced by (a) personality, (b) cultural affiliation, (c) prior schooling, and (d) teacher expectations. (p. 63)

A language-rich classroom will be a key to success. Even if a second language learner doesn't appear to be participating, remember that silence is part of the normal developmental sequence. The teacher and peers are often a great source of spoken English for second language learners. Setting up meaningful interactions among peers is key to supporting language development for all students, especially for second language learners. Just remember that participation doesn't necessarily mean speaking. Through listening, the student can begin to formulate hypotheses about language patterns and try out these patterns later in a more private setting.

While selecting materials, keep in mind that materials should seem age appropriate as well as accessible for your students. Invite students to share their experiences and teach their peers so that they feel that they are a part of your classroom. Making lists and using art, charts, drawings, and other graphic organizers are ways to help students build vocabulary and learn the language system.

Weddel and Van Duzer (1997) suggest that beginning-level students can write in both English and their native language if necessary.

As students become more competent in English, the teacher can enlist them to assess their language needs by asking them questions such as "Where do you use English?" "For what purpose do you want to use English?" and "What language skills are you interested in developing?" Most important, we need to remember that language learning doesn't take place in isolation and is best taught in the context of meaningful social interactions.

To support such meaningful interactions, find out as much as you can about your second language learners. That means reading research, talking with support personnel such as ESL teachers, and, most important, talking with your students and their families. Tap the resources that students bring to your classroom, and invite them to share their experiences with others. Create opportunities for a mix of students to interact in nonthreatening ways. Enrich your verbal directions with nonlinguistic support such as artwork, drama, and role play. Most of all, create a climate of safety where all contributions are valued and difference is not a sign of deficit.

UNDERSTANDING AND DOCUMENTING STUDENT GROWTH

It's important for middle school teachers to understand that sometimes an "error" in a student's work is actually a developmental leap or experimentation with something that is just beyond the student's reach, something over which the student does not yet have control. You might notice that when you teach apostrophes to show ownership, for instance, apostrophes might begin appearing after almost any "s" that ends a word. It takes time, practice, and gentle reminders before young adolescents learn to recognize their own error patterns.

Similarly, second language learners often overgeneralize where language rules are concerned. This is not surprising when you think about how many languages contributed to the development of English. Our language shifted as the Celtic languages of the British Isles were infused with vocabulary and grammatical structures from invaders and immigrants such as the Germanic tribes, missionary priests, and the Vikings. With this confusing mix of language influences, it would be impossible to derive a set of simple and fixed rules for helping students to master the nuances of spelling, syntax, or grammar.

Students who have not heard particular words in use may generalize a language principle inappropriately. When ESL students or others apply past tense by adding "-ed" to a word such as "go," making it "goed," you should see this usage as a window on their cognitive development rather than a sign of incompetence. According to Samway and McKeon (2002), these errors for second language learners "are an integral part of the second language learning process, helping learners to refine and revise their understanding of how the second language works"(p. 63). This same principle applies to all of your middle school students. They may be making great leaps in language use that look like errors to you. An error pattern can be evidence of growth rather than a sign of incompetence.

Learning From (and About) Our Errors

Particularly in working with early adolescents, it's important to take the sting (and the boredom) out of grammar and usage instruction. On the other hand, it's important to realize that someone's use of language, much like his or her religion or politics, can carry a great deal of emotional and personal baggage. Janet Hart learns this the hard way in Classroom Case 7-3, when she designs a "Grammar Derby" for her middle school students.

Classroom Case 7-3

The Grammar Derby

As a first-year teacher, Janet Hart inherited an eighth-grade curriculum that caused her great discomfort. All of her students had been required to purchase three disposable workbooks, one each for grammar, vocabulary, and spelling. The second 9-week curriculum guide addressed grammar and usage. She didn't want to assign worksheets every day, but there was an expectation that students should use their workbooks. Writing was to come a couple of weeks later. Janet wanted an engaging way to teach grammar and usage in context, and she guessed from her own middle school experience that the isolated skills-driven approach would not pique their interest.

As a beginning teacher, Janet also didn't want to stray too far from the curriculum. So she decided to weave in some ideas from popular television, music, and current events that she thought would be of interest to middle school students. She designed a game that she called Grammar Derby, in which students were supposed to look for rule violations in their daily lives. She hoped to use these examples as a way of helping students to understand how context and expectations make a difference in the way rule violations were received. For example, in informal speech most people say, "Who did you go with?" even though "With whom did you go?" is more grammatically correct. For most people, the latter statement sounds—in the words of a popular joke—"like a fool or an English teacher." Janet began by handing out a game sheet that explained the task (see Figure 7-3). Examples of rule violations could come from popular magazines, newspapers, television shows, the Internet, or in students' daily interactions with others.

FIGURE 7-3   Grammar Derby

Grammar Derby

(Points: Adults, 5 points; children under 12, 1 point; characters on TV, 3; song lyrics, 3; in print, 5)

Usage Rule	Violation	Who Said It	Where Said	Points	Total Points
Subject-verb agreement	She don't look back.	Singer	Radio	3	3
Double negatives	You don't love me no more.	Singer	Radio	3	6

As you might guess, students were highly motivated. Some came with two or three sheets filled in a night. The activity was working just great, she thought. She was planning some discussion prompts to help her students understand the complexities of language in use one morning at 7:30 when Mr. Bilke, the eighth-grade math teacher on her team, stormed into her classroom. Without a greeting, he interrupted, "What's this grammar derby stuff you got the kids doing?"

Janet was caught off guard and began, "I asked my students to listen for errors and then. . . ."

"Well, it's interfering with my class. I said something, and about half the class took out a sheet of paper and started writing something down. They told me I said something like, 'can't not,' and they were smirking and laughing. I'm sure I didn't say it, but it was disrespectful, and I want it stopped."

Janet apologized and tried to explain that she wanted her students to understand that everybody doesn't follow the rules all the time. She was still trying to explain when Mr. Bilke turned away and walked out of her room. "I want it stopped" was all that he said.

For Discussion

In striving to make connections in the real world, Janet hadn't thought through how her activity might have placed students, parents, or teachers in disrespectful or embarrassing situations. She learned an important lesson about the personal and emotional dimensions of language. Are there ways that this language play activity might be salvaged next time around? If her goal was to show how language rules shift depending on context, how might she modify this activity so that real individuals are not harmed? Similarly, if she wanted to teach her middle school students how language is tied to issues of power and status, how might she change or extend her activity to encompass that goal?

Shaughnessy (1979) suggests that in addition to noting the errors a student makes, teachers need to understand the reasons for these errors. If you notice particular usage errors that seem to crop up in the writing or speech of most students, it's time for a mini-lesson or two. You can provide mini-lessons for an entire class or to just those students who need support with a particular skill. You don't want to embarrass students in front of peers, but you can address particular error patterns in brief lessons and then ask students to look through their writing folders for evidence of these errors or ask them to trade papers with friends and engage in a bit of peer editing. There are several ways to develop students' awareness of errors without humiliating or discouraging them. Here are just a few approaches you might pursue.

Student self-assessment.   Students can keep track of their individual language issues in a skills-building section of their writer's notebook. The purpose is to help middle school students understand their own errors and take responsibility for them. After you have taught a mini-lesson on a particular skill or set of skills, hold some revising conferences with students and identify one or two error patterns in their drafts. Ask the students to record comments on these patterns in a "skills to remember" section of their notebooks, along with some clever gimmicks or tricks to help them to notice the error. For example, by memorizing the sentence "A bad person behaves badly," they can remember the spelling difference between the adjective and adverb. The difference between "there" and "their" can be taught by pointing out that the word "there" contains the word "here" (a place), while "their" contains "heir" (someone who inherits or possesses something). Considering the illogical nature of English, we sometimes must do more "un-teaching" than teaching, to make our students aware of the many "exceptions" to grammatical and usage rules.

The editor role.   Rather than meticulously editing a student's written work, try circling a couple of persistent error patterns, and discuss these patterns in your next conference with the student. As students become more familiar with grammar and usage rules, they can try looking for error patterns with partners. When you feel comfortable scaling back your editing even more, you can begin placing a checkmark in the line where an error has occurred and asking students to figure what the error might be. Give extra credit for every error they correct and add to the "skills to remember" section of their writer's notebook. Figure 7-4 is an example of one teacher's guidelines, designed to help students to monitor their language use and development.

Goals and growth records.   Monitoring students' language development is no easy task. One way is to ask students to set goals and assess their own progress. This will take some modeling and practice, but it will help students learn to monitor

FIGURE 7-4   Monitoring Language Use

A Special Section of Your Writer's Notebook—"Skills to Remember"

It's important for you to understand the common spelling mistakes, punctuation conventions, and usage errors that you make. I would like you to take charge of your language learning this semester. In your Writer's Notebook, create a section called *"Skills to Remember."* Each time you hand in written work, I will make an *X* in the margin next to any errors I find. If I notice that you are making the same mistake over and over again, I will circle the *X*. It is your job to (a) discover what this error might be, and (b) find a trick or gimmick to help you remember the correct form. Sometimes we will be working on these together with all of your classmates. Sometimes I can meet with you individually. You can also ask someone in your writing group to help you if you can't find the error. And you can always look in your English book or in some of our classroom resources, specifically a few grammar and usage handbooks in our writing corner. This section of your notebook should be continually expanded as you progress through the semester and beyond.

their own development and take further responsibility for their own learning. Periodically ask students to set two or three language goals. Then regularly ask them to record their progress. Following is an example of a student's progress report from Mr. Maslow's sixth-grade classroom:

> Hey Mr. M,
>
> I had three goals. 1 bring my pencil to class. 2 write sentences 3 write its and it's right. how I am doing so far. I usully brang my pencil. thats good. I write sentences. I use a period and a question mark. I am good. I don't use its so no problem. next time you told me to make some more goals so I am.
>
> Your favorte student
>
> William S. Walters

Asking students like William to write periodic letters about their progress in learning about language conventions is a good way to promote self-awareness and to make your conferences more individualized and personal. It's not necessary to point out the grammatical and usage errors in William's letter, since Mr. Maslow will use future writing conferences to help William identify his error patterns. To do this, he must focus on two or three pressing and reachable goals, rather than editing every piece of writing that William turns in.

Although Mr. Maslow has more than 150 students, he keeps six small black notebooks behind his desk, one for each of six class periods. When he meets with William and other students, he makes anecdotal records of their goals and accomplishments. All of this record keeping is done at the time of the 3- to 5-minute conference. Although he would like to take more time, as a veteran teacher, Mr. Maslow knows that managing the paper load is vital to his success, so he has created a shorthand way of keeping track and has turned over some of the responsibility to his students. Figure 7-5 offers an example of the goals and growth records that he and his students keep together.

Portfolios.   Students can include evidence of their growth in language study through writing samples, audiotapes, self-assessments, and progress notes in portfolios. These student records and reflections on aspects of their language learning can reduce your paper load and help students to focus more acutely on their own issues.

Communication with parents.   As a middle school teacher, you'll find that it's not only important to know how to teach students about various aspects of their language, but it's equally important to communicate your beliefs about language study for the benefit of parents, colleagues, and other community members. Often parents become irate, for example, when their children's papers come home full of unedited grammatical or usage errors. Many don't understand the importance of ignoring errors in early drafts or informal writing-to-learn-activities such as quickwrites or learning logs. Fieldwork Journal 7-2 gives you a chance to articulate your own developing philosophy of language study.

FIGURE 7-5   Goals and Growth Record

Student's Name _____
Grading Period _____

Date	Goals Set	Conference Date Scheduled	Progress and Plans	Teacher and Student Agreed
Sept. 4	• Bring writing materials • Use end marks • Use *its* and *it's* correctly	Oct. 4 set	• Good job with pens • Periods and question marks are coming • Not so important	MJM + WSW 10/04
Oct. 5	• Use end marks • Use capital letters to start a sentence • Share in small group			

Fieldwork Journal 7-2

A Letter Home

Parents often bring a set of assumptions about what and how you should teach, based on the grammar and usage worksheets they used in their junior high school English classroom. Caregivers who don't understand your feelings about language variation may incorrectly believe that you are disrespecting the language of their home or community.

Your task is to write a letter to parents, explaining your philosophy of language study. Before you can do that, you will want to articulate some of these beliefs for yourself. Working with a partner or small group, think about the ways in which you might design learning experiences for your middle school students to address some or all of the goals listed on the chart in Figure 7-6.

Referring to some of these goals and strategies, write a brief letter to parents or caregivers, explaining some of the things their middle school children will be doing this year in your classroom and the philosophy behind these activities.

When you have completed your letter, discuss some other ways to communicate with parents and community members regarding your approach to language study. Explore how you might tap the expertise of families and community members to enhance and support the kind of language-rich classroom you envision.

FIGURE 7-6 Designing Language Experiences

Designing Language Experiences			
To analyze how social context affects language use	To learn English appropriate for many settings, including workplaces	To monitor their own language use	To understand how and why the English language varies and changes

In this chapter we hope we have helped you to "think about words" with some of the same enthusiasm that Anna expressed in the opening case study. Understanding how language varies and changes in different regions, across different discourse communities, and across time can support middle school students as they expand their repertoire of effective language practices. Tapping students' expertise with language can make your classroom a rich and productive discourse community.

In the following standards in Practice, we invite you to look at language study through the lens of your state standards.

Standards in Practice

How Does Your State Define Language Study?

Look back at Fieldwork Journal 7-2, in which you wrote a letter to parents. Make a list of the major assumptions in your philosophy statement. Your list might begin something like this:

- Middle school students can analyze how social context affects language in use.
- Middle school students show respect for language variations.
- Middle school students understand how and why the English language varies and changes across cultures, ethnic groups, geographic regions, and historic periods.

Now locate a copy of your state English language arts standards. Find the standards that specifically address language study, and try to unpack the assumptions from which your state seems to be operating. For example, consider how narrow or broad your state's definition of language seems to be. Is the primary focus on grammar and standard usage, or are other aspects of language (dialect variation, history, semantics, etc.) addressed within your state's standards? To what extent do your state standards define language study as a decontextualized activity or as integrated into students' authentic language use?

Look for points of agreement and disagreement between your developing philosophy and your state's standards. Then consider how easy or difficult it might be to prepare your middle school students for standardized tests based on your state's standards. How can you teach students to pass these high-stakes tests without abandoning your core beliefs about what language study is and how it should be taught?

REFERENCES

Christensen, L. (2002). Whose standard? Teaching standard English. In B. Power & R. Hubbard (Eds.), *Language development: A reader for teachers* (2nd ed., pp. 173–177). Upper Saddle River, NJ: Merrill/Prentice Hall.

Delpit, L. (2002). What should teachers do? Ebonics and culturally responsive instruction. In B. Power & R. Hubbard (Eds.), *Language development: A reader for teachers* (2nd ed, pp. 124–128). Upper Saddle River, NJ: Merrill/Prentice Hall.

Edelsky, C. (1992). A talk with Carole Edelsky. *Language Arts, 69,* 324–329.

Gee, J. (1990). *Social linguistics and literacies: Ideology in discourse.* New York: Falmer Press.

Heath, S. B. (1983). *Ways with words: Language, life, and work in communities and classrooms.* New York: Cambridge University Press.

Hymes, D. (1972). Models of the interaction of language and social life. In J. Gumperz & D. Hymes (Eds.), *Directions in sociolinguistics: The ethnography of communication* (pp. 35–71). New York: Holt, Rinehart and Winston.

Hymes, D. (1996). *Ethnography, linguistics, and narrative inequality: Toward an understanding of voice.* London: Taylor & Francis.

Levitt, P., Guralnick, E. S., & Stevens, J. (1999). *The weighty word book* (2nd ed.) Boulder, CO: Court Wayne Press.

Samway, K., & McKeon, D. (2002). Myths about acquiring a second language. In B. Power & R. Hubbard (Eds.), *Language development: A reader for teachers* (2nd ed., pp. 62–68). Upper Saddle River, NJ: Merrill/Prentice Hall.

Sebestyen, O. (1997). *Words by Heart.* New York: Yearling.

Shaughnessy, M. (1979). *Errors and expectations: A guide for the teacher of basic writing.* New York: Oxford University Press.

Stafford, W., & Dunning, S. (1992). *Getting the knack: 20 poetry exercises.* Urbana, IL: National Council of Teachers of English.

Weaver, C. (1996). *Teaching grammar in context.* Montclair, NJ: Boynton/Cook.

Weddel, K. S., & Van Duzer, C. (1997). *Needs assessment for adult ESL learners (ERIC Digest).* Washington, DC: National Clearinghouse for ESL Literacy Education. (ERIC Document Reproductive Services No. ED 407882).

RESOURCES

Print

Boran, S., & Comber, B. (2001). *Critiquing whole language and classroom inquiry.* Urbana, IL: National Council of Teachers of English.

Cazden, C. (1988). *Classroom discourse: The language of teaching and learning.* Portsmouth, NH: Heinemann.

De Jong, E., & Harper, C. (2005). Preparing mainstream teachers for English-language learners: Is being a good teacher good enough? *Teacher Education Quarterly, 32*(2), 101–124.

Dudley-Marling, C., & Edelsky, C. (2001). *The fate of progressive language policies and practices.* Urbana, IL: National Council of Teachers of English.

Edelsky, C. (1996). *With literacy and justice for all: Rethinking the social in language and education (Critical perspectives on literacy and education).* New York: Taylor & Francis.

González, R. D., & Melis, I. (2000). *Language ideologies: Critical perspectives on the official English movement. Volume 1: Education and the social implications of official language.* Urbana, IL: National Council of Teachers of English.

González, R. D., & Melis, I. (2001). *Language ideologies: Critical perspectives on the official English movement. Volume 2: History, theory, and policy.* Urbana, IL: National Council of Teachers of English.

Hall, S. (1981). Teaching about race. In A. James & R. Jeffcoate (Eds.), *The school in the multicultural society* (pp. 58–69). London: Harper.

Jimenez, R., Gerstein, R., & Rivera, A. (1996). Conversations with a Chicana teacher: Supporting students' transition from native to English language instruction. *The Elementary School Journal, 96*(3), 333–341.

McWhorter, J. (2000). *Spreading the word: Language and dialect in America.* Portsmouth, NH: Heinemann.

Ng, R., Staton, P., & Scane, J. (1995). *Anti-racism, feminism, and critical approaches to education.* Westport, CT: Bergin and Garvey.

Power, B., & Hubbard, R. (2002). *Language development: A reader for teachers* (2nd ed.). Upper Saddle River, NJ: Merrill/Prentice Hall.

Wallace, R., & Hunter, S. (1995). *The place of grammar in writing instruction: Past, present, future.* Montclair, NJ: Boynton/Cook.

Weaver, C. (1998). *Lessons to share on teaching grammar in context.* Montclair, NJ: Boynton/Cook.

Weaver, C., Gillmeiser-Krause, L., & Vento-Zogby, G. (1996). *Creating support for effective literacy education.* Portsmouth, NH: Heinemann.

Young, M. (1996). English (as a second) language arts teachers: The key to mainstreamed ESL student success. *The English Journal, 85*(8), 17–24.

See also a special issue on Educating Language Learners of *Educational Leadership,* December 2004/January 2005, Volume 62, Number 4.

Electronic

Center for Multilingual Multicultural Research

CMMR is an organized research unit at the University of Southern California. The center focuses on multilingual education, English as a second language, foreign language instruction, multicultural education, and related areas. The center's comprehensive Web site addresses language policies and rights and includes Asian-Pacific Island resources, Latino/Latina and Hispanic resources, Native American/American Indian, and African American resources.

http://www.usc.edu/dept/education/CMMR/

For a collection of articles on the Ebonics debate, visit

http://www-rcf.usc.edu/~cmmr/African_American.html#ebonics

Weblogs for Use with ESL Classes. This site offers information on using weblogs with ESL students. A weblog (or "blog") can be thought of as an online journal that an individual can continually update with his or her own words, ideas, and thoughts through software that enables one to easily do so.

http://iteslj.org/Techniques/Campbell-Weblogs.html

Example of blog and Web site that provides materials for ESL teachers and students: ESL Café www.eslcafe.com

International Reading Association. The IRA has two Web sites that address critical issues of language study: Focus on Critical Literacy, Focus on Language and Cultural Diversity, and Focus on Adolescent Literacy.

IRA Focus on Critical Literacy

This Web site was organized to help teachers and their students to understand, develop, and adopt a critical perspective on literacy. It offers online resources on critical literacy, including links to IRA journal articles, book chapters, programs, position statements, and more.

http://www.reading.org/resources/issues/focus_critical.html

IRA Focus on Language and Cultural Diversity

This Web site addresses issues related to teaching students whose first language is not the primary language of instruction and whose culture and values may differ from those in mainstream schools and of the larger community.

http://www.reading.org/resources/issues/focus_diversity.html

Karen's ESL Partyland. This site features lots of fun ideas for teachers and students alike. It's more appropriate for teachers in self-contained ESL classrooms, but you can easily modify the activities to suit your own teaching situation. Your ESL students might also benefit from taking some of Karen's quizzes.

http://www.eslpartyland.com/default.htm

On Line Writing Lab. The OWL at Purdue University provides a wealth of support for teaching second language learners as well as teaching grammar, punctuation, and spelling. This site includes an extensive list of links to other Web resources for ESL teachers and learners.

http://owl.english.purdue.edu/oldindex.html

William Safire's Rules for Writers. Visit this site and download a copy of this humorous list of grammar rules, including such pithy maxims as "Verbs have to agree with their subjects."

http://www.chem.gla.ac.uk/protein/pert/safire.rules.html

Language Varieties. This site is about varieties of language that differ from the standard variety that is normally used in the media and taught in the schools. It includes suggestions for teaching, links to other Web sites, and references.

http://www.une.edu.au/langnet/

http://www.une.edu.au/langnet/aave.htm

Language Varieties Network. The purposes of this network are to provide a forum for dialogue about variant-language issues in education, to provide a network of information about pidgins, creoles, and other stigmatized varieties, and to raise educators' awareness of issues of pidgins, creoles, and other stigmatized varieties.

http://www2.hawaii.edu/~gavinm/home.htm

Literacy Resources for Learners of English as a Second Language. This Web site offers access to a wide assortment of literacy ideas customized for classroom teachers of students who are learning English as a second language (ESL) or English as a foreign language (EFL).

http://www.literacy.uconn.edu/eslhome.htm

Chapter  8

Writing in the Middle Grades

GUIDING QUESTIONS

1. For what purposes do middle school students need to write?
2. What are the multiple ways that writing can be showcased in an integrated language arts classroom?
3. What are the key components of an effective middle school writing program?

A CASE FOR CONSIDERATION

To Assign or Not to Assign

Cristina Santos and Emily Lewis are co-teaching in an eighth-grade classroom for a 6-week student teaching placement. Although Cristina hated keeping journals during her own middle school days, she wants to assign them to her students. She writes in her fieldwork journal:

> When Emily and I were designing our unit, I insisted that the students keep journals. She and I agreed that I would be responsible for reading and responding to the journals. Although I hated keeping a journal as a student, I wanted to see how the students would respond if they receive a lot of personal feedback. Every time journals were collected, my students could expect a letter that was at least half a page long. My feedback was primarily praise or questions about what they had written, often asking them about their hobbies or experiences. I never gave negative feedback or corrected their writing.
>
> On the first day of class, Emily and I were discussing our policies and the grading rubric. I discussed the journal component with the class, explaining the rationale was that it would help us get to know the students better and would give them practice writing. At the end of the period, I assigned a journal entry for homework. It was to be at least a page, and the topic was "names." One girl raised her hand and commented, "You said that you wanted to get to know us through the journals but how do you expect to get to know us if you assign topics?" I didn't have a really good answer. Afraid of being wrong or of contradicting

what I had said already, I skirted the question. I did not modify the assignment and to my relief the bell rang.

That night I went home and thought about the girl's comment. I knew she was right, but I didn't know how to fix it; yet the answer seemed so simple. I could let the students select their own topics. This was a simple solution but one I didn't like. If the students wrote about what they wanted, then I was not in control. How would we be able to tie their journal entries to class discussion?

FOR DISCUSSION

Anyone who has ever taught writing in a middle school classroom has struggled with Cristina's questions: How do we invite students to write for authentic purposes? How much choice should we let students have, and when do we need to take charge? How do we make our goals coincide with theirs? And, selfishly, how do we handle the burden of all those half-page comments in the midst of our busy lives? Like Cristina, we believe that journal keeping can be an effective means for students to explore ideas and for us to document growth or change over time. Yet, like the eighth-grade girl in Cristina's class, students may see journals as one more thinly veiled exercise in teacher control—meaningless and contrived. It's also a good bet that, after a few weeks of those half-page responses, Cristina may come to regret assigning journals in the first place. What goals did Cristina appear to have for assigning journals, and what did she do to undercut those goals? How do you balance your need to develop students' writing skills and students' needs for freedom and choice? Considering that this student teacher had 129 students, what suggestions do you have for managing the "paper load"?

WRITING WITH MIDDLE SCHOOL STUDENTS

Although the focus of this chapter is writing, we believe that writing should be interwoven with other language arts to support students' confidence and competence as language users. In this chapter, we will attempt to demonstrate the ways that writing can both support and be developed through meaningful activities in all of the language arts.

But just for a moment, think back to your middle school or junior high school days. Try to remember an artifact, text, or teaching material your teachers might have used to teach writing. This artifact might be a grammar handbook, a workbook, a notebook, or an empty sheet of unlined paper. Perhaps, like many English language arts teachers, you can't remember being explicitly taught to write at all. What does this artifact (or lack of it) say about your former teachers' assumptions about learning to write? The difference between a workbook and a spiral notebook is probably vast in terms of the assumptions that lie with each of them. Keep these thoughts in mind as you explore some of your own assumptions about the teaching of writing in Fieldwork Journal 8-1.

Fieldwork Journal 8-1

Writing Assumptions

Part One: Examining Your Assumptions About Writing

Write for a few moments on the following prompts:

1. Writing is . . .
2. Writing is not . . .
3. If I were to create a metaphor for my own writing process, it would be . . .
4. I would rank the following aspect as most (1) to least (5) important in terms of what I hope to develop in my students:
   _____ writing as personal expression
   _____ writing as thinking
   _____ writing as crafting clear, polished, and correct texts
   _____ writing as communication
   _____ writing as socially transforming
5. The following expresses my sense of the prevailing middle school students' attitudes toward writing?
   a. They hate any form of writing.
   b. They love to write stories and poems.
   c. They see writing as less important now that they have access to computers and other technologies.
   d. _____

After you have written for a while, consider how your assumptions about writing and your own writing processes may have been influenced by the curriculum of your own middle or junior high school teachers.

Part Two: Student Survey

If you are currently teaching, ask students to respond to the first three questions in Part One. Then analyze their responses according to the following questions:

- How closely do your assumptions about writing match theirs?
- How might your writing curriculum have influenced their responses?
- Considering the diversity of the metaphors they chose to describe their writing processes, how can you reach all of the writers in your middle school classroom?

In your Fieldwork Journal exploration, you might have pondered a question that many literacy teachers struggle with: "How can I teach writing when I don't feel like a writer myself?"

In our work with teachers in classes and workshops, we have noticed that some excellent writing teachers feel great inadequacies in terms of their own writing abilities or feelings about writing. Some would rather do anything than write in a journal, write letters to friends, or even answer an email. Others have vivid memories of negative writing experiences in school that, even today, seem to hold them hostage to feelings of incompetence in writing. If you are one of these teachers, there is hope. First, you need to realize that many "closet nonwriters" are out there, and some have become outstanding teachers of writing and outstanding writers themselves. This is a dilemma that Herm Card worked out over the course of his teaching career. A veteran English teacher in a rural middle school as well as a poet and successful workshop facilitator, Herm describes his own transformation in Classroom Case 8-1.

Classroom Case 8-1

Back to Poetry

For some 10 years of my teaching career, I steadfastly avoided the curriculum's reference to poetry. I had been told, essentially, to teach "what works," and I was sure poetry wasn't going to work. The reason I made that assumption was that I didn't know much about it, and cared less. Not that I hadn't taken poetry courses, or read poetry, or written poetry. I had done all three. Unfortunately, the one poetry course I had taken pretty much did me in for poetry. It was horrible. Not horrible if you were a poetry scholar perhaps, but horrible if you were a college sophomore who fancied himself an aspiring poet, a poet who had written tons of love poems and another ton of angry, dark, '60s style poems, two of which had actually been published.

The poetry course was a semester devoted to rhyme, meter, and forms, with the word "poetic" seldom uttered by the professor. Having had this experience, I was so turned off to poetry that I stopped writing it and years later, when I entered the teaching profession, avoided teaching it. I realized that I knew nothing about poetry and really felt nothing for it. I assumed I was an anomaly, the poster boy for fear of poetry.

The bottom line is that some 10 years after I began teaching, I began writing poetry again, and I began reading poetry again. Soon after, I made the seemingly daring leap into teaching poetry.

The poster boy for fear of poetry. Over the years I have discovered that was not the case. As my career has evolved for some 8 years I have been presenting workshops on teaching poetry and writing to teachers. I have discovered the trepidation I felt about teaching poetry to be relatively common among teachers. Something about poetry makes them question their ability, question their knowledge, and, more important, question themselves. Many teachers do not consider themselves poetic. Most students do not consider themselves poetic, so it's not like the odds are against us. In my workshops, the very people who claimed to have never taken a poetic breath have produced some of the most astonishingly personal, sensitive, and beautiful poetry I have ever read. It is not unusual for a piece of writing from an "I can't write poetry" claimant to send people scurrying for the tissue box. I have had workshops nearly end because no one, including me, could imagine reading next after a piece that had reduced us all to tears or gales of laughter or sent us deep into nostalgic reverie.

For Discussion

It's probably true that Herm has not taught these teachers to write poetry any more than he can or does teach any student to write it. It is not teaching poetry that we strive for as much as it is allowing our students to become aware of and involved with poetry. What are some ways that Herm has specifically promoted his students' and his colleagues' involvement with poetry?

Perhaps a first step in developing our own identities as teachers who write is accepting the fact that both teaching and writing are enriched when we find the "comfortable pace and level" that Herm described, one that can support teachers and students alike to flourish and grow. We probably all agree that our former teachers had a great influence on our assumptions, feelings, and fears where the teaching of writing is concerned. Consider as well the role of popular media in shaping your assumptions. For years, media pundits have speculated on why "Johnny" can't write. In such public arenas, conceptions of teaching writing may be reduced to teaching and testing issues of correctness. With the arrival of computers, technology has often been touted as the answer to our writing problems.

Certainly, computers and other technologies can support the teaching of writing. Since the arrival of word processing, multiple drafts can be managed with more ease than middle school students are usually willing to devote to rewrites. The Internet makes the process of research more intriguing and accessible than ever before. But there are few easy solutions to the complexities of teaching writing. In fact, many have argued that computer technology only increases this complexity. Grammar and spelling checks and the polished look of word-processed texts can give students the impression that drafts are perfect just as they are. The barrage of information, advertising, and propaganda on the Internet heightens our responsibility to make students critical consumers and producers of electronic media.

Current literature about writing is flooded with talk of "new literacies," "technoliteracies," and "multiliteracies." With the arrival of new information and communication technologies comes an imperative that we expand old notions of a traditional writing curriculum. Texts may be face-to-face, virtual, and/or multimedia. New technologies give us rich opportunities to open up classrooms and our writing curriculum. Carrington and Luke (2003) critique literacy programs that remain traditional in a print format that is disconnected from a broader analysis of community, of environment, of the experiences and practices of globalization. The goal of a writing program is, according to Carrington and Luke, to engage children in critical use of both digital and print media. There is a growing attention to the need for teaching students how to become critical consumers and producers of texts, to understand the multiple dimensions of literacy, and to take critical perspectives. Approaches to classroom study can and should be a part of a larger critical analysis of who uses language, where, and with what power (Carrington & Luke, 2003; Comber & Simpson, 2001; Edelsky, 1996; Luke, Freebody, & Land, 2000).

In short, there is no quick fix or cure-all for the cries of politicians, pundits, and policy makers about the woes of poor John or Janie. Chances are that you will be pulled to teach a narrow writing curriculum geared to improve standardized test scores. You will be pushed by current scholars and educators to teach critical literacies with a focus on larger social issues. Convincing parents, administrators, and even students that writing is complicated, messy, and often difficult is no easy task. Teaching writing is many things. It is giving students access to the conventions of edited English, at the same time that we value and respect their home languages. It is making students aware of rhetorical choices and the social and political consequences of those choices, at the same time as we provide opportunities for private, informal exploration. Even today, after three decades of attention to the importance of teaching "processes as well as products," finished products are still seen by many as the end goal of a writing curriculum, a way of showcasing what students have already learned.

As you'll see, writing can be used to learn, to explore ideas, to rehearse and perform, and to develop language skills. Of course, writing skills are necessary for students to pass standardized tests, but this is only one small part of the purpose writing should play in the life of the early adolescent. In this chapter, we'll address strategies for writing to learn as well as learning to write.

Before we focus on the teaching and learning of writing, let's examine the ways in which writing may support multiple purposes and a varied array of other language arts. Often, the teaching of literature overshadows the teaching of writing in an English language arts classroom. Although book reports, essay exams, or research report writing may be integral parts of a middle school curriculum, other purposes may be overlooked. Think back to the language lenses presented in chapter 6. In what ways might writing support reading? How might writing serve to support language study or talking and listening? How might writing be used to make connections with the local community or the larger world?

Writing-to-learn activities give middle school students a chance to make predictions, record what they already know, ask questions, and explore their views. In addition to being a tool for learning, writing can enable students to share and to showcase, to forge connections with peers and family, and to reach out to the larger community. Let's explore those purposes in Fieldwork Journal 8-2.

Many writing activities such as journals or peer writing groups can seem deceptively simple on the surface: "Just assign a journal," you might think, "and kids will see writing as personally meaningful; put kids into groups and, magically, they'll love getting and giving feedback and response." As Patricia Lopez discovers in Classroom Case 8-2, however, these seemingly simple approaches to writing require a great deal of trial and error before they can be made to work in the classroom.

You'll want to design groups so all students have powerful roles in the classroom. Students who are proficient in languages other than English may be asked to be involved in activities that do not require language production—observing, pointing, collecting, constructing, for example. Consider what other extensions and adaptations you might try in your own classroom to ensure that all group members—even those who are still developing skill and fluency in English—have the chance to make a positive contribution to the groups.

Fieldwork Journal 8-2

Writing for Multiple Purposes

Consider all the ways that writing may be used in a middle school classroom. The chart in Figure 8-1 lists some of the many forms that writing may take in and beyond your classroom.

Think about this list of texts and techniques for writing and see how many you can add. Then, in your fieldwork journal, create a chart like the one in Figure 8-2. Pick one of the techniques in the list and experiment with the different purposes this technique might serve in your teaching of writing. Consider, for example, the journal. Rather than serving one narrow purpose in your writing classroom, the journal serves as an incredibly flexible tool with multiple uses, as we see it. After reading the example provided in the Purposes for Writing chart, choose another of the writing forms and techniques from Figure 8-1, and experiment with the different purposes it can serve in your curriculum.

In addition to sharing your ideas with others, you might want to reflect on the ease or difficulty you had in thinking of writing activities for each of the four purposes presented in the chart. Perhaps it was easy for you to list examples of writing to connect but more difficult to provide any examples of writing to learn about writing. If so, what might account for this difference? Just as any activity may support more than one of the language arts, a writing activity may clearly serve more than one purpose. For example, although we've placed them in the category of writing to connect and transform, dialogue journals (journals kept by two students who exchange them on a regular basis and respond to each other's work) may fit equally well under writing to explore. Ask yourself if you resonate with one of these writing purposes more than others or if you have strong positive or negative feelings about

FIGURE 8-1 Texts and Techniques for the Writing Classroom

Texts and Techniques for the Writing Classroom		
journals	sketches	Web pages
applications	critical reviews	response papers
songs	anecdotes	novels
stories	field notes	cartoons
commentaries	requests	photo essays
dialogues	proposals	directions
editorials	charts/graphs	diaries
research reports	monographs	fictional narratives
book reports	applications	story problems
letters	puzzles	autobiographies
résumés	scripts	drawings
essays	lists	diagrams
memos	notes	e-mail messages
poems	concept maps	

FIGURE 8-2   Purposes for Writing

Purposes for Writing				
Texts and Techniques for Writing	**Writing to Explore** How might students explore ideas and express themselves through writing?	**Writing to Learn About Writing** How might students become better producers of print and nonprint texts?	**Writing to Connect and Transform** How might students use writing to connect with others and make an impact on their world?	**Writing to Showcase** How might students share or demonstrate what they have learned through writing?
Journals and Logs	• Students Keep personal **journals** or **diaries** to record experiences that might lead to future writing topics. • Students keep **learning logs** for recording their growing understanding about particular readings or topics. • Students create **dialectical notebooks** (Berthoff, 1981) to record observations and inferences about their observations of everyday life.	• Students create writing **stylebooks** that include personal skill inventories, spelling lists, and examples of techniques borrowed from published writers. • Students keep **reading journals** or **literature logs** to record responses to literary styles. • Students keep **dialect journals** to record observations about language use in multiple social contexts.	• Students trade **dialogue journals** in which they write informally to their teacher or a peer about their learning experiences. • Students keep project journals as a repository of research citations, writing ideas, interview notes, and for other data on social action or community service projects.	• Students create **writers' notebooks** in which they showcase polished writing, keep notes on future writing ideas, and reflect on their progress over the course of time. • Students keep logs of Internet addresses with evaluation of the sources of information available.

particular activities on the list. What do your feelings and preferences imply for your own teaching of writing with students at the middle school level? Do you hold positive or negative views of any of these categories or any particular activities? What are the implications of these views for you as a middle school writing teacher?

Classroom Case 8-2

Writing Groups That Work

Patricia Lopez makes peer response groups a regular part of her classroom instruction. She admits to having struggled in the past with how to place students in groups:

I used to just number kids off by six or seven and ask them to get into groups. This was usually a disaster. There were always boys who didn't want to sit next to girls or kids from one neighborhood who didn't want to sit next to those from another. It was a mess. Now I plan for my writing groups. First I ask each student to write me a private note, listing people they would like to work with and any individuals they might have trouble working with. I use these lists as a starting point, but I reserve the right to veto anybody's choice if I think that cliques will form or work won't get done.

Then I follow a few rules of thumb:

1. *Each group should have a mix of kids in terms of race and gender.*
2. *Groups should include quiet as well as more talkative kids.*
3. *When I have students with special needs or whose first language isn't English, I try to place one or two of the more "tolerant" kids in that group—people who are likely to help out others and collaborate with those who need extra support.*
4. *Finally, for writing groups, I try to have around three or four per group. If you have more than this, each student doesn't get a chance to share writing. If you have less, and someone is absent, students can get stuck without a group.*

From this starting place, I create my first groupings. I like for kids to stick together for several weeks so that people feel comfortable sharing their writing, but I always reserve the right to break up groups that are too rowdy or not working productively. It's interesting, but I usually don't have to break up groups once they get started. Especially in the first few weeks, I make sure that I constantly circulate around the room, sometimes sitting in on a writing group that seems to be struggling or straying off task. Later, I can hold individual writing or reading conferences while peer groups are under way.

Next, there's the issue of how to respond to each other's writing beyond the usual "it's great" or "it sucks" language that middle school students tend to use. Sometimes I give them a page with three simple prompts and task them to: (a) listen to a writer read a piece aloud, (b) take notes for a few minutes, and (c) respond orally. The prompts are usually something like this:

1. *One thing I noticed about your writing was . . .*
2. *Some questions I had were . . .*
3. *For your next draft you might think about . . .*

For the first few weeks, students fill these forms out each time they give oral feedback on each other's writing. Later, groups can give feedback without writing out their comments first. I collect the written comments as a check on which students may be straying off task or are unclear about how to give productive feedback. Sometimes I give a little mini-lesson on helpful and unhelpful comments just as a reminder.

Eventually I lead students into more extensive types of response. I like to use a list of options I derived from Elbow's book, Writing without Teachers.

1. *Mirroring—paraphrase the writer's text or ideas back to him/her just as you heard them.*
2. *Movies of the Mind—describe your moment-to-moment responses, reactions, images, and feelings as you listened.*
3. *Nutshelling—sum up the writer's main point in a sentence or two.*
4. *Questioning—ask the writer questions about points you are wondering about or points that are unclear to you.*
5. *Pointing—tell the writer what words or phrases successfully "penetrated your skull" or those that were weak, hollow, or empty.*
6. *Potpourri—say whatever comes to mind after hearing the writing. (1973)*

On the first day I hand out this list, I usually cut the class into six sections and ask students sitting in each section to take one of the response options and write an anonymous response to a piece of writing I read aloud to them. I then collect their anonymous responses and read each one to the class, commenting on which responses were most and least helpful to me as a writer. The first time I place students into their writing groups, I ask them to choose one response type—usually "movies of the mind" because that's really fun for them—and to try giving this kind of oral feedback to each other. As weeks go by, they can try other ways of responding as they feel more comfortable as writers and as responders.

We only do writing response groups every week or two in my classroom so kids don't get bored with this activity. If interests begin to wane, I stop them for a while. Generally, though, with a little planning and structure on my part, the kids build their enthusiasm and confidence with a little help from their friends.

I wish I could say that these groups are an unqualified success. I have to admit there are times when students' responses are negative and not productive. There are also those students who enjoy making comments on each other's work but do little to revise their own work in terms of other students' comments. I still feel these group sessions are important. For one thing, students learn to work together. And they're only one part of my writing instruction. I always take the opportunity to hold conferences with students and make comments on some (but not all) of their written work so they have that feedback from me. The peer writing groups serve a couple of important purposes, though: They help kids to understand what it is to write for a real audience, and they make them aware of techniques that other students are using and that they might use in their own writing. For these reasons and many others, I'll continue to use peer groups in my classroom.

For Discussion

If you haven't already done so, try to use some of the response strategies that Patricia has suggested with your own students in peer response groups. In placing students into groups, Patricia tries to support particular students by placing them with more "tolerant" kids. Think about the effect (positive and negative) that this strategy has on the "tolerant" and the "tolerated," and make sure you mix up the arrangements from time to time.

Just as there is a need to create opportunities for social interactions around writing, there is a vital need to respect the privacy of students. Students need to explore their views without fear of the judgments from peers or the evaluation of teachers. As we set up our writing classrooms, we need to consider the obstacles and opportunities that our structures and activities might create for particular students. We need to decide how and when students should be given choices, not only about topics but about the social structure of the classroom as well. Clearly, no one structure is best for all students under all circumstances. We must often negotiate a fine balancing act between careful planning of writing activities and a willingness to adjust the moment-to-moment orchestration of our lessons as the social dynamics shift.

Language Study in Context

You may want your students to research the kinds of writing that their parents or future employers do, investigating what they write as well as the writing, reading, and oral language processes they engage in to accomplish their work. Your students could also explore the ways in which adults often cross disciplinary boundaries in their work. This research could be shared with the whole class through role play, speeches, or dramatic dialogues.

As we addressed in chapter 7, issues of edited English such as grammar, punctuation, and spelling are best taught in the context of students' own language activities. Concentrating on patterns of error rather than editing every error; helping students to keep personal skills inventories of spelling, punctuation, and usage errors; and making "progress, not perfection" your ultimate goal will go a long way in developing your students' knowledge of language conventions without stifling their enthusiasm and creativity.

Writing is one means by which the language arts curriculum can become real and relevant, especially if students are given opportunities to make real contributions to their local community and beyond.

Sometimes this type of writing will demand rigid adherence to particular conventions of edited American English that will allow students to have an impact on others. And sometimes rigid adherence to one set of conventions that do not carry currency in a particular context will prevent their voices from being heard. The ability to move among the multiple ways of writing and make appropriate choices for particular contexts will allow students to write their ways into the larger world.

CREATING A CLASSROOM FOR WRITERS

Clearly, we have a lot to think about in designing and implementing writing lessons. Even though it may appear almost overwhelming, we need to remember that middle school students are likely to meet writing with eagerness, especially if we approach the writing opportunities with enthusiasm, a confidence that all students have something important to say, and a belief that all students can learn.

It is now commonly understood that teachers and learners should attend to both the processes and products of writing. In many middle school classrooms, you may see wall charts and posters that list steps of "The Writing Process" that move linearly from prewriting to drafting, to revising, to editing, to publishing. A focus on both writing process and product has improved writing instruction, but the linear lockstep approach is problematic. Murray (1994) writes that he feels "no loyalty to a process" (p. 60), arguing that the process of writing should be considered always in the plural. He says that the processes change (a) according to the cognitive style of the writer, (b) according to the writing task, and (c) with experience. Murray goes on to identify the range of writing processes that vary from a three-step process (collect, plan, write), to a five-step process (focus, explore, plan, draft, clarify), and up to a seven-step process (focus, collect, share, order, develop, voice, edit).

The point here is to disrupt the notion that there is one linear progression in the writing process. Leading students through a sequence of writing steps may seem like effective writing instruction, but no two writers go through the same steps for all writing. As Murray and many others have demonstrated over the past three decades, writing is recursive rather than linear, and effective writers use only those steps needed for a particular project. As Murray notes, with experience, a writer will internalize some of the planning strategies that are demanded by more familiar tasks and may need extra support for less-familiar tasks.

Savvy middle school writers can co-opt any teacher's attempt to force all writers into the same linear process. They may, for example, complete final drafts first and then "mess it all up to make a first draft" for their teachers. Many of us may have been guilty ourselves of writing a final draft for our teachers and then going back and writing out our outlines after the project was completed. That said, we should focus time and instruction on the multiple processes needed for effective writing. Depending on the purposes and audiences for a particular writing project, some steps of the process should be stressed while some may be omitted altogether.

If our purpose for a particular writing prompt is for students to explore their views on an issue, then prewriting strategies such as brainstorming or concept mapping may be the most appropriate means to achieve that goal. Revision and editing may not come into play at all. By contrast, if a student's goal includes publishing in the local newspaper to enlist the support of community members for a particular position, then revision and editing would clearly be important. It is our hope that middle school students will begin to see that writing has real purposes and the potential for real effects.

Part of creating a welcoming yet honest climate in your writing classroom involves sharing your own writing processes and struggles. It's a good idea, for example, to write alongside your students. This is a quick way to gauge when a writing activity is confusing or bogus. Sharing your writing with students can also build camaraderie, but you must be careful not to set yourself up as the writing-expert-in-residence or the grammar guru. One way of making your writing process more accessible is to model your own drafting processes aloud for students. You could bring in a blank overhead transparency and ask your students to suggest a few

FIGURE 8-3 Observation Task for Composing Aloud Activity

Instructor to Observers

Group A, take notes on what **behaviors** you see as I write (for example, I put down my pen, stare into space, scratch my head, etc.).

Group B, take notes on times when I seem to be **struggling** with my writing. What seems to worry me (for example, what others might think about my language choices)?

Group C, take notes on any **decisions** I appear to be making as I write (for example, whether "frightening" or "scary" is a better word).

---

topics. Then you could proceed to "think aloud" as you move from selecting a topic to creating a rough draft. Before beginning, you might break students into three groups, each with its own task, as outlined in Figure 8-3.

After about 15 minutes, stop and ask students to make a list of at least three questions they would like to ask about your composing process. Then ask students to report on what they have noticed from their particular vantage point. After this discussion, students are free to ask any further questions about your writing processes.

Many years ago, Donald Murray spoke at the National Council of Teachers of English annual conference. Although we can't remember his exact words, the gist of his message went something like this: "We have an ethical responsibility to fail more often in front of our students." It's an interesting paradox that, within limits, the more vulnerable we become, the more powerful our teaching becomes. We would all do well to remember that adage as we nurture and develop the multiple writing processes of our middle school students.

We'd now like to focus on an increasingly popular approach that allows teachers to attend to the processes and products of student writing: the writers' workshop.

The Writers' Workshop as a Structure for Learning

A writers' workshop includes time to write, to respond to peers, to confer with the teacher and peers, to share, and to publish. There is no one correct way to set up a writers' workshop in your classroom. Some workshops last an entire semester, some for 3 to 6 weeks. Some teachers sponsor writers' workshops 2 days a week, whereas others hold workshops every day. Some workshop models allow students to be completely in control of what they write; others may be designed around a theme or genre. Atwell (1987) and Rief (1991) provide a wealth of information on how to facilitate a workshop.

In many workshop models, students enter the classroom and begin to work on their individual writing projects. The teacher may give a mini-lesson (5 to 20 minutes) for the whole class or for those needing to work on a particular strategy or skill.

A table may be set up in the corner of the room for conferences. In some versions, students sign up for a conference with their peers or their teacher on an as-needed basis; in others, teachers hold regular conferences on a rotating schedule. Often the students themselves determine when they are ready to share, but some workshops include regular "sharing circles" each week. Students may share their work in progress or polished pieces. Often classrooms are organized with an area set aside for sharing that includes an author's chair (Graves, 1982). The chair may be a rocking chair, an overstuffed chair, or simply a tall stool placed in a significant location in the room where the author sits to read to peers. Some middle school classrooms have a big couch and a rug for comfortable sharing times. The physical room arrangement may not be critical to a workshop's success, but attention to the physical arrangement can help to create opportunities for the kinds of activities that support young writers.

The writers' workshop can be an effective means by which students can learn from, support, and teach their peers. The workshop structure accommodates middle school students' needs for social interaction and self-expression, something the National Middle School Association and other middle school specialists advocate. According to the Carnegie Task Force on Education for Young Adolescents (1995), a focus on early adolescents' social needs has overshadowed their needs for academic rigor. Under the skilled and caring guidance of a middle school teacher, however, a writers' workshop can accommodate both academic rigor and social interaction. The writers' workshop in which students share their writing and their expertise will create opportunities for students to gain confidence and competence in themselves as writers and as learners. Workshops have proven effective because they balance individual and group work as well as explicit instruction and writing as rehearsal. Workshops often include sharing and publishing to make visible the ways in which writing can have a real impact on individual students, their peers, and the larger community. The photograph in Figure 8-4 shows the kind of involvement that can be achieved when students write collaboratively in a classroom setting.

Recording Students' Progress

In any writing workshop, the teacher must attend to record keeping. Students can take on many of the responsibilities by keeping a writer's record of their writing, their progress, their skills, and their publications. Such records may be kept in the classroom, or students may be expected to carry their writing folders to class each day. Because many middle school teachers have more than 150 students, it is vitally important to have a system of record keeping.

There is no one correct or easy way to manage the paper load. But without an effective and efficient system, the workshop is sure to fail. Harried teachers may simply drop the workshop for some other pedagogical practices that generate less paper. If you decide to set up a workshop, you must create a comfortable structure within which you and your students can thrive. Depending on the purposes and goals, a writers' workshop can be set in harmony with any approach to literacy teaching, such as text-centered, personal growth, or sociopolitical.

FIGURE 8-4 A Writers' Workshop in Progress

To illustrate more concretely one way in which a workshop might be implemented and monitored, we present Michael's story in Classroom Case 8-3. As you read his story, try to tease out the assumptions that appear to guide him in his teaching decisions.

Classroom Case 8-3

Facilitating One Writing Classroom

It was late January and Michael had been in his student teaching assignment for just 2 weeks when his mentor teacher suggested that he begin planning for a 3-week writing unit with his sixth-grade students at Irvin Middle School. Irvin is a rural middle school with a large bussed-in population. As students in a rural township school, all of Michael's students rode the bus at least 30 miles every day. Michael knew very little about his students except that most were farmers and most were working class or poor. Michael decided to tap the expertise of his students and organize a writing unit around the theme of animals, something many of them had already written about in detail.

After inquiring about a field trip to the zoo 60 miles away, he learned that the school's budget and bus scheduling wouldn't allow for such a trip. Refusing to be deterred, Michael began planning his writing unit. In an attempt to balance both student choice and attention to the department's language arts goals, Michael developed social and academic goals for his students that included punctuating dialogue correctly, using factual information to support a position, working collaboratively with a small group, and sharing writing in a public forum. After conferring with his mentor teacher about how to make this writing unit real and relevant, he decided that the culminating activity would be to write and perform scripts for a sixth-grade version of the television show *Animal Planet* and invite kindergarten and first-grade students to attend.

To support writing, Michael selected clips from the television shows *Dogs with Jobs* and *Animal Planet*. He also selected the short story "Dirk, The Protector" from *My Life in Dog Years* by Gary Paulsen (1999). From the public library, Michael checked out an audiotape of Paulsen discussing his preparation for the Iditarod, the great Alaskan dog sled race. He planned to ask students to conduct an interview with a pet owner and to invite Ms. Lawson to come in and speak about her seeing-eye dog.

Michael thought this unit would work well to teach his students about writing within a real-world context. Rather than emphasizing issues of correctness severed from context, Michael embedded these issues within students' own writing, helping them to learn that language choices are "correct" when they match the context in which they are used. As a mini-inquiry project, students would collect "bits of language" about pets from two sources: one informal source such as stories about pets from family and friends, and one more formal such as an encyclopedia entry, documentary, or pamphlet from a veterinarian's office. They would then analyze the ways in which the same animal was described in these different contexts and write about the similarities and differences. He also identified two skills he would address in writing lessons: punctuation marks and the use of paragraphing.

Michael began close to home. On the first day of the unit, he brought in a photograph of his cats, Betty Lou and Big Gray. After sharing a story about how he acquired Betty Lou, he asked students to share any stories they had about their own pets. He then conducted a mini-lesson on using quotation marks.

He asked students to pair up and write a brief imagined conversation between his cats and another person or animal. After about 10 minutes of working time, Michael asked if any partnership would like to come to the front of the class to read their dialogues. He shared his own short conversation about Betty Lou scolding Big Gray for being so rude to a visiting dog. As pairs read aloud, Michael pointed out when the paragraphs would change to indicate a new speaker and how quotation marks would be used to help readers keep track of who was talking.

Michael concluded that first day with an overview of the coming weeks. There would be workshop time to write stories of real or imaginary animals, small-group time to research and plan a script for their very own edition of *Animal World*, and partnership time to investigate how realistically animals are portrayed or treated in a movie or television show. He explained that one or two guest speakers would talk about caring for and being cared for by animals. He concluded the day with a short poem about cats by May Swenson.

During the following days, Michael provided much time for students to write individually about their pets and any other animals they found interesting. Their individual writing time was interspersed with whole-class discussions and some direct teaching. Each student was expected to complete a writing folder that included stories and poems about animals, one critical analysis of a television or movie with animals in it, and a television script with suggestions for costumes and stage directions.

Focus On
Reading and Viewing

Focus On
Language Study

Focus On
Reading and Viewing

Focus On
Talking and Listening

Focus On
Language Study

Over the course of 3 weeks, Michael's students worked collaboratively to create scripts and present 5-minute television programs for young children focused on different animals. Students brought in props, drawings, puppets, and even live animals. Michael videotaped these performances, and they were eventually shown to the first-grade and kindergarten classes. His students felt so proud as they saw their work on a television screen, and the eager response of these young people made the experience even more memorable.

For Discussion

You can see how Michael worked within the parameters of his department and school to provide meaningful writing opportunities for his students. While he was very disappointed that a trip to the zoo was not considered possible, he understood the economic constraints of such a trip and was pleased that his enthusiasm had been contagious. As a student teacher, Michael had developed plans and activities that were exceptional. He connected to his students' experiences, since most were farmers and many were members of the 4-H clubs. He built in choice and structure. Yet, in the end, he struggled with the same challenge that most beginning teachers face: How do teachers turn all of this into something to record in a grade book? Michael wanted the video presentations to serve as a celebration for learning rather than as an occasion for assessment, so he hesitated to assign a letter grade to the final videos. He didn't want to create any kind of competition among his students by judging the videos or awarding prizes, because he feared that might undermine his students' sense of collaboration and celebration. As you think about Michael's lessons, think about some concrete ways that he could build in both formative and summative assessments that tap the multiple academic and social competencies his students have acquired. What are some alternatives to grading or awarding prizes to those final videotapes?

The following section offers some ideas for assessment that might help you to answer these questions.

INTEGRATING ASSESSMENTS

It's important to distinguish between response, evaluation, and grading. Response involves giving students the benefit of your personal reaction to their writing. In contrast to response, evaluation involves judging student work against some kind of standard. Given that middle school students often make great strides in learning that are not evident in their final products, you will want to attend to the processes as well as the products of their writing, and you will want to make clear to students how you are attending to each.

In 1993 the NCTE Committee on Assessment was assigned the task of developing an official position statement aimed at securing the best assessment options for all students. The statement was approved for publication by the Conference on College Composition and Communication in 1995 and can be found in its entirety on the Web at *http://www.ncte.org/about/over/positions/category/assess/107610.htm.*

The document presents several important tenets in assessing writing, but three are particularly important for middle school writers:

- Writing is most effective where it accomplishes something the user wants to accomplish for particular listeners or readers. Additionally, assessment must be contextualized in terms of why, where, and for what purpose it is being undertaken; this context must also be clear to the students being assessed.
- Since language by definition is social, assessments that isolate students and forbid discussion and feedback from others conflict with current cognitive and psychological research about language use and the benefits of social interaction during the writing process.
- Writing "ability" is the sum of individual ability and a variety of skills employed in a diversity of contexts. Consequently one piece of writing—even if it is generated under the most desirable conditions—can never serve as an indicator of overall literacy, particularly for high-stakes decisions. Ideally, such literacy must be assessed by more than one piece of writing, in more than one genre, written on different occasions (accessed from the NCTE Web site on February 1, 2006, at *http://www.ncte.org/about/over/positions/category/assess/107610.htm.*

In sum, these tenets of assessment from NCTE seem to say that a competent assessment system should encourage middle school students to write for purposes and audiences that are real and important to them; demonstrate their writing abilities through more than one writing sample; be given time and resources to plan, draft, revise, and edit; and participate in the assessment of their own writing.

The next section will describe some ideas for assessing student progress before assigning that final grade.

Monitoring Progress: Formative Assessments

We begin with the premise that some writing will be abandoned before reaching any final draft stage. For any number of reasons, some middle school students who may have learned a great deal about or through writing will not complete a final writing project. We ask you to hold three action principles in the back of your mind as you think about formative as well as summative assessments for middle school writers: "practice without penalty," "processes and products," and "progress, not perfection."

Practice without penalty.   As a middle school teacher, you'll want to provide all students with opportunities for practice. Too many teachers assign writing without providing time for experimentation and rehearsal. Fear of the grade may inhibit students from experimenting with styles or rhetorical devices that they do not have command of. For example, give your students lots of opportunities to practice a rhetorical technique or an unfamiliar genre and then ask them to select one piece that they want to have graded. For some students, activities and projects like keeping a writer's notebook and producing a particular number of "polished" pieces of writing per marking periods work very well. As a way of supporting practice, part of your grade can be determined by a simple contract such as the one in Figure 8-5.

FIGURE 8-5 Grading Contract

Twenty percent of your grade for the next 6 weeks will be based on your creative writing. Grades will be determined as follows:

To earn an A:

- Hand in FOUR polished pieces (these pieces must be submitted to me in advance and judged as acceptable).
- Keep copies of all drafts for these and other writing in your writing journal.
- Get written feedback from at least one classmate on each of these four pieces-in-progress.

To earn a B:

- Follow the same procedure as above, producing THREE polished drafts.

To earn a C:

- Follow the same procedure as above in producing TWO polished drafts.

Create writing activities that are written with a partner or in a small group.

Ask your middle school students to read their writing with a partner to reduce the anxiety that may have inhibited learning. Create opportunities for students to play with language. Simply allow for many pieces to be abandoned.

Processes and products. Students make tremendous strides in learning that may never appear on any final draft, and errors may actually be signs of growth. It may sound simple to assess the processes as well as the products along the way, but it's often hard to get a handle on exactly what processes to assess and how you might see evidence of them, much less assess them. Below are just a few examples of record-keeping systems you might use for assessing students' writing folders and daily behaviors.

> **Language Study in Context**
>
> As you discover patterns of errors in students' written work, you might ask them to keep a skills inventory. In a three-column chart they can list (a) a description of the error, written in their own words, (b) two examples of the error in their own writing with corrections, and (c) a gimmick or trick to help them remember how to avoid the error.

And remember that writing can serve as a springboard that will lead to learning in multiple ways. Writing may be the process by which your middle school students learn and rehearse, which ultimately leads to a final product that is not text based. For example, after researching a topic of interest to them, students might document their learning by creating a Web page, a DVD, or a PowerPoint presentation. After learning how to compare and contrast in written form, for instance, they might use this learning to design a community-based project that has real application to their families.

Progress, not perfection. Just as one of your first sewing projects or welding projects may have had unsightly globs, clumps, or puckers, the fact that the sleeve or handle stayed on is evidence that you were making progress. We are not suggesting that the conventions of edited American English go untaught or unevaluated. Lisa Delpit (1988, 1991, 2002), among others, advocates for explicit instruction so that children who are not born into the dominant dialect may gain access to further opportunities that are often denied them due to linguistic stereotyping and prejudice. We have already discussed the need to evaluate students on their growth as writers rather than their ability to produce error-free papers. We still can't do that. While clearly one goal will be to move students toward understanding and using the conventions of edited American English, middle school students may actually make more mistakes for a time as they are trying out new techniques. For example, if students' spelling seems to degenerate, they may simply be trying out complicated vocabulary or syntax patterns. If organization falls apart, they may be trying to write in a genre they've never tried before. Think about the last time you tried something completely new like learning a new software program. How many mistakes, computer crashes, and calls to support personnel did it take before you felt proficient? Writing is more like a heartbeat (with those inevitable peaks and dips) than a straight line to perfection. This leads to our third watch phrase—"progress, not perfection."

You can keep track of your students learning and document their progress in a variety of ways.

Anecdotal records.   Keeping anecdotal records in your journal or plan book is a good way to document student progress and to remind yourself of issues you would like to bring up in writing or evaluation conference. Remember that this list is only a starting place. You'll want to add to it as other ideas occur to you.

- Do students produce multiple drafts for at least some pieces of writing?
- Can they make local (word level) as well as global (paragraph level or larger) revisions?
- Do you see evidence that they are experimenting with literacy devices, rhetorical strategies, or new vocabulary?
- Can they give substantive oral and/or written feedback on writing to their peers?
- Do they appear to be on task during writing time?
- Can they describe the progress they made and their goals in writing conference with you?
- Can they articulate their writing decisions?
- Can they describe why one piece of their writing is better than another?
- Can they recognize problems in their own writing?
- Do they show progress on the goals you set in evaluation conferences?
- Can they generate writing topics of interest to them?

In addition to assessing processes, you will want to find effective and efficient means to manage the paper load. In the following sections, we present some examples of how you might balance student- and teacher-centered assessment in your writing curriculum.

Conferences.   In periodic evaluation conferences, you can ask students to look over their writing logs and address how they were accomplishing their goals. Instead of grading or responding to each piece of writing, you can ask students to select one piece of writing that they see as their best and compare it to a draft they wrote earlier in the year in terms of what it shows about their development as a writer. This procedure gives some of the responsibility to students and reduces your paper load, allowing more attention to the student-selected piece of writing.

Student self-evaluations.   Students can keep records of their writing in progress and periodically evaluate their development as writers. At particular points in the school year, ask students to record how they are spending their time and what skills they are currently targeting. After a writing conference with you, remind them to record their weekly progress, including goals and accomplishments. Periodically, ask students to create an overall progress report based on their log entries. Depending on their level of comfort and expertise in assessing their own work, you will want to guide their self-evaluation accordingly (see Figure 8-6).

FIGURE 8-6   Self-Evaluation

Name _____

Week _____ to Week _____ (include dates since last evaluation conference)

The goals that I have worked on for the past 3 weeks are:

I have done the following to achieve these goals:

My best piece of writing for the past 3 weeks is (give title and dates of all drafts):

I think it is the best because (state at least three specific reasons):

I have read the following (books/chapters) for independent reading:

Based on the work described above, I believe that I deserve a grade of _____.

For example, you might ask students to respond to the following prompts just prior to each marking period:

- What are your strengths as a writer?
- What are two goals that you have set for yourself?
- What are two goals that you and I have set for you, and how have you met them?

Writers' notebooks. Similar to learning logs, writers' notebooks may be places where writers reflect on their writing. You might want to assign some focused activities such as exercises for generating topics, short writing prompts, and guided self-assessment prompts for students to include in their notebooks. Short excerpts from books on writing by authors such as Anne Lamott (1994), Natalie Goldberg (1986), and Ralph Fletcher (1996) stimulate ideas for students' own writing about writing in their writer's notebooks.

There's no doubt that, given the class load of the average middle school teacher, we cannot afford to read and respond to every entry in our students' journals. One technique to monitor progress and turn over some of the responsibility to students is to periodically give students two sticky notes or paper clips and ask them to read through their own journals, selecting one or two entries for which they would like some response. You may then select one or two more at random. In self-selecting the entries for you to read, students have greatly reduced your paper load. More important, they have analyzed and reread their journals with a critical eye.

Peer group records and checkpoints. Asking groups to evaluate their processes is tricky but important. In many group situations, one or two students carry the others; if we value group work, we need to evaluate how groups are functioning. Just as with individual projects, group work can produce a great deal of student learning that is not readily visible in the final project. Periodically, you can ask each group member to write a brief summary, listing what the group has accomplished to date and specifically addressing the ways that individual participants contributed to the group's progress.

Creating in-progress checkpoints for understanding may help some groups to efficiently organize their time and attend to the tasks at hand. Likewise, these checkpoints will reduce the likelihood that students can simply plagiarize their writing project or procrastinate until the quality is compromised. You may provide a progress checklist or create one collaboratively with your students. These checkpoints will help you to keep tabs on both the group dynamics and the production schedule. For example, say a group is planning to write a script for a radio show to be taped and played for classmates. Their checklist might look something like this:

_____ Day 3: All group members have chosen topics. Topics approved by teacher.
_____ Day 5: Notes from interviews shared with all group members.
_____ Day 6: Drafts of new reports written and shared with group members.
_____ Day 7: Order of reports decided. Oral practice of reports. Introductions written.
_____ Day 8: Practiced with visuals, costumes, and props.
_____ Day 9: Videotape show.

FIGURE 8-7 How We Talk About Our Animals

As part of our animal unit, select an animal in which you are especially interested. You will need to collect information for your report from at least two sources. One of your sources should be someone you know pretty well. Family, friends, or neighbors may be good sources of information about the animal you have selected. The other source should be considered an expert on the animal. You may find an encyclopedia, documentary, Internet site, zookeeper, pet storeowner, or veterinarian to help you. This is a big project and we'll be doing lots of practice in class. We will pay close attention to the different ways we talk about animals. You will have two parts to your report; a visual representation (that may be a graph, chart, or table) and your writing where you talk about the similarities and differences that you found in your research. Later we will use some of your research for our video project.

As noted earlier, middle school students sometimes invest an incredible amount of energy and make tremendous leaps in learning but fail to show these leaps in the finer details of a completed project. Designing checkpoints can assist you in providing structured support along the way for your students and can highlight both the processes and products of their learning.

Writing rubrics. A rubric can make your expectations visible and support learners who may not understand the task at hand. A rubric should be written in language that students understand, and often includes attention to both the processes and products of writing. It may include reflections on students' writing processes and their development as writers. A writing rubric should be intricately tied to writing tasks. Be leery of writing rubrics that are disconnected from the task, audience, or context in which the writing has occurred.

If you want students to participate in establishing criteria for the rubric, you can bring in a couple of points that are important to you, such as "Your essay should show a clear cause-effect organizational pattern," and then ask students to help you think of other criteria for the rubric. As part of his unit on animals, for example, Michael gave out the assignment sheet in Figure 8-7 to his students.

Some time before the project was due, Michael brought in a blank rubric on an overhead transparency and created the grading rubric in Figure 8-8 with his students. Some states have grade-level writing rubrics that will be used to assess students in a standardized testing situation. You should familiarize yourself with those rubrics so you can provide meaningful opportunities for your students to learn the content to be tested.

Writing portfolios. Writing portfolios should include more than copies of students' polished drafts. You may want students to keep drafts-in-progress as well as writing goals and self-assessments. You may ask students to keep process portfolios or showcase portfolios. If students do a great deal of writing in your classroom, writing portfolios can become unwieldy. Your room will certainly fill to overflowing. As you think about the portfolio as a tool to document growth over time, consider what central elements will be necessary. Whether your students' writing portfolios are kept in cereal boxes, notebooks, folders, or on Web pages, you will want to create

FIGURE 8-8 Grading Rubric for Animal Project

Research	Excellent	Good	Needs Work
	I have two sources. I give examples from each. I made a good selection for my sources.	I have two sources. I could have included more examples of the different ways that my animal is described.	I didn't have two sources.
Organization	I tell about the similarities and differences. It is easy to see on the graph what I learned. My report is easy to understand.	I jumped around just a little bit, but I did a pretty good job. I could take more time to help my readers follow my ideas.	I didn't help my readers to understand what I learned. My paper is confusing.
Skill Builders	I began a new paragraph when I presented different speakers or ideas. I used quotation marks when I included the exact words that someone said.	I used paragraphs much of the time. I used quotation marks at times, but I didn't always use them in the right places.	I didn't use what we have been learning in class about paragraphs and quotations. I need to put these on my skill-building chart.

something that is manageable. Many teachers discontinue portfolio keeping because they simply cannot physically handle all of the papers or containers. As one way of managing "portfolio overload," you could ask students to keep copies of everything they write in process portfolios. Periodically, ask them to select a finished piece to place in their showcase portfolio, which can be kept in a file cabinet, carton, or shelf in the classroom. Items from the process portfolio not included in the final showcase portfolio can be discarded or taken home.

Reflective windows.   Along with the pieces of writing that are placed into the showcase portfolio, you might ask students to search through their writers' notebooks and give you a "window" into their thinking about writing. In these reflective windows, students will write a commentary in which they address what they learned, what they did particularly well, why they consider this selection a representation of their best work, and how they plan to continue to grow as writers.

Students will need to learn to write differently for different contexts. Think about the many rhetorical decisions you make in writing for different classes, for different occupations, and for different people. Keep these differences in mind as you explore writing in the disciplines in Fieldwork Journal 8-3.

Fieldwork Journal 8-3

Writing Across the Disciplines

Our job as middle school teachers is to guide our students to use writing in more complex ways to reach their goals. Of course, our job is also to help our students make connections with other disciplines in school and beyond. Our students likely will be asked to write in all of their classes. Conduct an interview to find out what kinds of writing are demanded in science, math, social studies, or any other class you choose. If possible, interview a middle school teacher who is teaching many of the same students you are. You may be able to set up an interview at your next team meeting or simply ask to meet individually with this teacher.

During your interview, ask about the kinds of writing that students are expected to do in that class. Then ask about the writing demanded in a profession closely aligned to that subject matter. Be careful not to go in with an agenda to teach or judge your colleagues, and avoid writing jargon. Focus your interview questions on the kinds of writing your students must do to succeed in that class and what they must do to write well as scientists, artists, historians, or mathematicians.

You may want to share with others what you have learned about writing in the disciplines. Depending on your teaching circumstances, you may want to design supports for your students based on the writing demands you have identified. You may even be able to collaborate with those on your teaching team to design a writing project that straddles one or more subject areas.

Next, we'll discuss the impact of new technologies on your writing curriculum.

USING TECHNOLOGY EFFECTIVELY WITH MIDDLE SCHOOL WRITERS

It goes without saying that electronic and other technologies have transformed our definitions of what writing is and our writing processes as well. Jonathan Bush is an associate professor of English Education who has long been interested in ways of infusing technology into the middle school classroom. In Classroom Case 8-4, he shares what he has learned in working in middle schools as a teacher, in-service facilitator, and researcher.

Classroom Case 8-4

Information Technology

The middle school literacy classroom is an ideal place for the appropriate integration of new computer technologies. The thematic and interdisciplinary nature of the middle school context, combined with the emphasis on student development and expression, creates many opportunities for effective technology integration. The World Wide Web and other Internet technologies, including class discussion boards, real-time chat, and online document sharing, are effective tools for young writers. Technology also affords various means of publishing, such as Web publishing opportunities, document design, and digital video and audio.

But with these technologies come responsibilities and dilemmas. As teachers of middle school English language arts who use technology, we must consider our goals as teachers and work to ensure that the technologies we integrate into our classrooms do not work to subvert these goals. In particular, we need to consider some potential shoulds and shouldn'ts as we experiment with these technologies in our classrooms.

The list in Figure 8-9 represents some veteran middle school teachers' concepts of what should and should not occur when technology is integrated into the English language arts classroom. It is important, however, for individual teachers to develop their own guiding concepts of technology based on their unique classroom goals and contexts.

Here are some examples of potentially positive uses of some of these technologies in middle school English language arts.

To Expand the Dimensions of Literacy

- Students can explore the genre of the Web site and learn the characteristics of effective www-based communication, including means of evaluating online sources and their biases and potential credibility.
- Students can extend their knowledge and perspectives on issues by searching for Internet resources on project elements or classroom issues.

To Support Teaching

- Class Web sites can be used by teachers to organize information, communicate goals and strategies to parents, and support home-school connections.
- Email offers a way for parents to communicate with teachers.

FIGURE 8-9 Technology in Middle School Classrooms

Should	Shouldn't
• Work to validate individual students and empower their ability to achieve academic success.	• Replace complex language and development goals with more simplistic "learn the technology" goals.
• Enhance traditional print/literature/media materials.	• Replace traditional print/literature/media materials.
• Amplify students' means of expression and broaden their opportunities to reach meaningful audiences.	• Disrupt normal classroom community and critically based objectives.
• Deepen students' understanding of complex issues and enhance their ability to make global connections.	• Stifle students' ability to participate by favoring students with advantaged access to technology.
• Expand the dimensions of literacy.	• Deepen social and economic inequities.
• Facilitate an open forum for discussion that allows for more free and democratic participation.	• Replace teacher-student/student-student interaction.

- Free online teaching sites such as *blackboard.com* offer services that allow teachers to organize classes, archive information and student work, and generally assist in the integration of technologies in class activities.

To Support and Enhance Classroom Discussions
- Student-led, small-group, real-time chats and whole-class discussion boards can allow for more participation by normally shy or less confident students.
- Follow-up searches of online resources and ancillary materials can be conducted. If a topic/issue interests students during a class discussion, the technology can be used to explore it further.

To Create Opportunities For Expanded Publishing/Audiences
- Students can create group or individual Web sites as a means of sharing research findings with wider audiences.
- Students can interact with others, both locally and internationally, via email, discussion boards, or teacher-led, real-time chats in and outside class.
- Students can use visual technologies to create, manage, and design documents, thereby expanding their abilities to express their ideas through new means.

Technology can support our writing goals and those of the young writers in our classrooms.

For Discussion
Think about a lesson or set of lessons that you are preparing. What are some specific ways that you might include technology into the goals and activities? Are there ways that technology might assist you to cross disciplinary boundaries within these lessons? Are there ways that attention to technology might open your classroom door to other classrooms, local neighborhoods and/or international communities?

The role of the middle school teacher is to guide students to use writing in a more complex manner, to employ writing as a tool to reach their goals. As a middle school teacher, you'll want to help your students attend to the content as well as the conventions. Too often perhaps in middle school settings, writing is reduced to filling in the blanks. To gain independence as writers, middle school students need to create their own blanks, to decide what best serves their goals and purposes. But, of course, they will need support to learn to employ the most effective processes to achieve their writing goals. They will need guidance and direct instruction to learn what rhetorical decisions or technological tools to use, what writing steps to take, and what conventions to follow. They will need opportunities to practice making choices, making mistakes, and making connections.

In the next chapter, you'll have an opportunity to explore oral language and consider how to create effective speaking and performance activities with middle school students. We turn your attention now to the NCTE/IRA standards.

Standards in Practice

Viewing Your Writing Lessons Through the NCTE/IRA Standards

Locate a copy of the *NCTE/IRA Standards for the English Language Arts* (1996). For an explanation of the standards as well as a table of contents for the volume, an annotated listing of each standard, and chapter excerpts, consult the NCTE Web site at this address: *http://www.ncte.org/standards.*

All of the standards may be relevant to your writing classroom. But, for purposes of this exercise, we suggest you look most closely at Standards 5, 7, and 8. You will notice that within each standard are words or phrases that could be construed as subgoals for your writing classroom. Begin with Standard 5. What subgoals are embedded within this standard? Read this standard closely and attempt to tease apart the multiple goals embedded within it. Highlight the subgoals or list them separately on a piece of paper.

Standard five: Students employ a wide range of strategies as they write and use different writing process elements appropriate to communicate with different audiences for a variety of purposes.

Standard seven: Students conduct research on issues and interests by generating ideas and questions, and by posing problems. They gather, evaluate, and synthesize data from a variety of sources (e.g., print and non-print texts, artifacts, people) to communicate their discoveries in ways that suit their purpose and audience.

Standard eight: Students use a variety of technological and information resources (e.g., libraries, databases, computer networks, and videos) to gather and synthesize information and to create and communicate knowledge.

FIGURE 8-10   Addressing Standards in Our Practices

Addressing Standards in Our Practices	
Activities	**Connection to Standards**
• Complete a writing folder that includes stories and poems about animals.	• Employ a wide range of strategies as they write.
• One critical analysis of a television show or movie focused on animals.	• Use a variety of technological resources. • Synthesize data from a variety of sources.
• Videotape script.	• Use a variety of technological resources.
• Show video to kindergartners and first graders.	• Communicate with different audiences.

Now, look at a writing lesson you have created or one you are in the process of writing. If you aren't currently planning lessons of your own, you might want to refer to Michael's writing lessons about animals, presented in Classroom Case 8-3. For each activity in your lesson plan, try to tie it to one or more of the subgoals. As an example, we have paraphrased some of Michael's activities in Figure 8-10. Beside each activity, we placed the relevant subgoals. For practice, look through Michael's animal workshop against the backdrop of the three standards listed here. Do you note any subgoals that have not been addressed?

Although you can't address all standards in all lessons, on occasion you may want to look closely at the standards to determine how you are addressing them in relevant ways for your particular students in your particular community. There are valid reasons to emphasize some over others. If you find that you do not address some subgoals, you should consider why not. You may have valid reasons for such omissions.

REFERENCES

Atwell, N. (1987). *In the middle: Writing, reading, and learning with adolescents.* Portsmouth, NH: Boynton/Cook.

Berthoff, A. (1981). *The making of meaning: Metaphors, models, and maxims for writing teachers.* Upper Montclair, NJ: Boynton/Cook.

Carnegie Task Force on Education for Young Adolescents. (1995). Great transitions: Preparing adolescents for a new century. Washington, DC: Carnegie Council on Adolescent Development.

Carrington, V., & Luke, A. (2003). Reading, homes and families: From postmodern to modern? In A. van Kleeck, S. A. Stahl, & E. B. Bauer (Eds.), *On reading to children: Parents and teachers.* Mahwah, NJ: Lawrence Erlbaum.

Comber, B., & Simpson, A. (Eds.). (2001). *Negotiating critical literacies in the classroom.* Mahwah, NJ: Lawrence Erlbaum.

Delpit, L. (1988). The silenced dialogue: Power and pedagogy in educating other people's children. *Harvard Education Review, 58,* 280–298.

Delpit, L. (1991). A conversation with Lisa Delpit. *Language Arts, 68,* 541–547.

Delpit, L. (2002). What should teachers do?: Ebonics and culturally responsive instruction. In B. Power & R. Hubbard (Eds.), *Language development: A reader for teachers* (2nd ed., pp. 124–128). Upper Saddle River, NJ: Merrill/Prentice Hall.

Edelsky, C. (1996). *With literacy and justice for all: Rethinking the social in language and education (Critical perspectives on literacy and education).* New York: Taylor & Francis.

Elbow, P. (1973). Writing without teachers. Oxford, England: Oxford University Press.

Fletcher, R. (1996). *A writer's notebook: Unlocking the writer within you.* New York: Avon.

Goldberg, N. (1986). *Writing down the bones: Freeing the writer within.* New York: Random House.

Graves, D. (1982). *Writing: Teachers and children at work.* Portsmouth, NH: Heinemann.

Lamott, A. (1994). *Bird by bird: Some instructions on writing and life.* NY: Anchor.

Luke, A., & Carrington, V. (2002). Globalisation, literacy, curriculum practice. In R. Fisher, M. Lewis, & G. Brooks (Eds.), *Raising standards in literacy* (pp. 231–250). London: Routledge.

Luke, A., Freebody, P., & Land, R. (2000). *Literate futures: The Queensland state literacy strategy.* Brisbane, Australia: Education Queensland. [http://www.qed.qld.gov.au]

Murray, D. (1994). Knowing and not knowing In L. Tobin & T. Newkirk (Eds.), *Taking stock: The writing process movement in the'90s* (pp. 57-65). Portsmouth, NH: Boynton/Cook (Heinemann).

Paulsen, G. (1999). *My life in dog years.* New York: Bantam Doubleday Dell.

Rief, L. (1991). *Seeking diversity: Language arts with adolescents.* Portsmouth, NH: Heinemann.

RESOURCES

Print

Allen, J., & Gonzalez, K. (1998). *There's room for me here: Literacy workshops in the middle school.* Portland, ME: Stenhouse.

Alvermann, D. (2002). *New literacies and digital technologies: A focus on adolescent learners in new times.* New York: Peter Lang Publisher.

Alvermann, D. E., Moon, J. S., & Haygood, M. C. (1999). *Popular culture in the classroom: Teaching and researching critical media literacy.* Newark, DE: International Reading Association.

Atwell, N. (1998). *In the middle: New understandings about writing, reading, and learning* (2nd ed.). Portsmouth, NH: Boynton/Cook (Heinemann).

Atwell, N., & Newkirk, T. (1987). *Understanding writing: Ways of observing, learning, and teaching.* Portsmouth, NH: Heinemann.

Booth, D. (2001). *Reading and writing in the middle years.* Portland, ME: Stenhouse.

Butler, A., & Turbill, J. (1987). *Towards a reading-writing classroom.* Portsmouth, NH: Heinemann.

Christian, S. (1997). *Exchanging lives: Middle school writers online.* Urbana, IL: National Council of Teachers of English.

Dorn, L., & Soffos, C. (2001). *Scaffolding young writers: A writers' workshop approach.* Portland, ME: Stenhouse.

Fletcher, R. (1996). *Breathing in, breathing out: Keeping a writer's notebook.* Portsmouth, NH: Heinemann.

Fletcher, R., & Portalupi, J. (1998). *Craft lessons: Teaching writing K–8.* Portland, ME: Stenhouse.

Fountas, I. C., & Pinnell, G. S. (2001). *Guiding readers and writers (Grades 3-6): Teaching comprehension, genre, and content literacy.* Portsmouth, NH: Heinemann.

Graves, D. (1991). *Build a literate classroom (Reading/writing teacher's companion).* Portsmouth, NH: Heinemann.

Graves, D. (1994). *A fresh look at writing.* Portsmouth, NH: Heinemann.

Hall, S. (1981). Teaching about race. In A. James & R. Jeffcoate (Eds.), *The school in the multicultural society* (pp. 58–69). London: Harper.

Hull, G., & Schultz, K. (2002). *School's out! Bridging out-of-school literacies with classroom practice.* New York: Teachers College Press.

Lensmire, T. (1994). *When children write: Critical re-visions of the writing workshop.* New York: Teachers College Press.

Lensmire, T. (2000). *Powerful writing, responsible teaching.* New York: Teachers College Press.

Mahiri, J. (1998). *Shooting for excellence: African American and youth culture in new century schools.* Urbana, IL: NCTE.

National Council of Teachers of English. (1996). *Motivating writing in middle school. Standards Consensus Series.* Urbana, IL: Author.

Tobin, L., & Newkirk, T. (1994). *Taking stock: The writing process movement in the'90s.* Portsmouth, NH: Boynton/Cook (Heinemann).

Underwood, T. (1999). *The portfolio project: A study of assessment, instruction, and middle school reform.* Urbana, IL: National Council of Teachers of English.

Yagelski, R., & Leonard, S. (2002). *The relevance of English: Teaching that matters in students' lives.* New York: Teachers College Press.

Yancey, K. (1992). *Portfolios in the writing classroom: An introduction.* Urbana, IL: National Council of Teachers of English.

Electronic

Blackboard.com. Although Blackboard is a commercial software company that creates proprietary software for sale, the company also offers some free resources for teachers on its Web site. This site allows you to create your own course site, manage course documents, assist student groups, run course discussion boards and real-time chats, and use numerous other services.

http://www.blackboard.com

The National Writing Project. The mission of the NWP is to improve the teaching of writing and improve learning in the nation's schools. Through its professional development model, the National Writing Project recognizes the primary importance of teacher knowledge, expertise, and leadership.

http://www.writingproject.org/

NCTE Position on Writing Assessments. NCTE and IRA have created these standards for writing assessment.

http://www.ncte.org/edpolicy/writing/about/122373.htm?source-gs

Promising Young Writers. The Promising Young Writers program represents NCTE's commitment to early and continuing work in the development of writing. The program was established to motivate and recognize student writers and to emphasize the importance of writing among eighth-grade students.

http://www.ncte.org/about/awards/student/pyw/107525.htm

Chapter  9

Talking and Listening in the Middle Grades

GUIDING QUESTIONS

1. Why do some teachers feel uncomfortable sponsoring oral language activities in their middle school classrooms?
2. What purposes and forms might talk and listening take in the English language arts classroom?
3. How do issues of race, class, gender, and culture influence middle school students' attitudes toward oral language activities?

A CASE FOR CONSIDERATION

Beyond the "Official Meaning"

Janie, a masters student in her final semester, posted this message to the members of her student teaching listserv:

In one of my recent classes, I asked my students why James McBride uses images of water at the end of his book, The Color of Water. *Some students thought it was totally unintentional, while others began to ask questions that explored possible "deeper meanings" of the text. One student, however, responded in a way that totally shocked me. He said, "What does it matter if the book has a deeper meaning to us? It's whatever the author intended. We will never know what he intended, so there's no use making up stuff about the text."*

Well, this was by far the most engaged and passionate response I had received that day, so I asked the rest of the class to respond. Everyone began to join in on the conversation, which ranged from students' sharing of personal experiences with the book to how we make meaning out of information. I suggested that interpretation and personal response help us explore the author's intent and bring out the multiple perspectives of the people in a classroom. This is what makes literature rich, meaningful, and beautiful. The kids felt that literature was a "mirror" for their lives. . . .

[This experience] made me realize that I need to be aware of my "personal agenda" as a teacher. Maybe my student wasn't just responding to the "pointlessness of interpreting texts," but rather a teacher's way of bringing out one interpretation—her interpretation or the "official meaning." Teachers want their students to use critical thinking and interpretation, but it's not going to do them much good if their interpretations lead them to the teacher's answer or interpretation. Thus, I began to rethink how I've been leading discussion. I want to give my students access to various meanings of the text, but I also want to truly value each perspective and interpretation as adding to the meaning of the text. Any ideas about how this might look in practice???

FOR DISCUSSION

Janie articulates one of the biggest struggles that English language arts teachers face: How do we balance our agenda—what Janie calls the "official meaning"—with our students' ideas, issues, and concerns in the many forms of talk and listening we sponsor in our classrooms each day? Perhaps most troubling is the question that Janie poses at the end of her reflection: "Any ideas about how this might look in practice?" Let's begin by considering this and some related questions. How do you prepare for discussion in your middle school classroom (with a list of questions, an activity, or something else)?

This struggle is particularly compelling in the literature classroom, where we want to invite what Langer (1995) calls a "horizon" of interpretive possibilities in discussion. We must continually be mindful of whose ideas get the floor whenever we sponsor a class discussion, group sharing, or public performance. Who tends to "hold the floor" in your classroom and who stays out? How do issues of race, class, gender, and culture enter the picture? How do you consciously avoid making your agenda the centerpiece of classroom talk?

THE MANY FACES OF TALKING AND LISTENING

There's no doubt about it. Oral performance is scary stuff, particularly for early adolescents who are so conscious of peer approval. On the other hand, oral performance can enliven and enrich your English language arts classroom immeasurably. This is the dilemma of many of us who were trained to teach the (relatively private) subjects of reading and writing and have never stepped foot on a theater stage or a public speaking platform. Although we are always "performing" every time we get in front of a class, the idea of teaching theater arts, public speaking, oral interpretation, or other oral activities can feel pretty threatening for those of us without formal preparation.

Luckily, a range of oral language activities is available to us along a continuum from playful and exploratory to more rehearsed, public, and polished. As this chapter will demonstrate, it's not that difficult to give all of our middle school students this broad range of experiences with oral language.

PURPOSES AND FORMS OF TALK AND LISTENING

Consider all of the possibilities for talking and listening in your middle school classroom. One day your students might role-play a scene from a story they're reading; the next, they might hold a panel discussion or debate; the next, they might create scripts or readers' theater presentations for their classmates or parents. The possibilities range only as far as your (and their) imaginations extend. Far from being a solely performance-oriented art, oral language can involve both *talking to learn* and *learning to talk*. The same is true of listening. Think, for example, of the difference between listening for information to be remembered later on a test and listening for pure pleasure and enjoyment. Figure 9-1 presents just a few of many techniques and forms of talk and listening available to us.

We suggest four purposes for using talking and listening with middle school students: (1) to explore, (2) to learn about talking and listening, (3) to connect with others and transform their worlds, and (4) to showcase their learning. These four purposes are summarized in Figure 9-2.

FIGURE 9-1 Techniques and Forms of Oral Language and Listening

group discussions	interviews
debates	mock student congress
dramatic improvisations	memorized speeches
extemporaneous speeches	recitations
dramatic enactments	oral interpretations of literature
panel discussions	dramatic monologues
conversations	choral reading
"pair-shares"	poster sessions
collaborative learning groups	oral demonstrations
jokes	skits
storytelling	problem-solving groups
scripted dialogues	oral reports

FIGURE 9-2 Purposes for Talking and Listening

Techniques for Talking and Listening	Talking and Listening to Explore	Talking and Listening to Learn About Talking and Listening	Talking and Listening to Connect and Transform	Talking and Listening to Showcase
	How might students explore ideas and express themselves through oral language and listening?	How might students become better speakers, collaborators, and listeners?	How might students use talking and listening to connect with others and make an impact on their world?	How might students share or demonstrate what they have learned through talking and listening?

In Fieldwork Journal 9-1, we ask you to use this preliminary list as a starting place for considering how these forms and techniques might be used for a variety of purposes.

TALK AND LISTENING WITH MIDDLE SCHOOL STUDENTS

Moffett (1968) argues that drama is the matrix from which all other language experiences derive. Think about that concept for a moment. How much of our daily language is devoted to explaining what happened, narrating, or in some way experiencing, enacting, or creating real or imagined events through words? It's this near compulsion to use language as a way of acting on each other and the world that

---

Fieldwork Journal 9-1

Examining Talk and Listening in Your Own Teaching

First, look at the list in Figure 9-1. Feel free to add your own forms and techniques for talking and listening to this preliminary list.

Now, create a chart like the one in Figure 9-2. Pick one of the forms or techniques from Figure 9-1 and experiment with the different purposes it might serve in your teaching of writing, reading and viewing, and language study. Look at Figure 9-3 as one example.

When you've finished this exercise, you might want to share some of your ideas with others.

FIGURE 9-3 Purposes for Talking and Listening

Purposes for Talking and Listening				
Forms and Techniques for Talking and Listening	**Talking and Listening to Explore**	**Talking and Listening to Learn About Talking and Listening**	**Talking and Listening to Connect and Transform**	**Talking and Listening to Showcase**
	How might students explore ideas and express themselves through oral language and listening?	How might students become better speakers, collaborators, and listeners?	How might students use talking and listening to connect with others and make an impact on their world?	How might students share or demonstrate what they have learned through talking and listening?
Interviews	• Students interview each other and create commercials, "advertising" the best qualities and talents of their partner. • Students role-play interviews with characters from literature. • Students interview their classmates about early reading and writing experiences and create "literary biographies."	• Students study the language of talk-show hosts for the purpose of creating and videotaping their own talk shows. • Students interview members of their family for the purpose of studying their family's language patterns, pet phrases, and so on. • Students study the dialect in a piece of historical fiction, then stage mock interviews with characters in the dialect of the period.	• Students interview senior citizens about their experiences during the Great Depression as a prelude to reading a novel about this period in history. • Students interview the principal of the nearby high school for the purpose of understanding more about school violence in their area.	• Students conduct schoolwide interviews and create a video segment on attitudes toward teenage drinking in their school. • Students present oral "author studies," based on televised or print versions of interviews with famous literary figures. • Students present informative speeches, based on interviews with local experts.

makes talk and listening such a vital part of middle school life. At the same time, we cannot ignore the risks involved, especially for early adolescents who are not situated squarely in the mainstream.

Here are just a few considerations to ponder in creating opportunities for talking and listening with middle school students.

Considerations for Talking and Listening in the Middle School Classroom

- How do we allow opportunities for sharing and performance without putting shy or reluctant learners on the spot?
- How can we provide opportunities for our students to develop their oral language and listening skills with parents and other interested adults?
- How can we provide oral language opportunities for students from a variety of cultural and linguistic backgrounds?
- How can we get students out of their seats more often during the course of reading, writing, and language study?
- What roles can drawing, viewing, performing, and public presentation play in students' oral language and listening experiences?
- How can we accommodate our teaching to the vast array of communication styles in our classroom?
- How do we balance our responsibility to develop students' formal spoken language skills with their need for play, social interaction, and exploration?
- How can we sponsor activities for talking and listening to learn as well as talking to showcase learning?
- How can we encourage collaborative and cooperative behaviors among students of various abilities as well as linguistic and cultural backgrounds?
- How might we find authentic and appreciative audiences for students' public performances and demonstrations within and outside our classroom walls?
- How can our students use talk and listening as a way of exploring the world beyond their schools, communities, and country?
- How can oral language and listening promote students' involvement in social and political activities of importance to them?

LEVELING THE FIELD: RACE, CLASS, GENDER, CULTURE, AND ORAL LANGUAGE

Many complicating factors are related to oral language for early adolescents. Middle school students are becoming more conscious of peers as they develop their adolescent identities. For some, there are greater penalties for speaking out in class than for others. For example, gender plays a great role in who is likely to contribute and who is likely to stay out of group discussions. At times, discussions of sensitive topics like race or social class hold greater consequences for students from particular backgrounds. Emma, a preservice teacher in her first teaching placement, reflects on this dilemma in a message to the members of her student teaching seminar:

> *I was wondering what sort of experience you're having with your students in regards to their genders? Do you find girls are less or more talkative in discussion than boys?*

Do you see the same boys ruling the discussion? That's how it is with my [third period class]; however, [the girls in my fourth period class] are vocal and leaders. . . . I went to an all-girls' high school and can see a marked difference between how girls reacted in my high-school classes versus how they react in a coed atmosphere. Just today while working with one of [my host teacher's] classes, I encountered a loud, opinionated boy who reminded me why I chose an all-girls' high school—so I would have a voice that wouldn't be drowned out by one boy's objective to rule the class. However, I'm sure some of you have girls who also attempt to do this, but perhaps in a different manner. Any thoughts on leveling the field?

As Emma notes, no hard-and-fast rules dictate how gender, race, cultural background, or other factors figure into the likelihood that students will or will not participate in oral language activities. Think back to the earlier chapters in this text and consider how Emma's personal history might have shaped her views of teaching.

Researchers have discovered a few trends about the complexities of oral language and listening in your classroom. Often, adolescent girls are reluctant to participate in class discussions for fear of looking too smart and therefore jeopardizing their popularity (Sadker & Sadker, 1994). Many adolescent males are wary of enjoying traditionally "feminine" activities like keeping journals or reading and writing poetry for fear of losing their status as macho or athletic (Sadker & Sadker, 1994; Salisbury & Jackson, 1996).

The tenuous status of African American females in school and society is even more profound (Fine, 1995; Fordham, 1996; Grant, 1984; Hooks, 1989; McCarthy, 1996; Sadker & Sadker, 1994). According to Fordham (1993), Black teenage girls are more likely to be shunted to the margins of the classroom than any other group. As a result, they typically try to achieve academic success by being "phantoms in the opera." That is, they either remain "voiceless" or impersonate "a male image" (p. 10). Fordham argues that Black girls may unwittingly participate in their own exclusion by engaging in behaviors that alienate their teachers.

There are other complications to the classroom dynamic as well. Researchers have concluded the following, for instance:

- Often, mixed groups of males and females will choose a male as spokesperson, even though females may have done most of the work (Salisbury & Jackson, 1996).
- Teachers often mistake the active communication styles of students from certain racial or ethnic groups as rowdiness or disrespect (Cureton, 1985; Smitherman, 1986).
- Teachers often correct dialectical miscues, such as "He be going," whereas they tend to ignore nondialectical miscues, such as "Put it over there" instead of "Put it over here" (Cunningham, 1976–1977). This type of response sometimes makes students reluctant to read aloud or talk in classes.
- Students from some cultural backgrounds have been taught that respect equals silence and that asking questions of teachers means inappropriately questioning authority. Teachers unaware of these cultural differences may interpret their silence as apathy or disinterest.

- Teachers sometimes equate limited language production with limited academic or cognitive ability, ignoring the fact that second language learners can often understand significantly more than they can demonstrate through oral language.

We must be constantly mindful of these social and cultural complexities for our middle school classrooms, realizing that oral language activities like collaborative learning, sharing circles, group discussion, and public performances are not always equally enjoyable or easy for all students.

In addition, we must often reach across cultural boundaries to help students whose first language is not English or assist those whose communication styles diverge from what's considered "the norm" because of their family or cultural background. It should not be the burden of students of color or those from countries and cultures outside the United States to "educate" more mainstream students about linguistic stereotyping or insensitive comments about race or ethnicity in class discussions.

> **Language Study in Context**
>
> Invite students to generate a list of common situations (e.g., making a telephone call, asking to borrow something, inviting someone to their house). Have them role-play these situations and "code-switch," depending on their conversational partner (e.g., a teacher, parent, employer, best friend).

As teachers, we are responsible for offering not only oral language and listening experiences, but also opportunities to talk about and explore the many forms of oral language in our diverse society.

It's also important to recognize the varied definitions of "listening," particularly as they relate to high-stakes standardized testing. Often, statewide or district competency examinations equate listening with taking notes or memorizing details from materials read or presented orally. This limited view unfortunately blinds us to the rich variety of listening purposes beyond the gathering of information: listening empathically and responding in a socially appropriate way; listening critically; listening for the subtle nuances in the words of others; and listening for pure relaxation and enjoyment.

Creating a Learning Community

For productive talk and listening to occur in classrooms, middle school teachers need to create an environment that reduces stress and anxiety and that promotes acceptance of all students. In the middle grades, especially when students from different neighborhoods are coming together for the first time, it's vital to create a climate of high expectations for all, paired with a deep respect for students' cultural references and home language. Creating this community is no easy task. Oral language activities may be cause for great anxiety because oral language is typically equated with the public forum of a whole-class activity. And we know that middle school students may be cruelly critical to others marked as different. How we talk is not simply how we talk; our language competencies are tied to our identities. The intimate relationships between classroom discourse, language production, cultural norms, and cognitive language are complex and intertwined. As Abrams and Ferguson (2005) note, "Cultural values are part of every language learner's profile. Some types of behavior considered unacceptable in the dominant culture are not only acceptable but even encouraged in the student's home culture" (p. 65). ESL students, for example, often experience a conflict between learning a new language and retaining their native language and culture. Nowhere is the need to nurture and support competence in both home and school cultures more important than in the language arts classroom when students engage in talking and listening opportunities.

As we discussed in chapter 4, some excellent information on culturally relevant teaching is available from "Teaching Diverse Learners," a Web site sponsored by the Education Alliance at Brown University. Links to seven principles for Culturally Relevant Teaching can be found at *http://www.alliance.brown.edu/tdl/tl-strategies/ crt- principles.shtml.*

It's important to remember that language is such an integral part of culture and identity that when students put their talk and themselves "out there" to be scrutinized and evaluated by their teachers and peers, many feel exposed. For those students most at risk for failure due to poverty, limited English proficiency, or background knowledge and experiences that do not map easily onto school expectations, talking and listening activities may create barriers rather than bridges to learning.

For all voices to be heard, middle school teachers need to make clear the rules of engagement and provide multiple models for the way students participate in oral activities of all kinds, including whole-class or small-group discussions, final performances, or speculative conversations. Remember the watch words presented in chapter 8, "Practice without penalty"? In terms of oral language, provide all students with opportunities for practice in private or in a more comfortable small group before sharing in front of the whole class. Too many teachers ask students to speak publicly without providing time for experimentation and rehearsal.

Provide multiple pathways to learning. Douglas Barnes (1976) coined the term "exploratory talk," to describe oral language as a way (and not just an outcome) of learning. It's a good idea to promote multiple opportunities for this type of talk in your classroom. Middle school students who are trying to talk their way into deeper understandings do so best in whichever language or dialect they feel most confident and comfortable. To force students into compliance with the conventions of formal spoken English or to call attention to errors in students' speech is extremely counterproductive. Opportunities for exploratory talk should never be evaluated. Remember that it's best to deal with issues of standard language in writing than it is in speech. As long as students know up front that you expect them to use edited American English in their final written work, and as long as you focus on one or two errors at a time, students will usually take your private corrections on their writing in stride.

On the other hand, oral performance—whether formal or informal—carries a greater burden of risk than writing because of its public nature. Even in the context of a small group, what seems like an innocuous correction or comment on your part can be excruciatingly embarrassing for early adolescents. If performances or presentations are to be graded, consider creating an evaluation rubric with the input of class members well in advance of the final presentation. Give students a chance to practice and rate each others' performances in a low-risk setting before you assign grades.

Involve all students. Give all students active roles in the classroom, regardless of their culture or linguistic background. Sometimes teachers with the best of intentions do not ask students who are proficient in languages other than English to talk, for fear of embarrassing them. Believing that these students are unable to participate in class discussions, teachers may even move them to the side or back of the classroom and give them independent work. While this may be done with the best of intentions, it is not the best pedagogy. All students need opportunities to practice their language skills with peers.

If your class sits in groups, place newcomers with sociable English speakers. You may ask students who are proficient in languages other than English to be involved in activities that do not require language production—observing, pointing, collecting, constructing, for example. All students need to feel like valued members within the community of learners. Monitor your practice to ensure that you are tapping the expertise of each learner and showcasing the contributions of each.

Build and maintain a caring and respectful climate. Clearly, if students do not feel cared for or respected, they cannot be productive members in the learning community. If their teachers don't believe in them, middle school students are less likely to believe in themselves as literacy learners. Duncan (2002) concludes that many White teachers view their African American male students as "beyond love." Furthermore, Reid (1995; personal communication, February 7, 2006), noting the critical need for teachers to understand the unique issues that surround biracial children and their families, cautions middle school teachers not to assume that biracial middle school students automatically identify as people of color. She argues further that when teachers silence middle schoolers' curious questions about race, skin color, parents, or heritage, we are sending implicitly negative messages about identities to our students.

Middle school teachers can mitigate risk factors by challenging intolerance, showing respect, and holding high expectations for all learners. Respect is most often characterized as what the student holds for the teacher; but as Sara Lawrence Lightfoot, professor of education at Harvard University and author of *Respect: An Exploration* argues,

> I think when most of us think of respect, we think of a hierarchy. We think of approbation, deference offered to someone who is more knowledgeable. . . . And the picture is one of a triangle or a pyramid. My view of respect is a circle. It is about symmetry. It's about reciprocity. Even if there are differences in knowledge and status and power and resources and skills, that respect is a great equalizer. It is the ways in which we can be symmetric with one another, and it comes again through this sense of connection in relationships. (accessed on February 3, 2006, from *http://www. pbs.org/newshour/gergen/june99/respect_6-30.html*)

As you read this chapter, try to think of ways in which you might use talk and listening to create bridges rather than barriers. One key way is to support student participation, not just in your classroom, but in the many language communities (e.g., home, school, neighborhood, peer group) to which students belong.

In one middle school classroom, for example, a group of young women decided to investigate community-based agencies where teens could volunteer their services in improving their neighborhoods (see Figure 9-4).

FIGURE 9-4 Getting Socially Active

They created a pamphlet, detailing the names and contact information for these agencies, and made an oral presentation on their project, "Getting Socially Active" (see Figure 9-5).

The project "Getting Socially Active" involved using a rich array of oral language competencies for all four purposes. Through positive social interaction and collaboration, the girls used exploratory talk to conceptualize the community project. They had to rehearse and consider the ways to become better speakers as they met with community members when they conducted their research. Clearly the project is connected to the community with a potential impact on their community and as you see, from the photograph, seated at their presentation station, the girls used talk to showcase their learning. Thus this one project focused on all four purposes presented in Figure 9-2.

Designing a curriculum for talk and listening, a teacher shouldn't adhere too firmly to these boundaries between the purposes of language use. Teachers must be flexible and responsive to student needs for language use. The four purposes presented in figure 9-2 serve as a guide to help avoid focusing a curriculum too heavily on one purpose at the expense of the others.

FIGURE 9-5 Pamphlet of Community Agencies.

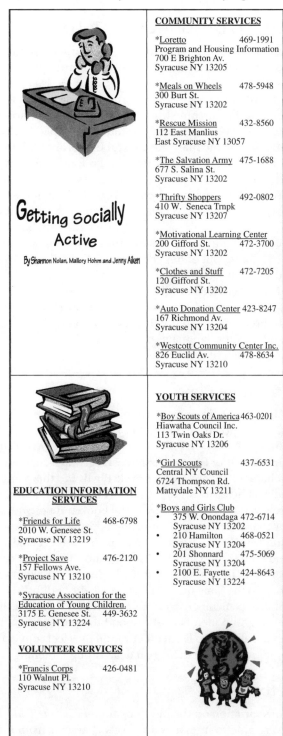

Getting Socially Active

By Shannon Nolan, Mallory Hohm and Jenny Aiken

COMMUNITY SERVICES

*Loretto   469-1991
Program and Housing Information
700 E Brighton Av.
Syracuse NY 13205

*Meals on Wheels   478-5948
300 Burt St.
Syracuse NY 13202

*Rescue Mission   432-8560
112 East Manlius
East Syracuse NY 13057

*The Salvation Army 475-1688
677 S. Salina St.
Syracuse NY 13202

*Thrifty Shoppers   492-0802
410 W. Seneca Trnpk
Syracuse NY 13207

*Motivational Learning Center
200 Gifford St.   472-3700
Syracuse NY 13202

*Clothes and Stuff   472-7205
120 Gifford St.
Syracuse NY 13202

*Auto Donation Center 423-8247
167 Richmond Av.
Syracuse NY 13204

*Westcott Community Center Inc.
826 Euclid Av.   478-8634
Syracuse NY 13210

**EDUCATION INFORMATION
SERVICES**

*Friends for Life   468-6798
2010 W. Genesee St.
Syracuse NY 13219

*Project Save   476-2120
157 Fellows Ave.
Syracuse NY 13210

*Syracuse Association for the
Education of Young Children.
3175 E. Genesee St.   449-3632
Syracuse NY 13224

VOLUNTEER SERVICES

*Francis Corps   426-0481
110 Walnut Pl.
Syracuse NY 13210

YOUTH SERVICES

*Boy Scouts of America 463-0201
Hiawatha Council Inc.
113 Twin Oaks Dr.
Syracuse NY 13206

*Girl Scouts   437-6531
Central NY Council
6724 Thompson Rd.
Mattydale NY 13211

*Boys and Girls Club
•   375 W. Onondaga 472-6714
     Syracuse NY 13202
•   210 Hamilton   468-0521
     Syracuse NY 13204
•   201 Shonnard   475-5069
     Syracuse NY 13204
•   2100 E. Fayette   424-8643
     Syracuse NY 13224

PROMOTING LANGUAGE GROWTH

In his student teaching placement, Jeff wanted to avoid the typical teacher-dominated class discussion in his suburban ninth-grade classroom. In preparation for teaching several vignettes from *The House on Mango Street* by Sandra Cisneros (1991), Jeff invited students to take turns creating a word web on the board. "Take a piece of chalk and write some words that remind you of home," Jeff began. After several minutes had passed, Jeff and his students stepped back to look at what they had written. Students "wrote many wonderful things about their homes," Jeff remarked. "They wrote about safety, security, family, food, modern conveniences, athletic equipment, big yards, big rooms, garages, and so on." In the discussion that followed, Jeff asked students to compare their more privileged home lives with that of Cisneros as a young girl, and finally, to create a metaphor for one of the characters in the vignettes. He observed, "This was a difficult assignment, but the students came up with many clever metaphors. One female student wrote: 'Esperanza is a butterfly, when she writes she comes out of her cocoon'. . . . Overall, it was a good day. I enjoyed this lesson, and so did my students."

As Jeff has discovered, talk and listening do not have to involve formal performance. The simple act of walking to the board and writing one word to describe "home" can break up a potentially dreary day and allow students to learn from and with each other. Oral language can be used in many other informal, exploratory ways. Here are just a few examples.

Character Role Plays

Place the desks or chairs in your room in a circle; then choose four or five characters from a story, poem, or novel you are reading. For example, say your students have just finished the novel *The Friends* by Guy (1973). Cluster your students into small groups of four or five and assign each group a character. You might choose the following characters from Guy's novel: Phylissia (the main character), Edith (her friend), Ruby (Phylissia's sister), Calvin (her father), and Ramona (her mother).

Choose several major events from the book and pose questions about those events to different character groups. For example, you might choose an event like Phylissia's first meeting with Edith. Read an excerpt from the book describing Phylissia's first reaction and then turn to the "Phylissia" group: "When you saw Edith for the first time, did you ever think the two of you would be friends?" Encourage more than one Phylissia to respond to the same question. Then ask the "Ediths" the same question, allowing any and all group members to respond. The more varied the responses, the better. Don't force all group members to respond to each question. Some students will learn more if they are allowed to listen quietly until they feel comfortable joining in. Whether they talk or not, they will learn a great deal through listening to the responses of others.

"To Tell the Truth"

Consider this variation on the old quiz show *To Tell the Truth*. Ask students to imagine that they were able to interview a famous character from literature. Choose a short text with a fairly unspecified narrator, such as "Stopping by Woods on a Snowy Evening" by Frost (1995). This is a good choice because the speaker in Frost's poem could be male or female, a farmer or a retired investment banker. After students read the poem a couple of times, ask them to write a paragraph as that character, trying to capture the "voice" of the narrator they imagined. Ask them to include information such as the narrator's name, occupation, reason for being in the woods, and so on.

When they've finished this task, put them into small groups and ask each group to imagine that Frost's narrator was going to visit their class. Ask students to generate a series of questions they might ask Frost's narrator in an interview. Questions might range from "What is your name and what were you doing in the woods that evening?" to "What did you mean by 'miles to go' before you sleep?"

When they've finished, ask for three or four volunteers, each of whom will roleplay the narrator in Frost's poem as they envisioned him or her. Have students in the audience take turns asking questions of all three narrators; then vote on which narrator was most convicing. At the end of the lesson, invite all students to read or talk about the different narrators they constructed in their opening writings.

TALK AND LISTENING AS INQUIRY

In previous chapters, we have discussed the value of inquiry projects that allow students to explore questions of authentic interest and to tap resources beyond traditional print materials found in libraries. Such exploration should be a vital and compelling component of your middle school English language arts program.

Handing over more of the authority to our students isn't easy, but it is perhaps most fully accomplished as we help students to see how their talk and listening can make an impact on the larger world. This is a lesson that Harry Webb learned in his first teaching job. Harry tells the story in his own words in Classroom Case 9-1.

Classroom Case 9-1

"A Foot in the Door": Service Learning in an Alternative Classroom

"Your main task will be to get these kids interested, just to get them to come to school." Those were the instructions I received from my principal during the interview for my first teaching job; I would be teaching "at-risk" eighth graders in an alternative classroom. Originally I thought of the job as my foot in the door of an "excelled" school district. The students had grown up in an educated, upper-middle class city whose citizens placed great importance on a quality school system. The writing skills of my students were not lacking, but their motivation was. Despite the achievements of my district, or any district for that matter, there will always be those students who slip through the cracks, and these were the kids I faced for the very first time 4 years ago in my classroom. I now know that I got my foot in the door of an exciting classroom with some amazing kids. But in the beginning I wasn't sure what to do.

Where did I go from there? How was I supposed to motivate 20 students to write? To read? To engage in school literacy? Students who all had juvenile officers and none with both biological parents at home? For one quarter I tried the methods that my college had taught me: journals, literary response letters, essays, reports, newspaper articles, etc. The students were doing little writing, some did nothing, and all did not care that they were failing. I quickly found that college had given me many great ideas on teaching motivated kids, but I held no strategies for the unmotivated ones. That's when I discovered service learning.

By working on service projects that moved them out of the classroom and into the community, my students had a greater desire to attend school and complete the educational tasks. They worked in the community to achieve tangible goals, and when they returned to the classroom, they had a shared concrete experience that inspired their writing. I used the same writing assignments as before but this time drew from their personal experiences during service learning.

In one of our projects, students wanted to improve their school grounds as a way of giving our school and community a better reputation. Students chose an element that needed improvement, gathered supplies, made a scale model, wrote letters, and made phone calls. The actual project involved buying supplies and learning new skills such as using power tools, pouring concrete, building, and landscaping (see Figure 9-6).

In addition to improving their written expression, students also increased their proficiency with oral language. Students needed to make phone calls. It was in that "need" that their oral skills came into play. They wanted projects to be successful, and they couldn't do it alone. They needed to communicate with each other, and they needed to go beyond the classroom for help. Much of their oral language development came in the process of getting the project off the ground. But they also needed to advertise their success beyond our classroom. I designed assignments to help them promote their projects and, more important, themselves. One such assignment was a reflection on the entire school year and all the service learning projects we had completed. The class put together a film documenting the many contributions to the community and the skills they used and learned as a result of their work. The film required a written script and voice narration. Once again, with a shared concrete experience and results in which they had pride, the students were able to complete the assignment in the classroom with much success.

Another successful example of "at-risk" students using oral proficiency by means of service learning was their elementary school presentations. The eighth-grade class took numerous trips to local elementary schools in the district to read stories, teach the youngsters about dangerous household chemicals, the dangers of strangers, and ways to avoid troublesome situations in their neighborhoods.

It was amazing to see kids who normally had a hard time talking in front of a group shine as they spoke about something they knew about in front of an audience of as many as 50 five- to seven-year-old children. As a great celebration for this particular assignment, the class was designated as the "Volunteers of the Month" by the city in which they lived and were granted the award in a ceremony by the mayor.

Last fall, my students decided that needy children might like to have bicycles for the holidays. Realizing that many community members would probably be willing to donate bikes that could be repaired with a little effort, they set about collecting and repairing bicycles for these children. They sent out flyers and made phone calls, asking for donations. In addition to gathering tools and creating a work area, they learned about bicycle repair and eventually created some special holiday gifts for children in our community (see Figure 9-7).

These "at-risk" students have routinely written reflections of their service work using journals, newspaper articles, reports, essays, scripts, skits, creative stories, poetry,

Focus On
Talking and Listening

Focus On
Writing

FIGURE 9-6   Service Learning Project—Improving School Grounds

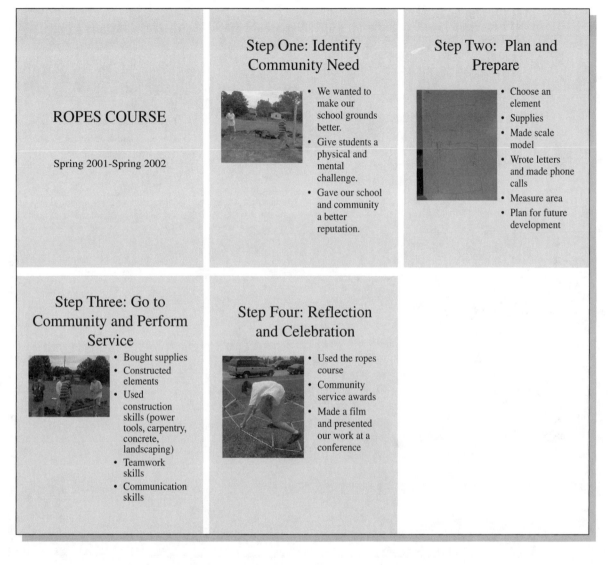

and letter formats. In addition, some of the actual work for the projects required writing as part of the preparation, proposals for grant money, letters of permission, flyers, storybooks for children, and public service announcements. Where do I go from here?

For Discussion

Harry understands that literacy is one piece in the complex puzzle of helping the "at-risk" child, though it is a large one. The job that started four years ago as his "foot in the door" continues to be the biggest and most rewarding challenge of his life. If Harry asked you where he should go from here, how might you answer him?

FIGURE 9-7 Service Learning Project—Bicycle Repair

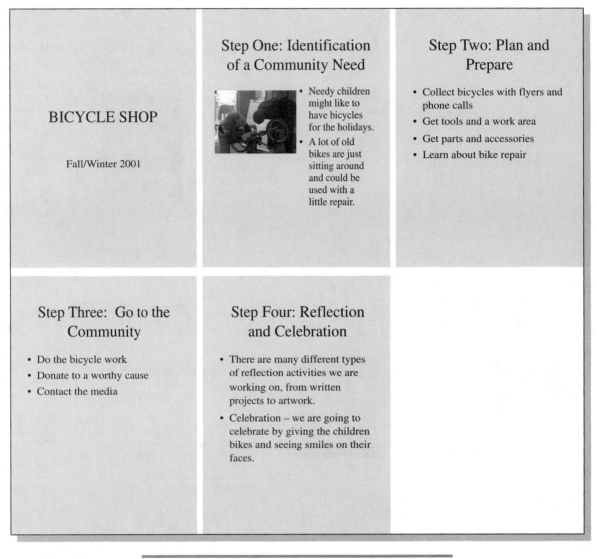

EXPLORING THE LANGUAGE OF SELF AND OTHERS

No chapter on oral language would be complete without a brief discussion of interpersonal communication and its role in students' literacy development. Under the general banner of interpersonal communication lie many important topics: impression formation in intra- and interpersonal communication, nonverbal communication, active listening, empathy, assertiveness, conflict management, and cross-cultural communication, to name a few. Although your classroom should never resemble an encounter group or a therapy session, students might explore several aspects of interpersonal communication as they learn about how talk and listening function in the social world.

Remember that the activities suggested in the following pages can be somewhat tricky. Students should never feel coerced to reveal personal information or delve too deeply into emotional issues. Especially with early adolescents, it's important to infuse humor and lightheartedness into your teaching so that students don't feel forced into uncomfortable self-disclosure. Whenever you ask them to write or talk about personal topics, be sure to offer them the opportunity to keep their views private. Here are just a few ideas for exploring the dimensions of interpersonal communication with your middle school students.

The Power of Names

Ask students to think for a moment about how they would like their friends and family members to view them. As soon as they have thought (and perhaps jotted some notes) about their "ideal selves," ask them to write a one-page "character description" of themselves, something that a novelist might write. Suggest that their description should be concrete enough that a stranger could recognize them from this single page and assure them that they may keep this information totally private. Next, tell them to make up a nickname that they would like to have for themselves, something by which they would like to be remembered. This could be a nickname that someone has already given them. Discuss the names they chose and why they chose them.

Now ask them to think about nicknames they have been called in the past. Explain that you don't want them to share the nicknames publicly (some of them may be negative); instead, ask them to consider the power of others in developing our self-concepts. What does it mean, for instance, when a child is labeled "the bookworm" or "the comedian" in a family?

You might also ask your students to talk about a piece of literature, paying particular attention to how characters and events are shaped by the way others talk about them. Choose a piece with multiple points of view like Avi's documentary novel *Nothing but the Truth* (1991), asking students to notice the ways that Phillip, his parents, Ms. Narwin, and other story characters label and describe each other through their diary entries, letters, reports, and other media. Discuss how labels and descriptors not only reflect people's views of us but actually play a part in how we see ourselves.

Active Listening in Literature and Life

Explain the difference between hearing (passively registering the gist or the details of what someone has said) and listening (giving nonverbal cues that let a speaker know that he or she has been heard).

Stress the fact that active listening involves more than just hearing; simple cues like facial expressions, nods, and short words of encouragement like "uh huh" or "how did that make you feel?" can go a long way in promoting successful conversations. Ask your students to make a list of situations in which they have felt listened to and situations in which they have been merely heard. Have them in

> **Language Study in Context**
>
> Have students observe the conversations of peers from a distance in the lunchroom or other location in the school. Stress the fact that they are not expected to eavesdrop on conversations, but to watch from a place far enough away to allow observation only. Ask them to note how others show they are listening through nonverbal behaviors.

groups or pairs work to make a list of the nonverbal and verbal behaviors of others that encouraged them to feel as they did.

Now, try a bit of modeling. Ask a student to pretend to be asking you for something—say a higher grade in your class. As the student begins talking, demonstrate some of the "hearing" behaviors from the list the students just generated: Shuffle papers as he or she speaks, look at your watch, yawn, stare into space, insert an occasional "uh huh" at an inappropriate moment, and make irrelevant or distracting comments. Now role-play the conversation again, this time demonstrating active listening skills: Make eye contact with your student, paraphrase to make sure you've heard what he or she said, ask questions that help you to clarify, and so on.

Once your students have an idea of the difference between hearing and listening, choose a situation of conflict in a piece of literature, preferably one that is alluded to but not specifically represented in dialogue. An example might be the opening of Myers's story, "The Treasure of Lemon Brown" (1997). As the story opens, 14-year-old Greg is suffering through a lecture by his father about Greg's poor math skills. A week before, Greg asked his father if he could play basketball with the Scorpions, a local team, and was told that the answer depended on his next report card. The conversation with Greg and his father is not directly represented in dialogue, but it's clear that a great lack of understanding separates Greg and his father.

Pair each student with a partner and ask them to take turns privately role-playing the scene between Greg and his dad in two different ways: first, using "hearing" techniques, and second, using "active listening" techniques. If you have students who are fairly comfortable with each other, pairs may want to share their improvisations with the whole class. Wrap up the experience by discussing how active listening can go a long way in preventing and mediating interpersonal conflicts.

Nonverbal Criminals

If handled sensitively and with plenty of forewarning about possible consequences, this exercise can be an enjoyable lesson in the "unwritten rules" of nonverbal behavior in social settings. First, ask students to brainstorm a list of "unspoken" nonverbal rules that people are supposed to follow in social situations. You might start them off with a few examples such as the following:

- When in an elevator, you are supposed to look at the ceiling or the numbers on the panel above the doors, and not at other people.
- When in a cafeteria, you are not supposed to sit with people you don't know and enter into their conversation as if you were an intimate member of their group.
- When you are in a library, your books and possessions should not invade the space of those at the table with you.

Once you have generated a good list of rules, create a corresponding list of "strategies for nonverbal criminals." For example, one strategy might be to "enter an elevator and turn toward the people standing behind you. Maintain eye contact with them throughout the entire ride." Although some of your students will probably want to push the boundaries, make sure the list covers petty and not major crimes such as staring at personal body parts or using offensive gestures in public.

For the next several days, have students go out in pairs and break at least two of these nonverbal rules. One student acts as observer and takes inconspicuous notes while the other student violates the rule. At the end of a few days, ask students to make brief reports on how others reacted to them.

As a connection to literature, ask students to read stories or poems, paying particular attention to the nonverbal details that the author chooses to describe characters. A good example might be the character Alphonso in Gary Soto's short story, "First Love" (1992). Throughout the course of the story, Alphonso, whose family cannot afford to get him braces, continually pushes on his front teeth in the hope that he can straighten them himself. Ask students why Soto may have chosen this and other nonverbal behaviors to portray Alphonso's character. Popular television shows with teenage characters are another good source of information about how characters are portrayed through nonverbal and verbal behaviors. Students can follow up these activities by writing their own stories or character sketches, concentrating on revealing character through nonverbal and verbal behaviors.

Dinner Table Study

This idea is taken from the famous discourse analysis of a family dinner table conducted by Tannen (1981). Although many students might enjoy studying the conversational patterns in their own family gatherings, there are many reasons not to make students' own families the centerpiece of an assignment. Issues of privacy and middle-class assumptions about families gathering around dinner tables can get dicey for certain students in your classroom. As an alternative, you might show a segment of a popular television show or movie that depicts a family eating dinner. A good choice might be the dinner table scenes from movies like *Meet the Parents* with Ben Stiller and Robert De Niro, *The Nutty Professor* with Eddie Murphy, or *Father of the Bride* with Steve Martin and Diane Keaton. Ask students to view the scene with an eye toward the nonverbal and verbal behaviors of family members. Assign different conversational features (words, phrases, nonverbal behaviors) to different observation groups and ask students to take notes on that particular aspect of the conversation. When they've finished, discuss what roles are revealed by the nonverbal behaviors of different family members. For example, who carves the meat, sits at the head of the table, goes to the kitchen? What is the family's conversational style: Do people take turns talking, have side conversations, argue, or share daily events? When you've finished with this informal discourse analysis, talk about the roles that people learn to play in conversations with peer groups, families, or other close-knit groups.

As you can see by these few examples, the English language arts classroom can be a place where students learn more about the art of effective interpersonal communication at the same time as they develop deeper understandings of the social and interpersonal dynamics of their reading, listening, viewing, and writing.

In previous chapters, we have presented many ways of inviting students to collaborate through talk, from peer writing conferences to group inquiry projects, literature circles, and teacher-student conferences. Although we believe that the bulk of talk and listening, especially for early adolescents, should involve these informal experiences, there is no denying that whole-class instruction remains the mainstay of the middle and secondary classroom. For this reason, we have decided to focus particular attention on making large-group discussion a forum for intellectual exploration, personal connection, and social transformation rather than a thinly veiled exercise in teacher control.

Breaking the I-R-E Pattern: Inviting Students' Genuine Responses in Class Discussion

Avoid known-information questions.

Many of us bring heavy baggage from experiences with teachers who relied on a steady diet of what Mehan (1979) called "known-information" questions, or questions to which they already know the answer. In an article called "What Time Is It Denise? . . ." Mehan presents the following conversation for consideration:

> What time is it, Denise?
>
> Two o'clock.
>
> Very good, Denise.

It doesn't take long to recognize that this conversation happened in a classroom. The line "Very good, Denise" is the tip-off. Imagine the response you'd get if you asked a passerby on a city street the time of day and then responded, "Very good." In the real world, of course, a simple "thanks" would suffice. The typical pattern of classroom questioning follows what Mehan and others have called an "I-R-E" or initiation, response, evaluation sequence; that is,

> What time is it? (*initiation*)
>
> Two o'clock. (*response*)
>
> Very good. (*evaluation*)

The evaluative nature of most classroom discourse lets students know that there is one correct answer to their teachers' questions. Lest we give the impression that it's easy to avoid the I-R-E trap, we'd like to make the point that all teachers, ourselves included, struggle with ways to step back from the center and invite our students' authentic responses into the conversation. The Center for Research on Education, Diversity & Excellence (CREDE) has articulated five standards of effective pedagogy. One standard addresses engaging in dialogue over lecture. The "Instructional Conversation" (IC), as they define it, engages students in more authentic talk than the more traditional classroom discussion. They make the following point:

> Thinking, and the abilities to form, express, and exchange ideas are best taught through dialogue, through questioning and sharing ideas and knowledge. In the Instructional Conversation (IC), the teacher listens carefully, makes guesses about intended meaning, and adjusts responses to assist students' efforts—just as in graduate seminars, or between mothers and toddlers. Here the teacher relates formal, school knowledge to the student's individual, family, and community knowledge. The IC provides opportunities for the development of the languages of instruction and subject matter. IC is a supportive and collaborative event that builds intersubjectivity

and a sense of community. IC achieves individualization of instruction; is best practiced during joint productive activity; is an ideal setting for language development; and allows sensitive contextualization, and precise, stimulating cognitive challenge. Accessed on February 3, 2006, from *http://www.crede.org/standards/5inst_con.shtml*)

You might be wondering what these "Instructional Conversations" look like in the everyday world of the middle school classroom. This is a topic that Susan tackles in Classroom Case 9-2.

Classroom Case 9-2

Teaching Off-Center

Four years ago, when Susan was invited by a friend to co-teach in a seventh grade classroom during a sabbatical from her university, she was excited but a little intimidated. She'd be walking into someone else's classroom, and she wanted to make this new crop of middle school students comfortable in exploring their ideas with a college professor. Early in the semester, she had a chance to try her luck at stepping out of the center where class discussion was concerned.

She and her teaching colleague were just beginning a unit on racism. One day, she opened the discussion by asking whether her students thought racism was still alive in America. Their responses stunned her: There were points of view all over the map, but the majority of students, Black and White alike, all seemed to agree that racism wasn't a daily part of their lives—it was something we had dealt with in the 1960s and was not really an issue in today's world.

Susan wanted to confront the assumption that racism had been "dealt with" without lecturing or dominating the discussion. After a bit of thinking, she decided that perhaps a picture would be worth the proverbial "thousand words." She went home that night and began to download some images of racism in America from the Internet, including the 1992 beating of Rodney King by a group of White police officers, the Los Angeles riots that followed, and the beating of Reginald Denny, a White truck driver who was attacked by a gang of Black youths during the riots.

That morning, instead of posing her usual teacher-made questions, she placed an image of a burning building in the Los Angeles riots on the overhead projector and asked students to write a short response to the following question: "What story does this picture seem to be telling?" After students wrote, she asked them to share their thoughts. One look at the following transcript shows just how powerful a simple request like "write (or tell) the story that's in your mind" can be in stimulating student-centered discussion.

Danielle:	It looks like it's in [an urban] area. And it looks like it's in the nighttime and maybe a mob might have burned it.
Susan:	What gives you a clue that maybe a mob might have burned it?
DeShawn:	Because the fire's sort of on the ground and it looks like there are maybe people walking around.
Susan:	That's a really good insight. You really looked into this picture.

Brooke:	Someone might have blew it up.
Susan:	What gives you that idea?
Brooke:	Because how, like the building is so high and there's like a little fire going on the street.
Susan:	So it kind of looks like a big explosion happened here, huh? . . .
Susan:	[pointing to a student] And your name is?
Christie:	Christie. Um, I thought that maybe it was racism. It looks like there's somebody there.
Susan:	It does look like there's somebody there, doesn't it? Now that I look at it, I see somebody there. I'm sorry [this picture is so fuzzy] I had to blow it up. I got it off the Internet. It was a tiny little picture. So you think it might be racism. What gives you the thought it might be racism? Christie?
Christie:	(Inaudible)
Selwyn:	I think somebody started it on purpose, um, somebody might have thought that in life they were losing and they have to let it out on other people.
Susan:	Oh that's really quite interesting. I'm not going to tell you what [this photo] is for a few minutes but, remember that [thought] . . .
Pat:	I think it was done by an enemy or something. I think they used a firebomb.
Susan:	A firebomb. And who do you think the enemy was, you know, an enemy of whom?
Pat:	The people who owned the store.

More exploratory discussion followed as, one by one, Susan placed photographs of the Rodney King beating, the Los Angeles riots, and the beating of Reginald Denny on the overhead, asking students to write or talk about "the story" that the photos suggested. Although her seventh grade students were only a few years old at the time of these incidents, it appeared that their modern-day experiences with violence had done much to inform their perceptions of past events, and that many of those perceptions were eerily on target. Even though the police cruiser was not visible in the Rodney King photo, one student immediately identified the scene as the result of a "wild police chase." Another suggested that maybe "[S]ome guys . . . want to beat up on the other person because he has a different idea or belief." The photos reminded one student of Jonny Gammage, a man from their city who had been stopped by police on a New York interstate and beaten to death when they supposedly mistook his cell phone for a gun. When one of her students remarked Gammage was his cousin, the issue of racism moved even closer to home. Susan explained:

What followed from that day of exploratory talk was a flurry of interest topics like hate, intolerance, racism, and homophobia. Students became interested in hate crimes like the Matthew Shepard murder, the dragging death of James Bird in Texas, the Columbine massacre, the death in our own state of Jonny Gammage and a few weeks later, the death of Amadeau Diallo in a New York City apartment hallway. In the days and weeks that followed, I was constantly reminded of the need to get rid of my own questions, allowing my students to explore their own authentic questions about events that touch their lives.

If you look back at the transcript of that discussion, you might wonder just what accounts for the more exploratory student-centered nature of the conversation. In terms of the sheer numbers of statements, it's clear that Susan talks as often as the students do. Yet, as she remarks,

> *Most of my questions were truly aimed at gathering information I really wondered about, questions like "What gives you the thought it might be racism?" or "What gives you a clue that maybe a mob might have burned it?" Some of my comments weren't even questions at all, but attempts to paraphrase students' responses so that others in the room could hear them ("It does look like there's somebody there, doesn't it?") or expressions of genuine surprise as students pointed out aspects of the photo I hadn't noticed before ("Now that I look at it, I see somebody there").*

If we want to break the "I-R-E" habit, it's not so much the number of times we talk, but our intentions behind what we say that counts. Making sure we ask no questions to which we already know the answer is a good way to start. After a bit of time, Susan reflected,

> *Did I know more than my students did about those photographs? Of course! Did I know everything they would teach me about their understanding of racism and violence in America? Of course not! And that, as Robert Frost would say, has "made all the difference." Despite my attempts to avoid such traps, I noticed when I looked at the transcripts I still fell back on traditional evaluation responses like "that's really quite interesting," or "that's a really good insight." However, I remember feeling a genuine spirit of respect and curiosity about students' comments, and their responses continued to amaze me throughout ensuing days.*

Transforming the patterns of talk in the classroom is only one way to place students more squarely in the center of their own learning, but it's an important one. The next time you plan a large group discussion, keep these ideas in mind:

- Ask no questions to which you already know (or think you know) the answer; in fact, try asking no questions at all.
- Allow for "wait time" and rehearsal (in the form of free writing, pair-shares, or just a brief "heads-down" time) before inviting all students into a large group discussion.
- Give students something to hold in their hands and their heads (a bit of writing, graphic organizer, drawing) before opening a discussion.
- Make abundant use of nonverbal prompts such as movies, songs, and photographs to stimulate student talk.
- Don't get obsessed with the amount of time that you hold the floor (teachers do often know more than students, after all), but try to bite your lip whenever a silence seems unbearable or sharing your own personal experience seems more tempting than waiting for students to share theirs.
- Find a way to recognize, but not spotlight, shy or reluctant students.

In Fieldwork Journal 9-2, we ask you to try your hand at analyzing the conversational patterns in your own classroom.

Fieldwork Journal 9-2

Classroom Inquiry—Discourse Analysis

If you are currently teaching, tape a small segment (roughly 15 minutes) of a discussion you are leading. If you don't have a classroom of your own, observe someone who is teaching and analyze the discussion together. If possible, take the tape home and transcribe the discussion or a part of it. Consider the following questions as you read through the transcript or listen to the tape. Take notes and write about the results of your analysis.

Focus on Your Language
- What kinds of roles do you seem to be playing at different points in the discussion (e.g., traffic cop, peacekeeper, fellow learner)? Do you tend to favor one role over the others?
- What kinds of questions do you seem to be asking at different points in the discussion? Do your questions appear to invite or shut down discussion?

Focus on Your Students' Language
- Do your students typically reply to you or to their classmates? Is their talk different when they direct it to you rather than to each other?
- When do students seem most invested in the discussion? What is their language like when they seem to be invested?
- When do students seem least invested? What is their language like at those times?

Focus on Interrelationships
- What is the proportion of teacher-to-student talk? Does this balance change at different times in the discussion? Try to mark those places on your transcript. Why do you think these changes are occurring?
- Who has the power at different times in the discussion? What's happening at moments when it seems to switch?

As we think about those teacher questions that shut down exploratory talk or rich interpretation—questions like "What is the name of . . ." or "What happened when . . ."—we would do well to plan some alternatives. One way you might do so is to ask students to jot down anonymously two or three questions on note cards before, during, or after a lesson. These could be questions pertaining to something you're reading ("Why did he do that?" "What did the author mean when she said . . .") or to larger issues ("Is it right for people to . . ." "What is the historical period of this story?")

"I wonder what his mother is like."). These should be questions that students are actually wondering about at that moment, not questions they think you want them to ask. Once the cards are handed in, shuffle the pack and call out the questions. Class discussion from these "wonderings" can last several minutes or a couple of class periods, depending on student interest. Questions related to longer or more provocative texts can serve as a seedbed for future research projects.

TALK AND LISTENING TO SHOWCASE AND PERFORM

Opportunities for performance can range from informal activities like reading or role playing to more elaborate performances such as public speeches, readers' theaters, skits, or plays. It is clearly beyond the scope of this book to describe all of these performance activities in depth. In the next few pages, we'll offer a few general suggestions for how you can enliven your English language arts classroom with performance opportunities suitable for early adolescents.

Speeches, Demonstrations, and Presentations

Often the formal nature of much public speaking intimidates students and teachers alike. Especially at the middle school level, we suggest that public speeches and presentations should be extemporaneous rather than heavily scripted and memorized. On occasion, you might want students to memorize a famous public address, skit, or dramatic monologue. Usually, however, you'll want your students to be adept at speaking from note cards or cue sheets rather than formal manuscripts.

It takes many years of practice to make a scripted presentation sound fresh, engaging, and spontaneous. This kind of practiced informality is beyond the scope of most middle school students, or their teachers, for that matter. Furthermore, we believe that presentations and speeches for this age group should range from a minute to no more than 4 or 5 minutes. Here are just a few suggestions for brief performance opportunities.

Soapbox speeches. One way of introducing students slowly to the concept of impromptu or extemporaneous speaking is to set up an area of the room and ask students to talk informally for no less than 1 and no more than 2 minutes on an item of current interest to them. Set up a small wooden box or platform in the front of your classroom. Explain how, in earlier days, speakers used to pull up a makeshift platform (often a wooden soap box) and make informal, impromptu speeches to anyone who would listen.

Tell your students you will devote the first 5 minutes of each class period to these "soapbox" speeches. Give students a couple of minutes after they settle in to make a few notes or think about what they might say. Then invite them to stand on the soap box and talk for a minute or so about topics ranging from opinions on current events to announcements about school plays, meetings, and dances. Invite them to tell funny stories or share interesting experiences. The idea is not to produce polished presentations, but to get students comfortable with the idea of getting up and talking in front of peers about something that engages them. Give students a check mark in your grade book each time they speak, making sure to give those who haven't spoken the first chance to do so each day. At the end of a marking period, you can refer to these marks in assigning class participation grades or deciding whether to move students who are between grades up to a higher grade.

Grab bag speeches.   Collect small objects and keep them in a paper bag in your classroom. Whenever you have a few moments left at the end of a class period, invite students to pull out an object. Give each student 1 minute to jot down ideas for an introduction, three major points, and a conclusion. They might create an advertisement for the object, describe its useful features, tell a story about "a day in the life" of that object, or draw some completely unexpected connections to it. You don't need to grade these speeches. Simple marks in your grade book will document how many times students have spoken. Give students a few "passes" during the grading period, so they don't feel forced to perform every time. Write a "P" in your book each time a student chooses to pass. Once all passes are used up, students must speak every time you call on them.

"Process" speeches and informative reports.   Periodically, or as a culmination to inquiry projects, students might present information about topics related to their expertise or experience. Consider asking them to create visuals such as charts, graphs, or electronic slide shows to assist them in making their presentations. Students might explain a process like "jump-starting an engine," a historical event like "the destruction of the World Trade Towers," or a skill like "planning a yard sale."

Mock legislatures.   Particularly if you are teaming with a social studies teacher, you could sponsor an informal classroom congress. The National Forensics League Home Page, listed in the Resources section of this chapter, gives rather lengthy rules for student congress; however, you needn't be this elaborate.

If you don't want to get caught up in the particulars of Robert's Rules of Order (Robert, 2000) or other complicated topics like how a bill becomes a law, consider asking students to work in teams of about four or five students, researching issues that involve some kind of change in our current laws or public policy (for example, eradicating homelessness or abolishing the death penalty). Ask each group to create at least two "bills" that could be debated in a student congress. (The National Forensic League Student Congress manual at *http://www.nflonline. org/AboutNFL/LeagueManuals* provides the format for a sample bill.)

Once each group has drafted at least two bills, set aside a class period for group representatives to make short presentations of the bills and submit them to the entire class for a vote. Depending on your time limits, you can narrow your choice to one bill or allow two or three bills for debate. Give students a few days to work in teams, gathering information to support or argue against the chosen bills. Eventually, each student should prepare an informal 2- or 3-minute persuasive speech for or against a bill, including evidence from reliable sources.

During the session (which can last one class period or several days), pull the desks together so that affirmative ("pro") speakers are on one side of the room and negative ("con") speakers are on the other side, with a podium in the middle. All students should have an equal chance to speak throughout the time period. Each student should speak no more than 3 minutes, with a 1-minute follow-up time for questions from the opposing side. Evaluate speeches on a 1-1 to 3-point scale and use these points to determine final grades.

Beyond Round-Robin Reading: Oral Interpretation, Choral Reading, and Readers' Theater

One of the most tried (or trite) and true approaches to reading dramatic literature in the secondary or middle school classroom is what has been called "round-robin reading." Although many students enjoy reading aloud in class, others find it dreadfully dull, and for good reason. How many of us can remember holding our collective breath as some poor classmate struggled to produce a cold reading of Shaw or Shakespeare?

If you are going to ask students to read aloud, consider assigning parts or characters a day beforehand and asking students to rehearse before coming to class. Better yet, avoid round-robin reading altogether and substitute a bit of choral reading, oral interpretation, or readers' theater. If you're at a loss about where to begin, lots of excellent books, articles, and Web sites are listed in the Resources section of this chapter. You might want to begin with Aaron Shepard's Web Page at *http://www.aaronshep.com*. Aaron sells his books and scripts, so this is a commercial site, but he also offers plenty of "resources and treats for teachers, librarians, storytellers, children's writers, parents, and young people" at no cost.

If you spend an hour surfing some of the Web sites at the conclusion of this chapter, you should return to your classroom armed with some good ideas and even a few scripts to begin your first foray into the world of oral interpretation. First, a few explanations. As opposed to presentational theater, where props, costumes, and settings are often realistic, oral interpretation is more like a theater of the mind, which allows the audience to imagine many aspects that would be presented to them in a stage play or movie. Since oral interpretation and its close relatives readers' theater and choral reading rely on minimal or no props, costumes, and settings, the audience is expected to participate imaginatively, as they would in reading a book as opposed to seeing a movie. Much of the interpretation is accomplished through the performers' expression, intonation, and limited movement and gestures rather than props, settings, or other trappings of traditional theater.

At its simplest level, oral interpretation involves the dramatic verbal and vocal representation of a piece of literature in a way that conveys a particular tone, mood, feeling, or other aspect of the interpreter's understanding. Many Web sites and books are available for teachers wishing to use readers' theater in their classrooms. Some are listed in the Resources section of this chapter. If you've ever seen a play such as *Our Town* by Thornton Wilder performed with minimal or no costumes, props, or scenery, you have an idea of what a readers' theater might look like. On a much simpler level, you might have seen performances of poetry or other literature such as *Spoon River Anthology* by Edgar Lee Masters in which interpreters sit on stools and read dramatically from scripts. The following basic decisions need to be made in planning performances of literature.

To stage or not to stage?   Interpreters can stand on platforms or risers, sit on stools, read from scripts, or use simplified props, blocking, and pantomime. The idea is to be representational rather than real. Characters can pantomime actions like drinking from a glass or opening a door. Sometimes a few stage props (a plant, framed photograph on the wall, chair) can say more about a story's setting than a more elaborate set. Slides and music can enhance elements of tone, characters' emotional states, or other aspects of the script.

To memorize or not to memorize?   Because it eliminates the need for scripts, memorization allows interpreters more freedom in moving around a stage, gesturing, and pantomiming. If students do memorize their parts, consider using what is called "offstage focus" (having interpreters look out at the audience as they are saying lines, rather than other characters on stage). This gives audience members a feeling of intimacy and allows them to see subtle facial expressions and other nonverbal nuances of the interpreters.

To costume or not to costume?   If you decide to use costumes, keep them to a minimum. One item of clothing (a scarf, pipe, or cane) can represent a character. As a way of minimizing expense, decide in advance which items of clothing students already have (e.g., black tee shirts and jeans) and use these rather than purchasing or making costumes.

Published versus student-created scripts?   Although a growing number of published readers' theater scripts are available (many of which are based on traditional materials with no copyright restrictions), we see more instructional value in having students cut scripts and assign parts themselves or with your help. Collaborative and critical skills are developed as students explore questions about the various possibilities for which speakers or "voices" to assign to different readers, when a line shifts perspective, or which poems seem to go together in the context of a larger script.

The book *Something Is Going to Happen: Poetry Performance for the Classroom* by Wolf (1990) is a great source for approaching poetry interpretation with middle school students. It includes commonsense descriptions of issues like blocking and script cutting and a nice variety of short sample scripts with suggested stage directions.

Planning Performances

Although the possibilities for readers' theater and oral interpretation in your English language arts classroom are nearly endless, here are just a few ideas for your consideration.

Performance anthology.   Decide on a unifying theme ("Life Cycles") and commission student writings on various aspects of the theme (e.g., growing up, childhood, teenage years, and parenting). Rather than creating a print anthology of student writing, create a performance anthology or a collection of oral renditions of student writings, arranged according to themes. Students can perform their own pieces or ask class members to do so. Consider using popular or original music, slides, and other artistic touches. Invite friends and family members to attend the final performance.

Collaborative script writing.   Engage your students in writing and performing a script for a soap opera or simple melodrama—the cornier, the better. Decide on a clever title (e.g., "As the Eyeball Turns"), a cast of characters, and a basic plot line. Together with your students, map an outline of the plot onto a piece of chart paper and break it into three or four short scenes. Assign each scene to a scripting group. Once the script is created, you can duplicate copies, assign parts, and read or perform it aloud.

Thematic montage.   Tie together several short pieces under some unifying theme with several subthemes. For example, excerpts of "The People, Yes" by Sandburg (1990) can be interwoven with other literature, music, and visual images of American life. If you have access to a stage, consider using lighting to add yet another dimension to the performance. Share your students' work in an assembly or on parents' night.

EVALUATING ORAL LANGUAGE AND LISTENING

Oral language and listening are perhaps the hardest language acts to grade and evaluate. Any kind of performance, whether a formal public speech or a class comment, is loaded with emotion and personal investment, especially for early adolescents. The question is how to encourage students to develop their oral language abilities without squelching their often tentative attempts at expression and fluency.

As noted previously, many times assessments should be designed as a means to choose more appropriate teaching strategies and interventions, not to rank order students. Consider negotiating the criteria for grading or evaluation with your students. This is perhaps most crucial in the areas of oral language and listening. Students need to know what is expected of them, and you must be adept at guessing what is appropriate to grade and what is best left ungraded.

Just as in the writing classroom, you should sponsor a large number of ungraded, exploratory oral activities before assigning a grade. Above all, don't use the forum of a public discussion or performance as an opportunity to correct students' grammar or usage. Simply rephrasing a grammatically incorrect statement in what has been called "the language of wider communication" as you respond orally to students will most likely let them know in a subtle way that they've made a mistake. Correcting errors directly and publicly can lead to frustration and makes students focus on form rather than meaning.

> Give credit for both preparation and performance.

Paula Kristmanson, in her article on the importance of considering affect in supporting second language acquisition (2006) notes, "Using more natural approaches (i.e., those often used in maternal language development) such as asking clarifying questions, rephrasing the statement in the correct manner, and creating situations where students can negotiate meaning, creates less stressful language learning environments." Further, Kristmanson suggests that statements such as "Can you tell me more" or "Très intéressant" can be more validating than corrections and can help

English language learners to focus on content rather than form in their oral language (Accessed on February 6, 2006, from *http://www.caslt.org/research/affect.htm*).

Once students become comfortable talking and listening in informal situations, you may want to assign more formal graded tasks like presentations or speeches. As an introduction to formal public speaking, consider making a humorous example of yourself. If you are a bit of a ham, walk into the classroom with your shirt untucked or hair mussed, and place a sheaf of notes on a podium. Make sure to drop the notes and rearrange them several times before beginning to speak. Announce your topic: "Ten Tips for Delivering a Public Speech." As you speak from a list of 10 pointers, illustrate each one by doing the exact opposite of what it says. For example, as you say "avoid distracting behaviors," rock the podium back and forth, pace from one end of the room to the other, or fiddle with your jewelry. As you say "be sure to make eye contact with each member of your audience," look at the floor or above the heads of the audience. Be sure to lower your voice so that even people in the front row can't hear you and clear your throat often. Your students will get the idea pretty quickly. Use this demonstration as a springboard for discussing a few general criteria on which you might judge their first public performance. Turn these criteria into a simple rubric and grade students on a 3- or 5-point scale for each criterion. Again, give your students time to practice without threat of evaluation.

If students are creating readers' theater presentations, you might want to grade aspects of the process (e.g., creating a script, contributing published or student writing, rehearsing) but leave the performance itself ungraded. Consider creating a contract in which students can lose points for failing to show up for rehearsals or using group time unproductively, but which leaves other, more risky, aspects of the performance ungraded. The contract could allow students to earn extra points for things like bringing in props, creating slides for a show, writing an original song, or creating a tape or CD of background music. These extra points could serve as a reward for shy students or those who have a limited knowledge of English and would rather not perform. You may need to create positive roles that do not include language production for some students. Listening is an active and important process step for second language users.

If you are serious about integrating the language arts in your classroom, you will have plenty of opportunities to grade or evaluate more formal and polished aspects of student work. Just as you wouldn't grade individual entries in a personal journal or learning log, you'll want to avoid assigning grades to students' tentative, exploratory attempts at talking and listening. Formal public speeches and debates lend themselves more readily to grading, but even these should be handled with care. Finally, we believe it's always important to give lots of formative evaluation (in the form of informal feedback at every stage of preparation) before arriving at a final grade.

The best advice we can offer applies not only to oral language and listening but to all language arts: Look closely, beneath the surface of a student's classroom behavior. Most students are like icebergs. A great deal of their interest, their skill, their preferences and proclivities, the key to what moves them to passion or bores them to death, is hidden beneath the surface of their classroom performances. Some are what Jim Jackson, a preservice teacher in his final placement, likes to call "slacker savants." Classroom Case 9-3 offers Jim's final reflection for the members of his student teaching seminar.

Classroom Case 9-3

The Slacker Savant

What's Going On

There is one student like this in every class. A student that is too withdrawn from everyone and everything to give a damn about school. This student might be the one that shouts out things that are irrelevant to class; it also may be the student sitting in the back corner asleep. Usually, this student might tend to turn in very little work, if any. Yet we, as educators, are enamored by this kind of mentality. "I came up with the most interesting community builder about yadda yadda, and all STUDENT X could do was sleep!" is our battle cry. Plagued with constant absences, trips to the office, detention, and expulsion, we are left to ask, where does it end?

Maybe we are asking the wrong questions. I think we should ask, where does it start?

Yesterday

There was a student in my 8/9 period class. For privacy reasons, let's call him Dan. Dan was the student that always stumbled into class late, orange juice in hand, Discman hidden under his hooded sweatshirt, five o'clock shadow on his face. He would pick his seat in the corner, slump into it, and nod off to sleep. He rarely turned in work and didn't contribute to class in a positive manner.

All in all, I had no reservations about who I believed Dan was. I pictured him a slacker, a student with no ambition and drive. I saw his multiple absences as cuts; not times he was sick, but days he just didn't feel like going to school. When pushed, I figured he would do as little as he could to survive and waste the rest of his, and my, time.

All this changed when Dan handed in his first writing assignment, 2 weeks late. It was a very polished, deep, dark poem on drug use. I was expecting something a lot more elementary, and I was floored. I read his poem over and over again, wondering how he could waste so much time during class and turn in a piece of work that was phenomenal. I then deemed Dan the Slacker Savant.

In keeping with Dan's love for music, I have decided to use popular song quotes for the headings of this reflection. This is important because, although it does have something to do with Dan's love for music, it also works to show where we have moved to and from as a teacher and a student, and a student and a teacher.

Right Now

Now that I had my beliefs about Dan disproved, I was ecstatic. I felt that it would be a whole new world for the two of us, as I would be able to ask things of him, and he would do them. In all actuality, things went back to the same way they were before, where he would come in, sit down, and "veg" out. This was troubling to me, as I wondered how I could bridge the gap between the two of us, find out what exactly made him act this way, and how I could get him to produce better, and more frequent, work.

I began by observing the way he acted in my class. I had him toward the end of the day in a class that was fairly small, so it was easy for me to keep an eye on him while I taught the class. At first, I noticed he liked to talk to some of the nearby students, but many kids in the class did this, so it didn't strike me as odd. I also noticed that when he was supposed to be reading his free-read book, which we provided time for in class, he had his head down and he was napping. I looked back roughly 5 minutes later to see him with his book open, reading.

On the next day, which was a writing day, again I followed his movements as I went about my daily routine. I didn't want him to know I was observing him, as I figured it would change what he was doing. During the mini-lesson, he had his head down, napping. When the class moved on to peer editing their writing pieces, he again took a few minutes more than everyone else, but he managed to begin editing his writing with another student.

Throughout the semester, I noticed he would never turn things in when we asked him to, but the quality of the work was always right there. I began to question what Dan's beliefs were about school and the school environment. In my own school days, I tended to produce the same habits as Dan because I was not a fan of the structure of school. I was a more independent learner and tended to do things on my own schedule. This was my hypothesis for the way Dan worked.

I thought it would be a great idea to talk with Dan about his final project, and I could then use the conversation as a gateway to a somewhat informal interview of Dan on his opinions toward his work, his study habits, and school in general. I believed that a normal interview wouldn't be a good idea because it would prove to be too regimented for Dan, and he would favor a conversation that went normally, as opposed to a conversation where I took down his words or taped them.

Dan and I talked about his final project, which would be on building soapbox racers. We then began talking about his inability to hand things in on time and often enough. When I asked Dan if he thought he was a good student, he said, "I dunno." When pressed, he said his work was average and he didn't like doing small assignments like the ones we had him doing because he felt they "wasted [his] time." When we moved on to talking about school, Dan said exactly what I believed he was going to say: "School sucks." He began detailing the fact that he didn't like school because he wasn't an early person and didn't like the fact that everything was so scheduled and organized. He said he liked doing things at his own pace and liked to take more time on things that he enjoyed because they meant more to him.

As my student teaching semester came to a close, I began to ask Dan's opinions on some of the lessons we had done in class. I was always happy that he would give me an honest response, which would really tell me how things went. The class we had fed off its own energy and we became a tighter knit class and got more work done as a result of it.

When I sat down to analyze Dan's literacy, I came to a resounding conclusion. Dan can do the work. It isn't a question of whether or not he can do it, because he can. The challenge is getting him to do the work. The thing I found out about Dan, and about slacker savants in general, is that in many cases they aren't lazy or slow. They just aren't into it. These students don't want to waste their time on busy-work, because they believe their time is worth more than that. In many ways, I agree with them.

Don't Stop Thinking About Tomorrow

Since we know what we know about Dan, we can use what we have learned about him to better the learning environment of our classes. What we must first realize is that we aren't going to get a classroom of 30 students just like Dan. Many students, if you ask them to recopy the dictionary, will get their pens ready. These are the students who not only want to succeed, but also might believe that every assignment we give them is going to be required for graduation. Now, I don't want to put any kind of student above another, but I favor a student who is resistant to learning. When you have a student who does everything you ask of him or her, there isn't much of a challenge. I had a challenge in Dan in that he challenged me to come up with lessons he would enjoy, lessons he would do, and lessons from which the entire class would benefit.

I agree with Dan that he should be assigned work that is worth his time. I think we might want to work toward giving students like these more independent roles inside and outside of the classroom. When I asked Dan about his final project, he was adamant about working on it. I believe he was enthralled with it because it involved something he enjoyed, and it wasn't tied down into the classroom. . . . If we give students who are more independent the opportunity to use their own time for their own reasons, we might see a better work output from them.

For Discussion

In what ways did Dan serve as Jim's teacher? All in all, students who push us, as educators, to adapt our needs to more than one kind of student are positive because they broaden who we are as educators. How might Jim have created ways to learn more from Dan?

From teaching our students to become better communicators and listeners to becoming more careful observers of their verbal and nonverbal behaviors in our classroom, much can be gained by making talk and listening a significant part of our English language arts curriculum. It may seem scary at first to think about performance activities like readers' theater, public speaking, debate, or drama, but the benefits far outweigh the costs. As Miss Frizzle says in the popular children's television show, *The Magic School Bus*, it's important to "take chances, make mistakes, get messy!" As Jim observes, our teaching, our students, and our classes are bound to be "the better for it."

Standards in Practice

Viewing Your Oral Language Lessons Through the NCTE/IRA Standards

Locate a copy of the *NCTE/IRA Standards for the English Language Arts* (1996). For an explanation of the standards, a table of contents for the volume, an annotated listing of each standard, and chapter excerpts, consult the NCTE Web site at this address: *http://www.ncte.org/standards*.

FIGURE 9-8 Standards-Based Learning

Activities	Connections to Standards
Landscaping Project	
• Choosing an element that needed improvement	• Students participate as *knowledgeable, reflective, creative,* and *critical members* of their classroom community.
• Making phone calls • Writing letters	• Students use spoken and written language to *accomplish their own purposes* (e.g., for *learning, persuasion,* and the *exchange of information*).
• Learning new skills	• Students use spoken language to *accomplish their own purposes* (e.g., for *learning and the exchange of information*).
• Writing reflections on the entire year	• Students use written language to *accomplish their own purposes* (e.g., *for learning*).

For purposes of this chapter, we suggest you look most closely at Standards 11 and 12. Read each standard closely and attempt to tease out the multiple goals embedded in each one. We have highlighted words and phrases in these standards that you might use in critically analyzing your own lessons.

NCTE/IRA Standard One

11. Standard Eleven: Students participate as knowledgeable, reflective, creative, and critical members of a variety of literacy communities.
12. Standard Twelve: Students use spoken, written, and visual language to accomplish their own purposes (e.g., for learning, enjoyment, persuasion, and the exchange of information).

Now, look at a lesson you have created or one you are in the process of creating that involves talk and listening. If you aren't currently planning lessons of your own, you might want to refer to Classroom Case 9-1 on Harry Webb's service learning projects presented earlier in this chapter. For each activity in your lesson plan, try to tie it to one or more of these subgoals. As an example, in Figure 9-8 we've paraphrased some of the activities in Harry Webb's service learning project. Beside each activity, we placed the relevant subgoals of Standard 11.

Critically examine one of your lessons (or Harry's) against the backdrop of the two standards listed at the beginning of this section. Do you note any subgoals that have not been addressed? Although you can't address all standards in all lessons, on occasion you may want to look closely at the standards to determine how you are addressing them in relevant ways for your students in your particular community. You may have valid reasons to emphasize some over others. You may find that you do not address some subgoals. If so, consider why that is the case.

REFERENCES

Abrams, J., & Ferguson, J. (2004/2005), Teaching Students from Many Nations. *Educational Leadership, 62*(4), 64–67.

Avi (1991). *Nothing but the truth.* New York: Avon Books.

Barnes, D. (1976). *From communication to curriculum.* Harmondsworth, England: Penguin.

Cisneros, S. (1991). *The house on Mango Street.* Madison, WI: Turtleback Books.

Cunningham, P. M. (1976–1977). Teachers' correction responses to black-dialect miscues which are non-meaning changing. *Reading Research Quarterly, 12*(4), 637–653.

Cureton, G. O. (1985). Using a black learning style. In C. K. Brooks, L. C. Scott, M. Chaplin, D. Lipscomb, W. Cook, & V. Davis (Eds.), *Tapping potential: English and language arts for the black learner* (pp. 102–108). Urbana, IL: National Council of Teachers of English.

Duncan, G. (2002). Beyond love: A critical race ethnography of the schooling of adolescent black males. *Equity and Excellence in Education, 35*(2), 131–143.

Fine, M. (1995). Silencing and literacy. In V. Gadsden & D. Wagner (Eds.), *Literacy among African-American youth: Issues in learning, teaching, and schooling* (pp. 201–222). Cresskill, NJ: Hampton Press.

Fordham, S. (1993). Those loud black girls: (Black) women, silence, and gender "passing" in the academy. *Anthropology and Education Quarterly, 24*(1), 3–32.

Fordham, S. (1996). *Blacked out: Dilemmas of race, identity, and success at Capital High.* Chicago: University of Chicago Press.

Frost, R. (1995). Stopping by woods on a snowy evening. In R. Frost, *Collected poems, prose, and plays.* New York: The Library of America.

Grant, L. (1984). Black females' "place" in desegregated classrooms. *Sociology of Education, 57*(2), 98–111.

Guy, R. (1973). *The friends.* New York: Holt Rinehart & Winston.

Hooks, B. (1989). *Talking back: Thinking feminist, thinking black.* Boston: South End Press.

Kristmanson, P. (2006). Affect in the second language classroom: How to create an emotional climate. (Accessed on February 6, 2006, from http://www.caslt.org/research/affect.htm)

Langer, J. (1995). *Envisioning literature: Literary understanding and literature instruction.* New York: Teachers College Press.

McCarthy, C. (1996). Multicultural policy discourses on racial inequality in American education. In R. Ng, P. Staton, & J. Scane (Eds.), *Anti-racism, feminism, and critical approaches to education* (pp. 21–44). Westport, CT: Bergin and Garvey.

Mehan, H. (1979). What time is it Denise? Asking known-information questions in classroom discourse. *Theory into Practice, 18*(4), 285–294.

Moffett, J. (1968). *Teaching the universe of discourse.* Boston: Houghton.

Myers, W. D. (1997). The treasure of Lemon Brown. *In the language of literature, 7th grade* (pp. 18–26). Evanston, IL: McDougal Littell.

Reid, E. (1995). Waiting to excel. Biracial students in American classrooms. In C. Grant (Ed.), *Educating for diversity* (pp. 263–273). Boston, MA: Allyn and Bacon.

Robert, H. M. (2000). *Robert's rules of order.* New York: HarperCollins.

Sadker, M., & Sadker, D. (1994). *Failing at fairness: How our schools cheat girls.* New York: Simon and Schuster.

Salisbury, J., & Jackson, D. (1996). *Challenging macho values: Practical ways of working with adolescent boys.* London: Falmer Press.

Sandburg, C. (1990). *The people, yes.* San Diego: Harcourt Trade Publishers.

Smitherman, G. (1986). *Talkin and testifyin: The language of black America.* Detroit, MI: Wayne State University Press.

Soto, G. (1992). First love. In J. C. Thomas (Ed.), *A gathering of flowers: Stories about being young in America* (pp. 135–151). New York: HarperCollins Children's Book Group.

Standards for the English language arts. (1996). Urbana, IL: National Council of Teachers of English/International Reading Association.

Tannen, D. (1981). New York Jewish conversational style. *International Journal of the Sociology of Language, 30,* 133–149.

Wolf, A. (1990). *Something is going to happen: Poetry performance for the classroom—A teacher's companion book.* Asheville, NC: Iambic Publications.

RESOURCES

Print

Drama

Barnes, D. (1968). *Drama in the English classroom.* Urbana, IL: National Council of Teachers of English.

Blau, L. (1997). *Favorite Folktales and Fabulous Fables: Multicultural Plays With Extended Activities.* One from the Heart.

Bowles, N. (2000). *Cootie Shots: Theatrical Inoculations against Bigotry for Kids, Parents, and Teachers.* New York: Theatre Communications Group.

Ellis, R. (1998). *Multicultural Theatre 2: Contemporary Hispanic, Asian and African-American Plays.* Colorado Springs, CO: Meriwether Publishing, Ltd.

Gerke, P. (1996). *Multicultural Plays for Children: Grades 4–6.* Mandester, NH: Smith & Kraus.

Johnson, L., & O'Neil, C. (Eds.). (1984). *Dorothy Heathcote: Collected writings on education and drama.* London: Hutchinson.

Manduke, J. (Producer/Director). (1975). *Cornbread, Earl, and me [Motion Picture].* United States: Orion Home Video.

O'Neil, C., & Lambert, A. (1982). *Drama structures: A handbook for teachers.* London: Hutchinson.

Wagner, B. J. L. (1998). *Educational drama and language arts: What research shows.* Portsmouth, NH: Heinemann.

Teacher Questioning

Bloome, D. (1986). Building literacy and the classroom community. *Theory into Practice, 25,* 71–76.

Dillon, J. T. (1990). *The practice of questioning.* New York: Routledge.

Hynds, S. (1991). Questions of difficulty in literary reading. In A. Purves (Ed.), *The idea of difficulty in literature* (pp. 117–139). Albany, NY: SUNY Press.

Hynds, S. (1992). Challenging questions in the teaching of literature. In J. A. Langer (Ed.), *Literature instruction: A focus on student response* (pp. 78–100). Urbana, IL: National Council of Teachers of English.

Raphael, T. (1986). Teaching question-answer relationships, revisited. *The Reading Teacher, 39*(6), 516–522.

Talk in the Classroom

Barnes, D., Britton, J., & Torbe, M. (1987). *Language, the learner and the school* (3rd ed.). Harmondsworth, England: Penguin.

Brice Heath, S. (1983). *Ways with words: Language, life, and work in communities and classrooms.* Cambridge, England: Cambridge University Press.

Cazden, C. (1988). *Classroom discourse: The language of teaching and learning.* Portsmouth, NH: Heinemann.

Gere, A. R. (1990). Talking in writing groups. In S. Hynds & D. L. Rubin (Eds.), *Perspectives on talk and learning* (pp. 115–128). Urbana, IL: National Council of Teachers of English.

Hynds, S., & Rubin, D. L. (Eds.). (1990). *Perspectives on talk and learning.* Urbana, IL: National Council of Teachers of English.

Lundsteen, S. W. (1979). *Listening.* Urbana, IL: National Council of Teachers of English.

Marshall, J. D., Smagorinsky, P., & Smith, M. W. (1995). *The language of interpretation: Patterns of discourse in discussions of literature.* NCTE Research Report No. 27. Urbana, IL: National Council of Teachers of English.

Mehan, H. (1979). What time is it Denise? Asking known-information questions in classroom discourse. *Theory into Practice 28*(4), 285–294.

Moffett, J., & Wagner, B. J. (1992). *Student-centered language arts,* K–12 (4th ed.). Portsmouth, NH: Boynton/Cook, Heinemann.

O'Keefe, V. (1995). *Speaking to think/thinking to speak: The importance of talk in the learning process.* Portsmouth, NH: Boynton/Cook, Heinemann.

Sorenson, M. (1993). Teaching each other: Connecting talking and writing. *English Journal, 82*(1), 42–47.

Sowder, W. H. (1993). Fostering discussion in the language arts classroom. *English Journal, 82*(6), 39–42.

Torbe, M., & Medway, P. (1981). *The climate for learning: Contexts for language.* Montclair, NJ: Boynton/Cook.

Weinberg, S. K. (1996). Unforgettable memories: Oral history in the middle school classroom. *Voices from the Middle, 3*(3), 18–25.

Wells, G. (1985). *The meaning makers: Children learning language and using language to learn.* Upper Montclair, NJ: Heinemann.

Electronic

International Listening Association Home Page. This site is a treasure trove of inspiration that includes thought-provoking, fun quotes about listening. A favorite of ours is from *Pooh's Little Instruction Book*: "If the person you are talking to doesn't appear to be listening, be patient. It may simply be that he has a small piece of fluff in his ear."

http://listen.org

The Internet Theatre Bookshop. This is a great site to browse for play scripts. You can search by genre, nation, author's name, or keyword. Includes a brief synopsis and casting requirements for each play.

http://www.stageplays.com/index.html

Gallery of Poets. Focused primarily on classic poets such as Poe and Frost, this is a good site for finding CDs, films, reviews, and other resources helpful for the oral performance of poetry.

http://www.galleryofpoets.com

Virtual Presentation Assistant. This site provides an online tutorial to help students develop public speaking skills such as determining purpose, topic selection, and so on. The site is intended for students at the college level, but the language is accessible to younger folks as well. Links to other sites focused on public speaking are also available.

http://www.ku.edu/~coms/virtual_assistant/VPA.html

Shakespeare Bookshelf. Sponsored by a group called the "Internet Public Library," this is a great source if you want to find full-text electronic versions of all the Shakespearean plays.

http://www.ipl.org/div/shakespeare/

Art of Speaking in Public. This nonprofit site includes several quick tips for beginning public speakers.

http://www.artofspeaking.com/main.htm

National Forensic League Home Page. If you sponsor or wish to work with a speech and debate program, several features on the National Forensic League (NFL) Web site might interest you, including a detailed description of the rules and regulations of "student congress," an explanation of different debate formats, and the current national topic for high school students.

http://www.nflonline.org/Main/HomePage

National Junior Forensic League (NJFL). The NJFL is an arm of the NFL designed for middle school students. Teacher sponsors can assign points to students for participation in various speech events. Membership information can be accessed at

http://debate.uvm.edu/NFL/AnnouncingNJFL.html

Middle School.Net Debate Sites. Advertised as a resource "for teachers by teachers," this site contains many valuable links for teachers interested in starting a debate program or using debate techniques in their classrooms.

http://www.middleschool.net/activities/debate.htm

McCoy's Guide to Theatre and Performance Studies. Beginning teachers are often "chosen" to sponsor the drama club, even though they may have no clue as to how to hold tryouts, plan a rehearsal schedule, or build a set. This site is a good place to start and includes a list of several excellent Web sites.

http://www.stetson.edu/csata/thr_guid.html

Aaron Shepard's Storytelling Page. As with his popular readers' theater page, Aaron Shepard again provides valuable resources for the middle school teacher—everything from articles on storytelling to sample scripts.

http://www.aaronshep.com/storytelling/index.html

Aaron Shepard's RT Page. Billed as a place to go for "scripts and tips" for readers' theater, this site provides just that. Aaron Shepard sells books and other materials, but you don't need to purchase a book to use the many informative materials and free scripts provided on this Web page. His tips on cutting your own scripts are particularly informative.

http://www.aaronshep.com/rt/

Poetry Alive. This organization brings oral interpretation techniques to teachers and schools through its workshop opportunities and assembly performances. Tapes, CDs, and books are available from this Web site. Of most interest to teachers are the free texts of poetry for various grade levels and the many links to author information and biography. Ideal for texts suitable for readers' theater scripts.

http://www.poetryalive.com

Dramatic Storytelling in the English Classroom Prepared by Dianne Pizarro and Ruth Buchanan. This site provides a commonsense explanation of the characteristics of readers' theater, along with sample texts and scripting techniques.

http://www.aspa.asn.au/Projects/english/rtheatre.htm

Learn Improv. This site is a good source for quick, creative dramatics exercises. You can also contribute an idea for other teachers to access if you're so inclined.

http://www.learnimprov.com/

Improv Games Collection. This is an excellent source for improvisational games.

http://www.humanpingpongball.com/gm.html

Creative Drama Lesson Plans. This Web site is created by a teacher for teachers. Great ideas for simple exercises you can use in your classroom.

http://www.childdrama.com/lessons.html

Tolerance.org. This is a good site for students interested in becoming active in social justice, service learning, or community service projects. Sponsored by the Southern Poverty Law Center, this site is dedicated to promoting tolerance and fighting hate. Students can access a feature called "Tolerance Watch" to be alerted to instances of hate and injustice, one called "Do Something" if they are interested in ways to become involved, or one called "Dig Deeper" if they want to examine their own prejudices and attitudes.

http://tolerance.org

Chapter 10

Reading and Viewing in the Middle Grades

GUIDING QUESTIONS

1. What different print and nonprint "texts" do middle school students encounter each day?
2. Considering this vast array of texts, how would you define "reading" at the dawn of the millennium?
3. How are reading and viewing alike and yet different?

A CASE FOR CONSIDERATION

Making Room for Poetry

Brendan Larsen is approaching his first student teaching placement in a suburban middle school. After consulting with his host teacher, he decides to create a unit on poetry for his eighth-grade students. As you can see in this excerpt from his unit plan, several issues trouble him as he prepares for his first teaching experience:

Campbell Middle School is a suburban, or perhaps it might be more accurate to say rural, school. One might presume this would mean a fairly homogeneous student population consisting mainly of white, middle class students. Indeed this was my naive assumption on my first visit to the school. We all know the code words. "Inner city" is taken to mean poor and black, and "suburban" means white and middle class. This is what I naturally assumed upon pulling into the parking lot of Campbell Middle School for my first classroom visit with Mrs. Martin and her eighth-grade English class. One look at the school confirmed my suspicions. . . . Most of the kids are white, neatly dressed (some look like they stepped out of the pages of a J. Crew catalog), and "into" school. . . . But after my first visit and my first conversation with Mrs. Martin, I understood that my assumptions were not in the least bit accurate. Campbell Middle School, in fact, consists of a very diverse student body. . . . Those J. Crew models might be in some way learning disabled, and those receiving the reduced and free lunches are among the most gifted. . . .

After deciding to teach a unit on poetry, my task was to find appropriate materials and activities. . . . My initial worry was not being able to find age-appropriate materials to work with. I don't want to have them working on simple elementary poems; they will just tune out. Nor do I want to work with poetry that is so obscure and remote that they will grow frustrated and resentful.

Fourteen is a difficult age. Kids are burgeoning adolescents. They are no longer children and hate to be thought of as such (in my experience, at least). They are starting to date. They worry about their experience and what peers think of them. One teacher said to me that it is all about being cool in junior high. But coolness is an ever-shifting definition. In researching this unit and the emotional and social development of the ages I will be working with, I found that adolescence is a period in life marked by an awareness of death. Kids begin to think about it for the first time. They start to become more existential in their thinking, but at the same time they listen to the Back Street Boys, throw spitballs at one another, and make crude jokes. In many ways they are still children; in others they are more complicated than ever before in their young lives. Considering all this, how then does one choose appropriate poetry? I don't want them rolling their eyes in boredom, nor do I want them tuning out because the selections I have chosen have zero relevance to them and what they are experiencing. Luckily for me, however, poetry seems like an ideal unit for us to work on together. There are volumes of poems and an endless list of poets on which I can draw. The difficulty has been in narrowing my selections.

As a student teacher, I didn't want to insert myself and my unit in a jarring or obtrusive way. I didn't want my unit to feel "tacked on." Above all, I wanted my unit to relate to what Mrs. Martin and her students have been doing all along. . . . They have just come off a unit on creative writing. I felt my job then was to relate poetry to the work they have done already. . . . I don't want the students to think that they are done with their short stories, that these will be stuffed away in a folder or in the bottom of their lockers never to be seen or heard from again. I especially don't want my instruction to be a side-show—a student teacher coming in two thirds of the way into the school year only to disappear again like some magic act after 6 weeks. I want my instruction to be as seamless as possible, and I think a way to achieve that is to relate it back to what the students have been doing all along. . . . So, how do I connect two seemingly unrelated genres in a meaningful and cohesive way?

FOR DISCUSSION

As Brendan's comments indicate, decisions about teaching reading (and, we will argue, viewing) in the middle school classroom are far more complicated than simply deciding on which texts to choose. As what he calls "burgeoning adolescents," his students are developing unique tastes and preferences for not only what they read, but also how, whether, and with whom. To complicate matters for Brendan, his relationship with a creative, experienced, and well-loved host teacher constrains his choices even further. Of the poems with which you are familiar, which would be most appropriate for middle school students and why? What forms of resistance to reading in general, and poetry in particular, might you expect, even among a seemingly "homogeneous" student population like the one in Brendan's student teaching placement? Do you worry about other people (parents, a host teacher, principal, or department chair) as you plan your students' reading and viewing experiences? If so, how do you deal with these constraints?

READING AND VIEWING IN NEW TIMES

Let's begin by examining our assumptions about what counts as "reading" in today's world. You'll notice that the title of this chapter covers "Reading and Viewing." This choice comes out of a belief that students in the 21st century need to become "active, critical, and creative users, not only of print and spoken language, but also of 'visual' language," according to the *NCTE/IRA Standards for the English Language Arts* (National Council of Teachers of English, IRA 1996, p. 5). Traditional notions of reading based on printed materials are no longer appropriate, as we understand that today's students must develop "multiliteracies" (New London Group, 1996), enabling them to adopt new ways of talking, feeling, acting, listening, and responding within and outside our classrooms (Gee, 2000; Luke, 1988).

> What is your definition of reading for the 21st century?

In this book, then, we define reading in rather broad strokes, including not only the reading of print-based materials, but also of electronic texts, video, film, television, and other media that surround middle school students at the dawn of the millennium.

> If you are working with a group of middle school students, ask them what Internet sites they read regularly.

As we define it, the term *reading* can involve many different varieties of texts from Instant Messaging posts to material on Internet sites, video games, television, and film, to name a few.

READING AND VIEWING FOR MULTIPLE PURPOSES

Consider the many texts and techniques for reading and viewing in the middle school classroom. The chart in Figure 10-1 represents only a few of the many options available.

In the following entry for Fieldwork Journal 10-1, we ask you to use this preliminary list as a springboard in considering how these texts and techniques might be used for a variety of purposes.

FIGURE 10-1   Texts and Techniques for the Reading and Viewing Classroom

political documentaries	newspaper editorials
literary fiction	nonfiction
music videos	movies
advertisements	electronic texts
silent reading	film critiques
learning logs	dramatic "spin-offs"
response guides	scene improvisations
reading/viewing journals	oral interpretation
critical essays	readers' theater
reviews	choral reading
book talks	cartoon illustrations
character sketches	imaginary dialogues
rewrites or parodies	multimedia presentations
inquiry projects	montages
author/director studies	Internet-based research
film production	scripts
class anthologies	oral reports on reading
literature circles	book clubs
television closed captioning	

READING AND VIEWING WITH MIDDLE SCHOOL STUDENTS

What's important to know about teaching reading and viewing to middle school students? First, because of their high need for activity and intellectual stimulation, middle school students quickly tire of skills-based "comprehension" activities that focus on contrived texts and "testable" experiences. Similarly, few are intellectually ready for the meticulous rendering of literary interpretation and the kind of close reading that have become the staple of many high school literature programs. They

---

Fieldwork Journal 10-1

Multiple Purposes

First, look at the list in Figure 10-1. Feel free to add your own texts and techniques for reading and viewing to this preliminary list. Now, create a chart like the one we've done for multimedia presentations in Figure 10-2. Pick one of the texts or techniques from Figure 10-1 and experiment with the different purposes it might serve in your teaching of reading and viewing. We've selected multimedia presentations as an example, but you should feel free to select other texts and techniques from Figure 10-1. When you've finished this exercise, you might want to share some of your ideas with others.

FIGURE 10-2   Purposes for Reading and Viewing

Purposes for Reading and Viewing				
	Reading and Viewing to Explore	**Reading and Viewing to Learn About Reading and Viewing**	**Reading and Viewing to Connect and Transform**	**Reading and Viewing to Showcase**
Techniques for Reading and Viewing	How might students explore ideas and express themselves through the reading of literature, nonfiction, film, or electronic texts?	How might students become better readers of print and nonprint texts?	How might students use reading and viewing to connect with others and make an impact on their world?	How might students share or demonstrate what they have learned through reading and viewing?
Multimedia Presentations	Students read self-selected books, keeping track of their responses through multiple genres of writing, drawing, and so on.	Students explore how the same story is presented in multiple media (e.g., film, novel, documentary, etc.).	Groups of students create and share multimedia presentations based upon their responses to "book club" selections.	After completing inquiry projects, individuals or groups create multimedia presentations to showcase what they've learned.

need chances to read books, stories, and poems that are full of compelling action, to share their choices and opinions in the comfortable forum of their peer group, to discover reading's dramatic potential, and to read nonfiction texts with depth and insight. Because they are moving toward high school (and in most cases, high-stakes testing), many middle school students do need help with reading comprehension.

It's important to remember, though, that middle school students need a particular kind of help to think deeply about important issues while they are developing reading skills. As teachers, we do not have the luxury of teaching them to think after we've finished teaching them the basics of decoding, comprehension, and critical analysis. This is all the more reason to offer multiple ways of responding and showcasing what students have learned through print as well as nonprint media. Middle school students respond particularly well to the incorporation of drawing, dramatic enactment, visual representation, music, film, video, and electronic texts into their reading and viewing experiences.

Whether they are "reading" fiction, film, music videos, or electronic media, middle school students are at a crucial period of developing identities, tastes, and preferences that will carry them into high school and adulthood. To teachers, they may seem hopelessly stuck on a steady diet of Harry Potter, Britney Spears, Spike Lee, or *Teen People*. However, these obsessions and binges are often the seeds of students' developing identities as readers and critical viewers.

> How can you balance choice and control in the reading and viewing experiences you design?

Sharing reading materials and ideas through book clubs or dialogue journals and having a great deal of choice in selecting (or abandoning) particular texts are crucial at this stage. At the same time, ironically, too much choice in texts and topics can be limiting, considering the fact that students will soon be expected to read, view, and understand materials about people, ideas, cultures, and topics that are often remote from their personal experience. More important, it is crucial for early adolescents to develop a critical sense of the content of the many texts that bombard them, the way in which these texts are marketed to young people, and their impact on society at large.

CONSIDERATIONS FOR READING AND VIEWING WITH MIDDLE SCHOOL STUDENTS

It would be impossible to list "best practices" for the reading and viewing classroom, since every middle school, community, and group of students has particular constraints that shape what those practices might be. Instead, we offer some considerations for you to explore in creating opportunities for reading and viewing in your classroom. The following list is based on a selection of items from the National Middle School Association "key developmental needs of young adolescents" introduced in Chapter 1 (for the full list, visit the NMSA Web site at *http://www.nmsa.org/Research/ResearchSummaries/ Summary5/tabid/257/Default.aspx*). As you review your own lessons and unit plans, you might want to periodically review these questions and considerations.

Considerations for Reading and Viewing in the Middle School Classroom

- When is it important for students to read and interact with texts freely and privately as opposed to publicly?
- In what ways can teachers become collaborators with students in their encounters with print and nonprint texts?
- How can we balance middle school students' need for greater autonomy with the need for greater social interactions?
- How can reading and viewing become active rather than passive pursuits?
- How do we support physical activities that prepare students for reading and viewing?
- When is it important for students to draw, talk, demonstrate, or perform their responses to texts?
- How do we facilitate students' choices of texts, while expanding their range of competencies with unfamiliar texts?
- How can students create their own print and nonprint texts for other students to read, view, and enjoy?

- How can we provide opportunities for reading and viewing that are not graded or evaluated, along with those that are?
- How do we connect students' lives outside the classroom with their reading and viewing experiences?
- How do we help them to become critical consumers of the texts that surround their daily lives?
- How can reading and viewing promote students' involvement in social and political activities outside the classroom?

DIFFERENCES BETWEEN LITERARY AND NONLITERARY READING

It's probably safe to say that the person who revolutionized the teaching of literature to adolescents was Rosenblatt. In her landmark work, *Literature as Exploration* (1995, originally published in 1938), she heralded what would become a truism for teach-

> How can you provide both aesthetic and efferent reading opportunities?

ers over the past several decades: There are as many individual responses to literature as there are readers of literature. Rosenblatt (1994) made us aware of the differences between what she called "efferent" and "aesthetic" reading. Taken from the Latin word *effere* ("to carry away"), *efferent reading* is for the purpose of gathering information to be used at some later time. Much reading in schools, Rosenblatt argued, is efferent reading, as opposed to the near-total absorption in the reading act, or "aesthetic reading" that literature requires.

Language in Context

You might ask students to select some of their favorite blog sites or other Web sites and do an investigation of the ways particular groups use "insider" language to show themselves as members in good standing.

Reading nonfiction requires a different stance from that used in literary reading. When we read information, we maintain what Langer (1995) calls a "point of reference" (p. 30). Literary reading, on the other hand, involves exploring what Langer calls "horizons of possibilities" (p. 26). For example, on the day the twin towers of the World Trade Center were destroyed, we all read or viewed the news reports, grasping for the details. The exact language of the reporters and newscasters did not register with us.

Reading a poem is very different from this sort of nonliterary reading. Poetry and other literature invite us to explore a variety of possible meanings, personal and aesthetic as well as intellectual. As middle school teachers, we must remember these differences when we sponsor reading and viewing in our classrooms.

INVITING STUDENTS' RESPONSES TO LITERATURE: STANCES VERSUS HIERARCHIES

For many years, and even today, some literature anthologies followed each literary selection with a list of questions in a hierarchy beginning with "literal" and proceeding through some variant of "interpretive" and "inferential" levels. Yet we know this isn't how real reading happens. Think of the last book or story you read. Did you begin by noting a list of literal details and then proceed neatly toward the other levels of the hierarchy? Of course not! Maybe you said something like "This book stinks. I'm going to put it down!" (an interpretive, evaluative level). Or maybe you read the first few pages and thought, "This is a typical murder mystery" (an inferential stance).

In contrast to the idea of reading levels, we'd like you to consider the intellectual stances that readers move through at various phases of their reading (see Figure 10-3). You might begin a lesson from a connecting or extending stance, for example, asking students to make predictions from illustrations or cover art as a way of introducing a text. Or you could ask them to take a few minutes and free write about their first understandings. One rule of thumb in dealing with aesthetic reading, however, is that it's best to allow students to experience the text on their own terms before leading them into rigidly teacher-directed activities. Feel free to modify the order presented in Figure 10-3, depending on the particular text and students you are teaching.

As a way of making these stances more concrete, you may want to think of your own reading process as you began this chapter. In the experiencing phase, you were probably focused on gathering impressions of what the chapter might be about. Perhaps you were underlining words or phrases with a highlighting pen or just trying to grasp the gist of the chapter without bothering about specific details. Brendan's story in the Case for Consideration at the beginning of the chapter might have set up a connecting stance, in which you were judging his experience against your own. The exercise in Fieldwork Journal 10-1 on "Reading and Viewing for Multiple Purposes" was designed to bring you into an extending stance, where you created new understandings about your own teaching. As readers, we shuttle imperceptibly among these three stances.

FIGURE 10-3　Stances for Reading and Viewing

Experiencing—In this stance, readers are simply gathering their first impressions of the book, movie, visual, or aural representation. They may be creating mental images, following random associations, forming a kind of gut response to an author's words or a filmmaker's images. They might be completely oblivious to events around them, as they immerse themselves aesthetically in what they are reading or viewing. Especially in the early phases of *experiencing*, they may be unable or unwilling to verbalize their response because they are so deeply engaged in forming their initial impression.

Connecting—In this stance, readers are thinking about similarities and differences. They might be comparing a movie with a book or holding characters and plot events up against their own lives. Perhaps they are rereading, rethinking, revising their initial impressions, looking closer at language and image, changing or enriching an earlier impression.

Extending—In this stance, readers are making broader connections between the text and other texts, ideas, or events in the world beyond. As part of an *extending* stance, they might be pondering what might come next or even creating their own classroom "literature," film, or artistic representation. As an extension of their reading and viewing, they may also be researching ideas and dramatizing or performing texts.

They do not occur in a lockstep order and are not mutually exclusive. Connecting and extending often occur simultaneously and are often a part of our first experiences with a text. It is important, however, to consider what stances you invite in your reading and viewing lessons.

STRATEGIES FOR COMPREHENSION AND UNDERSTANDING

Regardless of the myriad innovative ideas for teaching reading and literature that have proliferated in our professional conferences and in journals, the one staple of the middle or high school English language arts class seems to be the teacher question. How many of our own English language arts teachers have followed each literature lesson with those teacher-created questions, and how many of us have dutifully crafted them in our own lesson plans, assignments, and examinations, only to look out at a blank sea of student faces when we pose those "no-fail" queries about our interpretations of their reading?

The best advice we can offer is to avoid what Mehan (1979) has called "known information" questions, or those to which we already know the answer. Literal questions immediately after reading can do more to stifle discussion than they can to promote it. We covered the art of conducting whole-class discussions more thoroughly in Chapter 9. Now we invite you to consider ways to develop your students' understanding and response without relying on a steady diet of known information questions that set up a "one-correct-answer" atmosphere in your reading and viewing classroom. We'll begin by proposing six basic reading strategies that you might use in encouraging your students to read a variety of texts from fiction to nonfiction to visual and electronic (see Figure 10-4).

FIGURE 10-4   Strategies for Reading and Understanding

Predicting: Figuring out what might happen next, what a text might be about, how it might end, or what might happen at some future time.

Visualizing: Creating "mind pictures" of characters, setting, story events, or other aspects alluded to but not directly presented.

Connecting: Making associations between texts and related ideas, texts and personal experiences, texts and other texts.

Questioning: Posing questions about plot, characters, information, or issues raised during reading or viewing.

Clarifying: Reviewing, rereading, researching, or searching out resources to assist understanding.

Evaluating: Forming opinions about the quality of texts, motivations behind characters' actions, and other issues raised during reading and viewing.

To make these strategies more concrete, think again about your own reading of this chapter. You might have scanned the headings or opening questions in an attempt to predict the chapter content. As you read the vignettes about other teachers' classrooms, you were probably making connections or asking questions like "Has this ever happened to me?" or "What would I do in this situation?" You might have been visualizing what someone else's classroom looked like or evaluating the worth of an idea. Throughout the whole process, you were probably clarifying unfamiliar ideas by making notes in the margins, writing down questions you intend to ask in class, or rereading key passages. As with the stances for reading, these strategies are not neat and tidy. They are messy, recursive, and overlapping. Good readers use them in varied ways. Unfortunately, not all of our students have them at their command. As a way of thinking about how you might help your students to be more strategic readers without destroying the aesthetic stance so necessary for literary reading, try the following artifact analysis in Fieldwork Journal 10-2.

Fieldwork Journal 10-2

Artifact Analysis: Stances and Strategies in Your Reading and Viewing Lessons

We'd like you to consider the stances and strategies presented here as they pertain to your own teaching. First, find a lesson or unit plan involving reading and/or viewing that you've already taught or one you're currently planning. Think about the three stances of experiencing, connecting, and extending in Figure 10-3; then ask yourself:

- Are students allowed to experience a text on their own terms before moving into a connecting or extending stance? If not, do you have a good reason for your choices?
- Do you seem to prefer one stance over the others in this lesson? That is, do you rely heavily on personal connections, rarely asking students to extend their original interpretations into the realm of larger ideas or issues?
- Conversely, do you plunge students into an extending stance too soon? Do you, for instance, push them to find a "theme" for everything they read before they've fully experienced the text?

Now think about the reading strategies you set up in the lesson you've chosen in terms of the six reading strategies presented in Figure 10-4.

- Do you begin with literal questions or prompts designed to help students clarify what they've read? If so, consider whether these questions actually clarify ideas, or whether students feel put on the spot or encouraged to search for trivial answers rather than forming more global impressions of what they read.
- How often do you ask students to make connections between their reading and their own lives? Other texts? The larger world?

- How can you encourage students' curiosity and engagement by asking them to predict, generate their own questions, or follow up on ideas they are reading about with some additional research?
- How can you encourage multiple ways of responding, including visualizing or visual representation in your reading lessons?
- Do you encourage students to move beyond grasping the ideas in a text toward more critical understanding that requires them to evaluate the worth of those ideas and their larger implications?

STRATEGIES FOR CRITICAL READING AND VIEWING

In her book, *Critical Encounters in High School English: Teaching Literary Theory to Adolescents* (2000), Appleman observes:

> What could poststructuralism, new historicism, deconstruction, Marxism, and feminist literary theory possibly have to do with the average adolescent, just struggling to grow up, stay alive, get through school, and make the most of things? Why it sounds almost like I'm suggesting that passengers taste truffles as the Titanic sinks. It sounds as if I'm promoting a sort of theoretical fiddling while the Rome of our sacred vision of successful public education burns. . . . Nothing, however, could be further from the truth. . . . [C]ontemporary literary theory provides a useful way for all students to read and interpret not only literary texts but their lives—both in and out of school. In its own way, reading with theory is a radical educational reform! . . . Literary theories augment our sometimes failing sight. They bring into relief things we fail to notice. Literary theories recontextualize the familiar and comfortable, making us reappraise it. They make the strange seem oddly familiar. As we view the dynamic world around us, literary theories can become critical lenses to guide, inform, and instruct us. (p. 2)

In his large-scale study of literature teaching in the United States, Applebee (1993) revealed that, despite the broad expansion of literary critical theory in the past few decades, two approaches still dominate American schools: New Criticism and Reader-Response Criticism. With its text-based focus on literary devices, "close reading," and definitive interpretations, New Criticism remains popular in many high school and middle school classrooms today. On the other hand, Reader-Response Criticism, with activities designed to foster students' highly personal and individual responses to literature, is perhaps more conducive to teaching at the middle school level. Unfortunately, both reader-focused and text-focused approaches have overshadowed many other valuable approaches to literary reading that Appleman and others have begun to bring to the fore. Although it's beyond the scope of this book to present either current literary theories or their complex implications for adolescents' reading, we'd like to offer just a taste of how you might introduce your own students to the practice of looking at texts through what Appleman calls "critical lenses." Remember, though, that Classroom Case 10-1 offers only a glimpse of the complicated topics discussed in Appleman's book and other sources included in the Resources section at the end of this chapter (see "Resources for Young Adult Literature").

Classroom Case 10-1

Popular Culture Through Critical Lenses

Althea Hudson wanted to introduce her eighth-grade students to view aspects of their popular culture through a variety of critical lenses. She began by asking her students to look in their backpacks for any kinds of advertisements for products marketed to teenagers. In a blink of an eye, students pulled catalogs for everything from sports equipment to video games from their purses and backpacks. Then she asked them to look at their clothing and other belongings for evidence of advertising logos or visible brand names.

Althea challenged them: "Is there anybody in this room who has absolutely no logos or brand names on their clothing or belongings?" Not a single hand was raised. After a lively discussion about the fact that teenagers are quite literally "walking billboards," Althea challenged each of her students to go home and look for advertisements targeted toward people of their age group. She asked them to bring some of these advertisements to class. They could be from popular magazines, catalogs, taped television segments, or any other source. When students returned with their advertisements, she put them into small groups and asked them analyze the "language" of advertisements through several critical lenses. Althea found a chart with a brief description of each of several critical lenses in Deborah Appleman's book, and she used it to make the following handout, which she explained before asking her students to begin working.

- **Reader Response:** What memories or emotions do these advertisements evoke in you? Do your feelings come from particular experiences you've had or your hopes and dreams for the future? How do advertisements like these shape your hopes and dreams?
- **New Criticism:** What techniques do these advertisers use to achieve their goals? Look at camera angles, interesting or unexpected use of words, metaphors, interesting placement of people or objects, and appeals to logic or emotion. What messages do these advertisements send to teenagers about how life should be lived?
- **Feminist Criticism:** How are males and females portrayed in each advertisement? How do advertisers "teach" us about what women are supposed to be? About what it means to be a man? About what men and women are supposed to desire? Is this a realistic portrayal?
- **Marxist Criticism:** How do these advertisements play upon people's desire for wealth and power? How do advertisements "teach" us about what it means to be happy? Successful? Powerful? Wealthy?
- **Historical Criticism:** If you came from outer space, what would you guess from these advertisements about teenagers in today's world? How do teenagers live, dress, and act? What is a "normal" teenager in the 21st century? How much do advertisements like these "teach" teenagers how to hope, dream, buy, and behave?

> **Language Study in Context**
>
> Ask students to keep a running list of verbs, nouns, adjectives, and adverbs associated with different kinds of products in advertisements. Talk about what images and emotions these images conjure and what associations advertisers are appealing to in their language. For example, what does it mean when words like "sleek" or "sexy" are used in automobile advertisements?

The advertisements evoked a spirited and sometimes contentious discussion among Althea's eighth-grade students. Some argued that advertisements didn't have as much power over teenagers as people believed—that teenagers knew the ads weren't real, and they still liked looking at the pictures of rich and beautiful people. Others disagreed—arguing that everything from how to dress to the amount of money spent by teenagers was influenced by advertising.

When the arguments died down, Althea invited her students to participate in an inquiry project, focused on some aspect of advertising and marketing for teenagers. To start things off, she gave students the addresses for three Internet sites and asked them to spend some time gathering some eye-opening facts about teen magazine readership and marketing to teens. One was a report called "What Teens Read" (*http://www. magazine. org/content/files/teenprofile04.pdf*), another focused on media stereotyping (*http:// www.media-awareness.ca/english/issues/stereotyping/*), and the third was a fact sheet on the Kaiser Foundation study of "Teens, Tweens, and Magazines" (*http://www. kff.org/ entmedia/upload/Tweens-Teens-and-Magazines-Fact-Sheet.pdf*).

After a few days of working with these materials, students broke into task groups and chose a topic of interest to them. The assignment was to produce a five-page paper and a visual (poster, PowerPoint presentation, handout) to be used in a 15-minute culminating presentation. On the day of the presentations, Althea's students explored a range of topics, from how advertisers promote eating disorders to how cigarette ads recruit teenage smokers.

For Discussion

As you can see by Althea's example, Reader Response and New Criticism need not be the only lenses through which your students can read and view the array of texts that surround them. Asking students to shift from among several critical stances in their reading and viewing doesn't mean you need to bog them down with technical details or academic discussion of literary criticism. The point is to help them discover the critical skills so necessary for participation in our media-saturated society. Consider a text that you are presently working with and attempt to chart out some ways that you might ask students to try out several critical stances.

INFORMATIONAL TEXTS

Middle school students read widely from informational texts. In fact many students, but particularly boys (Smith & Wilhelm, 2002), find nonfiction trade books, trading cards, magazines, or reference work more relevant to their interests beyond the school walls than the reading of literature. Middle school students often come to the English language arts classroom with much experience reading and hearing fiction read to them in school. They may have been assigned to read informational texts, especially outside English class, but have not been taught strategies to read informational texts in systematic ways. Effective reading focuses on exploration, investigation, conjecture, evidence, and reasoning. These strategies need to be explicitly modeled and taught in the context of real reading. Although most textbooks and standardized tests promote a kind of decontextualized reading that may or may not be relevant to the lives of teenagers, you should make it your business to provide authentic contexts within which students can read informational texts. Althea's students were already excited to begin exploring the topic of advertising and marketing to teenagers. This kind of context building is crucial if you want to capitalize on student investment and engagement. Strategy instruction alone cannot succeed if students read perfunctorily or for the purpose of remembering disconnected facts that might appear on a test.

There are also important details to consider as you plan lessons designed to foster your students' rich appreciation and understanding of informational materials. The first step is to consider the demands of the text.

Demands of the Text

As you read the texts you plan to assign, try to anticipate potential difficulties that students may encounter. Informational texts generally provide cognitive, affective, and linguistic challenges for many students. The following guidelines might be useful in examining texts you plan to teach.

Cognitive demands

- Consider the amount of information that is likely to be new.
- Consider the prior knowledge that is needed to understand and use this text.
- Consider the level of specificity and complexity of concepts.
- Consider the predictability or complexity of text layout and organizational features.
- Consider whether the text has headings, subheadings, summaries, or other features that make reading easier.
- Consider whether abstract concepts are accompanied by contextual features that aid comprehension (e.g., pictures, charts, graphics).
- Consider the genre (lab report, scientific article, textbook, laboratory manual, reference book, science magazine) and your students' familiarity with the structural and language conventions of the genre.
- Consider whether particular idioms or cultural references will be difficult for struggling readers or students whose first language is not English.

Affective demands

- Consider the kinds of personal experiences related to the topic that students might lack or bring to the text.
- Consider possible biases they may hold toward the subject presented (gender, racial, political, religious, socioeconomic, etc.)

Linguistic demands

- Consider the sentence complexity (for example, the number of clauses per sentence).
- Consider the vocabulary.

- Consider whether unfamiliar or strange syntactical patterns might impede comprehension (for example, frequent violations of the familiar subject-verb-object pattern).
- Consider whether texts are written in the passive voice or contain vague referents such as *this, it,* or *those,* making them difficult for some students to grasp.

Designing Instruction

In choosing what students will read, you may assign only particular passages rather than an entire book or chapter. You may provide different students with texts of varying complexity so that everyone can actively participate in the discussion. In addition, you can use several teaching strategies in making informational texts inviting and accessible to your students. Consider the following possibilities:

- Encourage interest in the reading by making connections to students' families, neighborhoods, and favorite activities.
- Identify complex vocabulary and academic language that may be particularly difficult for students and create engaging activities for practicing unfamiliar words.
- Revisit ideas and concepts over a period of time by providing different texts and classroom experiences of varying complexity.
- Teach students how to identify unfamiliar words from illustrations or other context clues.
- Provide culturally relevant examples of major concepts or themes and create structures that allow students to connect new learning to their personal backgrounds, interests, and expertise.
- Model the use of text features such as headings, charts, pictures, indexes, etc. Teach students to skim, scan, and sample.
- Create opportunities for students to predict, explore, investigate, and provide evidence.
- Avoid lots of teacher questions. Instead, ask students to create their own questions from reading, according to their experiences and interests.
- Encourage fluency by asking students to underline noncrucial words or concepts that puzzle them, rather than stopping the flow of reading to look up words.
- When responding to students, analyze answers for the students' line of reasoning rather than looking for the correct answer.

Reading With All Readers

As we discussed earlier, a growing number of middle school classrooms are based on a model of inclusion. Students with disabilities or special needs are included in the regular classroom, often with the assistance of a teacher's aide or resource specialist. It's likely that you will have students with physical, emotional, or learning disabilities in the same classroom with students who are not labeled. One of your greatest challenges will be finding a way to invite all students, regardless of ability, preference, or desire to become members of what Smith (1984) calls the "literacy club."

The difference between successful and unsuccessful readers is the ability to effectively apply strategies to difficult texts in different contexts. We are all struggling readers in some contexts. "Nonreader" is not so much a static attribute of a student as it is a mismatch between prior knowledge and present expectations. Struggling readers, for example, might need some prereading enrichment before tackling a futuristic novel like Lois Lowry's *The Giver* (1994). Students who are resistant toward or confused by poetry might begin by circling every reference to colors in a poem like Gary Soto's "Oranges" (1990) and then writing or talking about what those color references evoke in them. For students who are turned off to reading, you might want to entice them into the literacy club through aspects of their popular culture such as Internet sites, videos, popular music, and other forms of nonprint media.

When we look through our multiple language lenses, reading may primarily be a literature lesson. It might be a springboard for writing or talking. As you consider if you plan to focus on reading skills or literary appreciation or a call to community service, it's also important to be aware of cultural differences that influence and constrain students' reading and viewing processes. This is important not just in considering your text selections, but considering the ways in which you invite students to engage with the texts.

You may want to create some opportunities for students to engage by "jumping in," as noted in chapter 1, which is similar to the "call-response" pattern of communication in African American churches, where members of the congregation participate actively and vocally (Labov, 1972). When students call out responses without being formally recognized by teachers or move around the room without permission, we must realize that their behaviors do not necessarily signal disrespect. On the contrary, such talk and movement may lead to great leaps in learning.

Although it has become popular to base many activities on personal sharing, some students may see as many perils as potential benefits when they bring their personal experiences and reactions to the forum of a whole-class or even a small-group discussion. Consider, for example, the penalties of personal sharing for gay students, those whose parents may be neglectful or abusive, or those whose cultures may differ significantly from what their classmates consider to be the norm. Never force students to share private writing without a great deal of advance warning. Give students plenty of warning when you expect them to share ideas or writing, and be on hand to offer advice or counsel when students feel that their personal experiences are too risky to be shared.

Likewise, we must also be sensitive to early adolescent girls who are afraid of participating in a discussion for fear of looking "too smart" and boys who avoid traditional literacy activities like keeping journals (too personal) or reading poetry (too feminine). Depending on their cultural backgrounds, some of your students may have parents who believe that being "seen and not heard" is a sign of respect and that the best way of learning is silence.

Placing students into familiar "home groups" for collaborative learning activities and giving them advance notice of when they will be expected to read aloud or change activities will also go a long way in reducing the anxiety of "going public" in the classroom.

TEXT SELECTION IN THE MIDDLE SCHOOL CLASSROOM

If your school has a large budget (an unfortunately rare situation), you may be able to purchase class sets of paperbacks for your students' independent reading and a modern literature anthology full of engaging multicultural texts geared toward students of various backgrounds, abilities, and preferences. If you're like most teachers, however, you'll need to build a classroom library without going into substantial personal debt. Your school library should be your first stop. Most school librarians are happy to put together a cart of books for your classroom during a particular unit. For example, say you're teaching *Briar Rose* (1992), a holocaust novel by Yolen. Your school librarian could provide you with a shelf of books, newspaper articles, videos, DVDs, or books on the holocaust. Texts that your library doesn't own can often be borrowed from other libraries through an interlibrary loan program. Enterprising teachers browse used bookstores, thrift shops, and, of course, yard sales or garage sales. Sometimes local bookstores or libraries hold end-of-the-season book sales. If you're fortunate enough to attend a regional or national conference, visit the booths of publishing companies and get on their catalog or mailing lists. Once you start receiving catalogs and collecting books, you'll be surprised at how crowded your own bookshelves begin to be.

During her teaching career, Susan created a small classroom library of books and anthologies she had scavenged over the years. Never an expert at the art of record keeping, she placed her students on an honor system. If they took out a book from her classroom library, they had to return that book or a different book (subject to her approval). This system ensured a constantly fluid supply of different books and allowed students who had fallen in love with a particular book to make it their own. Luckily, many students not only returned the books they had taken out but voluntarily brought bags of other books from home. By the end of the year, she had to find additional shelf space for her classroom library.

Text Selection and Censorship

What constitutes quality? Texts, ranging from fairy tales to young adult novels, have been criticized because they seem to constrain the roles available to boys and girls. Like many fairy tales, popular book series are often written in such a way as to construct models of adulthood that reinforce stereotypes. Texts should represent the lives lived by middle school students. Those who work in adolescent literature often describe the role of texts as serving as "mirrors and windows." Literature should serve as "mirrors" for early adolescents to see themselves and as "windows" to view others with a deepening respect for the multiple ways that young people are growing in America. It is as important for all students to see themselves in literature as it is for them to see people unlike themselves. For all middle school students, it is important to learn to understand and respect adolescents who are growing up now and long ago. Now, more than ever, we need to embrace the rich diversity of our students and their literature. Any list of good literature should be cognizant of including children with disabilities, and non-stereotyped gendered roles. Books in your classroom should be populated with strong, authentic Asian, Hispanic, African-American, and Native American characters.

In recent years, our classroom bookshelves have expanded to include literature and nonfiction representing a variety of cultural, racial, and ethnic perspectives. At the same time, formerly taboo issues like sexual identity, teenage suicide, pregnancy, and teen violence have been making their way rapidly into books targeted for teenagers. In light of the spate of lawsuits brought against teachers and school systems, only you can decide for which reading materials you are willing to "go to the mat." Some English departments form selection boards made up of parents, students, and teachers that review books and other materials to ensure that teachers are not harassed for their decisions about which texts to teach or make available to students in the classroom. Parental permission letters or contracts for students' independent reading have become commonplace (see the Resources section on combating censorship at the end of this chapter). Remember, though, that there is a difference between censorship and text selection. When you exclude texts from your curriculum out of fear that students will be exposed to disturbing ideas or parents will retaliate, you are engaging in censorship. You should try not to operate from fear but out of reasoned choice.

For example, however limited your budget may be, try to offer variety in the racial, ethnic, and cultural perspectives in your textual choices. Don't make *To Kill a Mockingbird* (Lee, 2001) the one text that includes African American characters or *Anne Frank: The Diary of a Young Girl* (1988) the one representative text of the "Jewish experience." Consider how your

> Broaden racial and cultural perspectives in your choice of texts.

African American or Jewish students must feel when they see themselves reflected in servile characters or are made to feel that racism was an unfortunate situation "dealt with" in the 1960s and that anti-Semitism was obliterated after World War II. Go back to the Electronic Resources section at the end of chapter 4 for many recommended and award-winning books.

If you have time for only so many longer works like novels or plays, try to collect shorter works—poems, songs, primary source documents, short stories, or picture books—to broaden the perspective that students have on cultural and historical issues. A picture book like *Rose Blanche* by Innocenti (1996) makes a powerful companion to a holocaust novel like *Briar Rose* by Jane Yolen (1992). Spielberg's film *Survivors of the Holocaust* (Spielberg & Holzman, 1996) is a stunning documentary based on the experiences of a group of Hungarian Jews who were children during the Nazi occupation. Similarly, *Faithful Elephants* by Tsuchiya and Dykes (1988) portrays the poignant situation of Japanese citizens during World War II and would be a good companion to a book that portrays the American experience. These shorter texts could be presented in one or two class periods and are a marvelous supplement to longer pieces of literature and nonfiction.

Organizing Instruction

When planning units, choose an organization that best supports your goals for reading and viewing. For example, if you want students to explore broad ideas, you can pull together a variety of texts that all relate to the same theme or subthemes, such as "Making a Difference" or "The Search for Identity." An historical approach works best when you want to focus on a particular period in history. A social studies unit

Language Study in Context

Locate some primary source documents from the Japanese internment newspaper articles and editorials from the time and transcripts of congressional debates and executive orders are good sources. Ask students to pay close attention to the language used to describe Japanese Americans by politicians, journalists, and editorialists. Discuss the power of language in stereotyping racial groups and in justifying decisions like the internment of Japanese Americans during World War II.

on World War II can be enhanced by an English language arts unit on the Japanese internment in America.

Books like *Farewell to Manzanar* by Watkusaki Houston (1983) can be supplemented with poems like Dwight Okita's "In Response to Executive Order 9066: All Americans of Japanese Descent Must Report to Relocation Centers" (1991) and a collection of primary source documents from the children of the Poston internment camp called *Through Innocent Eyes: Teenagers' Impressions of WW2 Internment Camp Life* (Tajiri, 1990).

If you want to focus on the work of particular authors, a biographical approach makes the most sense. Some modern literature anthologies include "author studies," which offer short pieces in several genres by contemporary and classic authors like Maya Angelou, Gary Paulsen, Edgar Allen Poe, and Jack London. A variety of Web sites that feature biographical sketches and author interviews are included in the Resources section at the end of this chapter.

Finally, if you're interested in reading/writing connections, organizing by genre makes sense. A unit on poetry might include the free verse of e. e. cummings alongside the heavily metered and rhymed work of Alfred Noyes or Edgar Allen Poe. Tracing similar ideas across several genres is another interesting approach to genre study. For example, students might compare the myth of Pyramus and Thisbe with the play *The Fantasticks* (Schmidt & Jones, 1992), a video of Shakespeare's *Romeo and Juliet*, or one of the many film modernizations of this famous tale.

A blend of several approaches is often a good idea. Themes like "Taking a Stand" can be traced through different genres or explored through various historical epochs. Above all, try to avoid the orthodoxy of boiling everything down to one simple theme or proceeding in a lockstep manner through each of the literary genres. Be creative and don't let your organizational system impose itself on your common sense when planning reading and viewing experiences for your middle school students. In the next section, we ask you to consider the many ways in which you can invite your students into a supportive community of readers.

CREATING A CLASSROOM CLIMATE FOR READING AND VIEWING

Organizing for Whole-Class Instruction

For many of us, reading instruction in junior high or middle school was often in the form of whole-class reading of novels or nonfiction. Despite the proliferation of workshop models and independent reading programs in recent years (Atwell, 1987; Krogness, 1995; Reif, 1992), it seems that large-group instruction, in which all students read the same text at the same time, still remains a popular (if not the most popular) approach. In many recent discussions of reading and its teaching, whole-class reading is often thought of as hopelessly outdated and traditional, a stifling approach that ignores the unique needs and preferences of individual students. Although it's true that middle school students especially benefit from abundant opportunities for independent, private reading or talking about their reading in small groups or book clubs, it is not true that whole-class instruction is limiting or boring. In Classroom Case 10-2, consider the ways in which Jennifer, a student teacher in a suburban school, skillfully manages to weave the language acts of writing, talking, listening, and viewing into her whole-group reading experience.

Classroom Case 10-2

No Promises in the Wind

Jennifer is teaching Hunt's novel *No Promises in the Wind* (1986) to a group of eighth-grade students at a small suburban middle school. Her students, on the surface, are relatively homogeneous. Most come from what her host teacher describes as middle class "well-to-do" backgrounds, and most are White. Among her 45 eighth-grade students, only one is African American, for example. Yet within this seeming homogeneity is subtle diversity. Many of Jennifer's students live in single-parent households, and around 10% are from lower-middle class backgrounds. Three of Jennifer's students receive services from a special education teacher, and four have been diagnosed with reading difficulties. Understanding that even in a suburban setting, there is no such thing as a "homogeneous" classroom, Jennifer decides to begin by making sure all of her students have the necessary knowledge and resources for understanding Hunt's historical fiction about a young boy and his family during the Great Depression. She begins with a bit of prereading.

Writing to Build Background for Reading

Realizing that her students may not have family members who remember the Depression, Jennifer decides to engage her students in several informal writing tasks, using graphic organizers as a way of building background for their reading. Due to block scheduling, her class periods are 80 minutes long. On the first day, she reads the first page of the book from a handout as students circle words or phrases that jump out at them, write comments in the margins, or underline particularly striking or confusing passages. She then asks them to fill in a first impressions chart (see Figure 10-5). For each prediction, they must also write down some evidence from the passage that supports their hunches.

Focus On Writing

FIGURE 10-5 First Impressions

First Impressions

Impressions	Questions	Predictions

Bringing It All Together

Focus On
Talking and Listening

The next day, after a brief review of the previous day's discussion, Jennifer asks students to jot down in their notebooks anything they know about the Great Depression along with what they might have learned from their reading. After they have written for a few moments, she helps them to create a concept map on an overhead transparency that includes what they know about this period in history (see Figure 10-6).

FIGURE 10-6   Concept Map

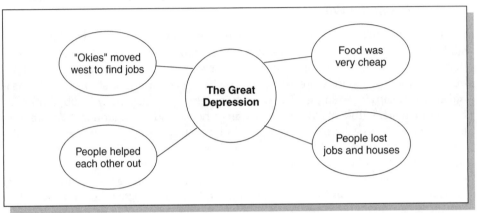

Building Background Through Film

Focus On
Viewing

After students discuss what they already know, Jennifer places them into small groups and shows a documentary film about the period while students "round robin" a sheet of paper in which they take turns noting important information from their viewing (see Figure 10-7).

FIGURE 10-7   Viewing Sheet

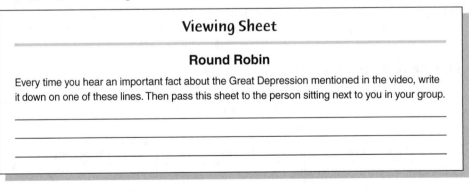

Learning About Historical Fiction

Focus On
Talking and Listening

The next day, to familiarize students with the characteristics of historical fiction, Jennifer begins a "guided imagery" exercise (see Figure 10-8) in which she asks students to envision themselves as characters in history.

FIGURE 10-8 Guided Imagery

Guided Imagery

Close your eyes. Tell all your muscles to relax. You are entering a time machine that looks like the one in *Back to the Future.* You sit inside the time capsule, which has soft, plushy seats. Suddenly, the machine starts its engine and begins to speed up. You quickly realize that it is about to take you back in time to another destination. You look down at the screen: It reads "October 29, 1929." With your knowledge of this time era, you decide to relax and enjoy the ride. Besides, you have enough plutonium to get you back. You buckle your seat belt and the time machine goes faster and faster. Suddenly, there is a flash of light. Within a second you arrive on Wall Street in the year 1929. It is morning and the stock market is about to crash. As you step out of the time machine, you immediately notice hundreds of people frantically rushing to banks. They are in such a panic that they don't even see you. In fact, the mob of people almost pushes you down, but you manage to keep your ground. You move away from the crowd and stop by a newspaper stand. A show business newspaper called *Variety* has a headline that strikes you: "WALL STREET LAYS AN EGG." You suddenly remember what is in the future for these people, and you decide to return to the present as soon as possible. The year 1929 is beginning to depress you. You make it back to the time machine and start the engine. Before you know it, you are back where you started from, back in good ole Campbell Middle School. Tell your muscles to move. Now open your eyes.

What made your trip seem real?
What aspects of your trip are imaginary?

Learning, Sharing, and Performing

As students move into groups to discuss their first responses to the guided imagery, Jennifer gives them a handout describing the unique characteristics of historical fiction and asks them to consider how Hunt's novel fits within this genre. She then presents each group with some primary source materials from the Depression, including photographs, newspaper advertisements, and an article from *Variety* called "Wall Street Lays an Egg." Other items include a "Depression Shopping List" specifying prices of everything from a Pontiac Coupe ($565) to a box of corn flakes (8 cents).

She assigns a role to each group member, such as task organizer, recorder, time-keeper, or presenter, and asks the group to create a chart with two columns (see Figure 10-9). Using their novels, reading-response logs, class webs, and Depression artifacts, students perform several tasks. For example, they choose at least one aspect of the setting that is factual and one that is fictional. They do the same for aspects of the plot and for the story's characters. At the end, they are asked to discuss what Hunt needed to know and do as an author to help them as readers to experience what it was like to live during the Depression era. As a final wrap-up, group presenters share their graphic organizers and ideas with the class.

Focus On
Reading, Viewing,
Talking and Listening

FIGURE 10-9   Collaborative Learning Chart

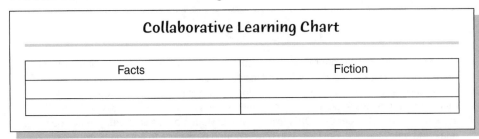

"Reading Like a Writer": Collaborative Story Making

Over the next several days, Jennifer asks students to engage in what Smith (1984) calls "reading like a writer." In groups, they create very short pieces of historical fiction (three to four paragraphs) that combine what they learned about the Great Depression with their knowledge of historical fiction. Group members explore various forms of collaborative writing. In some groups, each person takes turns contributing a sentence or two in a round-robin fashion. Others engage in what Jennifer calls "jump-in" writing; that is, any student is free to jump in with suggestions for plot, characters, or wording at any time. Students who are uncomfortable with such close collaboration can study the Depression-era photographs and create individual vignettes, eventually combining them into one piece.

Although the series of lessons presented in Classroom Case 10-2, taught over several days, relies heavily on whole-group instruction, we think you'll agree that it is hardly traditional and not a one-size-fits-all approach. Students constantly shift from among the language arts of reading, viewing, speaking, listening, and writing. They work collaboratively and alone, learning sophisticated reading skills, enlarging their understandings of Hunt's novel, making predictions about the outcome, and developing the necessary historical background knowledge for a rich and complicated reading. In addition, they are presented with a broad variety of evaluation and response options from visual to oral to more print based. In the following sections, you will see three different approaches to workshop teaching that allow for independent and whole-group reading experiences.

Organizing for Student-Selected Reading

We believe it's important to provide opportunities for free-choice reading in your middle school classroom for several reasons. First, if you consider yourself a lifetime reader (and remember that some English language arts teachers don't), it's at least partly because of your private reading experiences that are not monitored or assigned by others. If you don't consider yourself a lifetime reader, ask yourself whether your own teachers' criticisms or tests may have something to do with your negative perceptions about yourself as a reader. Whatever the case, as a teacher, you need to provide opportunities for reading that "counts" (i.e., carries some kind of reward or credit when grades are due) but does not *count against* your middle school readers.

We urge you to create a system of independent reading, in which students select their own reading and viewing experiences for at least part of their grade. Simply asking students to read so many books (or other texts) each marking period is a good way to start. Create a simple record-keeping system through which you check in periodically (once a week, for example) and ask students to tell you what they are reading and how much they have completed for that week. If you want to monitor their reading a bit more closely, consider holding periodic reading conferences, in which students take 5 minutes to tell you about their independent reading and you write simple notes about their progress in a folder. Or perhaps better still, invite four or five students at a time to hold an impromptu discussion about their independent reading while at the same time giving each other suggestions for what they might read next. If you don't have time for individual or small group conferences, you might hold a sharing circle each week or two, allowing students to give book talks or other informal presentations on their current independent reading experiences.

If you want to structure students' choice of response options, you might design a "menu" for students to use in deciding how to represent what they learned or experienced in their independent reading. Your menu could include choices that range from writing a critical review to artistic representation or oral performance. The idea is to open up the options for students to let you know that they have done their independent reading, while avoiding the fear of evaluation that often accompanies traditional tests, formal writing, or whole-class discussion.

Organizing for Small-Group Reading Experiences

As a supplement to your independent reading program, you might want to sponsor some opportunities for reading and viewing in the company of a small group of peers. For instance, you could hold literature circles in which students gather to read print or nonprint texts with or without your assistance.

Teacher-sponsored literature circles might be held on a regular basis (as often as 5 days per week, or as seldom as once every week or two). Students could have the choice of attending a literature circle with you or working independently on other assignments. You might also ask students to gather in small groups for student-led literature circles.

If you have access to sets of paperbacks (five or six copies of a few titles), you could create book clubs, which meet regularly to discuss common texts. Many modern paperbacks for adult readers are now being published with a list of discussion questions in the back. You could create similar lists for your students or simply ask them to come to each book club meeting with a list of questions they are wondering about at particular points in their reading. As one way of holding students accountable, you could offer a set of options for final projects, to be handed in at the end of the reading or presented for classmates. Options might include everything from research on related issues or topics to performance of key passages.

Organizing for Workshop Teaching

Perhaps the approach that offers the greatest flexibility for teachers who wish to combine whole-class, small-group, and independent reading is what is commonly called "workshop teaching" (Atwell, 1987; Reif, 1992). What makes workshop teaching unique is that it allows for a great deal of flexibility within structure. There is no one-size-fits-all workshop model. In general, workshop approaches allow students to follow their own pace and sequence, promote a balance of student and teacher choice, and allow students to work collaboratively and independently. In Classroom Case 10-3, you will see three different approaches to workshop teaching, though the possible configurations are practically limitless.

Classroom Case 10-3

Three Approaches to Reading Workshop

Ken: A Modified Workshop

The seventh-grade students in Ken's city classroom are primarily from impoverished or working-class backgrounds. Although his school has adopted many aspects of the middle school model such as team advisement and interdisciplinary planning, block scheduling is not one of them. His class periods are 40 minutes long, leaving him little time for extensive group experiences, individual conferences with students, or other approaches typically associated with workshop teaching. Nevertheless, he has created a modified workshop, combining whole-class, small-group, and independent learning activities.

Although Ken combines all of the language arts in his teaching, this brief description focuses mainly on his teaching of reading. Two days a week (Tuesdays and Thursdays) are reserved for whole-group instruction. On these days, Ken makes great use of video, film, and television, often asking students to critique programs and advertising geared to teens. Mondays and Wednesdays are "learning center" days, when students work quietly at one of six learning centers: reading, drafting, editing, free reading, conferencing, and grammar/usage. A couch in the corner of the room serves as the free-reading center, where students can relax and enjoy a book of their choosing.

Students must complete at least one independent book by the end of every marking period and keep a reading log, which they either exchange with a partner or with Ken for feedback and response. Reading logs are kept in crates and left in the classroom each day. At the reading center, students sit at a table with five or six other students and respond individually or collaboratively to a short text, photograph, or piece of visual art that Ken has chosen for that particular day. Students often have choices to write, draw, perform, or discuss their responses. Fridays are reserved for sharing circle, where students take turns either sharing a piece of writing they created or talking about something they've read that week.

As you can see, Ken's modified workshop allows him to make the most out of a 40-minute class period, offering students many opportunities to read and view a variety of texts alone and with others.

Mary: Reading/Writing Workshop

In Mary's city classroom, students are on a block schedule of 80-minute class periods. Her seventh-grade students come to her every other day and attend a social studies class on alternate days. Within this broad structure, students know that each 80-minute period will be broken up in roughly the same way. As they enter the room, they take their assigned seats at small tables with five or six members of their "home group." In this arrangement, they spend 10 to 15 minutes copying the agenda from the overhead and responding to a brief writing prompt, usually related to the day's reading. After this initial "warm-up" time, Mary calls the roll and asks students to choose either reading/writing workshop (working independently on reading and writing activities or inquiry projects in the classroom or at the library) or literature circle. Her philosophy of reading is that it can't be separated from the other language arts; students learn skillful ways of reading the work of published authors as they become writers themselves. By the same token, oral language, listening, and an understanding of various media all contribute to a rich reading curriculum.

Literature circles are always held in an area with a couch, two large padded chairs, and several pillows. As students settle into soft seats, pull up chairs, or find spaces on the floor, Mary begins by tying each day's opening task writing prompt to the piece of literature or nonfiction she has selected. After a few minutes of sharing their writing, the students usually take turns reading the day's selection aloud. Like Ken, Mary keeps track of students' choices in her plan book. If students choose reading/writing workshop 2 days in a row, they must come to literature circle the next time it's offered.

In addition to attending literature circles, students choose independent reading books roughly every 2 weeks. They keep track of their independent reading in logs, which are discussed with Mary and the other students periodically. Roughly every month, students conduct inquiry projects, based on some of the reading and writing they have been doing. Inquiry projects give them the opportunity to combine nonfiction, fiction, and electronic texts.

As you can see, Mary's workshop model is based on a great deal of student choice, balanced with more teacher-structured activities. Students have chances to read, write, talk, and engage in projects independently or with others. They have regular conferences with Mary for responding to writing or reading, goal setting, and evaluation. Each year, language activities are organized around a major theme and several subthemes. This kind of balance is crucial for middle school students, who are poised between dependence on adults and the development of their own identities and preferences.

Jerome: A Workshop in a Day

Jerome is starting a student teaching placement with a host teacher who has already established a successful set of routines and procedures in her sixth-grade classroom. He is wary of making large changes in her comfortable and predictable routine. After all, his placement is only for 11 weeks, and his host teacher must take over when he leaves. Nevertheless, she is willing for him to experiment a bit with the approach. With that in mind, Jerome embarks on his first instructional unit on short stories. He has already chosen a theme for the unit: "Searching for Self." Within this theme, he has collected stories by writers like Maya Angelou, Sandra Cisneros, Gary Paulsen, Toni Cade Bambera, Gary Soto, and other popular young adult authors. Because he wants students to explore the differences between short stories and other genres, he plans to bring in a short video, poetry, nonfiction, and other texts for comparison. At the same time, he plans to continue with some of the procedures his host teacher already uses: "Daily Oral Language," in which students identify grammar and usage problems for a few minutes at the beginning of each period; weekly vocabulary or spelling quizzes; and regular journal writing on teacher- or student-selected topics. He decides to devote 1 day per week to reading workshop.

Because most of Jerome's students have never experienced a workshop model, he prepares a handout, explaining what is expected of them on workshop day, which he plans to sponsor each Friday. For the first 3 weeks of the unit, students use their Friday workshop day in one of two ways: reading and discussing short stories together in a kind of book club arrangement or reading silently and responding privately to one of five different stories, copies of which he has placed on tables around the room. Students respond in ways that include drawing, visual representation, or oral performance, as well as more traditional writing activities. During the 4th week, his students gather in one area of the room to share what they learned about the unit theme, "Searching for Self," from their workshop experiences.

For the next 3 weeks, students use their workshop days to craft their own short stories, either independently or with others. As students work quietly around the room, Jerome holds conferences with them, helping them to generate ideas, reviewing their progress, or helping them to revise their writing. For the final 3 weeks, students are expected to work in small groups on various inquiry projects, focused on the unit theme. Toward the end of the unit, Jerome decides to expand workshop to 3 days per week, allowing more time for students to work together in the library, the computer lab, or the classroom, collecting resources and planning their final projects.

On the final workshop day, students invite their parents and other interested adults to attend a "share fair." Refreshments are served as visitors walk around the room, enjoying the many posters and displays that students have created to represent their learning for the past 11 weeks.

For Discussion

Considering the broad diversity of practices and procedures in these three scenarios, what sets workshop teaching apart from other approaches? Look back through these workshops and attempt to tease out what makes a workshop a workshop.

Now that we've covered these different approaches to creating a reading and viewing curriculum, we come to the thorniest and perhaps most important issue: an evaluation system.

ASSESSMENT ISSUES IN THE READING AND VIEWING CLASSROOM

First, we need to distinguish between response, evaluation, and grading. Response involves giving students the benefit of your personal reaction to their ideas and their work. It can encompass everything from recognizing and enlarging on their comments in class discussions to writing in the margins of their reader-response journals.

> Model effective responses and create opportunities for students to respond to each other's reading and viewing journals.

In contrast to evaluation and grading, response should generally begin with "I" statements: "I wondered about this when you said that," "I was moved by your story about your grandmother," "I can suggest other books by that author," and so on. Your intent should be to support students in voicing and elaborating on their ideas and insights.

In contrast to response, evaluation involves judging student work against some kind of standard. It's not quite as final as grading, in which students are given a summative appraisal of their work to be filed in a grade book or sent home on a report card. Evaluation can be performed in conferences with students, when you help them to see areas where they have grown or are in need of help. It can also be done in the form of comments on papers or check marks on a rubric designed for particular projects.

Whatever grading scheme you use, remember that students quickly learn to "read" your grading and evaluation system for evidence of how reading and viewing should proceed in your classroom. If every reading or viewing experience culminates in a multiple-choice test, students will learn to read literature efferently, making notes of "important" details to be remembered later for the test. If every reading experience begins with a vocabulary quiz, students may not be encouraged to figure out words in context. Remember that literature is not driver's education. Because it's important for inexperienced drivers to know the difference between a yield and a stop sign, an objective test on the rules of the road is probably necessary for obtaining a driver's license. Creating lifetime readers is a more delicate issue, requiring sophisticated response, grading, and evaluation procedures that mirror our true goals for students' reading in our classroom and in their lives outside school.

Responding

One of the most popular ways of keeping track of students' responses is to ask them to keep a journal or log. Students may simply stop at various points in their reading (at the end of each class period or the end of each book chapter) and jot down what they are wondering about, thinking, and feeling. Such jottings can be helpful if you plan to conduct conferences with students (either individually or in small groups of four or five students). Mary McCrone, a middle school teacher in an urban district, asks students to write three sentences at the end of each day they spend in reading workshop. She then uses these short log entries to talk in more depth with them about the books they've chosen for their independent reading. Other teachers like to structure the experience a bit more, asking students to choose from a menu of writing options such as the one in Figure 10-10.

There's no denying that students need response to their work and lots of it. As teachers, however, we also need to protect our personal lives. When you find yourself lugging response journals home every weekend or making copious marks in your grade book, you're probably headed for burnout. As an alternative, each morning you could ask students to call out the page number and title of their independent

FIGURE 10-10   Reading Menu

Reader's Choice—Perhaps there is something you are dying to write. Go to it! Choose any form that's comfortable and begin to write.

Personal Connections—Does this text remind you of anything in your own life? Try to capture that experience as closely as you can. Choose any form you like.

Playing With Form—Take one of the ideas in this text and write it into another form. Write a story, a letter, an essay, a dialogue, or monologue.

Futurizing—Write about what might happen to the characters at some future time. Choose one or more characters and pick a time a few minutes later or several years later. Choose any comfortable form.

Role Playing—Take the perspective of a character other than the speaker and write about the same incident from that character's viewpoint.

reading book as you call the roll. A quick notation system like this gives you a quick glance at the reading tastes and progress of your students. Of course, you need to combine this system with more concrete evidence of their reading such as journals or conferences with you. If you need to know whether students are being honest with you about their independent reading, consider giving brief independent reading quizzes on a regular basis. For example, you could give students a writing prompt such as "Who is the most memorable character in your book and why?" or "What has just happened in your book and what lesson can you learn from it?" A 5-minute free write can give you a pretty good idea about who is reading and who is not. You can make a point to confer with students whose responses are vague or questionable.

Holding conferences with small groups of students about their independent reading and making brief notes in your plan book (check, check plus, check minus) can be a healthy alternative to writing those laborious comments in the response notebooks of 100 to 120 students.

You might also consider dialogue journals, in which students write back and forth to a peer about their reading. Another idea is to collect a small number of journals each week and ask students to place a paper clip on an entry they'd most like to share with you. This entry, plus one that you choose randomly, could serve as a basis for a brief response.

Remember that a few honest and well-timed responses from you can be as valuable as a lengthy dialogue in a student's journal or the margins of a paper. Try to make a personal connection with each student about his or her reading at least once a week. Your response might be something as simple as a quick remark before class ("You're reading Harry Potter. Why do you think so many kids like that series?"), a comment during class discussion ("Josh, I know you like mystery stories. What do you think of this one?"), or a special act ("I brought in this book because I know you like this author so much."). The important thing is to create a classroom climate in which reading and viewing are held in high regard and in which students and teachers alike feel free to share their responses to everything from books to films to television programs.

Evaluating

A colleague of ours likes to distinguish between "responding" and "response" to reading. Because response is always necessarily private and hard to tap, teachers must create more public ways of responding that can be evaluated and eventually graded. Your choice of responding experiences will strongly shape the future responses of students and their reading processes and strategies. If you want students to respond aesthetically to literature, giving a factual test or assigning a literary essay on the front end will pretty much rule out this kind of response. This doesn't mean that every reading and viewing experience needs to be nebulous or highly personal. Reading a nonfiction piece on violence in America or homelessness can be followed by a formal writing assignment requiring critical analysis or an extended research project. It may be followed by the creation of a mini-video documentary that includes interviews with community members. It may culminate in a series of school announcements or a newspaper article with a call to action for changes in playground behaviors or school lunch activities to raise funds for the local shelter. Consider the skills learned and how best students might demonstrate them in use in a particular context. Community projects are often a way to add relevance for students, but given the constraints of time, you won't be able to do this with all reading and viewing materials.

Many teachers find it helpful to create a simple evaluation rubric for more formal papers and projects. Questions like "Does the paper/presentation reveal a thorough understanding of major issues?" or "Is the language clear, lively, and engaging?" can provide a comfortable yet clear structure for giving students feedback on their work. Rubrics can include a Likert scale, which allows you to circle numbers from 1 (poor) to 5 (outstanding) and to write qualitative comments in the space below.

Regular evaluation and goal-setting conferences can also be very useful to teachers and students alike. In preparation for such conferences, students can complete self-evaluation forms that include responses to prompts such as "How many books did you read on your own this marking period?" or "Give some examples of how you have grown as a reader over the past several weeks." As you and your students discuss their self-evaluation, you can negotiate two or three goals to be completed before the next evaluation conference. Goal statements such as "Jordan will read at least two books in a genre other than mystery" or "Shaliah will read from her independent book and write in her response journal at least twice each week" can be noted in the student's reading log and discussed during the next evaluation conference.

If you don't want to grade students' class participation or informal writing in a formal way, you might consider walking around the room during silent work time and placing "check plus" or "check minus" next to the names of students who seem particularly engaged or off task. A similar evaluation system can be used to give students credit for journal entries or informal writings that are especially thought provoking or to cue them that they are not putting enough effort into these assignments.

Grading

As you construct your grading system, you should try to balance student-controlled, teacher-controlled, and negotiated grading opportunities. In the past few pages, we have discussed teacher-controlled approaches from conferences to quizzes.

FIGURE 10-11 Grading Contract for Independent Reading

A: Read four books for the next marking period and produce a minimum of 12 entries
   of at least one page in your response notebook.
B: Read three books and produce a minimum of 9 entries.
C: Read two books and produce a minimum of 6 entries.
D: Read one book and produce a minimum of 3 entries.
F: Little or no evidence of independent reading.

Contract grading is an example of a more student-controlled activity. For independent reading, for example, you could create a contract such as the example in Figure 10-11.

In the case of formal projects and papers, you and your students may negotiate a grading rubric. If you have strong opinions about what needs to be included in grading a particular assignment, begin by writing these "givens" on an overhead transparency or a flip chart. Statements like "The paper must be seven pages long and typewritten" or "Each student must show evidence of his or her contribution to the project" can be written on the top of the list. Then, in an open discussion, students can suggest items they would like included in the rubric.

Teacher-controlled grading must be handled with care and consideration. Ask yourself what is most acceptable, considering where the students are at any particular moment. You may begin a school year with a large number of teacher-controlled activities, and then gradually shift to student-controlled or negotiated approaches as students prove they can handle such opportunities in a mature and conscientious way.

Consider the multiple pathways in which students might demonstrate emerging competencies. Consider the real-life contexts of your students and attempt to design assessments that have real-world applications as much as possible.

In planning your grading and evaluation system, remember to keep in close contact with resource personnel, providing alternative assessments for students with special needs and abilities. Particular students may need extra time for papers, quizzes, and projects, or they may need printed materials to be read aloud. Remember that some students may be reluctant to write about what they consider private thoughts in journals or logs, and others may find oral conferences with teachers torturous. Try to provide opportunities for all students to succeed. Draw upon multiple intelligences (Gardner, 1993) in the grading and evaluation experiences you provide. Notice, for example, the literacies involved in the board game a seventh-grade student created to represent his reading of *The Sword and the Stone* by White (see Figure 10-12).

Not only did this student use his knowledge of game construction, but he cleverly incorporated elements of the story's plot into each stage of the game.

Whatever your choices for response, evaluation, and grading in your reading and viewing classroom, remember that beyond the goal of creating intelligent, informed, and critical readers, it is also your responsibility to create citizens who will actually put these competencies to use in their daily lives beyond their years of formal schooling.

FIGURE 10-12 Board Game from *The Sword and the Stone*

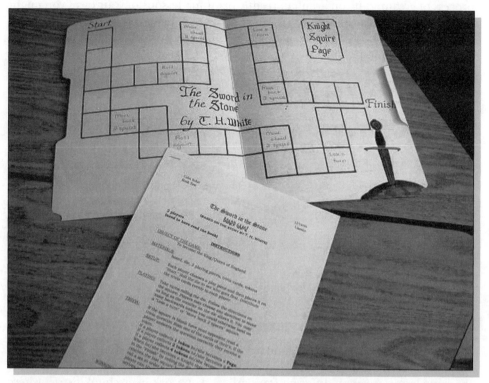

━━━━━━━━━━━━━━━ **Standards in Practice** ━━━━━━

Viewing Your Reading and Viewing Lessons Through the NCTE/IRA Standards

Locate a copy of the *NCTE/IRA Standards for the English Language Arts* (1996). For an explanation of the standards, a table of contents for the volume, an annotated listing of each standard, and chapter excerpts, consult the NCTE Web site: *http:// www. ncte.org/standards.*

Although all of the standards are relevant to your reading and viewing classroom, for purposes of this exercise, we suggest you look most closely at Standards 1, 2, 3, and 11. You will notice that within each standard are words or phrases that could be construed as subgoals for your reading and viewing classroom. Begin with the first standard and highlight the subgoals within this standard as we have done in this example:

NCTE/IRA Standard One
1. Students read a wide range of print and nonprint texts to build an understanding of texts, of themselves, and of the cultures of the United States and the world; to acquire new information; to respond to the needs of society and the workplace; and for personal fulfillment. Among these texts are fiction and nonfiction, classic and contemporary works.

Now locate a reading and viewing lesson you have created or one you are in the process of creating. If you aren't currently planning lessons of your own, you might want to refer to Classroom Case 10-2 on *No Promises in the Wind*. For each activity in your lesson plan, try to tie it to one or more of these subgoals from Standard 1. As an example, in figure 10-13 we've paraphrased some of the activities in Jennifer's unit. Beside each activity, we have placed the relevant subgoals of Standard 1.

FIGURE 10-13   Standards-Based Learning

Activities	Connections to Standards
Historical Fiction Project • Taking notes while watching a documentary • Listening to "guided imagery" • Considering unique characteristics of fiction • Discussing primary sources and considering which aspects might be fact or fiction	• Students read print and nonprint texts; acquire new information. • Students understand themselves and understand cultures. • Students understand texts. • Students read fiction and nonfiction, and understand texts.

When you've finished with Standard 1, you might want to do the same for Standards 2, 3, and 11. If you are working in a group, perhaps different groups can view the same lesson through different standards. If you work in a school district where state or national standards are important, it's a good idea to begin tying all of your lessons to those standards in this way.

REFERENCES

Applebee, A. N. (1993). *Literature in the secondary school: Studies of curriculum and instruction in the United States.* Urbana, IL: National Council of Teachers of English.

Appleman, D. (2000). *Critical encounters in high school English: Teaching literary theory to adolescents.* New York: Teachers College Press.

Atwell, N. (1987). *In the middle: Writing, reading, and learning with adolescents.* Montclair, NJ: Boynton/Cook.

Frank, A. (1988). *Anne Frank: The diary of a young girl.* New York: Bantam Books.

Gardner, H. (1993). *Frames of mind: The theory of multiple intelligences.* New York: Basic Books.

Gee, J. P. (2000). Teenagers in new times: A new literacy studies perspective. *Journal of Adolescent and Adult Literacy, 43*(5), 412–420.

Hunt, I. (1986). *No promises in the wind.* New York: Berkeley Publishing Group.

Innocenti, R. (1996). *Rose blanche.* Madison, WI: Turtleback Books.

Krogness, M. M. (1995). *Just teach me, Mrs. K.: Talking, reading, and writing with resistant adolescent learners.* Portsmouth, NH: Heinemann.

Labov, W. (1972). *Language in the inner city: Studies in the black English vernacular.* Philadelphia: University of Pennsylvania Press.

Langer, J. (1995). *Envisioning literature: Literary understanding and literature instruction.* New York: Teachers College Press.

Lee, H. (2001). *To kill a mockingbird.* New York: Harper Trade.

Lowry, L. (1994). *The giver.* New York: Bantam Doubleday Dell.

Luke, A. (1988). *Literacy, textbooks and ideology: Postwar literacy instruction and the mythology of Dick and Jane.* Bristol, PA: Taylor & Francis.

Mehan, H. (1979). What time is it Denise?: Asking known information questions in classroom discourse. *Theory into Practice, 18*(4), 285–294.

National Council of Teachers of English. (1996). *Standards for the English language arts.* Urbana, IL: Author.

New London Group. (1996). A pedagogy of multiliteracies: Designing social futures. *Harvard Educational Review, 66*(1), 60–92.

Okita, D. (1991). In response to executive order 9066: All Americans of Japanese descent must report to relocation centers. In Minnesota Humanities Commission/Minnesota Council of Teachers of English, *Braided lives: An anthology of multicultural American writing* (pp. 280–281). Saint Paul: Minnesota Humanities Commission.

Reif, L. (1992). *Seeking diversity: Language arts with adolescents.* Portsmouth, NH: Heinemann.

Rosenblatt, L. M. (1994). *The reader, the text, the poem: The transactional theory of the literary work.* Carbondale: Southern Illinois University Press.

Rosenblatt, L. M. (1995). Literature as exploration. New York: Modern Language Association. (Original work published 1938)

Schmidt, H., & Jones, T. (1992). *The fantasticks.* New York: Applause Theatre Books.

Smith, F. (1984). Reading like a writer. In J. Jensen (Ed.), *Composing and comprehending* (pp. 47–56). Urbana, IL: National Council of Teachers of English.

Smith, M. W., & Wilhelm, J. D. (2002). *Reading don't fix no Chevys: Literacy in the lives of young men.* Portsmouth, NH: Heinemann.

Soto, G. (1990). Oranges. In *Braided lives: An anthology of multicultural American writing* (pp. 134–135). Minneapolis: Minnesota Council on the Humanities.

Spielberg, S. (Producer), & Holzman, A. (Director). (1996). *Survivors of the Holocaust* [Documentary]. United States: Shoah Foundation.

Tajiri, V. (1990). *Through innocent eyes: Teenagers' impressions of WW2 internment camp life.* Los Angeles: Keiro Services.

Tsuchiya, Y., & Dykes, T. T. (1988). *Faithful elephants.* New York: Houghton Mifflin.

Watkusaki Houston, J. (1983). *Farewell to Manzanar.* Madison, WI: Turtleback Books.

Yolen, J. (1992). *Briar rose.* New York: Tor Books.

RESOURCES

Print

Resources for Readers' Workshop

Allen, J., & Gonzalez, K. (1997). *There's room for me here: Literacy workshop in the middle school.* York, ME: Stenhouse.

Bomer, R. (1995). *Time for meaning: Crafting literate lives in middle and high school.* Portsmouth, NH: Heinemann.

Conn, J. L. (1994). The Christian coalition: Behind the mask. *Church & State,* 4–7.

Daniels, H. (1996). *Literature circles: Voice and choice in the classroom.* York, ME: Stenhouse.

Hagerty, P. (1992). *Readers workshop: Real reading.* Richmond Hill, Ontario: Scholastic, Canada.

McKenzie, J. (Ed.). (1992). *Readers' workshop: Bridging literature and literacy.* Toronto: Irvin.

Pollack Day, J., Spiegel, D. L., McLellan, J., & Brown, V. B. (2002). *Moving forward with literature circles: How to plan, manage, and evaluate literature circles that deepen understanding and foster a love of reading.* New York: Scholastic.

Raphael, T., & McMahan, S. (Eds.). (1997). *The book club connection: Literacy learning and classroom talk.* New York: Teachers College Press.

General Resources on Reading

Beers, K. (1996). *Into focus: Understanding and creating middle school readers.* Norwood, MA: ChristopherGordon.

Burke, J. (2004). *Illuminating texts: How to teach students to read the world.* Portsmouth, NH: Heinemann.

Fountas, I. C., & Pinnell, G. S. (2001). *Guiding readers and writers grades 3–6: Teaching comprehension, genre, and content literacy.* Portsmouth, NH: Heinemann.

Janeczko, P. B. (2004). *Opening a door: Reading poetry in the middle school classroom.* New York: Scholastic.

National Council of Teachers of English. (1996). *Teaching literature in middle school: Fiction.* Urbana, IL: Author.

Robb, L. (2000). *Teaching reading in middle school (grades 5 & up).* New York: Scholastic Professional Book Division.

Schoenbach, R., Greenleaf, C., Cziko, C., & Hurwitz, L. (Eds.) (1999). *Reading for understanding: A guide to improving reading in middle and high school classrooms.* New York: Jossey-Bass.

Sloan, G. (2003). *Give them poetry! A guide for sharing poetry with children K–8.* New York: Teachers College Press.

Soter, A. (1999). *Young adult literature and the new literary theories: Developing critical readers in middle school.* New York: Teachers College Press.

Wilhelm, J. (1996). *You gotta be the book: Teaching engaged and reflective reading with adolescents.* New York: Teachers College Press.

Wilhelm, J. (2001). *Strategic reading: Guiding students to lifelong literacy, 6–12.* Portsmouth, NH: Boynton/Cook.

Wilhelm, J. D. (2004). *Reading is seeing: Learning to visualize scenes, characters, ideas, and text worlds to improve comprehension and reflective reading.* New York: Scholastic.

Including All Readers

Barbieri, M. (2002). *"Change my life forever": Giving Voice to English-Language Learners.* Portsmouth, NH: Heinemann.

Delpit, L., & Dowdy, J. K. (2002). *The skin that we speak: Thoughts on language and culture in the classroom.* New York: The New Press.

Freedman, D., & Freedman, Y. (2000). *Teaching reading in multilingual classrooms.* Portsmouth, NH: Heinemann.

Ladson-Billings, G. (1994). *The dreamkeepers: Successful teachers of African American Children.* San Francisco: Jossey Bass.

Ladson-Billings, G. (2001). *Crossing over to Canaan: The journey of new teachers in diverse classrooms.* San Francisco: Jossey Bass.

Ohanian, S. (2001). *Caught in the middle: Nonstandard kids and a killing curriculum.* Portsmouth, NH: Heinemann.

Resources for Young Adult Literature

Hurst, C., & Otis, R. (1999). *Using literature in the middle school curriculum.* Worthington, OH: Linworth Publishing.

The Lure of Young Adult Literature. (2001). *English Journal, 90*(3). [Special themed issue; articles by Cindy O'Donnell Allen et al. and Marshall George are particularly useful.]

Stover, L. (1996). *Young adult literature: The heart of the middle school classroom.* Portsmouth, NH: Boynton/Cook-Heinemann.

Resources on Informational Texts and Technology

Duke, N., & Bennett-Armistead, S. (2003). *Reading & writing informational text in the primary grades: Research-based practices.* New York: Scholastic.

Hoyt, L. (2002). *Make it real: Strategies for success with informational texts.* Portsmouth, NH: Heinemann.

Kist, W. (2004). *New literacies in action: Teaching and learning in multiple media.* New York: Teachers College Press.

Kristo, J., & Bamford, R. (2004). *Nonfiction in focus: A comprehensive framework for helping students become independent readers and writers of nonfiction, K–6.* New York: Scholastic.

Purcell-Gates, V., & Duke, N. K. (2001, August). *Explicit explanation/teaching of informational text genres: A model for research.* Paper presented at Crossing Borders: Connecting Science and Literacy conference, a conference sponsored by the National Science Foundation, Baltimore, MD.

Wood, J. (2004). *Literacy online: New tools for struggling readers and writers.* Portsmouth, NH: Heinemann.

Resources for Combating Censorship

Anaya, R. (1992). The censorship of neglect. *English Journal, 81*(5), 1992.

Applebee, A. N. (1992). Stability and change in the high school canon. *English Journal, 81*(5), 27–32.

The Bell Curve: How a dangerous book won legitimacy. (1994, Winter). *Rethinking Schools: An Urban Educational Journal, 1,* 14, 16.

Duke, D. (1993, Summer). Are fundamentalists taking over your school? How the Christian right organizes. *Rethinking Schools: An Urban Educational Journal,* 4–5.

English Journal, 81(4), 1992.

Fawcett, G. (1993–1994). Tom didn't say anything. *Educational Leadership, 51*(4), 35–36.

Garden, N. (1994). Banned: Lesbian and gay kids' books under fire. *Lambda Book Report: A Review of Contemporary Gay and Lesbian Literature, 4*(7), 11–13.

Lee, N., Murphy, D., & Ucelli, J. (1991). Whose kids? Our kids! Race, sexuality and the right in New York City's curriculum battles. *Radical America, 25*(1), 9–21.

National Council of Teachers of English. (1982). *Statement of censorship and professional guidelines.* Urbana, IL: Author.

National Council of Teachers of English. (1999). *Guidelines for dealing with censorship of nonprint materials.* Urbana, IL: Author.

Noll, E. (1994). The ripple effect of censorship: Silencing in the classroom. *English Journal, 83*(8), 59–64.

On Huck, criticism and censorship. (1984). *Interracial Books for Children Bulletin, 15*(1, 2, 3).

Peterson, B. (1993, Winter). What should kids learn: A teacher looks at E. D. Hirsch's work on "cultural literacy." *Rethinking Schools: An Urban Educational Journal, 1,* 8–11.

Pollard, B. (1990, October 15). To see one's face in the mirror: Teaching black American literature. *New York Teacher,* 19.

Reed, A. J. S. (1994). Censorship and the young adult book. In A. J. S. Reed (Ed.), *Reaching adolescents: The young adult book and the school.* Upper Saddle River, NJ: Merrill/Prentice Hall.

Electronic

The ALAN Review Digital Library and Archives.

http://scholar.lib.vt.edu/ejournals/ALAN

The Horn Book. *The Horn Book Magazine* and *The Horn Book Guide* are distinguished in the field of children's and young adult literature, and this site offers helpful reviews of young adult literature.

http://www.hbook.com/

Young Adult Library Services. Sponsored by the American Library Association, this site has many helpful features, including information about conferences and events, as well as several sites linking to award-winning books for young adults.

http://www.ala.org/yalsa

Reading Online: A Journal of K–12 Practice and Research. Published by the International Reading Association. This online journal has several helpful articles for practitioners by well-known practitioners and researchers in the field of reading. A chat line and helpful ideas for integrating technology into the literacy classroom are also offered.

http://www.readingonline.org

PBS TeacherSource Arts and Literature Page. This site provides a great source of fiction, nonfiction, and information on various topics relevant to the language arts classroom. Subjects range from slavery to immigration, architecture, and music, to name a few. The site is a great way to introduce students to print and nonprint resources for inquiry projects related to their reading.

http://www.pbs.org/teachersource/arts_lit.htm

The *New York Times* Daily Lesson Plans. Developed in partnership with the Bank Street College of Education, this site provides ways for teachers to use the newspaper to teach reading and other skills.

http://www.nytimes.com/learning/teachers/lessons

Internet School Library Media Center Index to Children's Authors and Illustrators Page. This is a good place to hook students up with information about authors and illustrators of their favorite books. The home page also provides an index to additional Internet sites featuring young adult authors and illustrators.

http://falcon.jmu.edu/~ramseyil

Center on English Language and Achievement Web Site. CELA is an OERI-funded research center dedicated to promoting English and literacy achievement in schools across America. Its Web site links teachers to relevant research in the area of literacy education. Many of the reports focus on reading and literature instruction.

http://cela.albany.edu

KidLit Web Site. This site is designed for children and adults interested in quality children's literature. One of the best features is the "KidLit Reviews," where students can write (and publish) reviews of their favorite books.

http://mgfx.com/kidlit

Links to Young Adult Authors

Several Web sites feature interviews, biographical sketches, and links to the Web sites of authors whose work is directed toward adolescents and young adults. The Web sites of most major publishers (especially those that publish anthologies for middle and high school students) feature regular biographies and interviews with young adult authors. Three other sites are particularly useful:

Dmoz Open Directory Project. This site has extensive links to Web sites focused on literature for young adults.

http://dmoz.org/Arts/Literature/Authors/Young_Adult

The Teen Place. This site is also a good source of links to popular young adult authors.

http://www.cantonpl.org/ya/arts.html

Kay E. Vandergrift's Special Interest Page. This site is an excellent resource for locating authors of children's and adolescent literature, and for picking up interesting teaching ideas.

http://www.scils.rutgers.edu/~kvander

Index